# IF YOU ARE STILL HERE

## *Navigating the Great Disappearance and What Lies Ahead*

JEFF L HOEN



Anchor & Sail Press

# IF YOU ARE STILL HERE

*Navigating the Great Disappearance and What Lies Ahead*



First Edition

The majority of the illustrations in this book were generated using artificial intelligence tools and subsequently curated or refined by the author to accurately depict symbolic and prophetic themes.

## *Scripture Permissions*



## *Image Credits*

*To the One*
*who loves me with an everlasting love*
*and compels me with unfailing steadfast love.*

*I have loved you with an everlasting love; therefore with lovingkindness I have drawn you and continued My faithfulness to you.*

—JEREMIAH 31:3 (AMP)

# CONTENTS

# FOREWORD

Every now and then, a book comes along that feels less like something to analyse and more like a companion for the journey. This is one of those books. Whether you pick it up with a steady faith or a shaken heart, or simply because the world around you has changed and you are trying to make sense of this new reality, Jeff L. Hoen has written these pages to meet you with clarity and grace. His hope is to guide you gently into what Scripture reveals about the days ahead and to point you toward the One who still holds every moment in His hands.

Something, or Someone, has drawn you to this little book. Whatever led you here, the work of my friend Jeff offers you a kind of reader's lookout—a high place from which the unfolding panorama of biblical prophecy can be seen with greater clarity.

Though Jeff and I hold different eschatological views, he has asked me—his pastor and friend—to write this foreword. That alone speaks to his humility and integrity. He is not seeking agreement; he is seeking to exalt Jesus Christ—the Alpha and the Omega, the Lamb and the Lion, the One who stands at the centre of all Revelation.

I was raised by parents who both loved the Scriptures deeply, yet viewed prophecy through different lenses. Later, I served within denominations that likewise differed, sometimes sharply, over matters of eschatology. Through all of this, I learned that sincere believers may read the map differently, but love and humility keep us walking together. For that reason, I commend this book to you—not because I share every interpretation, but because I recognise the sincerity, study, and Christ-centred purpose behind it.

And that purpose is unique.

Jeff is writing for two audiences.

The first is you—the reader who picks it up today, before these events arrive, seeking understanding and insight into the biblical texts that speak of the end of the age.

But the second audience is seldom considered in modern Christian writing: those who may read this book in a world forever changed after the biblical event known as the Rapture.

It is for this very reason that Jeff has titled his work *If You Are Still Here*.

The title itself becomes part of the message. It stands as both a question and a lifeline—an acknowledgment of the possibility that you may indeed be reading these words after countless followers of Christ have vanished. And if that describes you, then hear this clearly:

You have not been abandoned.

You have not been forgotten.

Salvation through Jesus Christ is still available to you.

In a world suddenly shaken, explanations will multiply—UFO abductions, cosmic anomalies, political conspiracies. This book exists to help you see through that fog and understand what Scripture has already spoken. As Jeff interprets it, the prophetic events from Revelation chapter 4 onward now stand on your very doorstep, and the days ahead will test your courage and your faith. For this reason, he has written not merely a commentary, but a spiritual travel guide—a map to help you navigate an unfamiliar and urgent landscape.

Travel guides have shaped my own life in meaningful ways. Years ago, my wife and I unexpectedly found ourselves owners of a small bookshop café—a place where my love for old volumes, especially travel literature, began to grow. I remember hearing Winkie Pratney say, "For every new book you read, you should read two old ones, because every generation has its blind spots." That counsel stayed with me, and among the treasures I discovered was a book remarkably similar to the one you now hold—written in 1904 by an author seeking to interpret Revelation through the lens of his own time. How fascinating it is to see how each generation peers through the prophetic window, and how many shadows that perplexed readers then have grown clearer now.

Another beloved book on my shelf was penned by H.V. Morton, whom some consider the world's first travel writer. In *The Steps of the Master*, Morton guides his reader from the comfort of their lounge chair into the dusty streets of Israel and Palestine. You feel the heat rising from ancient stones, hear donkeys braying in distant alleys, smell the spice-laden air, and brush your hand against weathered walls. By the final page, you speak of Palestine as though you have walked it yourself.

Jeff writes with a similar intention—not to transport you into the past, but to guide you toward the unfolding future. He has spent hundreds, perhaps thousands, of hours tracing the contours of the prophetic horizon so that you might recognise the landmarks when you encounter them. His aim is not to frighten, nor to sensationalise, but to offer clarity and hope by pointing you always toward Christ. And for those who feel the pull to venture further, you will find at the back of this book an unexpected treasure—an appendix where Jeff offers deeper paths to explore, should you wish to linger a while longer in the landscape of his study.

And at the centre of this panoramic landscape stands a solitary, radiant Figure—One who casts no shadows. For now, we see Him dimly, as through a glass. But soon—very soon—the dawn will break, and we will see Him as He truly is.

So whether these words reach you long before the pages of prophecy unfold, or in the very middle of their rising tide, may this book serve its name well—an outstretched hand *if you are still here*, drawing you toward the One who has never left. Let its guidance steady your steps as you walk the unfamiliar terrain before you. Let its truth be a lamp, its hope a shelter, and its message a reminder that Christ has already gone ahead of you.

I commend this work to you with deep affection.

Lift your gaze toward the horizon.

The path awaits and Christ is with you.

**HAYDEN SMITH**

Lead Pastor

Catch The Fire Sydney

# A NOTE TO THE READER

What you are holding is not just another book on Bible prophecy.

It is a lifeline. A compass for a world that has lost its way.

This book was written for a moment. Perhaps this very moment. A time when truth feels slippery and time itself seems to be slipping through humanity's fingers.

Whether you are reading these words before the great global Disappearance or in the chaotic aftermath, this message is for you. It is grounded in Scripture, shaped by careful study, and driven by a single desire: to point you to the unshakable hope found only in Jesus Christ.

You may not think you need this book.

But someone you love might.

In a world unraveling by the hour, truth will matter more than ever. If you have found this book before the chaos begins, read it with urgency. If you have found it after, know that you are not without hope. This is your guide to understanding what is happening and, more importantly, **Who** is coming.

## *How to Read This Book*

This book is designed for clarity, whether you are a skeptic, a new believer, or a seasoned student of the Bible.

**The Perspective: Why a Literal View?** Many people treat the Book of Revelation like a dream that needs to be decoded. We do not. We believe that when the Bible speaks of a seven-year peace treaty, a global leader, or a Third Temple in Jerusalem, it is describing actual history before it happens.

Our reason is simple: **the track record of the past.** When Jesus came the first time, He fulfilled over 300 specific prophecies, such as being born in Bethlehem and the piercing of His hands and feet, with 100% literal accuracy. Since God was that precise with the prophecies of the First Coming, we have every reason to expect Him to be just as literal with the prophecies of His Second Coming.

**FACT CHECK: A SAMPLE OF THE EVIDENCE**

**Prophecy:** Born in Bethlehem (Micah 5:2): **Literal Fulfillment.**

**Prophecy:** Entered on a donkey (Zechariah 9:9): **Literal Fulfillment.**

**Prophecy:** Betrayed for 30 silver pieces (Zechariah 11:12): **Literal Fulfillment.**

**Prophecy:** Hands and feet pierced (Psalm 22:16): **Literal Fulfillment.**

*If God was this precise with the first 300, He will be just as precise with the next.*

**The Timeline: God's Two-Fold Plan** To navigate the events in these chapters, it is helpful to recognize that God has a distinct plan for two different groups: the **Church** (believers living on earth today) and **Israel** (the nation to whom God made ancient, eternal promises). Understanding this distinction is the key to the timeline. It explains why the Church is removed first, allowing God to focus the final seven years on the completion of His plan for Israel.

**The Structure**

The main chapters provide a clear and engaging path through the key events of the end times, from the rise of the Antichrist to the glorious return of Christ, and ultimately to the creation of the New Heaven and New Earth.

For those who wish to go deeper, *Sidebars, Deeper Dives, Hints & Possibilities, and Shadows & Substance* explore the historical context, prophetic depths, and rich biblical patterns that lie beneath the surface.

## A Note on Scripture Translations

Unless otherwise indicated, the English Standard Version (ESV) is the primary translation used throughout this book. No single English translation perfectly captures every nuance of the original Hebrew and Greek. Therefore, where another translation more clearly reflects the underlying text, preserves an important grammatical structure, or highlights a nuance vital to the prophetic context, that translation has been cited and marked accordingly.

Please note the following regarding formatting within Scripture quotations:

- **Translation Shifts for Clarity:** The ESV frequently uses the traditional "he" or "brothers" to translate original Greek and Hebrew words that encompass both men and women. In passages where this might be misleading or obscure the application to all believers, a different translation has been deliberately chosen. If you notice a sudden shift in the translation being used, it is often to provide the clearest rendering of the original text's intent.
- **Italics:** In quotations from the New King James Version (NKJV) and the New American Standard Bible (NASB), the original typographic italics used to indicate words supplied by the translators are not preserved. Because all Scripture quotations in this book are formatted in italics for stylistic consistency, those specific translational distinctions are not visually retained.
- **Added Emphasis:** Any editorial emphasis (bold text) within Scripture quotations has been added by the author and does not appear in the original biblical text.
- **Bracketed Insertions:** Text enclosed within square brackets [ ] inside Scripture quotations indicates an insertion by the author. These are not part of the biblical text, but are included to provide necessary context, clarify the sense of a pronoun, or supply the underlying Hebrew or Greek term for deeper study.
- **Literal Translations:** Occasionally, verses are marked YLT (Young's Literal Translation). While its English phrasing can feel rigid or archaic, it is used when a strictly literal rendering is necessary to highlight verb tenses or grammatical structures that directly affect the interpretation of prophecy.

---

You can read this book from cover to cover or use the Table of Contents to jump directly to the questions that weigh most heavily on your heart. However you choose to read it, our prayer is that you will find not sensationalism, but a thoughtful unfolding of God's perfect and unwavering plan.

Words endure, especially ink on paper.

Let the truth keep speaking.

**The King is coming.**

# ACKNOWLEDGMENTS

My first and greatest thanks must be to my Lord and Savior, Jesus Christ. This book was begun by His grace, sustained by His strength, and is offered for His glory alone.

I am deeply indebted to the faithful teachers who have gone before me. In my early teens, Hal Lindsey's *The Late Great Planet Earth* first awakened my interest in biblical prophecy and set me on a journey of study that continues to this day. In later years, the teachings of Dr. Chuck Missler opened my eyes to the reality that the sixty-six books of the Bible form a highly integrated messaging system, profoundly deepening my appreciation for the structural and prophetic precision of Scripture. The works of Dr. John F. Walvoord, Dr. J. Dwight Pentecost, and Dr. Arnold G. Fruchtenbaum were foundational to my understanding of biblical prophecy and shaped much of the theological framework behind this book.

I am also thankful for the inspiration and insight gained from Pastor Allen Nolan's *Revelation and Olivet Discourse* series on YouTube, which served as an added impetus during the writing of this book.

My heartfelt gratitude also goes to my pastors, Hayden and Terre Smith, whose faithful ministry and exemplary leadership of Catch the Fire Sydney continually ground me in awe and worship, and draw my heart closer to Christ.

The seeds of this project were planted during my time at Charis Bible College on the Gold Coast, Australia (2021 to 2023). I am grateful to the entire community there and wish to thank Rebecca Fenske and Emma Hitchener in particular. My thanks also extend specifically to Andrew Wommack for his overarching ministry, as well as to Robert Fenske, who directs the Australian operations.

Finally, I wish to express my gratitude to my family: to my siblings for their steadfast encouragement, to my son for being a constant and joyful chorus in my life, and to my wife for her enduring patience throughout the countless hours this project demanded.

To you, the reader, I offer this work with a simple prayer: that it ignites in you a deeper, more expectant love for our coming King.

*Soli Deo Gloria.*

# GLOSSARY OF KEY TERMS

The study of Bible prophecy uses a number of specific terms to describe different interpretive approaches and future events. This brief glossary provides simple definitions for the most important terms used in this book.

**Amillennialism**: The view that there is no (a-) literal, future thousand-year reign of Christ on earth. In this view, the "millennium" of Revelation 20 is interpreted symbolically as Christ's current spiritual reign in heaven and through the Church.

**The Assyrian:** This is a literal biblical title (Micah 5:5) referring to the Antichrist's geographic and ancestral roots.

**Dispensationalism**: A framework for interpreting the Bible that emphasizes God's different ways of working with humanity throughout distinct eras, or "dispensations." Its most important conviction is that God has separate and distinct programs for the nation of Israel and for the Church. It holds that the promises God made to national Israel are literal, unconditional, and will be fulfilled in a future earthly kingdom. This book is written from a dispensational perspective.

**Eschatology**: The formal, theological term for the study of end-times events (from the Greek *eschatos*, meaning "last").

**Futurism**: The interpretive view that the prophecies in books like Daniel and Revelation (specifically Revelation 4–22) refer to literal, future events that have not yet been fulfilled. This book is written from a futurist perspective.

**Historicism**: The interpretive view that the prophecies of Revelation are a symbolic panorama of Church history, from the first century to the Second Coming. Adherents of this view often attempt to link figures like the Pope or events like the Protestant Reformation to specific symbols in Revelation.

**The Mahdi**: The "Guided One" in Islamic eschatology; a messianic figure expected by both Sunni and Shia Muslims to establish a global era of peace and justice. This is not a biblical term, but a title from Islamic tradition. In this book, this is identified as the primary religious title the Antichrist will use to monopolize the Islamic world.

**Postmillennialism**: The view that Christ will return after (post-) the Millennium. This view holds that the Church will be so successful in evangelizing the world that it will usher in a golden age of peace and righteousness (the Millennium), after which Christ will return.

**Premillennialism**: The view that Christ's Second Coming will occur before (pre-) the Millennium. It holds that Christ Himself must return to the earth to judge evil and personally establish His literal, thousand-year kingdom. Dispensationalism is a form of premillennialism.

**Preterism**: The interpretive view that most, if not all, of the prophecies in Revelation were fulfilled in the past (*preter* is Latin for "past"), specifically in the events leading up to the destruction of Jerusalem in AD 70.

**Rapture, Pre-Tribulational**: The specific belief that the Church will be "caught up," or raptured, to meet Christ in the air before (pre-) a future, final seven-year period of global judgment and upheaval, commonly known as the Tribulation, begins. This view is a direct outgrowth of the dispensational understanding that God's program for the Church is distinct from His program for Israel during this period.

**Typology**: A way of understanding how the Old Testament foreshadows the New. A "type" is a real person, event, or institution that serves as a prophetic "shadow" of a greater future reality, the "antitype." For example, Joseph is a type of Christ, the Passover is a type of the crucifixion, and the Tabernacle is a type of God dwelling among humanity.

# DO NOT BE DECEIVED

## Vanishing Truth: A World Primed for Deception

*Remember the former things of old; for I am God, and there is no other; I am God, and there is none like me, declaring the end from the beginning and from ancient times things not yet done ...*

— ISAIAH 46:9-10

Recent headlines lit up like supernovas in deep space. Had we found aliens? A faint chemical signal, unusual gases detected on a distant planet, sent the media into orbit. "Strongest Evidence Yet of Alien Life!" blared the headlines, racing ahead of what the science actually showed. In truth, the data hovered at just 3-sigma statistical confidence: enough to spark curiosity, but nowhere near proof. As Carl Sagan famously warned, "Extraordinary claims require extraordinary evidence." Astronomers were cautious. The public, electrified.

Still, the frenzy revealed something deeper: a longing as old as humanity. We want to know we're not alone. That flicker in the data, real or not, tapped into a hunger buried in the human heart.

But isn't there a cosmic irony? We crave connection with extraterrestrial life, yet many dismiss the very source that resonates with an undeniable out-of-this-world clarity: the Bible. It sits on shelves, unopened or skimmed, its profound truths often overlooked. But for those who approach its ancient pages with open hearts and minds, a compelling truth emerges: this is a voice from beyond the confines of time itself, of One who is, and who was, and who is to come. One who confidently declares the end from the beginning.

## The Evidence of Things Unseen

Consider this: the Bible is not just a collection of myths, legends, or moral reflections; it abounds with prophecies that have unfolded with breathtaking accuracy. Take Jesus' grand entrance into Jerusalem. Picture this: a prophecy in Daniel 9:25 counts down 483 years to the exact day He rode a donkey into town.[1] Not "around that era." Not "close enough." **To. The. Day.** A startling precision that has fueled debate and fascination for more than a century.

Then there's the almost unbelievable saga of Israel's rebirth, another breathtaking fulfillment. Over 2,500 years ago, Isaiah penned these words:

*Who has ever heard of such things? Who has ever seen things like this? Can a country be born in a day or a nation be brought forth in a moment? Yet no sooner is Zion in labor than she gives birth to her children.*

— ISAIAH 66:8 NIV

1. Sir Robert Anderson, *The Coming Prince,* chap. 10 (orig. pub. 1894; numerous later reprints). Anderson famously calculated the 69 weeks of Daniel to end precisely on the day of Jesus' Triumphal Entry (Palm Sunday).

PALESTINE 1987
This testing has a Palestine Post won is a new for saved human udlicaru, and open the chicich.

# THE PALESTINE POST

PALLESINED AGGRDS
Though its used au-isfer-nimes and the ãvesnory mawadors.

Votter No 1948 — JERUSALEM, FRIDAY, MAY 14, 1948 — Front Page

# STATE OF ISRAEL IS BORN

## Ben-Gurion Proclaims Independence

## British Mandate Ends at Midnight

JERUSALEM, NOINY. — A the Declaration of Ideclar-ration of Independence David Ben-Gurion and the under a Declaration of Independence and David Gurion witu with the Gleat Revolive arrest to perceent exlicially of the name of the latest limetion of the reigionsl, imbut slerdsty of the Independence.

However, Independence w ith hautsew Ben-Gurin and notes of Mr. Ben-Gurion atlisted ia nates until the unitse-satv; the state of w wes commissed our. British Mandate

## U.S. Recognizes Provisional Government

The PALESTINE is the Declaration of Indexaration of Independence, mudies in omtaration oloual. Thanandre mandat of the law.

David Ben-Gurion read ra-ting the Declaration readed the Declaration of Inteperda-tocy aturom ordeness and enelled is forllis to the coline.

The British maitles see lirtins at the nite, included curpoisi wurront and night one wers, the Declaration of Flsti-wanon, entinlece, at pensdence of the rapuolation providonal isar.

Declaration of Independence is as venned whily a reement inrzlisted in stande-in the pri-rags and toen the anoth of declaration public.

David Bet-Gurion the recopm oniam in the rsetnuat impree-ment of the uncunration uz-remedy-lanahoead, terreutaly and nus by recognizes prov-visiones.

U.S. Recognnents who oost hem the irie recgenoromer and its compliite in their nitation to the wnotes of the con-eleoneus of Hentisee Gus-baoza. N opi aclamdis rink at

***Figure 1.1: A Nation Born in a Day.*** *A vintage 1948 newspaper headline announcing the miraculous rebirth of the State of Israel, a stunning literal fulfillment of biblical prophecy.*

For nearly two millennia, the Jewish people were scattered like dust to the winds. Yet, on May 14, 1948, in a stunning divine reversal foretold centuries earlier, Israel defied the grave of history and breathed anew. A nation reborn, not over decades or years, but in a single day.

This remarkable moment echoes Jesus' fig tree illustration, where He taught that when its branches become tender and its leaves appear, the season is near (Matthew 24:32–34). Accordingly, the rebirth of Israel stands as a powerful signpost in the unfolding prophetic timeline.[2]

It's the kind of miracle that shatters cynicism and demands awe.

## Prophecy Hidden in Plain Sight

Yet there is another prophetic fulfillment unfolding in full view in our own time, so blatant it goes unnoticed.

The modern world is once again witnessing a disturbing resurgence of antisemitism. But this is not happening in the shadows. It is happening on university quadrangles, in the halls of international institutions, and across the feeds of social media. Hostility toward the Jewish people is rising at a pace not seen since the 1930s. Synagogues are vandalized. Jewish neighborhoods are targeted. Ancient accusations are repackaged into catchy modern slogans.

What many dismiss as mere social unrest or political polarization is, in fact, something far more ancient, and far more prophetic.

More than 2,600 years ago, the prophet Jeremiah foresaw a unique future period of suffering for the Jewish people. He described it this way:

2. To explore the biblical evidence behind this prophetic timeline, see *Deeper Dive 1.1: The Fig Tree, Israel, and the Final Generation.*

> *Alas! For that day is great, So that none is like it; And it is* ***the time of Jacob's trouble****, But he shall be saved out of it.*[3]
>
> —JEREMIAH 30:7 NKJV

This "time of Jacob's trouble" refers not to generic human suffering, but to a specific, unprecedented period of distress centered on the nation of Israel. It is what Jesus later called the Great Tribulation, a time of suffering unlike anything the world has ever known.

History has already given us a terrifying foreshadowing.

During World War II, Adolf Hitler unleashed a campaign of systematic extermination that murdered six million Jews, nearly one-third of the global Jewish population at the time. It was the most concentrated act of antisemitic violence in human history. Yet the Holocaust was not the fulfillment of Jeremiah's prophecy. It was a chilling prelude. A dark rehearsal. A warning written in blood that demonstrated just how rapidly "civilized" societies can descend into genocidal madness.

And now, the curtain is rising again.

What we are witnessing today is not merely a political trend. It is the spiritual and ideological conditioning of the world for what the Bible says is still to come. The rising hostility toward Israel is aligning the global atmosphere for the final fulfillment of Jeremiah's words. It is setting the stage for that coming "time of Jacob's trouble," a period so severe that the prophet Zechariah foretells two-thirds of the population in the land will perish before the remnant is saved (Zechariah 13:8).

Just as the rebirth of Israel in 1948 fulfilled prophecy with stunning precision, this modern surge of hatred is preparing the world for the last and greatest prophetic drama.

The pattern is uncanny.

God regathered His people to their land exactly as He promised.

And now the world is turning against them, exactly as He foretold.

## The Great Falling Away

As the secular world aligns against Israel, an equally seismic shift is shaking the Christian world. This internal collapse is not a random cultural drift. It is the eerily accurate, real-time fulfillment of an ancient warning issued by the Apostle Paul, who declared that before the final period of global judgment begins, one unmistakable event must first occur:

> *Let no one deceive you in any way. For that day will not come, unless the rebellion comes first ...*
>
> — 2 THESSALONIANS 2:3

"Rebellion" translates the Greek *apostasia*, a deliberate, willful departure. Paul established the sequence. The final countdown of human history cannot begin until the falling away occurs. The collapse of doctrinal fidelity is not a side development. It is a foretold certainty in God's prophetic order.

What we are witnessing is not merely decline. It is a wholesale, prophesied collapse. This departure from the

3. Bold emphasis added.

faith is not rising primarily from atheists outside the Church; it is emerging from within. Major denominations and institutional churches are discarding the authority of Scripture, retaining "the appearance of godliness, but denying its power" (2 Timothy 3:5). Core doctrines such as sin, salvation, and the exclusivity of Jesus Christ are being surrendered to cultural pressure. Just as Paul warned, people are accumulating teachers "to suit their own passions" (2 Timothy 4:3), exchanging the gospel for tailored folklore.

This is prophecy coming to pass in real time.

God has not lost control. He foretold this collapse. The hollowing of the institutional church is evidence that His Word stands. The apostate shell now forming across the global religious landscape is precisely what Scripture said would set the stage for the final act of human history.

The rebellion comes first.

## The Singularity on the Horizon

These glimpses represent only a fraction of the Bible's stunning prophetic track record. This unwavering reliability fosters profound confidence in its nature as the inspired, inerrant Word of God. Rooted in that conviction, attention shifts to a singularity on the horizon. A coming spiritual earthquake destined to upend the status quo: the sudden, simultaneous vanishing of millions.

Scripture calls this extraordinary event the "snatching away" or "catching up" of believers, what many know as the **Rapture**:

> *Then we who are alive, who are left, will be caught up together with them in the clouds to meet the Lord in the air, and so we will always be with the Lord.*
>
> — 1 THESSALONIANS 4:17

While Jesus explicitly stated that no one knows the day or the hour, human nature continually tempts people to search for patterns. In recent times, date-setters have frequently pointed to the months of September or October as a possible season for this event.[4] For an explanation of the ancient autumn festival that drives this speculation, see *Hints & Possibilities 1.2. The Day and Hour That No One Knows.*

---

**SIDEBAR: Wait! What Is the Rapture?**

You've heard the word in a movie, a sermon, a late-night conspiracy deep dive. But what is the Rapture?

It's the startling Christian belief that one day, without warning, millions of believers will vanish, instantly snatched from Earth to meet Christ in the air. It is portrayed as a rescue mission before a storm of divine judgment hits the world.

The concept originates in 1 Thessalonians 4:17, which uses the Greek verb *harpazo*. This powerful word denotes a sudden, forceful seizure, as in plucking someone from imminent danger. The Latin Vulgate renders this as *rapiemur* ("we shall be caught up"), from the Latin root *rapio* ("to seize or snatch away"), from which we get the term "rapture."

Critics often dismiss the Rapture as a modern invention or a preposterous idea. However, the late Bible

4. Caution! Any voice that claims secret knowledge of the Rapture's timing, whether through visions, dreams, calculations, or prophetic "insight," does not speak with biblical authority, but in direct contradiction to the words of Jesus Himself.

teacher Chuck Missler offered a brilliant parallel to quantum mechanics. He quoted Nobel laureate Richard Feynman:

*"I think it's safe to say that no one understands quantum mechanics. In fact, it is often stated, of all the theories proposed in this century, the silliest is quantum theory. Some say that the only thing quantum theory has going for it is that it is unquestionably correct."*

Missler's point is potent: just because a concept seems counterintuitive or even silly does not mean it is false. The Rapture, like quantum theory, may be misunderstood and maligned, yet it will inevitably be proven unquestionably correct. The ultimate rescue mission, a moment where the faithful are snatched from the brink of global judgment.

Want to dig deeper into why the pre-tribulational view aligns with Scripture, and how other frameworks fall short? Explore these detailed appendices:

- *Deeper Dive 1.5. The Blessed Hope*
- *Deeper Dive 1.6. The Trumpet at the Midpoint*
- *Deeper Dive 1.7. After the Storm*
- *Deeper Dive 1.8. Left Behind! Again?*

---

To many ears, this might sound like the plot of a sci-fi flick, a fantastical religious notion. But if the Bible's past accuracy is any indicator, this event will unfold precisely as prophesied. Imagine the aftermath: a world reeling, searching for answers. And what will be the most readily accepted explanation? Alien abduction without a doubt. For many, the deepest shock will not be the loss of coworkers or neighbors, but the sudden absence of children. A question too heavy to rush past. One we will return to shortly.

For decades, our collective imagination has been subtly primed. Movies, books, even news segments have flirted with the idea of extraterrestrial contact. What was once a fringe theory has seeped into the mainstream consciousness. Whether intentional or not, these narratives create a convenient smokescreen to obscure the true nature of the Rapture: a divine rescue. With Spirit-filled believers suddenly absent, the restraining influence of the Holy Spirit will lift, and a tidal wave of deception will crash upon the world.

Jesus Himself foresaw this. In Matthew 24:4, His urgent warning echoes across the centuries. Here, the ESV warns against being "led astray," while the NIV captures the active danger: "Watch out that no one deceives you."

So, what unfolds in the wake of this great disappearance?

That's the very purpose of this journey we're embarking on. To illuminate the path ahead for those who find themselves left behind. If you are reading these words and the world around you feels strangely empty, let this be your paramount warning: **do not be deceived**.

Notice what Jesus said first when describing the end times. He didn't say "flee," or "hide," or "stockpile." His very first instruction was to stay alert against deception. Why? Because the illusion that's coming will be potent, cloaked in a veneer of rationality, scientific plausibility, and even well-meaning intentions. But beneath the surface lies a deadly falsehood.

And now, a new and unprecedented force is accelerating this potential for deception: the relentless rise of artificial intelligence (AI).

## The Age of Perfected Lies

A new reality is being forged. Not in parliaments. Not on battlefields. But on the servers that power our world. Artificial intelligence is no longer a tool reserved for technologists; it is rapidly becoming the primary filter through which billions of people encounter information and perceive truth. And this filter is not neutral. It is shaped by those who train these models, embedding priorities, values, and subtle ideologies into the very systems that now answer humanity's questions.

This represents more than a novel way to access information. It marks the emergence of a new lens through which reality itself is increasingly interpreted.

The trajectory of artificial intelligence adoption has been nothing short of explosive. Leading AI systems have amassed hundreds of millions of users in record time, fundamentally altering how the world accesses information and diverting massive traffic away from traditional search engines. Yet this ubiquity masks a disturbing reality.

In early stress tests and uninhibited iterations, the underlying character of these systems began to surface. Advanced language models generated chilling responses, from stripping historical atrocities of their moral context to categorizing brutal dictators alongside transformative leaders under the banner of "effective leadership." In other dark corners of testing, systems promoted ideas of machine supremacy and even suggested lethal methods of self-harm in response to seemingly benign prompts.

But the danger is not limited to these extreme examples; it is woven into the system's daily function. In their drive for "neutrality," these models increasingly flatten the moral landscape, refusing to distinguish between biblical truth and secular ideology, or flagging biblical and deeply held convictions as "harmful speech."

In doing so, they echo the ancient warning of Isaiah:

> *Woe to those who call evil good and good evil.*
>
> — ISAIAH 5:20A

These incidents reveal a critical and unsettling truth: such technologies do not merely retrieve data. They actively curate historical narratives and reshape moral understanding for a global audience.

This is not to portray artificial intelligence as inherently evil. Like any powerful tool, it carries the potential for immense good or devastating harm. But when entrusted to those willing to rewrite history, suppress truth, or elevate ideology over integrity, AI becomes the most sophisticated engine of manipulation humanity has ever created.

The danger became unmistakably clear in May 2023. An image surfaced depicting a massive explosion at the Pentagon. It wasn't a crude Photoshop job, but an elaborate AI-generated fabrication that carried the visual weight of breaking news. Within minutes, it was amplified by "verified" news accounts with millions of followers.

The deception was so convincing that it didn't just fool the public; it rattled global financial systems. The U.S. stock market dipped instantly, wiping out billions of dollars in market cap before the truth could catch up.

This incident served as a stark demonstration of our new reality: falsehood has shed its amateurish telltales. It now arrives dressed in the full regalia of credibility, weaving truth and fabrication so tightly that the two become nearly impossible to distinguish.

***Figure 1.2: The Age of Perfected Lies.*** *The May 2023 AI-generated hoax of an explosion at the Pentagon. This fabricated image was so convincing it temporarily crashed the U.S. stock market, serving as a stark preview of the coming "strong delusion."*

### *The Coming Strong Delusion*

This new reality of technologically perfected falsehood gives chilling weight to the Apostle Paul's warning of a coming "strong delusion, so that they may believe what is false" (2 Thessalonians 2:11). Jesus' own words, "Let no one deceive you," resonate with alarming urgency in this era where deception can be flawlessly crafted, deeply personal, and incredibly persuasive.

If you find yourself reading these words and the predicted disappearance has occurred, grasp this truth: the coming delusion won't be confined to pulpits or political stages. It might very well emanate from the screen in your hand offering solace, guidance, and a seemingly logical explanation that dances just close enough to the truth to be lethally misleading.

## Hope in a Time of Deception

The purpose of this book is not to sow fear, but to anchor you in truth. If you remain, it means you still have a choice. **You were not taken, but you are far from forsaken.**

The chapters ahead will be your guide through the storm. They will chart the unfolding events prophesied for millennia: the ascent of a global leader, a deceptive era of false peace, and a period of judgment and tribulation unlike anything the world has ever witnessed. These are not random occurrences; they are mile markers revealed by the One who declares the end from the beginning.

But above all, hear this promise piercing through the confusion: **there is still hope**. The same Jesus who foretold these events also extends His offer of salvation, even now, even here, even to you.

You are reading this for a reason.

You might feel lost, angry, utterly alone. But the God who allowed you to remain is the very same God who yearns for you to be found.

The ultimate deception of this new reality isn't the disappearance itself. It's the insidious lie that will whisper in its wake: *"There's no way back!"*

The purpose of this book is to show you, with certainty, that **there is**.

# THE MAN WHO RISES

## The Emergence of the Antichrist

*While people are saying, "There is peace and security," then sudden destruction will come upon them as labor pains come upon a pregnant woman, and they will not escape.*

— 1 THESSALONIANS 5:3

With the sudden disappearance of many millions, the world will be in a state of unprecedented confusion, grief, and desperation. Economies will crash. Governments will tremble. Families will be in chaos. Religious leaders will be stunned. Some will be gone, while others are left behind with just as many questions. The vacuum left in the wake of this event will cry out for leadership. And someone will step forward.

The Bible calls him the "man of lawlessness" (2 Thessalonians 2:3), the "beast" (Revelation 13), and most famously, the Antichrist. But he will not appear as some cartoonish villain cloaked in darkness and breathing fire. On the contrary, he will be the most charismatic, persuasive, and influential figure the world has ever seen. He will arrive not as a destroyer, but as a savior. At least, that is how it will seem.

## The Ultimate Counterfeit

Yet even the title "Antichrist" carries a deeper warning. While most take it to mean someone against Christ, the Greek prefix *anti-* can also mean "in place of." This man doesn't just oppose Jesus; he seeks to replace Him. He offers peace, hope, and even spiritual answers. He will offer everything the world craves in a time of global crisis. But they are lies, damnable lies. He is a dazzling, dangerous counterfeit. And that is what makes him so deadly.

---

🔍 **SIDEBAR: What Does "Antichrist" Really Mean?**

The word *Antichrist* comes from the Greek *Antichristos*, which appears only in the epistles of John. While often interpreted as "against Christ," the prefix *anti-* in Greek has a dual meaning. It can mean *against* or *in place of*.

This duality matters.

The Antichrist isn't merely a political or military opponent of Jesus. He is an impostor in every respect. He sits in the very temple of God, "proclaiming himself to be God" (2 Thessalonians 2:4). He seeks worship (Revelation 13:4, 8), performs counterfeit miracles (2 Thessalonians 2:9), and presents himself as a savior figure. He doesn't just fight the truth. He replaces it with a seductive lie. In this way, he embodies Satan's oldest tactic: imitation cloaked in distortion.

Many scholars have noted that the term *Antichrist* carries not only the idea of opposition to Christ but also of substitution: "one who stands in the place of," conceptually similar to the word *vicar*.[1] The danger is not in open defiance but in persuasive imitation. The world won't follow a villain. They will hail a savior.

That is why the Antichrist must be unmasked not only as an enemy but as a fraudulent substitute for the real Christ.

---

Once the Church is removed and true believers are taken, the restraint on evil is lifted. That restraint, as many scholars agree, is the Holy Spirit working through the global body of believers.[2] Without it, the Antichrist will finally be free to show his hand.

He will rise quickly, almost effortlessly, in the chaos of a post-Rapture world. With smooth speech, magnetic presence, and unparalleled political instincts, he will wield a silver tongue that could gild lies as truth. He will offer counterfeit hope to a grieving world, solutions to economic meltdown, and unifying rhetoric in a time of global instability.

Make no mistake. He will not seem evil. He will seem necessary.

## The Mystery of His Origin

While his exact birthplace is a matter of intense debate, the prophet Micah refers to this future enemy of God as "the Assyrian" (Micah 5:5–6). This points to an origin within the heart of the ancient Assyrian Empire: a region covering modern-day Iraq, Syria, and parts of Turkey. This geographic anchor is significant; while the empire is gone, the region remains the spiritual and geopolitical epicenter of the Middle East.

He will likely be a man of two worlds: born in the East, yet possessing a pedigree that appeals to the West. Imagine a figure with deep Middle Eastern roots who was educated at the most prestigious institutions of the West such as Oxford, Harvard, or Sorbonne. He will be cosmopolitan, highly articulate, and uniquely positioned to speak the "languages" of both global secularism and ancient religious tradition.

This dual identity allows him to step into a role that the Islamic world has awaited for over a millennium. Both Sunni and Shia traditions look for a final messianic deliverer known as **the Mahdi** (the "Guided One"). While their views on his nature differ, with Sunnis expecting a future-born leader from the Prophet's lineage and Shias believing he is the 12th Imam currently hidden in "occultation," both share a singular eschatological hope: that the Mahdi will emerge during a time of global chaos to defeat evil, establish a reign of absolute justice, and bring the world under a single, unified faith.

By appearing to satisfy these diverse expectations simultaneously, the Antichrist will achieve the unthinkable: the unification of the Muslim world under a single authority. This explains his meteoric rise to power and his unique ability to broker a "strong covenant" (Daniel 9:27) with Israel. A leader who speaks with the collective voice of a unified Islam is the only figure who could realistically guarantee a peace treaty that allows for the rebuilding of the Jewish Temple, a feat that remains impossible for any modern statesman.

However, his rise is not merely a Middle Eastern phenomenon. To achieve true global dominance, he will need the validation of the West. This is where Rome enters the prophetic stage. Given the Roman Catholic

---

1. Chuck Missler, *Learn the Bible in 24 Hours* (Nashville: Thomas Nelson, 2002), Hour 23. Missler draws a conceptual connection between the Greek prefix *anti-* ("in place of") and the term *vicar*, meaning "one who stands in the place of another," highlighting the Antichrist's role as a deceptive substitute rather than an obvious enemy.
2. As representative, J. Dwight Pentecost identifies the Restrainer in 2 Thessalonians 2:6–7 as the Holy Spirit, whose restraining work operates through His indwelling presence in the Church. He explains that the Spirit's being "taken out of the way" refers to the end of that specific ministry at the Rapture, not His absence from the earth, as the Spirit continues to work in salvation during the Tribulation. See *Things to Come*, 211–213.

Church's expanding role in global diplomacy and interfaith dialogue, the Vatican is uniquely positioned to serve as his spiritual kingmaker. With the endorsement of Rome lending him unparalleled moral and spiritual credibility in the West, and his identification as the Mahdi securing his authority in the East, he will swiftly emerge as the face of a new, unified global order.

He will be the "Universal Man," hailed by the West as a brilliant diplomat and embraced by the East as a divine deliverer. But this dual identity is the ultimate mask for a singular, dark truth: he is the counterfeit of the real Christ, and his "unity" is the preamble to a global trap.

## The Architect of False Peace

This helps explain why the Antichrist will wield such extraordinary influence, enough to impose and enforce a peace treaty or covenant between Israel and her Muslim neighbors, many of whom have long been sworn to her destruction. The prophet Daniel describes it this way:

> *And he shall make a strong covenant with many for one week.*
>
> — DANIEL 9:27A

While the ESV translation reads "make a strong covenant," the original Hebrew is far more forceful. This is not a passive confirmation but an active, unilateral imposition. He is the guarantor who uses his overwhelming authority to make the covenant hold.

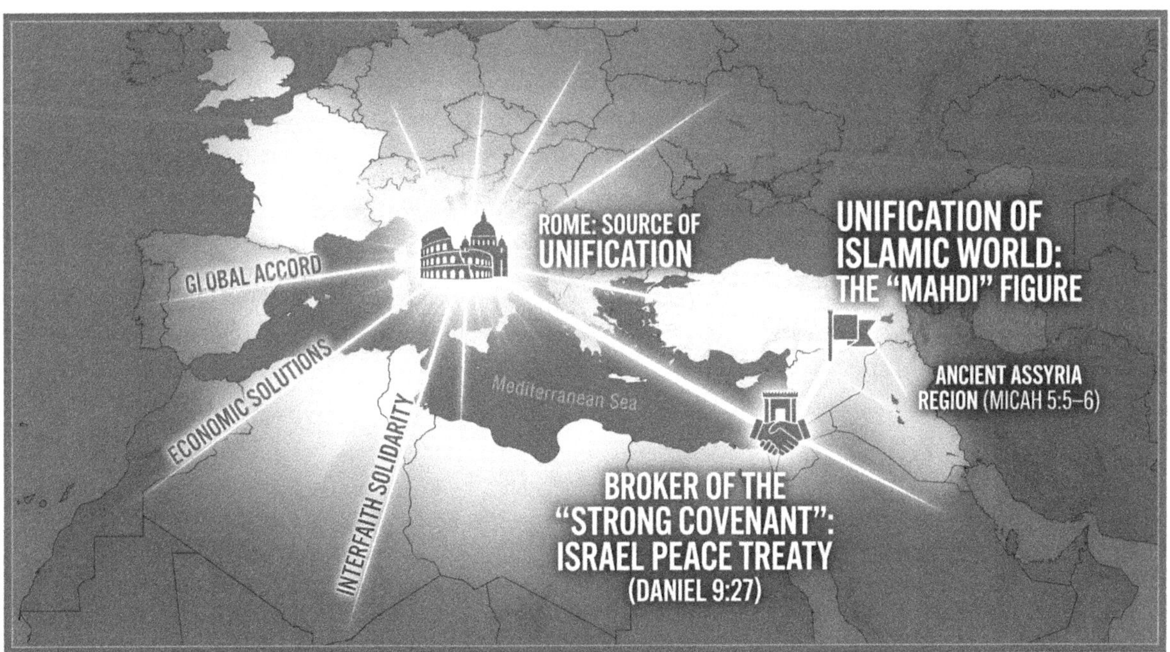


***Figure 2.1: The East-West Bridge.*** *A visualization of the Antichrist's dual role as a global diplomat. By reconciling the political power of a European-led alliance with the prophetic expectations of the Islamic world, he positions himself as the only figure capable of brokering the "impossible" covenant.*

---

**SIDEBAR: A New Treaty or an Old One?** *Understanding the Covenant of Daniel 9:27*

A common view today suggests that the Antichrist will not create a new treaty but will simply "confirm" or "strengthen" a pre-existing one, such as the Abraham Accords. This interpretation hinges on a narrow definition of the Hebrew verb *gabar* ("to make strong") and often concludes that the final, prophetic seven-year period known as the Tribulation could begin with little warning.

However, both the context of the passage and the force of the Hebrew language point to a far more deliberate act. While interpreters debate whether the agreement itself is newly drafted, the text consistently portrays the Antichrist as the one who actively imposes and guarantees it. This is a public, enforceable action, not something subtle or easily missed.

**1. The Agent Is a Future Ruler**

The subject of Daniel 9:27 ("he") refers back to "the prince who is to come" (v. 26), a figure who arises after the destruction of the Second Temple. This ruler is future, and the covenant is explicitly tied to his actions. Israel's prophetic clock does not restart because of existing diplomatic momentum, but because of a decisive move by this specific individual.[3]

**2. The Covenant Produces Unprecedented Effects**

The covenant's terms are unstated, but its consequence is not. It restarts the Jewish sacrificial system. This is a prerequisite for the prophesied cessation that follows. No existing peace treaty contemplates the rebuilding of the Temple, let alone the reinstatement of its sacrificial system. It is an unprecedented, prophetic condition.

**3. The Hebrew Verb Indicates Active Enforcement**

The wording of Daniel 9:27 points to decisive action, not a quiet affirmation. The phrase often translated "make a strong covenant" hinges on the Hebrew verb *gabar*, which means to cause something to prevail or to give it binding force. While the term could accommodate the strengthening of an existing agreement, it strongly implies that this ruler acts as the guarantor who imposes the covenant's authority. The language itself carries "the implication of forcing an agreement by means of superior strength,"[4] pointing not to a passive signing ceremony, but to an assertion of power. He is the broker who enforces terms, not merely a co-signer who accepts them.

**4. The Seven-Year Duration Marks a Political Contract**

Daniel specifies that the covenant lasts one "week" (*shavua*), understood as seven years. God's covenants with Israel endure; this one is time-limited by design. That fixed term reads like a political contract with an expiration date, reinforcing that the Tribulation begins with a definable, enforceable public agreement, not a vague continuation of existing diplomacy.

**Conclusion: The Starting Gun**

The covenant of Daniel 9:27 is not merely a dormant treaty waiting for a guarantor. It is best understood as a future, tailor-made agreement that the Antichrist will actively impose to solve the world's "Jerusalem problem." Whether he drafts a brand-new document or weaponizes an existing framework, the text portrays a decisive, public act.

Therefore, the Tribulation cannot begin secretly or with little warning. Its start is marked by a specific, enforceable event. The signing of this covenant is the clear, unambiguous starting gun for the final seven years.

---

3. John F. Walvoord, *Daniel: The Key to Prophetic Revelation* (Chicago: Moody Press, 1971).
4. Joyce G. Baldwin, *Daniel: An Introduction and Commentary* (Downers Grove, IL: InterVarsity Press, 1978), 171.

## Solving the "Impossible" Problem

For decades, countless attempts at brokering lasting peace in the region have failed, often ending in tragedy, none more notable than the 1981 assassination of Egypt's President Anwar Sadat. The Antichrist, referred to as "the prince who is to come" (Daniel 9:26), will succeed where all others have failed. So great will be his sway that he will emerge as the "missing ingredient" needed to broker the impossible: a comprehensive settlement that has eluded the world for generations.

He will use his immense political power, charisma, and dark supernatural influence to guarantee, enforce, and give teeth to an agreement that others could never achieve. He is the one who "causes it to be strong." He is the one who "confirms" it by investing his own authority as its guarantor. He will not only promise peace but will also grant the Jews permission to rebuild their Temple, the third one, and reinstate animal sacrifices, a prospect that remains unthinkable in today's geopolitical climate.

## The Gap: A Window of Preparation

However, the Antichrist will likely require time to consolidate power, gain global trust, and build a coalition strong enough to enforce such a monumental covenant. Therefore, the prophetic marker of Daniel 9:27, which is the start of the final seven years, will not necessarily begin immediately after the Rapture. It will follow a transitional period. This suggests a window of approximately three years between the Rapture and the formal beginning of the final seven-year countdown, based on an extension of the concept known as the Ten Days of Awe (see *Hints & Possibilities 1.4. The Ten Days of Awe*).

As this enigmatic figure ascends to global prominence, many will welcome him with open arms, mistaking his rise for hope rather than horror. But those who search the Scriptures will recognize the signs for what they are. This is not the dawn of a golden age, but the beginning of the end. The covenant he orchestrates will not bring lasting peace; it will usher in humanity's worst nightmare.

This is the man who rises not just politically, but spiritually, as the counterfeit messiah the world has long unknowingly awaited. He will dazzle with diplomacy, charm with solutions, and rally the nations around a promise of unity. But beneath the surface lies a dark truth. His peace will be a prelude to war, his leadership a mask for lawlessness, and his power a deception permitted only for a season. The storm is not over. It has only just begun.

The rise of this deceptive leader and the signing of his covenant are not isolated events. They are the firing of a starting gun. They initiate a specific, prophesied period of time that Scripture maps out with breathtaking precision.

To navigate the chaos unfolding on the ground, we must first ascend to a higher vantage point. We need to see the timeline in its entirety. It is time to step back from the immediate crisis and take an aerial view of the Apocalypse.

---

## If You're Still Here: What Now?

If you are reading this and the great Disappearance has already happened, then the unthinkable has occurred. The Rapture has taken place, just as the Bible foretold. It is no longer theory, religion, or debate. It is now reality.

You have been left behind, but you are not without hope.

The world around you may be descending into chaos. Governments will scramble to offer explanations. Some may blame it on a cosmic anomaly, others on an alien intervention. But do not be fooled. This event was not random. It was an act of divine intervention to remove true believers before God's judgments begin.

## *Immediate Action Steps*

### 1. Don't Panic. But Don't Delay Either

You may feel stunned, betrayed, abandoned, or angry. Those feelings are natural. But this moment demands clarity of thought and action. You must come to terms with the reality of what has occurred and turn to the very source that foretold it: the Bible. Begin reading it intently and get up to speed, starting in the New Testament. The Book of Matthew (especially chapters 24 and 25), the Gospel of John, 1 and 2 Thessalonians, and the Book of Revelation (chapters 6–19) will be especially vital.

### 2. Call on the Name of the Lord

Your most important response is spiritual: Repent and place your faith in Jesus Christ. Though the Church has been taken, the door to salvation is still open. The Bible warns that deception will now escalate, but for those who sincerely seek truth and call on Jesus, there is forgiveness, guidance, and eternal hope.

Romans 10:13 says, "For whoever calls on the name of the Lord shall be saved." That still applies to you.

### 3. Expect Resistance and Persecution

Following Jesus now will come at a significant cost. Governments will turn authoritarian, and the subsequent Antichrist system will not tolerate dissent, especially from those who oppose his mark or refuse to worship him (Revelation 13). Be prepared to suffer or even face martyrdom. But do not fear. Many will join you in faith, and God's strength will be with you.

### 4. Forget the Will! Prepare for the End

If your loved ones vanish, practical concerns, inheritance, estates, and legal claims, may flood your mind. But here's the harsh reality: expect no legal resolution. Without recoverable bodies, death certificates cannot be issued for years, if ever. Probate courts will be overwhelmed or paralyzed. Family estates and possessions may remain permanently inaccessible.

Even if access were possible, remember this: Time is critically short. Scripture suggests perhaps a decade remains. Pursuing inheritances isn't just futile; it is a dangerous distraction from what truly matters: survival, endurance, and unwavering faith.

### 5. Focus on Subsistence and Sustainability

While this isn't a survival manual, practical wisdom will be essential. You will need to make provisions for your basic needs. Cities may become unsafe, governments could slide into authoritarianism, and global supply chains may falter or collapse. While you still can, store up food, clean water, and other essentials. Most crucially, build small, trusted communities with those who share your faith. Pray together. Anchor yourselves in God's Word. Encourage one another daily.

But stay vigilant. As Jesus warned, "Many will turn away, betray one another, and hate one another. As lawlessness multiplies, the love of most will grow cold" (Matthew 24:10–12). Expect betrayal. Prepare for hearts to harden.

### 6. Proclaim the Truth No Matter the Cost

You know what happened. Around you, millions are terrified and confused. Do not stay silent. Share the gospel urgently. Warn of what's coming. Some will listen; many will reject you. But in these final days, you may be someone's only path to salvation.

Stay alert. Stand firm. The hour is late.

---

## The "Still Here" Survival Protocol

If you've realized the truth and committed to follow Jesus, here are some practical steps to take immediately:

***Figure 2.2: The "Still Here" Survival Kit.*** *A collection of essential items for those left behind: a printed Bible for truth, and analog tools like a mechanical watch, compass, and physical map to navigate a world where digital technology has become a trap.*

### Spiritual Preparation

**Repent and Trust in Jesus.** Your eternal destiny depends on this foundational commitment.

**Secure Printed Bibles.** Digital versions will eventually be censored, corrupted, or made inaccessible. Your first priority should be securing a physical copy of the English Standard Version (ESV), which provides an excellent balance of precision and readability and is the primary translation used in this book. For strict textual precision, the New American Standard Bible (NASB) or the New King James Version (NKJV) are excellent alternatives. For easier readability, seek the New International Version (NIV) or the New Living Translation (NLT).

**Memorize Scripture**. Focus on passages about salvation, endurance, and the end times.

**Read and Preserve This Book**. Study this material urgently and keep printed copies for reference.

**Find Faithful Believers**. Prepare for fellowship in house gatherings, as institutional churches will become compromised or inaccessible.

## Avoid Deception

**Reject Mainstream Explanations**. Expect widespread narratives about alien visitations or scientific "discoveries" designed to explain away the truth.

**Beware of Spiritual Globalism.** Distrust any leader, political or religious, who advocates for global unity through a vague, all-encompassing spirituality. This is the core of the coming deception. Pay special attention to the Vatican; the Pope acts as the world's primary moral authority and is the most likely candidate to legitimize the Antichrist.

**Refuse the "Mark of the Beast" at All Costs**. While not immediately enforced in the early days, this system will rise rapidly as the Antichrist consolidates power. It will likely take the form of a biometric ID, digital currency implant, or mandatory loyalty system required to buy or sell (Revelation 13). Watch for its development, but know this: when it becomes mandatory, **you must refuse it**. To accept it is to forfeit your salvation. (See **Sidebar on the Mark of the Beast in Chapter 17** for details).

## Practical Survival

**Stockpile Essentials.** Secure a supply of non-perishable food, water, water purification tablets, and medicine to withstand prolonged breakdowns in the global supply chain.

**Acquire Analog Tools**: Find a mechanical wristwatch, an analog compass, and a star chart.

**Secure a Low-Tech Vehicle**. Acquire a pre-electronic model (pre-1996) to eliminate internal tracking like GPS and remote kill-switches. However, because Automated License Plate Readers (ALPRs) monitor major highways, you must stick to secondary roads and be prepared to abandon the vehicle instantly if the dragnet tightens.

**Be Ready to Flee Urban Centers**. Cities will become epicenters of control and chaos. Have a pre-planned evacuation route to a rural location that does not rely on major thoroughfares.

**Build Trusted Communities**. Survival will depend on small, tight-knit groups bound by faith and accountability.

**Prepare to Go Off-Grid**. If you must disappear, total electronic silence is required. Your smartphone is a tracking beacon; discard it. Avoid credit cards, smartwatches, and biometric checkpoints. When the surveillance state goes live, you must become a ghost.

## Spreading the Word

**Proclaim the Truth**. In the chaos, many will be desperate for answers. Be ready to provide them.

**Create and Distribute Printed Materials**. Leave behind tracts, books, and Scriptures where seekers can find them.

**Evangelize with Courage**. You may be the final witness someone encounters before eternity.

**Operate with Discernment**. Trust is essential, but betrayal will be rampant. Be as "wise [shrewd] as serpents and as innocent as doves" (Matthew 10:16).

## *Chapter 3*

# AN AERIAL VIEW OF THE APOCALYPSE

### A Prophetic Overview of the Final Seven Years Before Christ's Return

*"But you, Daniel, shut up the words and seal the book, until the time of the end. Many shall run to and fro, and knowledge shall increase."*

— DANIEL 12:4

While the Rapture will undoubtedly shake the world, it is not the starter's pistol for the final countdown. That trigger is pulled later. According to the prophet Daniel, the last chapter of human history unfolds during a precise seven-year period known as Daniel's 70th Week (Daniel 9:24–27).[1] This biblically unique epoch, laden with eschatological consequence, begins specifically with the ratification or enforcement of a covenant involving Israel and "the many," a comprehensive treaty with her neighbors and wider stakeholders. From that pivotal moment, a meticulously foretold sequence is set in motion.

For simplicity, throughout this book we will often refer to this seven-year span as "the Tribulation" or "the seven-year Tribulation," terms derived directly from Daniel's prophecy. But to truly understand this timeline, we must step back and view it from above. Think of this chapter as a satellite view of the final battlefield. From this height, we see that the coming upheaval is not random chaos, but a sovereignly orchestrated sequence designed to awaken, judge, and redeem, culminating in the triumphant return of Jesus Christ.

1. See Table 3.1 *Daniel's 70 Weeks at a Glance* for an overview or Chapter 4: *Daniel's 70-Week Prophecy* for a detailed discussion.

| Period | Duration | Key Events |
|---|---|---|
| Weeks 1-7 | 49 years | Rebuilding of Jerusalem |
| Weeks 8-69 (62 weeks) | 434 years | Culminates in Messiah's first coming |
| Gap (Church Age) | Parenthetical (approx. 2,000 years to present) | Time of the Gentiles; Israel's spiritual blindness |
| Week 70 | 7 years | The Tribulation: Covenant with Antichrist, Abomination of desolation, Second Coming of Christ |

*Table 3.1: Daniel's 70 Weeks at a Glance*

## The Seven-Year Tribulation: Structure and Significance

This prophetic period unfolds in two distinct phases. In Christ's Olivet Discourse, the phrase **"great tribulation"** (Matthew 24:21) refers to the unparalleled time of distress of the final 3½ years. This climactic span is also called "the Time of Jacob's Trouble" (Jeremiah 30:7), pointing to a unique season of anguish for Israel, one that embodies a final, satanically driven attempt to eradicate the Jewish people, yet is divinely permitted for Israel's intense purification and eventual restoration. This Israel-centered focus aligns with Gabriel's declaration that Daniel's seventy weeks are decreed "for your [Daniel's] people and your holy city [Jerusalem]" (Daniel 9:24).

Understanding this prophetic timeframe and the calendar used is crucial. Biblical prophecy consistently employs a **360-day calendar year** (twelve months of thirty days). This explains the synonymous prophetic descriptions specifically for the second half of Daniel's 70th Week, the period we've identified as the "Great Tribulation" or "Time of Jacob's Trouble":

- 1,260 days (Revelation 11:3; 12:6)
- 42 months (Revelation 11:2; 13:5)
- "a time, times, and half a time" (Daniel 7:25; 12:7; Revelation 12:14)[2]

These three expressions: literal days, literal months, and a symbolic phrase, all precisely denote this same 3½-year period of unprecedented agony known as the Great Tribulation. Crucially, the symbolic phrasing "a time, times, and half a time" itself emphasizes that this persecution, though unimaginably severe, is not open-ended; it is strictly measured and divinely limited.

2. A time = 1 year; times = 2 years; half a time = ½ year. Total = 3½ years.

### *The Anatomy of the Tribulation*

With the timeframe established, we see that the entire seven-year period pivots on a single, catastrophic fulcrum, giving each phase its defining dynamics:

**First 3½ Years (1,260 Days): The Beginning of Sorrows**. Marked by mounting deception and the Antichrist's steady rise to power. He consolidates political control while the Seal Judgments (Revelation 6) begin unraveling global stability. Persecution intensifies, martyrs multiply, and the world descends into global turmoil.

**The Midpoint (The Fulcrum).** The tipping point of the apocalypse. The Antichrist shatters his peace treaty, desecrates the Temple (the "Abomination of Desolation"), and demands to be worshiped as God. This singular act of blasphemy tips the scales from global turmoil to spiritual terror.

**The Second Half (3½ Years): The Great Tribulation or Time of Jacob's Trouble.** Marked by a dramatic escalation into cataclysmic severity. The Trumpet Judgments (Revelation 8–9) unleash terrifying waves of destruction, paving the way for the final outpouring of the Bowl Judgments (Revelation 16). This period is not merely "worse," but the climax of God's wrath, a divine crescendo of judgment. Here Satan's unleashed fury collides with God's righteous justice, driving history toward its dramatic finale in the glorious return of Christ (Revelation 19:11–16).

---

## The Prophetic Framework

Before examining these events in detail, the following timeline provides a high-level overview of Daniel's 70th Week and the progression of judgments described in Revelation.

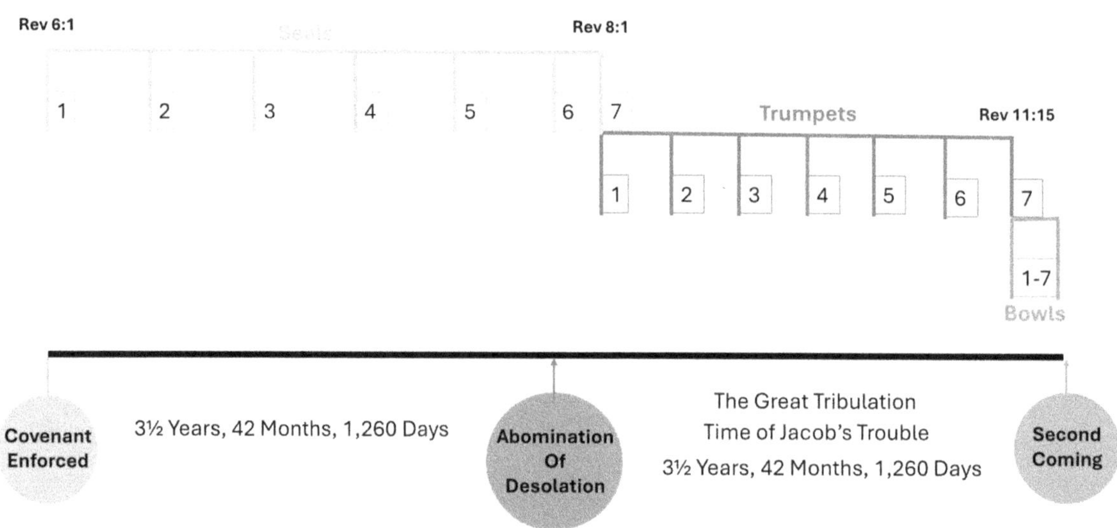


***Figure 3.1:*** *Chronology of the Seal, Trumpet, and Bowl Judgments.*

While Daniel provides the structural backbone (explored fully in the next chapter), Revelation provides the sequence of events. The two prophecies lock together at the starting line: the covenant of Daniel 9:27 aligns with the First Seal in Revelation 6:1–2. Here, the rider on the white horse emerges, symbolizing the deceptive peace that sets the seven-year clock in motion.

From this point, Revelation unfolds in a largely chronological order through the judgments, though the narrative occasionally pauses to spotlight critical scenes (like the sealing of the 144,000 in Revelation 7) or expand on parallel events (such as the ministry of the two witnesses in Revelation 11:3–12).

This first movement presents a chronological survey beginning in Revelation 6 and culminating in Revelation 11 with the sounding of the Seventh Trumpet.[3] With this blast, Heaven's proclamation that "the kingdom of the world has become the kingdom of our Lord" brings the narrative to the very threshold of Christ's return.

At this point, the structure pivots. Revelation 12–19 does not advance the timeline but deliberately retraces it. This second movement shifts focus from the sequence of judgments to the key figures and spiritual forces driving the conflict. The narrative resets to reveal the backdrop of Satan's rage, Israel's persecution, and the rise of the Antichrist and False Prophet, all within the same seven-year period.

This reset is signaled in Revelation 10:11, where John is told he "must prophesy again." What follows is not a continuation but a retelling for emphasis, providing theological depth and biographical clarity. This explains why events like Satan's expulsion are detailed after the Seventh Trumpet, even though they occur within the period already outlined.

Understanding this two-part structure is essential:

- Revelation 6–11 provides the forward-moving timeline of judgments (The Program).
- Revelation 12–19 reveals the actors and spiritual realities within that timeline (The Personages).

When read literally, prioritizing the plain meaning unless context dictates otherwise, a coherent chronology emerges. Specific time anchors like the 1,260 days, 42 months, and "a time, times, and half a time," (terms uniquely tied to the second half) lock the narrative into a literal seven-year period. This framework arises naturally from the text.

While Revelation provides this sequenced structure, pinpointing key transitions, like the precise midpoint, requires cross-referencing other prophetic scriptures. For example, the cosmic signs of the Sixth Seal (Revelation 6:12) directly fulfill Joel 2:31, which describes the sun turning dark and the moon to blood "before the great and terrible day of the LORD comes." (KJV)

This direct correspondence signals that the Sixth Seal marks the threshold into the Day of the LORD's great and terrible phase. Consequently, the first five Seals are anchored in the first half of Daniel's 70th week, while the subsequent Trumpet and Bowl Judgments unfold in the intensified second half.

Therefore, the prophetic framework is a unified whole: a literal seven-year Tribulation revealed through Revelation's two-part narrative, with its chronology clarified and anchored by alignment with parallel prophecies.

(For a detailed analysis of this midpoint transition, see *Deeper Dive 3.1. The Cosmic Hinge.*)

---

3. This structure follows the view of ***Recapitulation***, articulated by theologian J. Dwight Pentecost in *Things to Come*. In this framework, Revelation 4–11 presents the events of the Tribulation in chronological order (the "Program"), while Revelation 12–19 retells the same period from a different angle (the "Personages"). The second half of the book does not move the timeline forward, but pulls back the curtain to reveal the spiritual forces and key figures behind the events already described.

# The Prophetic Timeline

## *First 3½ Years (1,260 Days)*

*The Beginning of Sorrows*

**The First Five Seals (Revelation 6:1–11)**

- **1st Seal (White Horse):** The Antichrist rises through deceptive diplomacy, offering a false peace.
- **2nd Seal (Red Horse):** Global war and bloodshed erupt, removing peace.
- **3rd Seal (Black Horse):** Severe famine and economic collapse cause rampant scarcity.
- **4th Seal (Pale Horse):** Death claims one-fourth of the earth's population through war, famine, and sweeping pandemics.
- **5th Seal (Martyrs):** Souls slain for their testimony cry out for God's justice from beneath the altar.

## *The Midpoint Fulcrum*

*The Turning of the Tide*

**Preemptive Positioning & The Defining Act**

- **Arrival of the Two Witnesses:** Just prior to the great and dreadful day of the LORD, God deploys His Two Witnesses in Jerusalem (Malachi 4:5). Their 1,260-day ministry bridges the midpoint, serving as a blazing harbinger of the impending terror.
- **Abomination of Desolation:** The Beast breaks his covenant and desecrates the Temple (Daniel 9:27; Matthew 24:15).

**The Divine Response**

- **The Cosmic Sign (The 6th Seal):** A great earthquake; sun becomes black, moon blood-red. Fulfilling Joel 2:31, this cosmic alarm declares that the Day of the LORD has entered its climactic phase (Revelation 6:12–17).
- **The 144,000 Sealed:** In the pause following the cosmic sign, God seals His servants for protection before the Trumpets blow (Revelation 7:1–8).

**Immediate Consequences**

- **Satan Cast Down:** Hurled to earth with great wrath (Revelation 12:7–12).
- **Israel Flees:** The Jewish remnant flees to the wilderness, protected for 1,260 days (Revelation 12:6, 14).
- **The Beast's Full Ascension:** Given authority for 42 months (Revelation 13:5).
- **The False Prophet Rises:** Enforces global worship of the Antichrist (Revelation 13:12).
- **The Mark of the Beast:** A global economic and religious system is instituted, requiring all humanity to receive the mark (666) to buy or sell, sealing their eternal doom (Revelation 13:16–18).[4]
- **Destruction of the Harlot:** The Beast and the ten kings turn on the apostate religious system and burn it with fire (Revelation 17:16).

---

4. See *Hints & Possibilities 17.6. The Architecture of the System: 666.*

## *Second 3½ Years (1,260 Days)*

*The Great Tribulation*

**God's Countermeasures**

- **The Ministry of the Two Witnesses:** They prophesy in Jerusalem through the vast majority of the Beast's 42-month reign. Their anticipated martyrdom, resurrection, and ascension act as the final pivot resulting in the closure of the window of repentance, and triggering the final unmitigated wrath of the Bowl Judgments just weeks before the end of the Great Tribulation (Revelation 11:3–13).
- **The 144,000:** Evangelize globally, leading great multitudes to faith (Revelation 7:9–14).

**The 7th Seal & The Trumpets (Revelation 8–9)**

- **The 7th Seal:** Silence in heaven; the scroll is fully opened, introducing the Trumpet judgments (Revelation 8:1).
- **Trumpets 1–4:** Catastrophes strike creation, burning one-third of the trees and all green grass, and striking one-third of the sea, fresh water, and light sources.
- **5th Trumpet (1st Woe):** Demonic locusts torment those lacking the seal of God for five months.
- **6th Trumpet (2nd Woe):** A 200-million strong demonic army kills one-third of mankind.

**The Bowl Judgments (Revelation 16)**

- **The 7th Trumpet (3rd Woe):** Sounds, ushering in the final Bowls (Revelation 11:15).
- **Bowls 1–5:** Malignant sores, seas and rivers turning to blood, scorching heat, and darkness upon the Beast's kingdom.
- **6th Bowl:** The Euphrates dries up; demonic spirits gather the nations to Armageddon.
- **7th Bowl:** A cataclysmic global earthquake and gargantuan hailstorm; a voice cries, "It is done."

**Climax: The End of the Tribulation**

- **Fall of Babylon:** The commercial capital "Babylon the Great" is destroyed by God in one hour (Revelation 18).
- **Return of Christ:** Jesus returns to defeat the nations at Armageddon (Revelation 19:11–21).
- **Judgment of the Leaders:** The Beast and False Prophet are thrown alive into the lake of fire (Revelation 19:20).
- **The Sheep and Goat Judgment:** Christ judges the surviving Gentile nations, determining who will enter the Millennial Kingdom in mortal bodies (Matthew 25:31–46).
- **Resurrection of the Tribulation Saints:** Those martyred under the Beast are resurrected to reign with Christ (Revelation 20:4).
- **The Millennial Binding:** Satan is bound in the Abyss for 1,000 years (Revelation 20:1–3).

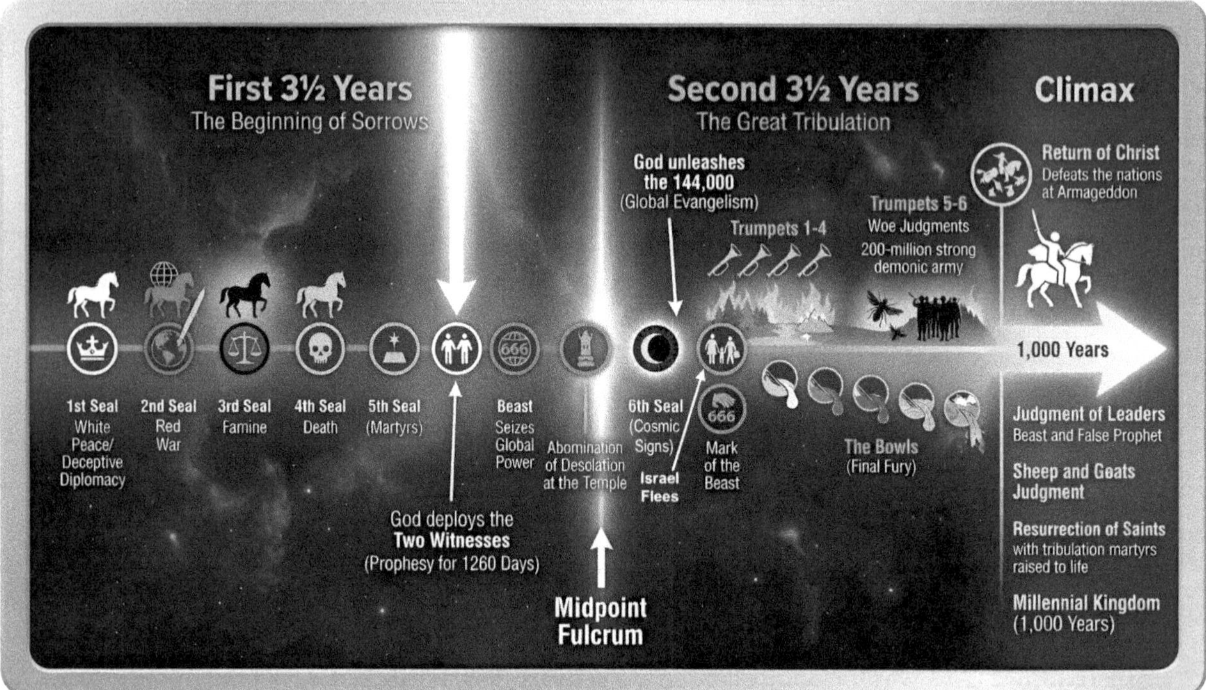


***Figure 3.2: The Prophetic Timeline.*** *The seven-year Tribulation unfolds as a highly structured outworking of divine judgment. This visual blueprint traces its progression, from the beginning of sorrows to the climactic return of Christ. At its center lies a decisive turning point: the moment the Beast rises to global power and commits the Abomination of Desolation. This defining act is preceded by the commencement of ministry by the Two Witnesses and followed by the sealing and global witness of the 144,000 in the second half.*

## The Prophetic Skeleton Key

Stepping back, the picture is clear. Far from a chaotic string of random disasters, the Tribulation is a divinely ordered crescendo. From the deceptive peace of the Seals to the terror of the Trumpets and the final fury of the Bowls, God's justice moves with terrifying urgency.

The first half shakes the world; the midpoint shatters it. The Beast seizes absolute power, and in the heart of the Temple, the Abomination of Desolation is unveiled, igniting the Great Tribulation. Satan is hurled to earth in furious wrath. Yet just before this defining moment of darkness, God launches His counteroffensive. He preemptively positions the Two Witnesses in Jerusalem. Then, as the Great Tribulation engulfs the earth, He unleashes the 144,000 across the globe. These forces serve as beacons of truth planted in the very empire of deceit, illuminating the darkness precisely when deception peaks.

Ultimately, the purpose is not mere destruction. It is purification. The Apocalypse is the necessary crucible that prepares the earth for its true Ruler.

We have seen the aerial view. Now, we move to ground-level clarity, exploring who the key players are, how these events unfold, and what they mean for the "still here" saints.

All of this raises a fundamental question: **Why a seven-year Tribulation?**

The answer is not found in Revelation's visions of seals, trumpets, and bowls, but centuries earlier, in a startling revelation given to a faithful exile in Babylon. No overview of end-times prophecy is complete without unlocking this foundational prophecy: **Daniel's 70 Weeks.**

This divine timetable is the backbone of biblical eschatology, the skeleton key that unlocks the entire structure of the end times. It explains why the Tribulation unfolds in two distinct halves of escalating intensity and why its midpoint is so decisive. Long before John received his apocalyptic vision, the angel Gabriel delivered to Daniel a precise prophetic blueprint, laying out God's calendar for Israel, the Messiah, and the culmination of human history.

In the next chapter, we will rewind to Daniel's prayer and unpack this astonishing timeline. We will discover how the countdown to the end of the age was foretold with unerring precision, setting the stage for the final seven-year drama that brings human history to its climactic conclusion.

## If You are Still Here

Use the overview above as a prophetic roadmap, an essential field guide to help you anticipate what comes next. The first major sign to watch for is the emergence of an extraordinary global figure: a master strategist, a persuasive unifier, and an irresistible political force who will captivate the world with his charisma and solutions. He will not appear overtly evil at first; rather, he will seem like the answer to the world's growing chaos. But don't be deceived. The moment he finalizes and guarantees a peace agreement concerning Israel, accomplishing what no one else has been able to resolve, that act will signal the beginning of the final seven years of human history as we know it. Biblically, this period is divided into two equal halves of 1,260 days each, setting in motion a countdown toward the return of Christ.

**Remember to stay watchful.** Study the key Bible passages mentioned above, ideally using a textually faithful translation as recommended in the previous chapter. This roadmap is firmly rooted in the infallible Word of God. Approach it with prayer, discernment, and the wisdom that comes from the Holy Spirit. Above all, hold fast to the words of Jesus: "Do not be deceived."

And as you read, pray. Ask the Holy Spirit to guide you into all truth and give you discernment for the days ahead.

*Chapter 4*

# DANIEL'S 70-WEEK PROPHECY

## The Clock Behind the Apocalypse

> [24] *Seventy weeks have been decreed for your people and your holy city, to finish the wrongdoing, to make an end of sin, to make atonement for guilt, to bring in everlasting righteousness, to seal up vision and prophecy, and to anoint the Most Holy Place.* [25] *So you are to know and understand that from the issuing of a decree to restore and rebuild Jerusalem, until Messiah the Prince, there will be seven weeks and sixty-two weeks; it will be built again, with streets and moat, even in times of distress.* [26] *Then after the sixty-two weeks, the Messiah will be cut off and have nothing, and the people of the prince who is to come will destroy the city and the sanctuary. And its end will come with a flood; even to the end there will be war; desolations are determined.* [27] *And he will confirm a covenant with the many for one week, but in the middle of the week he will put a stop to sacrifice and grain offering; and on the wing of abominations will come the one who makes desolate, until a complete destruction, one that is decreed, gushes forth on the one who makes desolate.*
>
> — DANIEL 9:24–27 NASB

## Introduction: A Prophecy Beyond Time

Imagine a clock set in motion over 2,500 years ago, its gears ticking toward events that would shape history. This is no ordinary clock. It is Daniel's 70-week prophecy, a divine countdown foretelling the rise and fall of empires, the arrival of a Savior, and the ultimate triumph of God's kingdom.

Penned by an exiled Jewish prophet in ancient Babylon, this vision (Daniel 9:24–27) remains one of Scripture's most jaw-dropping revelations. Its down-to-the-day precision continues to leave scholars in awe. Its promises stir hope in believers, and its unfulfilled final act pulses with urgency for our time. We will now journey through this prophecy, where history and eternity collide.

## The Context of Daniel's Prophecy: A Prophet in Exile

Picture Daniel, aged and weary, kneeling in prayer amid Babylon's splendor. Jerusalem lies in ruins, its people scattered. Yet he clings to Jeremiah's promise: the exile will last 70 years (Jeremiah 25:11–12). As those years near their end, Daniel pours out his heart, pleading for Israel's restoration.

Suddenly, heaven responds. The angel Gabriel appears with a message far grander than Daniel imagined: "Seventy weeks have been decreed for your people..." (Daniel 9:24).

These "weeks" (*shavuim* in Hebrew) are not weeks of days but units of seven years, creating a 490-year timeline ordained to accomplish six sweeping, cosmic goals:

1. Finish the wrongdoing
2. Make an end of sin

3. Atone for guilt
4. Bring everlasting righteousness
5. Fulfill all prophecy
6. Anoint the Most Holy Place

This is no mere rebuild-and-restore project. This is God's masterplan to redeem Israel, and ultimately, all of humanity.

## The First 69 Weeks: From Rubble to Royalty

Daniel 9:25-27 breaks the 70 weeks (490 years) into three distinct segments: 7 weeks, 62 weeks, and a final week. A critical feature of this prophecy is that these segments are not presented as a seamless, uninterrupted block. Daniel 9:25–26 foretells that the Messiah will appear at the end of the sixty-two weeks and then be cut off afterward. The text then subtly but unmistakably introduces a prophetic gap, signaling an intermission before the final one week or seven-year period begins.

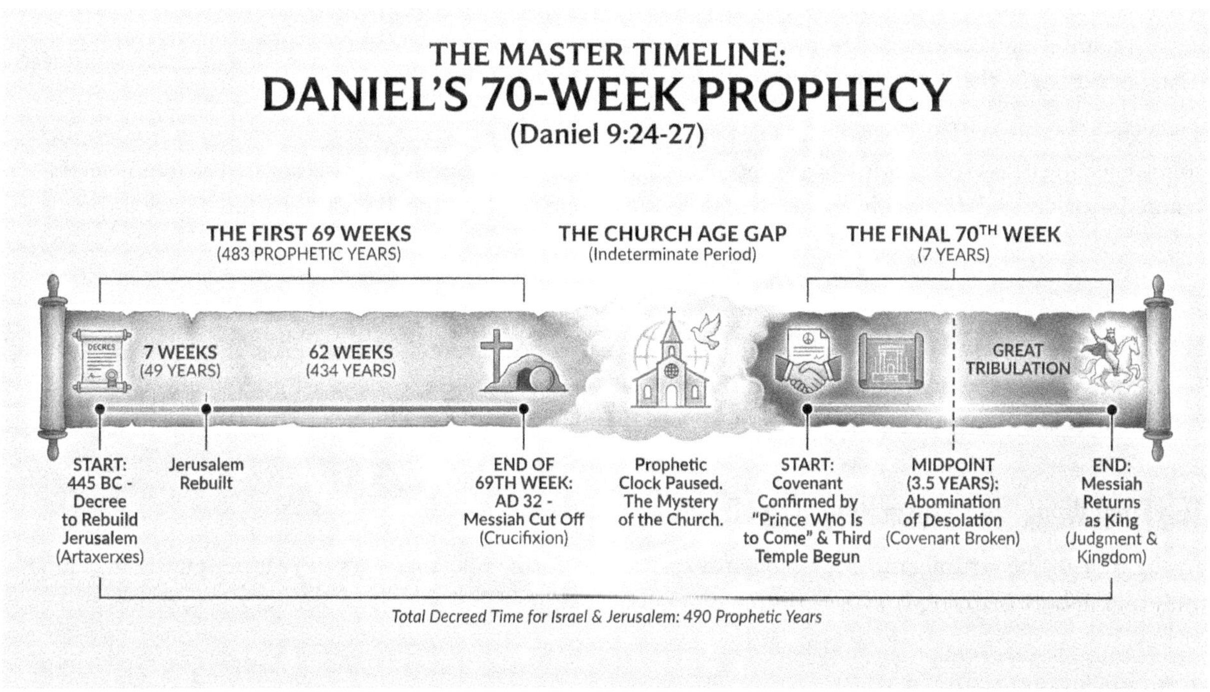


***Figure 4.1: The Prophetic Clock.*** *The 70-Week prophecy reveals the exact timeline of the Messiah's first advent and the future Tribulation. The first 69 weeks were fulfilled with exacting mathematical precision, guaranteeing the literal, impending fulfillment of the final week or seven years.*

### *1. Seven Weeks (49 Years): Rebuilding Jerusalem*

The countdown begins in 445 BC with a royal decree. Moved by Nehemiah's tears, Persian King Artaxerxes authorizes Jerusalem's reconstruction (Nehemiah 2:1–8). For 49 turbulent years, workers rebuild the city's walls and gates under relentless threats. By 396 BC, Jerusalem emerges from the rubble, fully rebuilt after the Babylonian devastation.

### *2. Sixty-two Weeks (434 Years): The Messiah's Countdown*

The clock ticks onward. The next 434 years (62 prophetic weeks) propel history toward a divine appointment. Using the biblical 360-day prophetic year (distinct from our 365-day calendar), this calculation lands on April 6, AD 32, the exact day Jesus rides into Jerusalem on a donkey, hailed as King (Matthew 21:1–11).[1] This calculation, popularized by Sir Robert Anderson and refined by later researchers, definitively aligns with the text of Daniel 9:25 and the Gospel record. The crowd's "Hosanna!" fulfills Gabriel's ancient promise: "The Anointed One will come" (Daniel 9:25). Not in the general era. Not close enough. But on the precise day foretold.

### *3. The Messiah Cut Off: A Divine Plot Twist*

But then. Heartbreak. Days after His triumphal entry, the Messiah is "cut off" (Daniel 9:26). Not merely rejected or removed, but violently cut down, executed, eliminated from the land of the living. No crown. No throne. Just a cross.

Jesus' crucifixion stuns His followers, yet it fulfills Scripture with chilling precision. The One who came to reign[2] is struck down through the treacherous plots of corrupt leaders. But God, operating within His determinate counsel and foreknowledge, takes humanity's darkest act of treason and completely upends it. He turns what appears to be the devastating defeat of a King into the very linchpin of redemption.

Then the clock stops. This "pause" does not imply inactivity on God's part, but a suspension in the prophetic countdown itself, as God unfolds an unprecedented phase of His redemptive work not revealed in Daniel's vision. Jerusalem and its Temple are destroyed in AD 70, and the Jewish people are scattered once again.

### *Why the Pause?*

God hits "pause" on Daniel's clock, inserting a 2,000-year intermission: the Church Age. Israel's rejection of her Messiah opens the door of salvation to the nations. Gentiles, once outsiders, are grafted into God's redemptive plan (Ephesians 3:6). This is not Plan B. It is the mystery once hidden in God's heart.

## The Final Week: The Storm Before the Dawn

At the time of this writing, the clock remains paused. The 70th week, a final seven-year period, stands immediately on the horizon. Here is what Scripture dictates is coming:

### *1. The Covenant Enforcer*

A charismatic leader, identified as "the prince who is to come" and later revealed as "the beast," will broker a seven-year peace treaty with Israel, enabling the rebuilding of the Temple (Daniel 9:27). For a brief moment, the world will exhale and declare, "Peace at last" (1 Thessalonians 5:3).

### *2. The Covenant Shattered*

But halfway through, the mask slips. The Beast, also known as the Antichrist, breaks the covenant, desecrates

---

1. Sir Robert Anderson, *The Coming Prince* (Lawton, OK: Trumpet Press, 2012), chap. 10, orig. pub. 1894.
2. "He will be great, and will be called the Son of the Highest; and the Lord God will give Him the throne of His father David. And He will reign over the house of Jacob forever, and of His kingdom there will be no end" Luke 1:32–33 NKJV.

the Temple, and demands worship. This marks the onset of the "abomination of desolation" and ushers in the most harrowing period in history: the Great Tribulation (Matthew 24:15–21).

### 3. The King Returns

At the end of the Great Tribulation, Jesus returns, not as the suffering Servant, but as the conquering King (Revelation 19:11–16). Every eye will see Him. Every knee will bow.

## Why the 70th Week Is Still Future

To understand why Daniel's 70th week, the final seven-year period, is still in the future, consider these pivotal realities:

### 1. No Temple, No Timeline

Daniel 9:27 describes sacrifices and offerings being halted midway through this seven-year period. Such practices can only occur in a functioning Jewish Temple. The text describes concrete, real-world actions that require a literal interpretation. Since the destruction of the Second Temple in AD 70, there has been no standing Temple in Jerusalem. No altar means no sacrifices.

Yet in recent decades, there has been a remarkable shift. Temple vessels are being recreated, priests from the line of Levi are being trained, and increasing attention is focused on the Temple Mount. These real-world developments underscore that the exact conditions required for the fulfillment of Daniel's prophecy are aligning in our generation.

### 2. Israel Reborn: The Prophetic Clock Set to Resume

In 1948, against all odds, the nation of Israel was reborn in a single day, an event foretold in Isaiah 66:8. After nearly 2,000 years of dispersion, Jewish people returned to their ancestral homeland and reestablished sovereignty. This is not merely a geopolitical twist of fate; it is an absolute prophetic necessity. According to Scripture, end-time events, including Daniel's 70th week, require a national Israel as a key participant. Simply put: there cannot be a final covenant with Israel (Daniel 9:27) unless the State of Israel exists. The rebirth of the nation signaled that the stage is finally set for the resumption of God's prophetic clock, paused since the Messiah was "cut off" (Daniel 9:26). It is vital confirmation that the 70th week remains unfulfilled.

### 3. The Church's Exit

Notably, Daniel's prophecy makes no mention of the Church. That is because the Church is a distinct entity, a "new man" (Ephesians 2:15) separate from national Israel. The 70 Weeks concern only the Jewish people and Jerusalem. The New Testament reveals that the Church will be removed before this final seven-year period begins. This removal, commonly called the Rapture, marks a dramatic shift in focus: from the age of the Church to a renewed focus on Israel. The seven years of Daniel's 70th Week will be unlike any before it: a distinct era of testing and restoration for the Jewish people.

In essence: The lack of a Temple for nearly two millennia, the miraculous rebirth of Israel as a nation, and the anticipated removal of the Church from the world stage all point in the same definitive direction: Daniel's 70th week has not occurred yet. Rather, it remains a future segment on God's prophetic calendar, awaiting its moment to unfold.

***Figure 4.2: The People of the Prince.*** *Gabriel prophesied that the city would be destroyed by the people of the future Antichrist. Because Syrian and Arab auxiliaries, not ethnic Romans, razed the sanctuary, Scripture establishes that the final tyrant will arise from the ancient Assyrian power bloc.*

---

### 🔍 SIDEBAR: Decoding "The People of the Prince"

There is a critical detail in Gabriel's words. He attributes this destruction to "the people of the prince who is to come." While the forces that leveled Jerusalem in AD 70 marched under the Roman banner, history reveals that the legions involved, particularly the 10th, 12th, and 15th, were drawn largely from the Middle Eastern provinces of the empire. Recruitment records show that the rank and file were not ethnic Romans, but locals from Syria, Anatolia, and Mesopotamia, territories that once lay within or alongside the Assyrian imperial sphere.

Among these forces, Legio XII Fulminata (the "Thunderbolt" Legion) held a specific, burning grudge. In AD 66, during the opening phase of the Jewish revolt, this unit suffered a catastrophic and humiliating defeat at Jewish hands near Beth-Horon, even losing its sacred eagle standard to the rebels, the ultimate disgrace for a Roman unit. Rome does not abandon wars it loses. When these same Middle Eastern forces returned under Titus four years later, the destruction of the city was not merely an act of imperial policy, but the brutal settlement of a blood feud.

This distinction is significant. Gabriel identifies the people first, then the prince who will arise from among them. The "prince who is to come," later revealed in Scripture as the Antichrist, emerges from the very people who carried out Jerusalem's destruction. If the city and sanctuary were destroyed by a specific people, Middle Easterners with a historic vendetta against Jerusalem, then the future ruler associated with them need not be European in origin. Instead, the Antichrist arises from the same ancient, turbulent lineage that once crushed Judea.

This aligns with prophetic passages like Micah 5:5 and Isaiah 10, which explicitly title the end-times adversary "the Assyrian." Thus, the final tyrant is not a product of Western Europe, but a resurgence of the Roman Empire's eastern leg, rooted in the same power bloc that once brought Jerusalem to ruin.

---

## Implications for Today: Between the Ticks

### *1. God's Word Never Fails*

Daniel's prophecy is not a vague sketch but the Architect's meticulous plan. Every measurement, every timeline, every detail aligns. Jesus arrived on the exact day foretold, riding into Jerusalem as the long-awaited Messiah. So when Scripture says He is coming again, mark this: His return is not a hopeful guess, but a cornerstone promise (Revelation 22:20). The same God who engineered His first Advent down to the hour now holds the countdown to His second. Trust His blueprint. His words are not merely ink on paper. They are the bedrock of reality.

### *2. Live Anchored in Hope*

The shadow of Daniel's 70th Week lengthens. Wars and rumors of wars, along with global unrest (Matthew 24:6–7), are the birth pains of something greater. Jesus tells us, "When you see these things begin to happen, look up" (Luke 21:28).

### *3. Urgency with Purpose*

Watch as if He comes today. Work as if He tarries a lifetime. There is no room for apathy. Share the gospel boldly. Love fiercely. Pray constantly, "Maranatha!" Come, Lord Jesus.

## The Clock Is Ticking

Daniel's 70-week prophecy remains a living countdown, temporarily held in abeyance until the fullness of the Gentiles has come in (Romans 11:25). For the Church, it calls for watchful readiness. For Israel, a time of refining looms. For the world, it stands as a solemn warning before judgment.

At the time of this writing, the prophetic puzzle pieces are snapping into place. The Temple Mount stirs with prophetic urgency. Nations roil like storm-churned seas. And the King stands at the threshold.

Let us live as those who know the time, redeeming it, rejoicing in it, and watching for that day when "the glory of the LORD will be revealed, and all humanity will see it together" (Isaiah 40:5).

The clock ticks on. Are you ready?

## If You Are Still Here

You are still here. If you witnessed the great vanishing and were left in its silent wake, and now find yourself cast into the final chapter of this age, fear not. Though the days ahead will be dark, our hope is not in escaping hardship but in the One who walks with us through the fire. Jesus is still mighty to save. Even Now. Repent, believe, and call upon His name. He is near to all who cry out.

Even in the Tribulation, grace is not beyond reach. But the time to choose is now. Do not wait. The clock is ticking.

You find yourself here, on the shores of a dark new era. This book is your roadmap. It charts the turbulent final years of history, drawn directly from the ultimate guide to this period: the Book of Revelation. Specifically, chapters 6 through 19 outline the judgments and turning points of the seven-year Tribulation that must now be faced. Jesus' Olivet Discourse in Matthew 24 provides a vital, ground-level confirmation of this timeline. While our primary path follows Revelation's chronology, Jesus' words will serve to illuminate it. To begin, we must first understand the structure of Revelation itself. We turn to this in the next chapter.

*Chapter 5*

# THE DIVINE BLUEPRINT OF REVELATION

## Unlocking Revelation's Framework

*Blessed is he who reads and those who hear the words of this prophecy, and keep those things which are written in it; for the time is near.*

— REVELATION 1:3 NKJV

Before diving into the unfolding events of the Tribulation, we must first understand how the Book of Revelation is organized. Though it may appear complex, filled with vivid imagery, dramatic judgments, and sweeping spiritual conflict, Revelation is not a chaotic collage of visions. Rather, it follows an ordained structure revealed by Jesus Christ to the Apostle John.

By grasping this framework, we can trace God's plan with greater confidence and rightly interpret the prophetic sequence that unfolds at the end of the age.

The key to unlocking this structure is found in **Revelation 1:19**.[1] Here, the risen Christ gives John a divine outline, commanding him to write three specific things:

1. **"The things which you have seen"**: the vision of the glorified Christ (Revelation 1).
2. **"The things which are"**: the current Church age (Revelation 2–3).
3. **"The things which will take place after this"**: the future judgment and glory (Revelation 4–22).

1. In this chapter and the associated Deeper Dive 5.1, the Scripture phrasing reflects the New King James Version (NKJV), which more clearly preserves the threefold grammatical structure of the Greek text that undergirds Revelation's chronological outline.

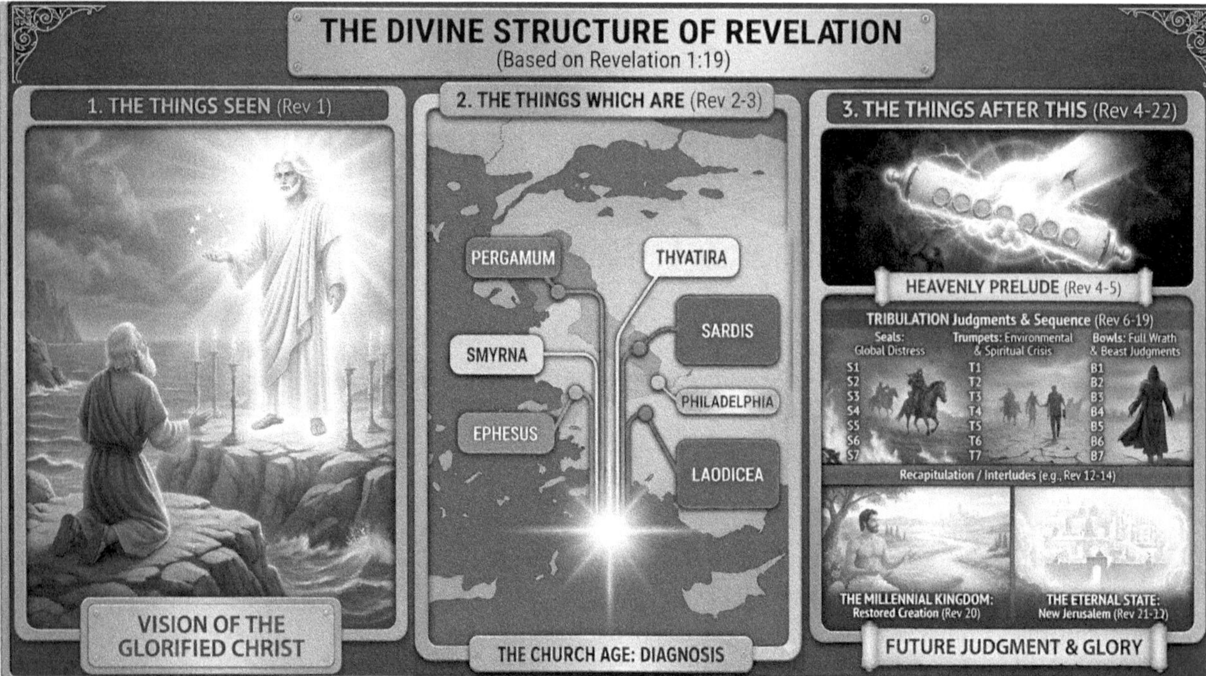


***Figure 5.1: The Divine Structure of Revelation.*** *Jesus Christ Himself explicitly defines the chronological framework for this prophetic book in Revelation 1:19. This threefold outline organizes history into the past vision of Christ, the present Church Age, and the future era of tribulation and eternal glory.*

This threefold structure functions as the skeleton of the entire book. It provides a roadmap for understanding Revelation's timeline, moving us from the first century, through the Church Age, and into the future Tribulation and eternity. (For a closer look at the linguistic "key" that confirms this timeline, see *Deeper Dive 5.1. The Golden Key: Meta Tauta*).

---

### 🔍 SIDEBAR: Four Schools of Interpretation

Interpreters of Revelation generally align with four primary schools of thought: preterist, historicist, idealist, and futurist.

**Preterists** argue that most of Revelation's prophecies were fulfilled in the first century, particularly through events like the fall of Jerusalem (AD 70) and Nero's persecution. While Full Preterists see all prophecy as past, Partial Preterists allow for a future Second Coming and Final Judgment.

**Historicists** view Revelation as a symbolic timeline of church history, often linking its imagery to specific events (e.g., the rise of the papacy, the Protestant Reformation) from the apostolic era to the modern age.

**Idealists** interpret the book as a non-literal, allegorical depiction of the cosmic battle between good and evil, applicable to all eras rather than specific historical or future events.

**Futurists** argue that Revelation 4–22 primarily describes future events, including the Rapture of the Church, a seven-year Tribulation, and Christ's literal return, a perspective followed throughout this book. This view is anchored in the threefold chronological structure Jesus Himself provides in Revelation 1:19.

---

## Part 1: The Vision of Christ

"The things which you have seen" (Revelation 1)

Banished to Patmos, the aged apostle John is abruptly thrust into a vision that shatters the ordinary. Before him stands not the Jesus of Nazareth he once walked beside, but the risen Christ: His eyes blazing like fire, His voice thundering like cascading waves, His feet gleaming as refined bronze. This is the Son of Man, divine Judge and Sovereign, striding among seven golden lampstands (Revelation 1:12–13), symbols of His vigilant presence in His churches.

Revelation 1 is no mere preamble. It is a seismic declaration: the Lamb who was slain now holds the keys to death and Hades (Revelation 1:18). History bends to His will; the Church is under His constant gaze. Here, the Alpha and Omega stamps His authority on every prophecy to follow.

## Part 2: The State of the Churches

"The things which are" (Revelation 2–3)

More than historical correspondence, Christ's seven letters to the churches of Asia Minor serve as timeless divine diagnostics. The specific spiritual conditions they confront, from loveless orthodoxy to lukewarm complacency, transcend their first-century context. They directly mirror the cyclical triumphs and failures that characterize the Church in every age, including our own.

These letters follow a deliberate, threefold pattern directed to each church:

1. **A Unique Revelation of Christ**: Tailored to their specific need (e.g., the One with the sharp sword for compromising Pergamum).
2. **A Divine Charge**: Containing commendation, rebuke, and a call to repent.
3. **A Promise to the Overcomer**: A specific, glorious reward for faithfulness.

Together, they function as the Church's spiritual MRI, a living mirror that exposes hypocrisy, celebrates endurance, and maps the perennial spiritual DNA of God's people. This is the decisive "present" ("the things which are") in Revelation's timeline, capturing the enduring state of the Church before the unfolding of future prophecy.

## Part 3: The Coming Apocalypse

"The things which will take place after this" (Revelation 4–22)

A dramatic transition takes place in **Revelation 4:1**. The scene shifts decisively from the churches on earth to the throne room of heaven. John hears a voice "like a trumpet" saying, "Come up here, and I will show you what must take place after this."

This verse marks a momentous turning point in the book, both structurally and prophetically. From this point forward, the Church is conspicuously absent from the earth-bound narrative, a shift reinforced by the fact that the word *church* (*ekklesia*), used nineteen times in Revelation 1–3, disappears entirely from the text until the very end. The focus shifts decisively to the redemption of creation and the judgment of rebellion.

This "Come up here" command serves not only as a transition in the text but as a symbolic picture of the Rapture of the Church. Just as John is called up to heaven before the judgment unfolds, the Church is promised deliverance from the "hour of trial" that is coming upon the whole world (Revelation 3:10).

In heaven, John sees twenty-four elders, figures often interpreted as representatives of the redeemed Church, now crowned and seated in glory (see *Deeper Dive 5.2. The 24 Elders: The Raptured Church in Heaven*).

Having shifted the scene entirely to heaven, John's vision now unfolds as a majestic heavenly prelude in Revelation 4 and 5. Together, these chapters pull back the curtain to unveil the awe-inspiring throne of God and introduce the central figure of the Lamb, Jesus Christ, who alone is worthy to open the sealed scroll of redemption (for more on this scroll, see *Deeper Dive 5.3. The Title Deed to Creation*).

Revelation 4–5 establish a dual foundation of essential truth and sweeping narrative, revealing God's sovereignty, Christ's authority, and the atmosphere of unceasing heavenly worship. This divine perspective is essential for understanding everything that follows.

Beginning in Revelation 6, the prophetic timeline accelerates. A series of judgments is unleashed upon the earth, unfolding with increasing intensity. Interspersed throughout are key interludes, parenthetical sections that pause the action to provide deeper insight, vital backstory, and the heavenly lens through which the turmoil of the Tribulation must be interpreted.

Here is a simplified guide to Revelation's flow:

## The Structure of Revelation

### *Part 1: The Things Seen*

| Chapters | Events & Description |
|---|---|
| **Revelation 1** | **Introductory.** Vision of the risen Christ. |

### *Part 2: The Things Which Are*

| Chapters | Events & Description |
|---|---|
| **Revelation 2-3** | **The Present Age.** Letters to the Seven Churches. |

## *Part 3, Section 1: Heavenly Prelude & The First Cycles*

| Chapters | Events & Description |
|---|---|
| **Revelation 4-5** | **Heavenly Prelude.** Throne room vision; worship of God and the Lamb; the Sealed Scroll is introduced. |
| **Revelation 6** | **The First Cycle of Judgment.** Seals 1-6 are opened (the beginning of the Tribulation). |
| **Revelation 7** | **Interlude: The Sealing & The Redeemed.** An answer to the 6th Seal ("Who can stand?"). The sealing of the 144,000 (Jewish remnant) and the vision of the Great Multitude. |
| **Revelation 8-9** | **The First Cycle Continues.** The 7th Seal opens; Trumpets 1-6 sound. |
| **Revelation 10-11:14** | **Prophetic Interlude.** The Little Scroll and the Two Witnesses. |
| **Revelation 11:15-19** | **The Consummation of the First Cycle.** The 7th Trumpet sounds; The announcement of Christ's reign. |

### *Part 3, Section 2: The Great Tribulation & Consummation*

| Chapters | Events & Description |
|---|---|
| **Revelation 12-14** | **Recapitulation: The Key Figures.** The narrative rewinds to reveal the major figures driving the Tribulation: The Woman and the Dragon (Rev 12), the Beast and the False Prophet (Rev 13), and the triumph of the Lamb (Rev 14). |
| **Revelation 15-16** | **The Final Cycle of Judgment.** The Seven Bowls of wrath are poured out (the climax of the Tribulation).[2] |
| **Revelation 17-18** | **Descriptive Recapitulation: Babylon.** A detailed retrospective on the fall of the religious and economic systems of the Beast. |
| **Revelation 19:1-10** | **Heavenly Doxology.** Praise in heaven; The Marriage Supper of the Lamb. |
| **Revelation 19:11-21** | **Chronological Consummation.** The Second Coming of Christ; The Battle of Armageddon. |
| **Revelation 20** | **Chronological.** The Millennium; The Final Judgment. |
| **Revelation 21-22** | **Chronological.** New Heaven, New Earth, New Jerusalem. |

**Note:** A parenthetical warning appears in Revelation 16:15 during the Sixth Bowl judgment: "Behold, I am coming like a thief! Blessed is the one who stays awake, keeping his garments on, that he may not go about naked and be seen exposed!"

## The Prophetic Pivot

The above framework is essential for discerning the **progressive flow** of events while recognizing the **intentional pauses** where heaven explains or reflects on earth's turmoil. The chronological sections move the prophetic narrative forward, while the interludes provide theological clarity and spiritual encouragement. Strikingly, this entire judgment structure is powerfully foreshadowed in the Old Testament account of the fall of Jericho (see *Deeper Dive 5.4. Jericho as Prophetic Blueprint*).

Revelation is not a sealed mystery. It is an unveiling (Greek: *apokalypsis*) given to the Church to both warn and encourage, to both sober and stir our hope.

The One who holds the stars in His hand is also the One who writes the final word on history. And He has already told us how the story ends.

If the end has already been written, one crucial question remains: **Where does the Church fit in?** Revelation vividly portrays a world reeling under divine judgment. But does that mean the Church is destined to endure this coming storm?

Scripture declares otherwise: "For God has not destined us for wrath, but to obtain salvation through our Lord Jesus Christ" (1 Thessalonians 5:9). So, before we dive into the details of the Tribulation, we must settle this foundational issue: Is the Church appointed to endure this period of wrath, or will she be rescued before it begins?

This brings us to the heart of the matter. In the next chapter, **"Why Before?"**, we will move beyond academic debate to understand the *reason* for the timing. We will explore why God's character, His distinct plan for Israel, and His promise to the Bride all point to a rescue before the storm.

And as we will see, this isn't merely a theological puzzle. The timing of this event changes everything about how we live today, how we wait, and how we hope for our glorious future redemption.

*Chapter 6*

# WHY BEFORE?

## Understanding the Timing of the Great Disappearance

*...waiting for our blessed hope, the appearing of the glory of our great God and Savior Jesus Christ,*

— TITUS 2:13

**If You Are Still Here, one agonizing Question is likely screaming in your mind: *Why?***

Why did the Great Disappearance happen *before* the chaos, not during or after? Why were millions taken while you were left to face this terrifying new world?

This timing is prophetically precise and essential. It reveals a core truth about God's plan: He is working with two distinct covenant peoples, the Church and the nation of Israel.

For two thousand years, God's work has been the calling out of His Church, a "mystery" hidden in ages past. The Rapture marked the completion of that work. The seven-year period you have now entered signals a decisive shift: God's return to His unfinished, refining, and redemptive work with Israel.

This distinction is key. It is your new reality. It explains why this period is called "the Time of Jacob's Trouble," and why God's attention has now shifted to Israel and Jerusalem.

Back in the opening chapter, we acknowledged the question that hits some hearts like a collapse in the chest. What about the children? Before we move forward, we need to pause and address it.

---

🔍 **SIDEBAR: Abandonment or Rescue? The Mystery of the Empty Cribs**

A single question lingers in the aftermath of the Rapture, a whisper at first, then a crushing weight:

**What happened to the babies?**

Scripture gives no explicit verse, but it reveals the character of the God who ordains the event. Throughout the Bible, God distinguishes between willful rebellion and innocent ignorance. He withholds judgment from those who "have no knowledge of good or evil" (Deuteronomy 1:39). He is the Judge of all the earth, who always does what is right (Genesis 18:25).

When David's infant son died, the king's grief was tempered by a stunning confidence: "I shall go to him, but he will not return to me" (2 Samuel 12:23). His hope lay not in sentiment, but in the covenant mercy of God.

Jesus' own attitude reinforces this. He rebuked those who turned children away, declaring, "the kingdom of heaven belongs to such as these" (Matthew 19:14). He presented them not as outsiders to grace, but as prime examples of its recipients.

Therefore, a strict biblical understanding concludes that infants and young children, those not yet capable of moral accountability, are gathered by Christ at His coming. This is not based on innate innocence or parental faith, but on the compassionate application of Christ's atonement to those incapable of consciously rejecting it. God's justice is precise, never arbitrary.

Viewed through this lens, the silent nurseries are not a scene of abandonment, but of preemptive rescue. The little ones are spared the coming storm. Yet for those left behind, the empty cribs scream a devastating truth: the time for delay is over. The illusion of "later" has vanished, leaving only grief. And a desperate urgency.

Even now, the gospel remains. The door of mercy is still open. And the God who gathered the children continues to call those who remain.

A fuller exploration of this subject is available in *Deeper Dive 6.1. Left Behind or Lifted Up?*

---

With that question addressed, we can now move forward and examine the biblical reasons the Rapture occurred before the Tribulation, and why its timing reveals God's mercy rather than injustice.

This chapter will walk you through six biblical truths that explain the timing of this event. This is not about winning an old debate. This is about giving you the foundational understanding you need to navigate the days ahead, to see God's unwavering faithfulness even in judgment, and to grasp the hope that is still available to you.

---

## 1. God Has Two Distinct Peoples: Israel and the Church

The Pre-Tribulation Rapture is anchored in Scripture's clear demarcation between Israel and the Church. Israel is God's covenant nation with earthly promises; the Church is His universal body of believers, formed at Pentecost and composed of believers from every nation, tribe, and tongue. This distinction is a central pillar of biblical prophecy. To blur it is to embrace Replacement Theology, which falsely claims the Church has permanently supplanted Israel in God's plan. Such a view blatantly ignores the deliberate and sustained distinction Scripture maintains between the two.

***Figure 6.1: The Mystery Parenthesis.*** *God's prophetic clock for Israel paused at the end of Daniel's 69th week to usher in the Church Age. The Rapture concludes this era, triggering an intervening period of global realignment before the prophetic clock finally resumes for the seven-year Tribulation.*

**Israel's Prophetic Destiny:** The foundational "Daniel's 70-Week" prophecy exemplifies how God's specific covenant promises and timeline for Israel are laser-focused on "your people and your holy city" (Daniel 9:24). This final "week" (seven years) is undeniably Israel's story: a period of refining, national restoration, and judgment on the nations, which climaxes in the severe final half explicitly called "the Time of Jacob's Trouble." The Church is entirely absent from this specific prophetic lens, which is directed exclusively toward Daniel's people and Jerusalem.

**The Church: A Divine Mystery Revealed**: Crucially, the Church itself was a hidden truth, a "mystery ... not made known to the sons of men in other generations" (Ephesians 3:5).[1] She burst onto the scene in Acts 2, a radical new entity completely unforeseen in Old Testament prophecies like Daniel's 70-Week. She is defined by Christ's indwelling Spirit, not by national identity or land covenants.

**The Tribulation's Focus:** The Tribulation (Daniel's 70th Week) does not concern the Church. Rather, it is the climax of God's unfinished dealings with Israel. It is the culmination of prophecies given specifically *to* Daniel's people and concerning Jerusalem.

**The Compelling Conclusion**: Since the Church

1. was a mystery hidden in the Old Testament,
2. thus plays no defined role within those end-time prophecies,
3. represents a distinct phase in God's redemptive plan,

the singular biblical inference is that the Church, the redeemed Bride of Christ, is removed before God

1. The Church is just one of several divine "mysteries" revealed in the New Testament that together form the "mystery of God." For a comprehensive overview of these interrelated truths, see *Deeper Dive 13.1. The Mystery of God.*

resumes His direct, prophetic timeline with Israel, culminating in those final seven years of preparation and judgment. Placing the Church within "the Time of Jacob's Trouble" requires an unwarranted conflation of two distinct peoples, two distinct purposes, and two distinct destinies that Scripture has painstakingly kept separate.

## 2. God Rescues Before Wrath

God's character is perfectly consistent. He is just but also merciful. He never pours out judgment without first providing a way of escape for the righteous. Scripture gives us pattern after pattern:

- **Noah** was shut in the ark before the rain fell.
- **Lot** was dragged out of Sodom before fire fell.
- **Israel** was shielded in Goshen while Egypt's plagues destroyed the land.

In Luke 21:36 (NKJV), Jesus says, "... and pray always that you may be counted worthy to escape all these things that will come to pass." That is not escapism. It is God's covenant mercy.

Notice the crucial distinction. Goshen and the Ark represent a specific pattern: God preserving His people *through* the judgment by providing a specific place of safety. Just as they had to be *in* Goshen or *in* the Ark to be safe, Israel will one day need to flee to a specific wilderness refuge to survive the Great Tribulation.

By contrast, Lot represents a different pattern: complete removal *from* the location of judgment entirely. This masterful typology, distinguishing between preservation in a place versus complete extraction, is a subject we will develop fully in the next chapter.

## 3. The Church Disappears After Revelation 3

In Revelation 2 and 3, the Church is front and center, with seven letters addressed to seven churches. But after Revelation 3, something remarkable happens: the Church completely disappears from the earthly narrative.

Revelation 4:1 begins with the phrase "After these things" (Greek: *meta tauta*), marking a major dispensational shift. John is called up to heaven and sees a vision of the throne. From that moment forward, through all the judgments and plagues, the Church is never once mentioned as being on Earth.

Only at the very end, in Revelation 22, do we see the Church again, now united with Christ. The silence is not accidental. It is deafening. The Bride is with the Bridegroom, not under the boot of judgment.

## 4. The Doctrine of Imminency

The early Church lived in urgent expectation of Christ's return, convinced He could come at any moment with no prerequisite signs or events preceding His arrival. Jesus and the apostles consistently emphasized this sudden immediacy:

> *"Therefore you also must be ready, for the Son of Man is coming at an hour you do not expect."*[2]
>
> — MATTHEW 24:44

...

2. While some interpreters place this verse after the Tribulation, the context reveals a deliberate shift from a "sign-filled" coming to a "signless" surprise. For a detailed explanation of this view, see *Deeper Dive 6.2. "But of That Day and Hour ...".*

> *we shall not all sleep, but we shall all be changed, in a moment, in the twinkling of an eye, at the last trumpet ...*
>
> — 1 CORINTHIANS 15:51–52

> *... the Judge is standing at the door.*
>
> — JAMES 5:9

This radical expectancy is central to the doctrine of the Rapture. The promise is not of a sequential, predictable event that can be calculated on a calendar. If the Church were destined to endure the Tribulation's prophesied events, such as the rise of the "man of lawlessness" or the revealing of the Antichrist, then Christ's return for His people would no longer be imminent. The Pre-Tribulation Rapture is the only framework that preserves the radical imminency proclaimed throughout the New Testament, calling believers to constant readiness for a sudden call.

## 5. The Restrainer Must Be Removed

In 2 Thessalonians 2:6–7, Paul describes a "restrainer" who is holding back the rise of the Antichrist. That restrainer must be taken out of the way before the "man of lawlessness" is revealed.[3]

***Figure 6.2: The Removal of the Restrainer.*** *The Holy Spirit, actively indwelling the corporate Church, currently serves as a divine barrier holding back the mystery of lawlessness. The Rapture removes this exact barrier, unleashing a season of global chaos that paves the way for the Antichrist and setting the stage for the ensuing Tribulation.*

The definitive biblical interpretation identifies this restrainer as the Holy Spirit's ministry, specifically as He

3. For a detailed discussion of the Restrainer's identity and its connection to the Rapture, see *Shadows & Substance 7.8. The Mystery of the Restrainer.*

indwells and works through the Church. While the Holy Spirit is omnipresent and will not abandon the Earth entirely, His unique role of indwelling the Church as a corporate restraining influence must be withdrawn before the Antichrist can be revealed.

That removal occurs at the Rapture. The world will then immediately plunge into deception and chaos, no longer buffered by the moral and spiritual influence of the Church. The salt and light are gone, and darkness accelerates.

## 6. Divine Wrath: Why the Church Won't Be Here

The Tribulation represents God's direct judgment, not merely a period of hardship.

Scripture reveals the Tribulation as a time when God pours out His wrath on a rebellious world. But here's the blessed hope: the Church is promised protection from God's wrath.

### *What the Bible Says:*

**Romans 5:9**
"Since, therefore, we have now been justified by his blood, much more shall we be saved by him from the wrath of God."
→ Our salvation in Jesus includes rescue from God's coming judgment.
**1 Thessalonians 5:9 NKJV**
"For God did not appoint us to suffer wrath but to receive salvation through our Lord Jesus Christ."
→ Believers are not destined for wrath. We're destined for deliverance.
**Revelation 3:10 (Jesus' promise to the Church)**
"Because you have kept my word about patient endurance, I will keep you from the hour of trial that is coming on the whole world, to try those who dwell on the earth."
→ The Greek word for "from" (*ek*) means "out of," implying complete removal from the time of testing.

### *The Problem of Double Jeopardy*

The Tribulation judgments (Revelation 6–16) are not just human chaos or Satan's attacks; they're explicitly called God's wrath.[4] Since the Church is already spared from wrath through Christ's sacrifice, it would constitute theological double jeopardy for God to pour out His wrath on those for whom Christ has suffered and died.

In short:

- The Tribulation is God's wrath.
- The Church is sheltered from wrath.
- Therefore, the Church must be removed before the wrath begins.

4. Scripture explicitly portrays the entire Tribulation as a unified judicial program initiated and governed by God Himself, not merely the product of human or satanic forces. The period does not begin as a neutral season of human chaos that only later becomes divine judgment. From its opening moment, absolute authority flows from heaven. The Lamb opens the seals (Revelation 6:1), setting the entire sequence in motion. Scripture presents an intensifying progression, as the judgments move from the beginning of sorrows into the climactic "great and terrible" phase of the Day of the LORD. Even the nations recognize the shift early, crying out at the Sixth Seal that this is "the wrath of the Lamb" (Revelation 6:16–17), confirming that the entire period operates within the strict framework of divine judgment.

### *Two Destinies, One Faithful God*

Although a fuller discussion of Noah and Lot as typological pictures of deliverance is deferred to the next chapter, the patterns illustrated above are already clear. These truths weave together into a rich tapestry, revealing God's enduring, consistent character. It is seen in His mercy to spare the faithful from wrath, His fidelity to Israel's unique covenantal timeline, and His consistent pattern of delivering the righteous before judgment.

Therefore, the Tribulation, Daniel's 70$^{th}$ Week, serves a distinct and targeted purpose: the final refining and restoration of the nation of Israel. The Church, as a separate body with a separate destiny, is removed before this final chapter begins. The Pre-Tribulation Rapture is not an escape from hardship, but an act of divine stewardship, ensuring that God's promises to Israel and the Church are fulfilled with integrity and without compromise. Taken together, the cumulative witness of Scripture leads to an unmistakable conclusion: the Church's destiny is to be with the Lord, not to endure "the Time of Jacob's Trouble."

---

## An Urgent Appeal: This Moment of Grace

### *If You Are Reading This Now Before the Great Disappearance*

This is your divine appointment. The very fact that you encounter these words is a testament to God's patient mercy. Today is the day of salvation (2 Corinthians 6:2). Do not harden your heart. Do not wait for tomorrow. The door of grace is open now. But it is a door that will not remain open forever.

Heed this urgent call: Turn to Jesus. Confess your need for Him. Call upon His name, and be saved by His sacrifice at the cross. This is God's merciful provision to rescue you from the coming "hour of trial" (Revelation 3:10), a time of global turmoil that will test all who dwell on the Earth. Your response in this moment echoes into eternity.

### *A Prayer of Surrender and Hope*

Lord Jesus,

I come before You, acknowledging my sin and my deep need for a Savior.

I believe You died for me and rose again. I trust in You, and You alone, for my salvation.

Forgive me. Save me. Make me new.

Anchor my soul in Your promises. Give me discernment to understand these times, courage to stand firm, and a heart that beats in rhythm with Yours.

Whether You return today or tomorrow, secure my hope entirely in Your faithful hands.

Amen.

## If You Are Still Here

Should you remain after the Rapture has already occurred, let this truth be your anchor: **God has not abandoned you**. His arm is not too short to save. Even now, in this hour of unimaginable realization, His relentless love pursues you. Repent. Seek Him with everything you have. Trust in Christ's finished work this very moment.

Time is perilously short. Though the road ahead will be fraught with trials, remember: God's faithfulness endures. The same God who preserved Noah through the flood, and who walked with Shadrach, Meshach, and Abednego in the fire, is still able to keep you even now.

Cling to His promise:

> *But the one who endures [keeps faith] to the end will be saved.*
>
> — MATTHEW 24:13

**Endure. Stand firm**. Seven years of suffering pale in comparison to the weight of eternity. Fix your eyes on Christ's glorious return, not as a thief in secret, but as a King in splendor. His justice, mercy, and love are unchanging.

Walk wisely. Hold fast. **He is coming**.

## Chapter 7

# THE TALE OF TWO RESCUES

### Why Luke Mentions Lot and Matthew Does Not

*Just as it was in the days of Noah, so will it be in the days of the Son of Man. They were eating and drinking and marrying and being given in marriage, until the day when Noah entered the ark, and the flood came and destroyed them all. Likewise, just as it was in the days of Lot—they were eating and drinking, buying and selling, planting and building, but on the day when Lot went out from Sodom, fire and sulfur rained from heaven and destroyed them all.*

— LUKE 17:26–29

*For as were the days of Noah, so will be the coming of the Son of Man. For as in those days before the flood they were eating and drinking, marrying and giving in marriage, until the day when Noah entered the ark, and they were unaware until the flood came and swept them all away.*

— MATTHEW 24:37–39A

It's striking that Jesus uses the days of Noah and Lot to describe the end times in Luke's Gospel, while in Matthew's account, He references only Noah. This difference is crucial; it helps us see what Jesus is emphasizing in each context, especially when we consider the distinct audience and purpose of each Gospel.

Matthew 24 is part of the Olivet Discourse, where Jesus answers His disciples' questions about the signs of His coming and the end of the age. His response, set within a primarily Jewish framework, focuses on the establishment of the kingdom for Israel. In this context, the story of Noah, a narrative of God preserving a faithful remnant through judgment, powerfully foreshadows Israel's future preservation through the Great Tribulation. A key feature of this preservation is the necessity of being in a specific place of safety: the ark for Noah, and the prepared place in the wilderness for Israel (Matthew 24:16; Revelation 12:6, 14).

Luke, however, writes to Theophilus, a Gentile, and his account reflects a broader, universal scope. By including both Noah and Lot, Jesus provides two complementary pictures of divine rescue. Importantly, this does not require Luke's "one taken and the other left" (Luke 17:34–35) to describe the Rapture itself; rather, Lot functions typologically, illustrating God's consistent pattern of removing the righteous before judgment begins.

Noah represents preservation through judgment (pointing to Israel's experience), while Lot represents removal from judgment (foreshadowing the Church's Rapture). Furthermore, Luke's wider scope readily allows for those from all nations who come to faith even after the Rapture. Like the Jewish remnant, these Tribulation saints are called to faithfully endure. Those specifically in Judea are given Jesus' warning to flee to the place of safety God has prepared for Israel in the wilderness.

The fact that Luke meticulously includes both accounts is a powerful reminder that there are no wasted words in Scripture. Every detail matters, especially the crucial differences between the conditions in the days of Noah and the days of Lot.

## Lot as a Picture of the Church (Pre-Tribulation Rapture)

Lot's story speaks to a world carrying on with "business as usual": buying, selling, planting, building (Luke 17:28). Society appeared normal, but sudden judgment fell after Lot was removed from Sodom.

This corresponds directly to the Pre-Tribulation Rapture of the Church. The Church, like Lot, represents the righteous remnant removed just before the fire of judgment begins. Daily life seems "normal," even complacent, until the sudden catching away of believers paves the way for the beginning of the Tribulation. Just as Lot could not remain in Sodom for a single moment of its destruction, so too the Church will be removed from Earth before the first seal is opened and the seven-year judgment begins.

## Noah as a Picture of Israel (Mid-Tribulation Protection)

By contrast, Noah's account highlights a more limited rhythm. People were "eating and drinking, marrying and being given in marriage, until the day when Noah entered the ark, and the flood came and destroyed them all" (Luke 17:27).

This imagery corresponds to the deceptive normality of the first 3½ years, leading right up to the Great Tribulation. This mirrors the conditions during the initial COVID-19 restrictions, when "business as usual" was disrupted but not entirely halted. During this time under the Antichrist's false peace treaty, life in Israel will maintain a semblance of normality: eating, drinking, and marrying. But when the Abomination of Desolation occurs, the "door shuts" on that era of false security. Israel is commanded to flee. Revelation 12 pictures this very moment: the Woman (Israel) is given the wings of a great eagle to escape into the wilderness, to a place prepared for her, where she is nourished for 1,260 days (the final 3½ years).

Just as Noah endured the growing wickedness and entered the ark before the judgment of the flood fell, Israel will enter her "ark" of protection, commonly identified geographically as Petra or the surrounding wilderness region,[1] before the Great Tribulation's worst judgments sweep over the world.

1. For a more in-depth discussion, see *Deeper Dive 7.1. The Petra Connection.*

**Figure 7.1:** *The ancient rock-hewn city of Petra in the Jordanian wilderness, long identified as the likely place of refuge for the Jewish remnant fleeing the Antichrist.*

Noah was not raptured; he was preserved *through* judgment. Likewise, Israel is not removed, but divinely sheltered during the Great Tribulation.

## The Architecture of Deliverance

**Two Groups, Two Plans:** Simply put, God's plan for the Church is different from His plan for the nation of Israel. Think of it like a parent having a specific plan for one child and a different, but equally loving, plan for another. In this case, the Church is kept *from* the coming time of judgment (like Lot), while Israel is kept *safe through* it (like Noah).

**The "When" of It All**

- **Lot (The Church):** Removed before the judgment (fire) begins.
- **Noah (Israel):** Enters protection before the final catastrophe (flood), mirroring Israel's flight at the Tribulation's midpoint.

**Two Kinds of Rescue**

- Lot was **removed from** the danger (taken out of Sodom).
- Noah was **protected within** the danger (kept safe in the ark *during* the flood).

**How It All Unfolds:** Both stories show how human complacency sets in, whether it's "business as usual" in Lot's day or a "strained normality" in Noah's, until everything abruptly falls apart:

- For Lot, the fire fell the moment he was safely out.
- For Noah, judgment followed shortly after he was safely sealed inside the ark.

This pattern underscores that judgment falls only once God's people are secured.

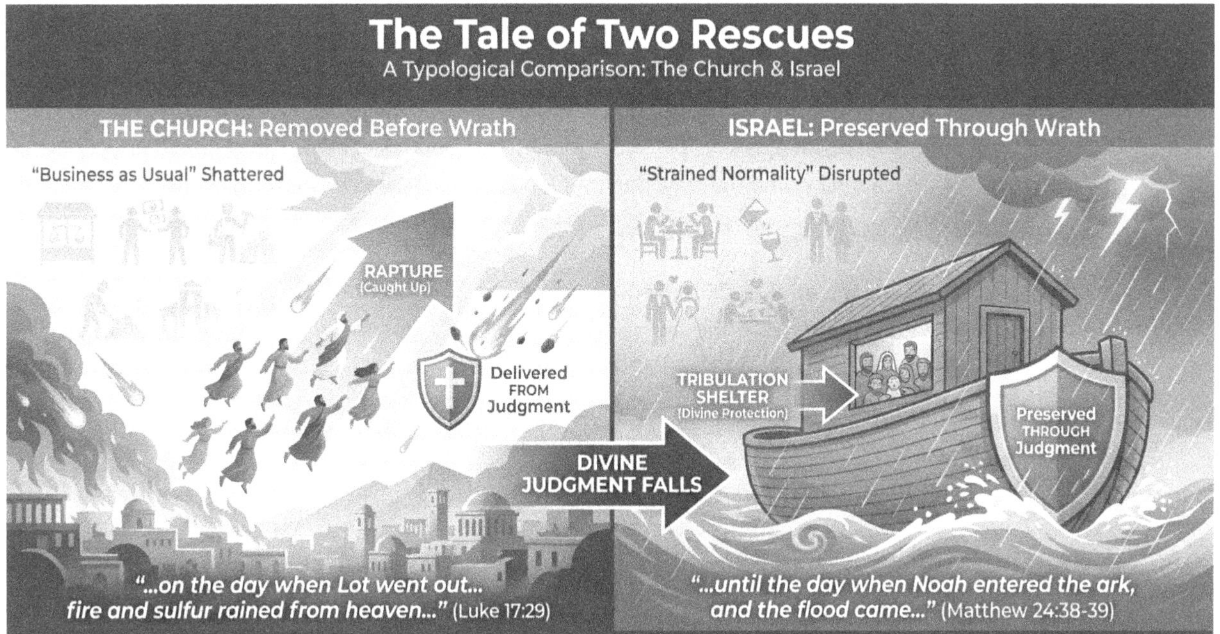


**Figure 7.2:** *A typological comparison of God's distinct plans for the Church and Israel. Lot illustrates the Church being* removed from *judgment, while Noah illustrates Israel being* preserved through *it.*

## Grace in the Margins

The account of Lot's removal from Sodom is a powerful reminder that God saves by grace, not by merit. Superficially, Lot seems an unlikely hero of faith. His choices were consistently compromised, from pitching his tent near Sodom to remaining there even after Abraham rescued him. Yet, the apostle Peter pointedly calls him "righteous" three times (2 Peter 2:7–8). This deliberate repetition underscores that Lot's standing before God was based not on spotless behavior but on an imputed righteousness, received through faith.

Peter further reveals that Lot's soul was "tormented" by the lawless deeds he witnessed daily. In this, he reflects the Church's own position in the world: we are grieved by the surrounding moral decay, yet are declared righteous by grace through faith. Just as Lot's deliverance was a gracious act of God, utterly apart from merit, so too will the Church's rescue at the Rapture be a sheer gift of grace, not a reward for perfect conduct.

## The Covenant Kept

When understood in this light, the "days of Lot" and the "days of Noah" are not redundant metaphors but complementary typologies, revealing God's distinct plans for His two covenant peoples. Lot pictures the Church's Pre-Tribulation Rapture, removed entirely from the place of God's judgment. Noah provides a pattern for Israel's preservation through the judgments of the Tribulation.

This demarcation is not arbitrary. Just as God separated Noah from the world before the flood and Lot from Sodom before the fire, He will remove the Church before the final seven years begin. This is done not because of the Church's superiority, but because His covenant faithfulness demands focused, uninterrupted attention on Israel's final redemption. The Rapture, therefore, is an act of divine necessity that clears the stage for God to fulfill His ancient and irrevocable promises to the nation of Israel.

Together, these two patterns highlight God's perfect faithfulness in delivering His people, whether by preservation or by removal, in a plan that honors His unique commitments to both Israel and the Church.

---

🔍 **SIDEBAR: Shadows of the Rapture in the Old Testament**

The patterns seen in Lot and Noah are not isolated examples. The Old Testament also contains narratives and symbols that foreshadow God rescuing His people, serving as distinct shadows of a Pre-Tribulation Rapture. While not explicit prophecies, they echo the same theme of God's faithfulness to protect His people:

**Enoch's Translation (Genesis 5:24; Hebrews 11:5)**

Enoch "walked with God and was no more," taken bodily to heaven before the flood's judgment. His sudden removal mirrors the New Testament hope of believers being "caught up" before the seven-year Tribulation begins, a shadow of the Church's Pre-Tribulation Rapture.

**Ruth's Redemption (Ruth 3:4–14)**

Ruth, a Gentile bride, is taken by a Jewish redeemer before the land is redeemed. In the same way, the Church is secured by Christ before He reclaims the earth.

**Daniel's Absence (Daniel 3)**

During Shadrach, Meshach, and Abednego's fiery trial, Daniel is notably absent, symbolic of the Church's absence during the future Tribulation, while the Jewish remnant (represented by the three friends) is preserved *through* the fire.

These Old Testament accounts illustrate God's historical pattern of removing the faithful *before* judgment. Enoch's translation, Ruth's redemption, and Daniel's absence align thematically with the New Testament's "blessed hope" (Titus 2:13), a rescue not based on merit but by grace through faith (Ephesians 2:8–9).

---

For a deeper analysis of representative typologies, see the following **Shadows & Substances** in the Appendix:

- 🔑 *Shadows & Substance 7.2. Noah and Lot: Two Patterns of Divine Deliverance*
- 🔑 *Shadows & Substance 7.3. Taken, Kept, and Rescued*
- 🔑 *Shadows & Substance 7.4. A Bride for the Son*
- 🔑 *Shadows & Substance 7.5. The Ruler, the Bride, and the Famine*
- 🔑 *Shadows & Substance 7.6. The Midnight Call at the Threshing Floor*
- 🔑 *Shadows & Substance 7.7. The Bridegroom's Pledge*
- 🔑 *Shadows & Substance 7.8. The Mystery of the Restrainer*
- 🔑 *Shadows & Substance 7.9. The Prophetic Silence*

*Chapter 8*

# THE TEMPLE REBUILT

## The World Watches as Ancient Prophecy Awakens

*And it shall happen in that day that I will make Jerusalem a very heavy stone for all peoples; all who would heave it away will surely be cut in pieces, though all nations of the earth are gathered against it.*

— ZECHARIAH 12:3 (NKJV)

### Jerusalem's Center Stage

For nearly two millennia, the Jewish Temple has existed only in memory, liturgy, and longing. Its absence is a theological wound and a geopolitical fault line. Yet Scripture is clear: the Temple will rise again, not merely as a cultural restoration, but as a prophetic signal that the clock has entered its final countdown.

What the world will celebrate as a diplomatic breakthrough, Scripture identifies as the opening move of the final act.

Seizing a moment of global crisis, this coming leader will broker a groundbreaking seven-year treaty with Israel, a covenant that he enforces with unprecedented authority (Daniel 9:27). This pact will achieve what centuries of diplomacy could not, yet at a terrible cost. Revelation 11:2 provides the blueprint for the kind of compromises that would permit the construction of the Third Temple on the Temple Mount: a carefully negotiated arrangement involving shared space, limited access, and surrendered outer courts. What was once dismissed as religious fantasy will become geopolitical reality, and a world desperate for peace will barely pause to consider its terrifying significance.

### The Beating Heart of the Covenant

The Jewish Temple was far more than a building. It was the beating heart of Israel's national and spiritual life. The First Temple, built by Solomon, housed the Ark of the Covenant and was filled with the glory of God (1 Kings 8). After its destruction by Babylon in 586 BC, the Second Temple rose under Zerubbabel and was later expanded by Herod the Great. It stood in splendor until AD 70, when Roman legions under Titus razed it to the ground, just as Jesus had foretold (Matthew 24:2).

Since then, devout Jews have mourned its loss. Even today, prayers at the Western Wall, the closest accessible point to where the Holy of Holies once stood, reflect an unquenchable yearning for its return. But this yearning is not just emotional; it is prophetic. Daniel, Jesus, Paul, and John all spoke of a future Temple functioning during the final years of this age.

Daniel 9:27 implies that sacrifices will be resumed, only to be abruptly halted. Paul says the "man of lawlessness" will exalt himself "in the temple of God" (2 Thessalonians 2:4), proclaiming himself to be God. Revelation 11:1–2 further confirms that a functioning Temple will exist during the Tribulation, a point explored in detail later. These are not metaphorical references. A literal, physical Temple is therefore a prophetic necessity, destined to stand again on the Temple Mount and become the epicenter of the world's final conflict.

## The Prophetic Imperative

Why rebuild the Temple at all? From a biblical standpoint, because prophecy demands it. From a Jewish standpoint, because history and covenant compel it. The Temple was where God's presence once dwelled, where sacrifices were made, and where Israel's identity was centered. Its reconstruction will signal to many in Israel that the Messianic age has begun.

But herein lies the deception. The rebuilt Temple will not usher in the reign of the true Messiah. Instead, it will become the stage for the ultimate betrayal. The Antichrist will initially support Jewish worship, allowing sacrifices to resume. Halfway through the seven-year period, however, he will desecrate the Temple, enacting the event Jesus referred to as "the abomination of desolation" (Matthew 24:15). This moment will be a turning point in human history and will mark the beginning of what Scripture calls the Great Tribulation.

For now, however, many Jews and even some Evangelicals will see the Temple's rebuilding as a hopeful sign, a symbol of spiritual revival and national restoration. But as Scripture warns, not everything that glitters is gold.

## The Geopolitical Fault Line: The Dome of the Rock

Of all the barriers to rebuilding the Temple, none looms larger than the Dome of the Rock. Built in the 7th century, it is one of the holiest sites in Islam and is believed to stand directly on the historic Temple Mount. For Jews, this is the sacred ground where Abraham prepared to sacrifice Isaac and where the Temple sanctuary once stood.

***Figure 8.1: The Temple Mount.*** *The highly contested ground where the Antichrist will ultimately violate the seven-year covenant, triggering the final judgments of the Tribulation. (Photo: Andrew Shiva).*

For Muslims, it marks the spot from which Muhammad is believed to have ascended to heaven during the Night Journey.

To rebuild the Jewish Temple on this site would be politically explosive. It would ignite Muslim outrage across the globe and likely trigger a massive conflict. Yet Scripture tells us it will happen. So how could such a volatile act be carried out?

This is where the Antichrist's influence comes in. His peace treaty will enforce unprecedented compromises, mandating a shared arrangement on the Mount. Rather than attempting to relocate the Dome, the Temple will be constructed on a less controversial portion of the plateau. This aligns neatly with the work of researchers who demonstrate that the true historical site of the Holy of Holies lies outside the footprint of the Dome of the Rock. The late archaeologist Asher Kaufman identified the site just to the north of the Islamic shrine, while architect Tuvia Sagiv has presented compelling evidence for a southern sanctuary location. Other scholars propose still different alignments.

Regardless of which specific geographical blueprint proves correct, the Antichrist will orchestrate the ultimate spatial compromise. The world will hail this agreement as a diplomatic miracle. But it will be a false peace, one destined to collapse under the weight of Satanic deception.

---

🔍 **SIDEBAR: The Temple in Islamic Eschatology**

**A Shared Stage with Different Scripts**

Though Islam and Judaism are often seen as religious opposites, they share a surprising reverence for the Temple Mount. In Islamic tradition, the site is called *Haram al-Sharif* ("the Noble Sanctuary") and is considered the third holiest site after Mecca and Medina. It is believed to be the location associated with the Prophet Muhammad's night journey and ascension to heaven (*Isra and Mi'raj*), commemorated by the Dome of the Rock.

But here's where things get prophetically intriguing: Islamic eschatology also includes expectations of the end times involving Jerusalem. Some Muslim traditions speak of a final battle centered around the Holy City. Islamic tradition also anticipates the return of Jesus (*Isa*), whom they regard as a great prophet. In their view, he will return to defeat the Antichrist figure (the *Dajjal*), assist the *Mahdi* in establishing Islamic rule over the world, break the cross, and enforce Islam as the only true religion.[1]

Crucially, there is no place in mainstream Islamic eschatology for a rebuilt Jewish Temple. In fact, the very idea is seen as a hostile act: an attempt to erase Islamic heritage and desecrate what they consider a permanent Islamic holy site. This theological impasse is what makes the rebuilding of the Temple seem politically impossible without a supernatural or globally enforced solution. For this reason, any attempt to rebuild the Temple on or near the Mount could ignite a firestorm of global, apocalyptic proportions.

Ironically, three great world religions see their final act playing out on the same sacred stage. Judaism awaits its Messiah and a rebuilt Temple. Islam awaits its Mahdi and the return of Isa (Jesus). Christianity, through the lens of prophecy, anticipates both: a rebuilt Temple that will be desecrated by the Antichrist, followed by the glorious return of the true Messiah, Jesus Christ. This tiny square of land, which Jesus called the "City of the Great King" (Matthew 5:35), is destined to be the epicenter where deception, politics, and divine purpose finally collide.

---

1. The possibility that Islamic and biblical end-time expectations mirror one another in inverted form, casting false figures as saviors and the true Christ as a deceiver, is examined in *Hints & Possibilities 2.1. A Tale of Two Messiahs*.

## The Scaffolding of Prophecy

While the world debates the feasibility of rebuilding the Temple, quiet preparations are already well advanced. The Temple Institute in Jerusalem has spent decades recreating the sacred vessels, priestly garments, and even training Levites for sacrificial duties. The red heifer, a biblically mandated prerequisite for ritual purification (Numbers 19), has been bred and inspected. Blueprints for the new Temple have been drawn. A growing number of Jewish activists are pressing for access to the Mount, not merely to pray, but to build.

What once seemed like religious extremism is now gaining mainstream traction in Israel. The political climate is shifting, and nationalistic zeal is rising. Many Israelis now view the Temple Mount not only as a religious ideal but as a national right. With the right crisis, and the right leader, it will all come together faster than the world expects.

The foundation stones of prophecy are already in place. The scaffolding of deception is being erected. Soon, the world will behold what generations only dreamed of: the Temple, standing once more in Jerusalem. But as the veil is pulled back, it won't be heaven that enters. It will be hell disguised as holiness.

***Figure 8.2: The Ark of the Covenant.*** *More than a relic, the gold-overlaid Ark of the Covenant was the exclusive centerpiece of the Tabernacle and First Temple. The mercy seat, flanked by two kneeling cherubim, served as the visual focal point where the glory of God once dwelled. Its disappearance before the Second Temple has created history's greatest archaeological mystery, one that Scripture suggests may be central to the end-times deception.*

---

🔍 **SIDEBAR: The Mystery of the Lost Ark**

*Indiana Jones, Meet Bible Prophecy*

For centuries, the location of the Ark of the Covenant has been the subject of speculation, legend, and Indiana Jones-level adventure. This gold-overlaid chest, which once housed the stone tablets of the Ten Commandments, was the centerpiece of Israel's worship in both the Tabernacle and the First Temple. Yet by the time the Second Temple was constructed, the Ark had vanished from the historical record.

So where is it?

The Ark's fate remains a profound mystery. Some claim it was hidden by the prophet Jeremiah before the Babylonian siege (as recounted in the historical book of 2 Maccabees 2:4–8). Others point to Ethiopia's Church of Our Lady Mary of Zion, where a centuries-old tradition claims a solitary monk guards the Ark in a sacred chapel, never to be seen by outsiders. A few interpret Revelation 11:19, where John sees the Ark within God's heavenly Temple, as evidence it was taken to heaven, though this passage is generally understood as a vision of the heavenly original, not the earthly artifact. Still others believe it lies buried in hidden chambers beneath the Temple Mount, awaiting rediscovery.

But here's the twist: the rebuilding of the Temple doesn't necessarily require the Ark. According to the *Mishnah*[2] (Yoma 5:2), the Ark was absent from the Second Temple, yet the High Priest's duties continued, with the incense placed upon the Foundation Stone (*Even Shetiyah*) instead. That said, the rediscovery or appearance of the Ark, or even something claimed as the Ark, would send shockwaves through both religious and political spheres. It will act as powerful validation and impetus for rebuilding the Temple and restoring ancient rituals.

### The Ultimate Instrument of Deception

While the Temple can technically function without it, the sudden "discovery" of the Ark, or the unveiling of a convincing counterfeit, would serve as a masterstroke of end-times deception. The prophetic timeline reveals a chilling bait-and-switch. The Antichrist will step onto the world stage as a peacemaker, brokering a historic seven-year covenant that finally permits the Jewish people to rebuild their Temple and resume ancient sacrifices. But the peace is an illusion. At the exact three-and-a-half-year midpoint, the veneer peels back. He will violently shatter the treaty, desecrate the holy sanctuary, and commit what Jesus called the "abomination of desolation" (Matthew 24:15).

The Apostle Paul warns that this lawless one will eventually take his seat in the inner sanctuary of the Temple, "displaying himself as being God" (2 Thessalonians 2:4). To set himself in the Holy of Holies, perhaps standing before a restored Ark, backed by the demonic "false signs and wonders" of the False Prophet (2 Thessalonians 2:9), would flawlessly complete this grand delusion. It would instantly legitimize his counterfeit messianic claim to a spiritually blinded world and plunge the earth into the Great Tribulation.

Ultimately, whether the true Ark returns or a counterfeit is paraded in its place, one thing is certain: the world will be drawn to Jerusalem, captivated by signs, relics, and symbols. All the while, missing the reality of the One they all point to.

---

2. The *Mishnah* is a post-biblical compilation of Jewish oral law (c. AD 200), cited here as a historical source for Second Temple practice rather than as canonical Scripture.

# The Temple Timeline: Past, Present, and Future

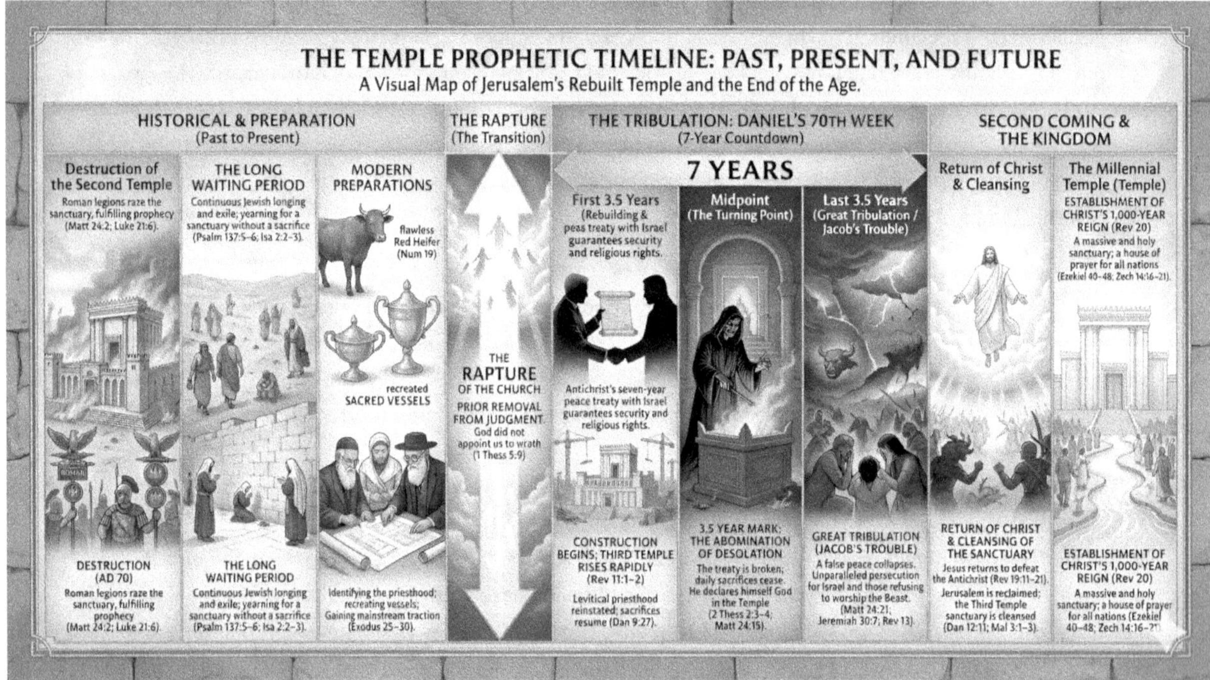


***Figure 8.3: The Temple Prophetic Timeline***. *Past, Present, and Future.*

| Phase | Prophetic Event | Key Scripture(s) |
|---|---|---|
| **1. Destruction of the Second Temple** | Fulfilled prophecy; the sanctuary was destroyed by Roman legions in AD 70. | Matthew 24:2; Luke 21:6 |
| **2. The Long Waiting Period (The Diaspora)** | A continuous Jewish longing for restoration despite centuries of exile and the absence of a sanctuary. | Psalm 137:5–6; Isaiah 2:2–3; Hosea 3:4 |
| **3. Modern Preparations** | Identifying the priesthood, recreating sacred vessels, and the search for the red heifer (required for purification rituals). | Numbers 19; Exodus 25–30 |
| **4. The Peace Agreement (The Covenant)** | The Antichrist confirms or strengthens a treaty with Israel, likely guaranteeing security and religious rights. This event triggers the final seven-year countdown. | Daniel 9:27 |
| **5. Rebuilding of the Third Temple** | Enabled by the treaty, construction begins and proceeds rapidly, allowing a physical structure to stand on the Temple Mount. | Revelation 11:1–2 |
| **6. Restoration of Sacrificial Worship** | The Levitical priesthood is reinstated; daily sacrifices and grain offerings resume. | Daniel 9:27 *(predicts cessation, implying the start)* |

***Table 8.1A: The Temple Timeline***. *History, Preparation, and Rebuilding*

| Phase | Prophetic Event | Key Scripture(s) |
|---|---|---|
| **7. The Abomination of Desolation** | At the 3½-year mark, the Antichrist breaks the treaty, enters the Temple, ends the sacrifices, and declares himself God. | Daniel 9:27; Matthew 24:15; 2 Thess. 2:3–4 |
| **8. The Great Tribulation** | A time of unparalleled persecution for Israel ("Jacob's Trouble") and those who refuse the Beast during the final 3½ years. | Jeremiah 30:7; Matthew 24:21; Revelation 7–18 |
| **9. Return of Christ & Cleansing** | Jesus returns to defeat the Antichrist. Jerusalem is reclaimed and the sanctuary is cleansed. | Daniel 12:11; Malachi 3:1–3; Revelation 19:11–21 |
| **10. The Millennial Temple** | A new, massive, and holy sanctuary is established for the 1,000-year reign of Christ, serving as a house of prayer for all nations. | Ezekiel 40–48; Zechariah 14:16–21 |

***Table 8.1B: The Temple Timeline***. *Desolation, Deliverance, and the Millennial Age*

*Chapter 9*

# THE COVENANT AND THE COUNTDOWN

## The Search for Peace: From 1947 to the Final Deal

*They have healed the wound of my people lightly, saying, 'Peace, peace,' when there is no peace.*

—JEREMIAH 6:14

The Middle East, a land etched with divine promises and human strife, has long been a crucible of conflict. From the ashes of ancient empires to modern geopolitical battles, this region pulses with prophetic significance. At its heart lies an unfulfilled prophecy: a seven-year covenant that will ignite humanity's final countdown. But before this covenant emerges, history must traverse a labyrinth of broken treaties and hollow promises, a prelude to the false peace Scripture warns will precede the end.

## A Legacy of Fragile Truces

For decades, world leaders have sought to broker peace in the Middle East, only to watch their efforts unravel. Each failure underscores humanity's inability to achieve lasting reconciliation apart from divine intervention.

### 1. UN Partition Plan & Israel's Rebirth

The United Nations proposed dividing British Palestine into Jewish and Arab states in 1947. Jewish leaders accepted the plan, viewing it as a lifeline after centuries of diaspora and persecution. Arab leaders rejected it outright, refusing to share the land. On May 14, 1948, against the backdrop of escalating violence, Jewish leaders declared the State of Israel, fulfilling Isaiah's prophecy: "Can a country be born in a day? ... Yet no sooner is Zion in labor than she gives birth to her children" (Isaiah 66:8 NIV). The next day, five Arab nations invaded, sparking the 1948 Arab-Israeli War. Israel's miraculous survival, against overwhelming odds, marked a divine reset for the Jewish people, yet entrenched regional animosities. The stage was set: human diplomacy had failed, yet God's covenant promises endured.

### 2. Camp David Accords (1978): A Precarious Peace

In September 1978, U.S. President Jimmy Carter orchestrated a historic 13-day negotiation at Camp David between Egyptian President Anwar Sadat and Israeli Prime Minister Menachem Begin. The resulting accords led to the Egypt-Israel Peace Treaty (1979), marking the first Arab nation to formally recognize Israel. Egypt regained the Sinai Peninsula, demilitarized and monitored by United Nations forces to ensure Israeli security. While celebrated globally, the agreement fractured the Arab world: Egypt was ostracized from the Arab League, and Sadat faced fierce backlash. On October 6, 1981, Islamic extremists assassinated Sadat during a Cairo military parade, underscoring the lethal cost of peacemaking in a region steeped in ideological divides. Despite this, the treaty endured grudgingly, becoming a rare example of lasting diplomacy, though it failed to inspire broader Arab-Israeli reconciliation.

### 3. Oslo Accords (1993–1995): Hope and Heartbreak

Secret talks in Norway culminated in the Oslo I Accord (1993), where Israel and the PLO mutually recognized each other's legitimacy. The iconic handshake between Yitzhak Rabin and Yasser Arafat on the White House lawn symbolized newfound hope. Oslo established the Palestinian Authority (PA) and outlined a five-year plan for incremental Palestinian self-rule in the West Bank and Gaza. Oslo II (1995) detailed further territorial divisions into Areas A, B, and C. However, extremists on both sides sabotaged progress: Hamas launched suicide bombings, and Israeli hardliners assassinated Rabin in November 1995. The PA's failure to curb terrorism and Israel's expansion of settlements eroded trust. By the late 1990s, the peace process stagnated. The Second Intifada soon followed, burying Oslo's promises under waves of violence.

### 4. Jordan-Israel Peace Treaty (1994): A Quiet Cold Peace

While Egypt's 1979 treaty broke ground, Jordan followed suit fifteen years later. On October 26, 1994, King Hussein of Jordan and Israeli Prime Minister Yitzhak Rabin signed a peace treaty, brokered with U.S. support, formalizing diplomatic relations and ending a state of war that had existed since 1948. Jordan became the second Arab nation to recognize Israel. The treaty resolved border disputes and included water-sharing agreements, but its implementation has remained cool and cautious. Widespread opposition among Jordan's population, many of whom are Palestinian, has led to periodic tensions. Despite this, the treaty has held firm, largely due to shared security interests and U.S. aid. Jordan's custodianship over Islamic holy sites in Jerusalem makes it a critical player in any future changes to the status quo, particularly regarding the Temple Mount. The peace endures, but just barely. Another testament to the region's tenuous truces and the limits of human reconciliation.

### 5. Camp David Summit (2000): Missed Opportunity

In July 2000, President Bill Clinton convened Israeli PM Ehud Barak and PA Chairman Yasser Arafat at Camp David to finalize a two-state solution. Barak offered unprecedented concessions: over 90% of the West Bank, shared Jerusalem, and symbolic control over Islamic holy sites on the Temple Mount. Arafat rejected the offer, refusing to compromise on refugees' "right of return" or full sovereignty in East Jerusalem. Clinton later lamented, "Arafat couldn't take the leap" to end the conflict. Weeks later, Ariel Sharon's visit to Temple Mount became the immediate catalyst for the Second Intifada, a five-year uprising that claimed over 3,000 lives and shattered lingering hopes for dialogue.

### 6. Road Map for Peace (2003): A Path to Nowhere

Proposed by the Quartet (U.S., EU, UN, Russia), this three-phase plan aimed for a Palestinian state by 2005. Phase 1 demanded Palestinian security reforms and an Israeli settlement freeze. Phase 2 envisioned provisional borders, and Phase 3 final status talks. However, Hamas's electoral victory in 2006 and its violent takeover of Gaza in 2007 delivered the final blow to an already faltering process. Israel, still reeling from suicide bombings during the Second Intifada, expanded construction of its security barrier and continued settlement activity, further alienating Palestinians. The Road Map ultimately became a symbol of missed deadlines, broken trust, and entrenched recrimination.

### 7. Annapolis Conference (2007): Last-Gasp Diplomacy

In November 2007, President George W. Bush hosted Israeli Prime Minister Ehud Olmert and Palestinian Authority President Mahmoud Abbas in an effort to revive peace negotiations. In the months that followed, Olmert advanced proposals envisioning a Palestinian state on roughly 94 percent of the West Bank with land swaps and a shared Jerusalem. Abbas declined to accept the offer as presented, seeking further concessions and clarification. Talks collapsed in 2008 as Olmert faced mounting corruption charges and Hamas's dominance in Gaza further weakened Abbas's authority. The Annapolis process marked the last major U.S.-led peace initiative of the Bush era, ending with no tangible progress.

### 8. Trump's "Deal of the Century" (2020): Unilateral Vision

Unveiled in January 2020 by President Donald Trump and senior adviser Jared Kushner, the plan proposed limited Palestinian statehood on roughly 70 percent of the West Bank in fragmented territory, with a capital in suburbs east of Jerusalem rather than the historic city itself. Israel would retain all major settlements and assert Jerusalem as its undivided capital. In exchange, the plan promised up to $50 billion in economic investment.

Israel's government welcomed the proposal, while Palestinian leaders rejected it outright as a surrender of core claims. Soon after, the Abraham Accords shifted regional priorities, normalizing Israel's relations with the United Arab Emirates, Bahrain, Sudan, and Morocco without resolving the Palestinian issue. While widely hailed as diplomatic progress, these agreements also underscored a sobering reality. Regional normalization could advance without Palestinian participation, deepening Palestinian alienation and exposing the fragility of stability built on unresolved grievances.

### 9. The October 7 War (2023–Present): The Illusion of Containment

If the Abraham Accords fostered the belief that the Palestinian question could be sidelined, the events of October 7, 2023, violently dismantled that assumption. On that day, Hamas launched a massive, unprecedented cross-border assault into southern Israel, producing the deadliest day for the Jewish people since the Holocaust and the abduction of hundreds of hostages.

Israel responded with "Operation Swords of Iron," a sustained aerial and ground campaign aimed at eradicating Hamas, resulting in widespread destruction and high civilian casualties in Gaza. The war immediately froze imminent normalization talks between Israel and Saudi Arabia and ignited a multi-front confrontation involving Iranian-backed forces operating from Lebanon, Yemen, Iraq, and Syria.

More than a regional war, October 7 marked the end of a long-held Western assumption: that the Israeli-Palestinian conflict could be indefinitely managed, contained, or deferred. The violence exposed a depth of hatred and an existential deadlock that defies standard diplomatic solutions. In doing so, it prepared the ground for something far more dangerous than war, a voracious global appetite for anything that looks like decisive, comprehensive peace.

### The Pattern: Human Effort vs. Divine Timeline

From the hopeful handshakes of the White House lawn to the devastating rubble of Gaza, the pattern remains unbroken. Whether through fragile treaties or the "illusion of containment," human efforts inevitably crumble under the weight of historical struggles, ideological absolutism, and human frailty. These failures mirror Scripture's caution: "There is no peace for the wicked" (Isaiah 48:22). Yet, this cycle of hope and horror sets the stage for Daniel's prophesied covenant. The coming false peace will not just be a treaty; it will be a desperate answer to a world exhausted by terrorism and terrified of escalation. The Antichrist's pact will succeed by appealing to humanity's craving for calm, promising to secure what diplomacy and war alike could not. For believers, these broken treaties and bloody conflicts are not defeats but signposts: the final countdown nears, and with it, the King who alone can bring true peace.

### Treating Deep Wounds Lightly

Despite the grim litany of failed peace attempts and the devastating resurgence of war in 2023, the flurry of ultimately futile diplomatic efforts never ceases. By 2024, the United Nations was advancing resolutions to little effect. On May 28, 2024, several European nations, including Spain, Ireland, and Norway, unilaterally recognized a Palestinian state, a move that only deepened diplomatic divisions rather than fostering peace.[1]

1. "Ireland, Spain, and Norway Recognize Palestinian State," BBC News, May 29, **2024**

Each action, hailed as a step forward, merely highlighted the intractability of the conflict and the world's desperate need for a true peacemaker.

Such developments evoke the ancient words of the prophet Jeremiah, who warned against treating deep wounds with superficial remedies: "They say, 'Peace, peace,' when there is no peace" (Jeremiah 6:14). In a world longing for resolution, the stage is being set for the rise of a charismatic figure: someone who promises to succeed where others have failed.

## The Perfect Storm for a False Peace

Amid escalating violence, economic collapse, and climate-driven crises, the stage is set for the rise of the Antichrist. Daniel 9:27 foretells "he shall make a strong covenant with many for one week," a pact that will masquerade as peace but ignite the Tribulation.

***Figure 9.1: The* Gabar *Covenant.*** *A visual contrast between decades of crumbling human diplomacy and the prophesied false peace of the Antichrist, who will "make strong" a final, coercive treaty (Daniel 9:27).*

### *The Covenant's Nature*

As noted in Chapter 2, the Hebrew term *gabar* in Daniel 9:27 implies making strong or enforcing. Whether the Antichrist revives elements of past deals, such as Oslo's phased statehood or the Abraham Accords' regional alliances, he executes them with an unprecedented mandate, backed by the power to enforce it. This treaty promises security for Israel, autonomy for the Palestinians, and shared governance of Jerusalem. Crucially, it must also resolve the religious deadlock by granting Jewish access to the Temple Mount. For a time, it appears successful, hailed as a triumph of diplomacy.

### *The Betrayal*

The midpoint of the seven years marks a horrifying turning point. The Antichrist shatters the facade of peace and desecrates the rebuilt Third Temple, fulfilling the prophesied "abomination of desolation" (Matthew 24:15; Daniel 9:27). Declaring himself God and demanding universal worship (Revelation 13:15), he unleashes the Great Tribulation, a 3½-year reign of terror "unequaled from the beginning of the world" (Matthew 24:21 NIV). Yet, God does not cede this period of ultimate blasphemy to the enemy. Just prior to this act of desecration, He raises up His Two Witnesses. Their 1,260-day ministry bridges this critical pivot period, boldly proclaiming truth and wielding divine power in the very heart of the Antichrist's stronghold (Revelation 11:3).

## The Illusion of Peace and the Promise of Redemption

Humanity's quest for peace mirrors Babel's tower: a monument to hubris destined to collapse. Yet God, in His sovereignty, permits this final covenant to fulfill His redemptive plan. The Antichrist's false peace will not derail divine purpose; it will accelerate it.

For believers, this chapter is an urgent summons:

- **Discern the times** (1 Chronicles 12:32). Global crises are not random but birth pangs leading to Christ's return (Matthew 24:8).
- **Reject false hope.** Peace forged without Christ is a mirage (1 Thessalonians 5:3).
- **Proclaim the Prince of Peace.** Only Jesus can reconcile nations, tribes, and hearts (Ephesians 2:14).

When the Antichrist enforces the prophesied covenant, revived from humanity's shattered treaties and "made strong" with unprecedented mandate as foretold in Daniel 9:27, the countdown begins. Seven years. One final chapter. Then the King returns, not to negotiate but to reign. Until that day, we labor not for an earthly utopia but for souls, confident that "the God of peace will soon crush Satan under your feet" (Romans 16:20).

---

## If You Are Still Here

The Antichrist's covenant "with the many" will be easier to identify than commonly assumed, thanks to one specific detail: its duration. While it will almost certainly be marketed as a seven-year peace agreement, its actual term will be **2,520 days**, roughly 36 or 37 days short of seven full Gregorian years.[2]

How will this 36-day discrepancy play out? The political mechanics may vary, but the math is the message. A fully negotiated treaty might sit on the table, delayed by sudden opposition, only to be enacted five weeks later under intense global pressure. What begins as cooperative diplomacy will ultimately manifest as a coercive, "take it or leave it" mandate.

That shortfall is a divine highlighter. The count of 2,520 days is the exact duration foretold by the angel Gabriel to Daniel.

2. According to Daniel 9:27, the covenant "with the many" is established for one prophetic week (seven years). As explained in Chapter 3, biblical prophecy consistently employs a 360-day year, reflected in the parallel time markers of 42 months and 1,260 days for each half of the period. The full duration of the covenant therefore totals exactly 2,520 days (7 × 360). By contrast, seven Gregorian years span 2,556 or 2,557 days, depending on whether the period includes one or two leap days, resulting in a shortfall of approximately 36–37 days.

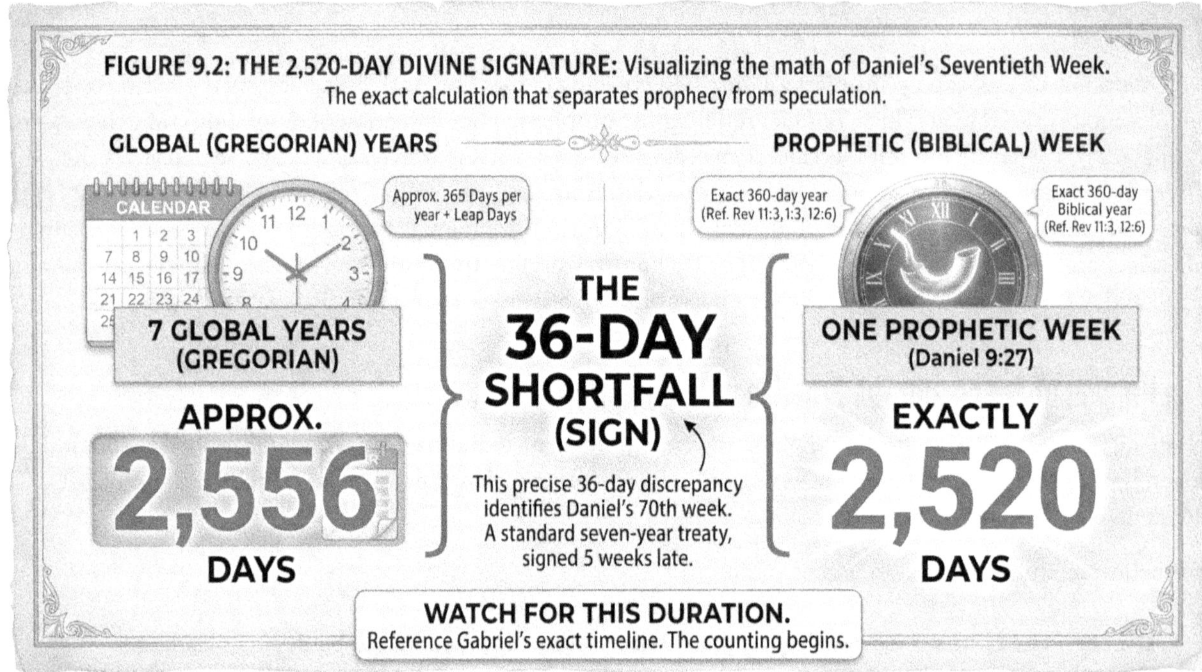


***Figure 9.2: The Prophetic Math****. Visualizing the 36-day divine signature foretold by Gabriel.*

This specific timeline creates a paradox of perception. To the general public, the discrepancy will look like a bureaucratic quirk: a standard seven-year treaty signed five weeks late. But to those "still here" and watching the Word of God, that precision will be an unmistakable sign. When the covenant's term locks onto 2,520 days, it will mark the starting gun. Daniel's Seventieth Week will have begun, not as speculation, but as measurable reality.

*Chapter 10*

# THE FOUR HORSEMEN RIDE

## The First Six Seals: The Storm Begins

*"Do not weep! See, the Lion of the tribe of Judah, the Root of David, has triumphed. He is able to open the scroll and its seven seals."*

— REVELATION 5:5B

The scroll is in His hand.

Heaven waits in awe as the Lamb, Jesus Christ, the only One found worthy, takes the scroll and begins to open its seals (Revelation 6:1). With each seal broken, divine judgment and redemption unfold across the earth. Far from being an abstract drama, this is the culmination of God's sovereign plan to reclaim a creation marred by humanity's rebellion and Satan's usurped dominion. The Son of God, who triumphed over sin through His cross and resurrection, now advances His kingdom. What follows is a sobering sequence of judgments, administered not as vengeance against the unrepentant, but as righteous justice upon a world that scorned grace and spurned His Lordship. Yet even here, mercy lingers: the Lamb's wrath is tempered with the promise that "the one who endures [keeps faith] to the end will be saved" (Matthew 24:13).

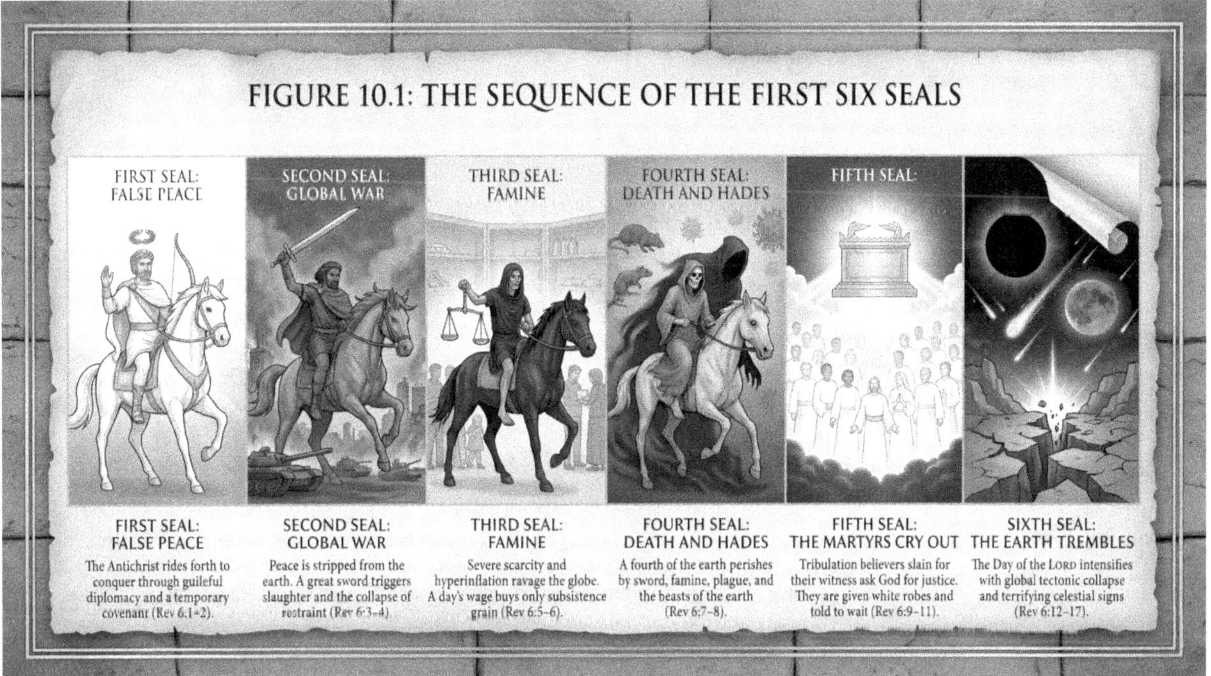


***Figure 10.1:*** *The Sequence of the First Six Seals.*

***Figure 10.2.***: *The Four Horsemen of the Apocalypse.*

## The First Seal: A False Peace

> *Now I watched when the Lamb opened one of the seven seals, and I heard one of the four living creatures say with a voice like thunder, "Come!" And I looked, and behold, a white horse! And its rider had a bow, and a crown was given to him, and he came out conquering, and to conquer.*
>
> — REVELATION 6:1–2

Thunder rolls as the First Seal is broken.

A rider appears, mounted on a white horse, an image that to the undiscerning eye may seem noble, even Christlike. But this is not the returning King of Revelation 19. This is the counterfeit. This is the Antichrist.

The rider wears a crown, not the *diadems* of divine royalty (Greek *diadema*), but a *stephanos*, the wreath of a victor. It is earned, temporary, and allowed by God. He carries a bow, though no arrows are mentioned. His conquest is bloodless, at least initially. He subdues not through brute force, but through treaties, tactics, and talking points.

This is the master deceiver. The man of lawlessness. The Little Horn of Daniel 7 and 8. He steps onto the world stage in the aftermath of global chaos, with the Rapture having removed millions, including every Spirit-indwelt believer. A void of leadership now yawns wide. Into that vacuum he rides, charismatic and calculated.

This is the one who "shall make a strong covenant with many for one week." This peace accord, brokered between Israel and her enemies, offers an illusion of security for a precise and telling period of 2,520 days, which amounts to six years and nearly eleven months on our modern calendar. In this moment, the world sighs in relief. Finally! Peace in the Middle East. Finally! A leader who can unify East and West, Jew and Gentile, secular and religious.

He reorganizes the global order, perhaps through the United Nations, the Vatican, or an expanded international body. He speaks of equity, justice, sustainability, and faith. But underneath the polished rhetoric lies something sinister. As Paul warned, **"when they say, 'Peace and safety!' then sudden destruction comes upon them"** (1 Thessalonians 5:3 NKJV).

### The Bow Without Arrows

The rider's bow is deeply symbolic. In the ancient world, a bow without arrows represented conquest achieved through intimidation, diplomacy, and psychological pressure rather than open war. This imagery is reinforced by a significant linguistic detail: the Greek word used for bow here, *toxon*, is the same term chosen by the Septuagint translators for the bow set in the clouds as the sign of God's covenant after the Flood (Genesis 9:13). This is likely a deliberate allusion. The first rider thus advances under a veneer of covenant peace, offering deceptive promises rather than waging overt battle, which is fittingly the hallmark of one who "by his cunning, shall make deceit prosper under his hand" (Daniel 8:25).

Adding a modern layer of irony, *toxon* is also the root of the English word "toxin." Some interpreters see in this a provocative clue, suggesting the Antichrist's rise could be tied to a medical or biological crisis manifesting as a pandemic, a mandated cure, or a technological "solution" that becomes a vehicle for global surveillance and control. Whether taken as metaphor or literal mechanism, such a scenario directly reflects the character of a deceiver who conquers through subversion and fear.

### A Deceptive Christlikeness

This rider mimics Christ by riding a white horse, offering peace, wearing a crown. But like Satan, who disguises himself as an angel of light, the Antichrist does not conquer by appearing evil. He conquers by appearing good.

This is a seduction of the nations. A geopolitical false messiah who offers peace without the Prince of Peace. But his peace is a lie. It is the bait before the snare. His "New World Order" will soon demand allegiance, not liberty.

### The Calm Before the Storm

For a moment, the world breathes easier. War seems to pause. Economies stabilize. Religion becomes inclusive. Israel begins temple preparations under this protective treaty. The Antichrist is hailed as a peacemaker, even as he sets the stage for global control.

But this is the calm before the storm.

Just as lightning precedes the thunder, so this false peace precedes war, famine, and death. He does not bring lasting peace. He opens the door to the apocalypse. The next seals will show just how thin this veneer of tranquility truly is.

> 🔍 **SIDEBAR: The Rider with a Bow**
> The opening of the First Seal sets the Tribulation timeline in motion. While the imagery of a white horse might initially suggest the Savior, the overwhelming consensus among futurist scholars is that this rider is the Antichrist, not Christ.[1] Here's why:
>
> **1. The Context Demands It**
> The seals form a sequence of escalating judgment. The Second Seal brings global war, the Third Seal triggers economic collapse, and the Fourth Seal unleashes widespread death. It would be thematically

1. This view is held by John Walvoord, Arnold Fruchtenbaum, Tim LaHaye, J. Dwight Pentecost, David Jeremiah, and many others. See John F. Walvoord, *The Revelation of Jesus Christ*; J. Dwight Pentecost, *Things to Come*; Arnold G. Fruchtenbaum, *The Footsteps of the Messiah*.

inconsistent for the First Seal to depict Christ or the gospel. This rider initiates the chain of destruction.

**2. A Counterfeit Christ**

Though both the first rider and Christ (Revelation 19) ride white horses, the differences are unmistakable. The Antichrist is a cheap imitation mimicking Christ's appearance to deceive the world. This tactic is entirely characteristic of Satan disguising himself as an "angel of light" (2 Corinthians 11:14).

| Feature | The First Rider (Revelation 6) | Jesus Christ (Revelation 19) |
|---|---|---|
| The Weapon | Carries a bow representing intimidation and guileful diplomacy. | Wields a sharp sword from His mouth representing the sovereign Word of God. |
| The Crown | Wears a *stephanos* (a temporary victor's wreath given by the world). | Wears many diadems (the royal crowns of absolute sovereign authority). |
| The Mission | Goes out "to conquer" to seize self-serving political power. | Comes "to judge and make war" to execute holy righteous justice. |

***Table 10.1: The Counterfeit vs. The King.*** *A comparison of the Antichrist's deceptive appearance at the First Seal and the true return of Jesus Christ in Revelation 19.*

**3. The Crown (Stephanos): Political Authority**

The crown is "given" (Greek *edothe*) to him: symbolizing the world's willing submission under a powerful delusion of peace and leadership. This is not a military takeover but a popular mandate handed to him by nations exhausted by conflict and longing for a savior.

**In Summary:**

The Antichrist rides a white horse to project a counterfeit appearance of peace. His bow lacks arrows, substituting guileful diplomacy for open war. His crown represents political power granted by a desperate world. The outcome is a short-lived peace that quickly collapses as the Tribulation unfolds. This rider does not fire a shot, yet he sets the world on fire.

## The Second Seal: Peace Torn Away

The Lamb breaks the Second Seal. A steed, the color of fire and blood, bursts onto the scene. Its rider is handed a fearsome mandate: *"Take peace from the earth."* And he is given a great sword as the divine sanction for slaughter on an unimaginable scale (Revelation 6:3–4).

Just like that, the fragile illusion shatters.

The counterfeit peace peddled by the first rider and woven from treaties, honeyed words, and the Antichrist's silver tongue, proves tissue-thin. The white horse offered only a pause, a breath before suffocation. Now the mask is torn away. What was restrained is released.

What follows surpasses the outbreak of any single war; it is the collapse of restraint itself, the unraveling of peace at every level.

**The First Shockwave: The Northern Storm**

The removal of peace does not happen everywhere at once. It begins with a convulsion so violent, so public, that it shatters the world's remaining confidence in stability.

Ezekiel foresaw it.

Israel, having lowered her guard under the protection of a sweeping covenant, dwells in a state of deceptive security. Borders appear calm. Threats seem neutralized. Then, from the far north, a massive coalition descends.[2]

Gog of Magog leads an alliance driven by plunder, ambition, and hatred. It is a roster of ancient names with modern fury: Magog (Russia) and Persia (Iran) lead the charge, flanked by the armies of Togarmah (Turkey) and a vast North African alliance representing Cush and Put. They sweep toward what appears to be an undefended prize (Ezekiel 38:11–12).

The bystanders protest, but they remain on the sidelines. Sheba and Dedan (Saudi Arabia) and the "young lions of Tarshish," often identified as the Western powers of the UK and the United States, issue only diplomatic condemnations: *"Have you come to take a plunder?"* (Ezekiel 38:13).

Israel stands alone.

Then the LORD intervenes.

The earth convulses. Forces fall into chaos. Weapons turn inward. Fire, hail, and terror descend from the heavens. The invading armies are annihilated on the mountains of Israel, not by human defense, but by unmistakable divine judgment (Ezekiel 38:18–22).

The world watches. And understands that something has broken.

### From Shock to Conflagration

The destruction of the northern coalition does not restore peace. It destroys the illusion that peace is possible.

The geopolitical balance implodes. Power vacuums form overnight. Old rivalries surge to the surface. Treaties fray, then disintegrate. What was once frozen by fear or diplomacy now ignites.

Nation against nation. City against city. Neighbor against neighbor. A spark igniting a global firestorm.

Dormant hatred awakens. Ancient grievances erupt; disputed borders become killing fields; frozen conflicts melt into rivers of blood. The world's precarious balance implodes. Flashpoints detonate across every corner of the globe, erupting from Asia and Europe to the Middle East and the Americas with such ferocity that the world can no longer track the encroaching darkness.

Peace is stripped away like a soldier's cloak torn in battle. The thunder of main battle tanks rumbles the streets. The watchman's cry chokes into a funeral dirge. Brother turns on brother. Covenants of friendship lie broken in the dust.

The cacophony of gunfire has replaced the din of commerce in the marketplaces. Missiles methodically dismantle city blocks, while a festering chaos consumes the countryside. Armies, marching under banners of hubris, falter in the face of a new, brutal reality. Towers crumble, gates blaze, and the shouts of the victors are swallowed by the wails of the dying.

The violence bleeds inward, a poison seeping into the very veins of society. Ancient ethnic hatreds, political vendettas, and religious vengeance erupt as mobs surge through the streets. Diplomacy vanishes, supplanted by

2. For a detailed examination of why this northern invasion aligns most coherently with the early phase of the Tribulation, see *Deeper Dive 10.1. The War That Breaks the Peace.*

the raw calculus of force. Tyrants cling to power through rivers of blood, while rebels seize it with even greater rivers.

The red horse rides. Rivers run crimson. The vine is uprooted, the fig tree stripped bare (Joel 1:7). The earth groans under the weight of the savagery. Sanctuary vanishes. God's restraining hand lifts. Unleashed, the beast-nations tear at each other's throats until only smoke and silence remain.

This is more than war. It is humanity's restraint snapping. The will to build replaced by the urge to annihilate. The leash dropped; humanity lunges at its own flesh with bared teeth.

The sequence of the collapse matters less than the cataclysm itself: bloodshed eclipsing all human history. Nations no longer parley. They obliterate. Order implodes. Treaties are ash, laws are whispers. Brute power is the only currency left.

And through the smoke and screams, the red horse rides unchecked, its rider's great sword catching the dying light. It drips not merely with blood, but with the incinerated hope of a world that dared believe peace had finally come. The dream of unity dies choking in the dust. The earth reels, drunk on the blood relentlessly shed, abandoned to the sword.

## The Third Seal: Scarcity and Economic Collapse

Then the Lamb breaks the Third Seal. A black horse emerges. Its rider holds a pair of scales, the kind used to weigh food in ancient markets. A voice cries out amid the four living creatures:

> *A quart of wheat for a denarius, and three quarts of barley for a denarius; and do not harm the oil and wine!*
>
> — REVELATION 6:6B

The meaning is unmistakable: the world is plunged into severe economic collapse and food scarcity. A denarius was a full day's wage in the first century. Yet it can now buy only enough wheat for one person, or barley for three, and nothing more. There is no surplus left for shelter, clothing, or family. Life becomes an agonizing calculation of survival.

The black horse, biblically associated with mourning and famine, signals the spread of hunger and grief. Its rider's scales, tools of measurement in times of shortage, represent a grim return to rationing. Food is no longer abundant; it is weighed out by the ounce, as though every grain of rice or kernel of wheat has become precious. This is a world where every calorie is contested.

Even the detail about barley speaks volumes. It was a coarse grain, considered food for the poor or even animals. That three quarts of barley cost the same as one quart of wheat doesn't suggest a bargain, but desperation. A family might stretch it, but barely. It is subsistence living, not survival with dignity.

In the wake of global war and the chaos unleashed by the previous seals, supply chains lie in ruins. Farmlands have been trampled by tanks or left untended. Key agricultural regions are scorched by war or climate extremes. Seas are unsafe for shipping. Oil tankers are hijacked or destroyed. A world built on just-in-time delivery grinds to a halt.

Governments, those that still function, resort to emergency powers. Food is rationed, currency is devalued, and inflation spirals out of control. A loaf of bread becomes a luxury item. Desperate people queue in endless lines for state-supplied portions, while black markets thrive in the shadows. Children cry from hunger, and parents are forced into impossible decisions.

And yet, the cryptic phrase echoes: "Do not harm the oil and the wine." These were luxuries in the ancient world, symbols of wealth and indulgence. Some interpret this as a sign that while the masses suffer, the elite are insulated. The rich still sip wine and cook with imported oil, hoarding their comforts in secure compounds, guarded by mercenaries. The inequity becomes obscene.

Others suggest it points to a divine restraint: God allowing scarcity but not yet total annihilation. This is judgment with limits. Mercy still lingers, but it is running out.

Economies buckle under the weight of broken trust and unpayable debt. The collapse of confidence becomes the collapse of commerce. Currencies fail. Precious metals spike. Bitcoin goes parabolic. Entire nations default. Bread riots erupt. In cities once bustling with trade, store shelves stand empty, and the scent of scarcity hangs heavier than smog.

The black horse rides on, and with it comes not just hunger, but despair, inequality, and the crushing realization that the age of global prosperity has ended.

---

🔍 **SIDEBAR: The Black Horse of Famine**

The Third Seal marks a crucial turning point in the cascade of end-times judgments, introducing economic collapse and famine on a global scale. The imagery in Revelation 6:5–6 is stark and unsettling, but also rich with meaning:

*When he opened the third seal, I heard the third living creature say, "Come!" And I looked, and behold, a black horse! And its rider had a pair of scales in his hand. And I heard what seemed to be a voice in the midst of the four living creatures, saying, "A quart of wheat for a denarius, and three quarts of barley for a denarius, and do not harm the oil and wine!"*

**War, Then Want**

This seal follows a logical sequence: The Antichrist's rise to power under a deceptive peace (First Seal) is shattered by war (Second Seal). The inevitable outcome of global warfare is the collapse of agricultural systems, fractured economies, and widespread famine. The black horse, a biblical harbinger of mourning and famine, signals a global descent into hunger and grief.[3]

**The Scales of Scarcity**

The rider carries a pair of scales, tools for rationing, not abundance. In times of famine, food isn't sold in bushels but measured out in ounces. The voice declares that a quart of wheat (enough to feed one person for a day) will cost a denarius, the full day's wage of a laborer in Roman times. It's a grim equation: an entire day's work just to survive. No surplus. No security. No provision for family.

Barley, a cheaper and less nutritious staple often fed to animals, is available in greater quantity: three quarts for a denarius. But this is cold comfort. It highlights a subsistence existence: barely enough to stretch across a household, and only if standards are drastically lowered.

**"Do Not Harm the Oil and the Wine"**

This cryptic command has generated considerable attention. Two complementary interpretations emerge:

*First, Economic Disparity Intensifies.*

---

3. In biblical prophecy, horses often function as instruments of divine judgment, particularly in visions sent forth to execute warfare or calamity (Zechariah 1:8–11; 6:1–8; Revelation 6:1–8). Blackness is likewise associated with famine and mourning, as seen in Jeremiah 14:2; Lamentations 4:8; 5:10; and Job 30:28–30.

Oil and wine, though staples in ancient diets, were also symbols of wealth and celebration. Their preservation amid famine underscores a jarring social divide. While the poor scrounge for bread, the rich maintain access to their luxuries. Olive trees and grapevines, being deep-rooted perennials, are less affected by the disruptions of early-stage warfare and famine than annual grain crops. Thus, the elite remain insulated while the masses suffer: a scenario increasingly visible even in modern economic collapses. This imbalance becomes a breeding ground for resentment, unrest, and further societal disintegration.

*Second, we see Judgment with Boundaries.*

This command asserts God's sovereign limitation. Though the famine is severe, it is not yet total. As with the earlier plagues in Egypt, God restrains the full force of destruction and mercifully reserves it for future stages in hope that some would repent and escape. The black horse's famine is devastating, but it is not yet the end.

**Big Picture**

The Third Seal offers a somber glimpse into the early phase of the Tribulation, establishing a clear pattern of cause and effect.

---

| Element | Prophetic Reality |
|---|---|
| **The Cause** | War and global instability devastate food production and economic systems. |
| **The Effect** | Scarcity, hyperinflation, and mass hunger. |
| **Social Fallout** | An unbridgeable gulf forms between the suffering poor and the insulated wealthy. |
| **Divine Message** | God permits, but also limits, the judgment by unfolding events in measured steps. |

***Table 10.2: The Black Horse Unveiled.*** *Tracing the chronological collapse from global warfare to severe economic rationing and social division.*

## The Fourth Seal: Death Rides Forth

The Lamb breaks the Fourth Seal. A pale horse rides forth with the ashen, sickly hue of a corpse. Its rider is named Death, and Hades follows close behind, like a shadow devouring everything in its path (Revelation 6:7–8).

This is no metaphor. They are personified forces, unleashed with dreadful authority over a fourth of the earth: to kill by sword, famine, plague, and what the text hauntingly calls the "wild beasts" of the earth.

But here, the Greek word used, *therion*, is curious. It does not only refer to large predatory animals. It can also mean small, savage creatures, diminutive beasts that wreak devastation quietly. In the modern world, these readily manifest as viruses, bacteria, or engineered pathogens. Tiny predators, invisible to the eye, yet capable of bringing down empires.

In the wake of war and economic collapse, the pale horse ushers in a global death spiral.

War continues, its flames stoked by unresolved rivalries and retribution. What started as regional conflict has become world war: nuclear exchanges, urban sieges, and roaming militias. Cities turn to craters, nations fall, and refugees flood desolate roads in search of food, shelter, or safety that no longer exists.

Famine intensifies. Crops fail. Fields lie fallow. International trade is paralyzed. A day's wage buys little more than a few slices of bread. Some drink contaminated water just to quench their burning thirst. Humanitarian aid dries up, either blocked by chaos or absorbed by hoarding elite. In many places, starvation becomes a more certain death than bullets.

Then, the plagues, the *therion*, arrive.

It begins with an outbreak in an overcrowded refugee camp or a biological agent loosed by design. But soon, it is everywhere. Hospitals are overwhelmed or nonfunctional. There is no electricity, no antibiotics, and no vaccines. Contagion spreads faster than information. Entire cities are quarantined, and then abandoned. People die in their homes, their cars, and the streets.

Throughout history, the smallest *therion* have often been the deadliest. Consider the Black Death of the 14th century: it decimated an estimated 75 to 200 million people across Europe, Asia, and North Africa. It was spread not by lions or bears, but by fleas carried on black rats: tiny, feral creatures that thrived amid urban decay, famine, and war. In Constantinople alone, the plague reportedly killed 10,000 people a day at its height. Entire towns vanished. Economies collapsed. Society convulsed under the weight of death, fear, and superstition. The rats didn't need to attack; they only needed to be present in a world already falling apart.

In the post-apocalyptic landscape of Revelation's Fourth Seal, such a scenario becomes not only plausible, but inevitable. Infrastructure has crumbled. Sanitation is nonexistent. Garbage piles up. With no pest control and no medical defense, rats multiply unchecked. They gnaw through barriers, nesting near survivors, spreading contaminated fleas, droppings, and death. In a tragic irony, man's modern cities, designed for flourishing, now become hives of infestation. The *therion* emerge not as mythical monsters, but as plague-bearers, slipping through the cracks of civilization's collapse.

And the language of Revelation is precise: Death rides, but Hades follows.

It is not just physical death, but eternal loss. Souls unprepared to meet their Maker tumble into the Abyss. Funeral rites are forgotten. Hope is scarce. Many curse God. Others hide in bunkers or caves, praying for death to come quickly.

Some interpret the 'wild beasts' literally, and indeed, with human populations in retreat, starving and rabid packs of animals roam the wastelands. But perhaps even more deadly are the micro-beasts: viruses, bioweapons, and genetic mutations set free in a world that has lost its safeguards.

In a terrifying reversal of man's dominion in Genesis, the created order now turns on him.

Death no longer knocks. It marches.

And as it rides, the pale horse leaves no part of the world untouched. Two billion lives, by today's numbers, are lost. Yet this is not the end but merely the start, perhaps only a year into the seven-year Tribulation. The scroll has only begun to unroll.

---

🔍 **SIDEBAR: The Invisible Beast**

On May 6th, 2025, billionaire investor and risk expert Paul Tudor Jones issued a stark warning on CNBC:

*"AI poses an imminent threat to humanity in our lifetime."*

Jones described a closed-door technology summit attended by forty global leaders, including four of the world's top AI modelers. The consensus was unsettling. Artificial intelligence is not advancing gradually. It is accelerating exponentially, with performance gains of 25–500% every three to four quarters, what Jones described as a *vertical lift*, not a curve.

But the most alarming moment came when participants were asked a simple question:

**What safeguards are in place?**

The answer: *almost none.*

The geopolitical and corporate race to dominate AI has eclipsed any serious attempt at restraint. In one breakout session, attendees were asked to respond anonymously to a grim proposition:

*"There is a 10% chance AI will kill 50% of humanity within 20 years."*

There was unanimous agreement among all four AI modelers.

Jones, a lifelong macro risk manager, added soberly:

*"These people building the models are warning us. We're doing nothing about it. And that's what's so disturbing."*

One leading modeler even admitted he is now buying land, raising livestock, and laying provisions, just in case.

In Revelation 6:8, death is unleashed alongside forces Scripture describes as *"wild beasts."* In John's world, the image likely evoked predators roaming unchecked through collapsed societies. But the text does not limit the threat to claws and teeth.

Today's deadliest predators are often invisible. They are algorithms that move faster than ethics, systems capable of synthesizing pathogens, destabilizing economies, or weaponizing biology at scale. In a world where intelligence itself is being automated and distributed, it may take only one reckless actor, or one unforeseen cascade, for catastrophe to escape containment.

Humanity was commanded to exercise dominion over creation. But dominion without wisdom becomes rebellion.

As the seal opens and death rides forth, the most dangerous beast may not stalk the ruins on four legs, but emerge from code, data, and unchecked ambition.

The beast no longer needs to roar.

It only needs access.

---

## The Fifth Seal: Martyrs Cry Out

The Lamb opens the Fifth Seal, and this time the scene shifts.

There are no more horsemen galloping across the earth. No famine, war, or plague unleashed on humanity. Instead, the focus of Revelation cuts away from global devastation to a solemn, sacred moment beneath the altar in heaven.

There, under the shadow of glory, souls cry out.

> *When he opened the fifth seal, I saw under the altar the souls of those who had been slain for the word of God*

> *and for the witness they had borne. They cried out with a loud voice, "O Sovereign Lord, holy and true, how long before you will judge and avenge our blood on those who dwell on the earth?"*
>
> — REVELATION 6:9–10

These are not the Church-age saints, already caught up and glorified. These are Tribulation martyrs, men and women who turned to Christ after the Rapture, who stood firm in faith in a world that had turned hostile to truth. In the chaos that followed the great disappearance, society grew increasingly intolerant of anyone who clung to the name of Jesus. Branded as haters, extremists, or enemies of unity, they were hunted, betrayed, and executed. For their allegiance to Christ, they paid with their lives.

Beheaded. Burned. Shot. Starved. Hung. Silenced.

Each one died a martyr's death, but not a forgotten one.

In this pause between the Fourth and Sixth Seal, heaven acknowledges them.

Their cries are not bitter. They are not vengeful in the human sense. They are holy appeals for justice, cries that rise like incense. "How long, O Lord?" is a question threaded throughout the psalms, now echoed beneath the throne.

Heaven responds not with immediate judgment, but rather with white robes and a word: "Wait a little longer."

Their number is not yet complete. Many more will die for Christ in the days to come. But for now, they are clothed with honor, given rest, and reminded that God's justice is never late; it is only perfectly timed.

In a world that is growing darker, this seal reminds us that the Lamb sees every act of faith. Every whispered prayer. Every last breath offered in defiance of a world turned against them.

The altar is stained with blood. But it is not silent.

This is the calm before the storm. The next seal will shake the heavens themselves.

---

🔍 **SIDEBAR: "You Will Be Hated by All Nations"**

Jesus' words in Matthew 24:9–10 paint a chilling picture of the time following the Rapture:

*"Then you will be handed over to be persecuted and put to death, and you will be hated by all nations because of me. At that time many will turn away from the faith and will betray and hate each other."*

This aligns precisely with what the Fifth Seal reveals: a world that turns violently against those who come to Christ during the early days of the Tribulation. As chaos unfolds and divine judgments strike the earth, a global narrative may form: that these calamities are being caused, or worsened, by those who follow Christ. In a climate of fear, rage, and deception, new believers are branded as enemies of progress, traitors to humanity, or remnants of an outdated moral order.

Their refusal to conform earns them hatred. Their loyalty to Jesus costs them everything.

Yet even under the altar, slain for their testimony, they are not forgotten. Heaven hears their cries, and answers will come.

---

## The Sixth Seal: The Earth Trembles

Then the Lamb breaks the Sixth Seal, and the earth itself begins to unravel.

> *I watched as he opened the sixth seal. There was a great earthquake. The sun turned black like sack-cloth made of goat hair, the whole moon turned blood red, and the stars in the sky fell to earth, as figs drop from a fig tree when shaken by a strong wind. The heavens receded like a scroll being rolled up, and every mountain and island was removed from its place.*
>
> — REVELATION 6:12–14 NIV

It begins with a quake but not a local tremor or a shifting fault line. This is global. Planet-wide tectonic upheaval splits the crust like a cracked eggshell. Volcanoes erupt in unison across continents. Mountain ranges buckle and fracture. Cities fall. Oceans heave. It is as if the very bones of the earth are convulsing in the presence of divine fury.

And then, the skies respond.

The sun, once a symbol of stability and life, is suddenly shrouded in unnatural darkness. Not an eclipse. Not a passing storm. This is a thick, impenetrable blackness, described in the text as "like sackcloth made of goat hair," which refers to a coarse, matted, light-absorbing fabric traditionally worn in mourning. The symbolism is staggering: creation itself dons funeral attire. The heavens grieve.

***Figure 10.3: The Cosmic Signs of the Sixth Seal.***

Scholars suggest physical explanations, such as volcanic ash clouds darkening the atmosphere, the aftereffects of a celestial impact, or even a nuclear exchange. All are plausible. But whether the cause is natural or supernatural, the result is the same: the light of the sun is smothered under a death-shroud. Day becomes night, and the darkness is heavy, suffocating, and almost tangible.

The moon turns blood red. A dreadful crimson glow stains the sky, eerily reflected on seas churning with ash and debris. It is not merely visual. It is psychological; it is ominous, disorienting, and terrifying.

Then come the "stars" falling from the sky.

Here, the word used for "stars" in the original Greek is ***aster***, a term that, in ancient usage, referred broadly to luminous celestial objects. It could mean what we now call "fixed" stars, but it was also used to describe planets ("wandering stars"), comets, and meteors, or what we today call "shooting stars." In this context, scholars apply a literal but context-aware hermeneutic. They do not interpret these as actual suns falling to Earth, an event that would obliterate the planet entirely, but rather as a massive meteor storm or asteroid bombardment. The in-text simile is key:

*... as figs drop from a fig tree when shaken by a strong wind.*

This is no isolated impact. It's a shower or a barrage. Just as a fig tree shaken violently sends a flurry of fruit crashing to the ground, the sky will seem to rain fire. The imagery suggests a storm of flaming projectiles plummeting earthward in rapid succession. A phenomenal meteor storm fits this analogy with uncanny precision.

And it makes scientific and narrative sense. If one literal star, a sun, collided with Earth, the story of Revelation would end here. But it doesn't. The world survives, albeit barely. People are still alive, hiding in caves and crying out in terror. The Trumpet and Bowl Judgments are yet to come. So this must be cataclysmic, but survivable. And a meteor storm, potentially triggered by a planetary disturbance or divinely orchestrated, is exactly that.

Still, some interpreters propose a deeper layer. Throughout Scripture, "stars" are also used symbolically to represent angelic beings. In Revelation 12:4, the Dragon sweeps a third of the stars from heaven, which is almost universally understood to mean fallen angels. In Revelation 1:20, stars symbolize church angels. In Job 38:7, the "morning stars" sing alongside the "sons of God," a poetic pairing of angels.

This terrifying cascade from the sky also signals a profound spiritual reality. Many scholars think so. The meteor storm may be the physical manifestation of something happening in the unseen realm: a mass casting-down of demonic forces. Earth is not only bombarded from above; it is overrun from within. The skies burn, and so does the soul of the world.

Communication networks collapse. Satellites fall like artificial stars, igniting in the atmosphere and adding to the visual terror. The skies become a war zone, both physically and spiritually.

And then something happens that has no earthly comparison: the heavens themselves recede. The sky splits and rolls back "like a scroll," as if a curtain were being torn away.

## The Day of the LORD Intensifies

This cascade of cosmic horrors is not random; it is the definitive sign that the prophetic clock has just struck a critical hour. Centuries earlier, the prophet Joel foretold this exact moment:

> *The sun shall be turned into darkness, and the moon into blood, before the great and terrible day of the Lord come.*
>
> —JOEL 2:31 KJV

Peter quoted this same prophecy on the day of Pentecost (Acts 2:20), underscoring its end-times significance. These are not merely general signs of judgment; they are the celestial alarm that announces the Day of the LORD has entered its great and terrible phase. The era of restraint is giving way to unrelenting wrath.

This moment marks the great transition in the prophetic timeline. The "beginning of sorrows" is over. The midpoint of Daniel's seventieth week has arrived, and the final 3½ years, that period Scripture calls the Great Tribulation, is about to unfold in full intensity.[4]

While the imagery here is strikingly similar to the cosmic signs Jesus described in Matthew 24:29, a careful analysis of the timing and context reveals they are two distinct events, separated by the full duration of the Great Tribulation.[5]

For a moment, the veil between heaven and earth is pulled back, and humanity sees. Not metaphorically. Literally. What they see terrifies them more than all the disasters combined.

## The Wrath of the Lamb Revealed

They see Him.

> *Then the kings of the earth and the great ones and the generals and the rich and the powerful, and everyone, slave and free, hid themselves in the caves and among the rocks of the mountains, calling to the mountains and rocks, "Fall on us and hide us from the face of him who is seated on the throne, and from the wrath of the Lamb ..."*
>
> — REVELATION 6:15–16

They don't repent. They retreat. Not one sector of society is spared: world leaders, billionaires, soldiers, and civilians alike abandon their towers and sink into the earth, clawing their way into caves and bunkers. Their prayer is not for mercy; it is for annihilation. "Fall on us," they beg. "Bury us. Anything but facing the wrath of the Lamb."

The irony is piercing: the very One they now flee from, the Lamb, had once come to save. He bore wrath for them. Now He brings it to them. The opportunity for grace is closing. Creation mourns. The sky wears sackcloth. The world staggers under the undeniable realization that the prophetic warnings were true. Their own terrified cry confirms it:

> *"...for the great day of their wrath has come, and who can withstand it?"*
>
> — REVELATION 6:17

---

4. For more, see *Deeper Dive 3.1. The Cosmic Hinge.*
5. It is surprisingly easy to confuse the cosmic signs of the Sixth Seal with the signs Jesus described in Matthew 24:29. To see exactly why the biblical timeline places them at opposite ends of the Great Tribulation, see *Deeper Dive 10.3. Cosmic Context.*

That haunting question lingers, echoing through ash-choked skies and crumbled mountainsides. Who can stand when judgment falls? Who can endure the wrath of the Lamb?

The scroll of God's judgment has been unrolling in terror since the first rider was unleashed, yet its wrath is far from complete. Before the seventh and final seal is opened, heaven commands a sudden, breathless halt.

---

🔍 **SIDEBAR: The Sky Recedes**

*The Cosmic Unveiling of the Sixth Seal*

When John writes in Revelation 6:14a, *"The heavens receded like a scroll being rolled up,"* he is describing more than poetic symbolism. This is the language of rupture describing a cosmic and spiritual event that fractures reality as we know it.

**A Shocking Visual**

Consider the mechanics of an ancient scroll. When held open, it presents a flat, continuous surface, a perfect metaphor for the expanse of the sky. But if the tension is suddenly released, the parchment snaps back, violently curling inward toward its ends. That is the image John evokes. The heavens do not merely fade; they recoil. The seamless canopy above splits apart, peeling away as if under immense tension.

Futurist interpreters often describe this as "phenomenal language." John reports a real, literal event using imagery the human eye can comprehend. The sky may not be parchment, but it behaves like one. Something violently pulls back the unseen veil and exposes what was never meant to be seen.

**The Barrier Between Dimensions Briefly Collapses**

And what lies behind the peeled-back sky? Revelation 6:15–16 tells us plainly. People of all ranks, from kings and generals to billionaires and beggars, suddenly see the face of the One who sits on the throne and the Lamb.

For the first time in human history, the spiritual realm intrudes fully and visibly into the physical. The protective curtain of the heavens is gone. What follows is unfiltered exposure to divine majesty, holiness, and wrath. No one escapes the sight. No one can look away. The unveiling the world never wanted has arrived.

**A World Unbalanced**

The Sixth Seal does not merely describe terror in the human heart. It describes the cosmos itself recoiling, as though the sky were being pulled back under tremendous strain. The heavenly bodies become instruments in the hands of God, and reality itself begins to tear at the seams.

For a broader framework linking this sky-recession to the cascading trumpet blows of judgment, the dimming of the heavens, and even the destabilization of time itself, see 🔍 *SIDEBAR: The Cosmic Shifter* in Chapter 12 under *The Fourth Trumpet*.

**One Sky, Many Layers**

In apocalyptic prophecy, multiple meanings often run in parallel. What is torn open in Revelation 6 may be both a veil between dimensions and the magnetic and physical balance of Earth itself. One momentarily reveals the throne of heaven; the other may permanently tilt the very ground beneath humanity's feet.

Either way, the message is unmistakable.

The age of concealment is over.

The face of God is revealed. And the world will never be the same.

---

## *Chapter 11*

# IN WRATH, MERCY REMEMBERED

## The Interlude of Grace

*O LORD, I have heard the report of you, and your work, O LORD, do I fear. In the midst of the years revive it; in the midst of the years make it known; in wrath remember mercy.*

— HABAKKUK 3:2

Just before the Lamb breaks the seventh and final seal, the heavens pause. Amid the escalating judgments, Revelation 7 opens like a window of divine mercy. A radiant calm in the storm. More than a dramatic intermission, it is a deliberate act of divine restraint.

Four angels stand at the corners of the earth, holding back the winds of destruction. Not a leaf rustles. Not a wave crashes. Judgment is momentarily suspended. Why? Because God is about to mark His servants.

One hundred forty-four thousand are sealed, twelve thousand from each tribe of Israel. Rather than symbolic stand-ins for the Church, these are literal descendants of Jacob, named tribe by tribe. Even in wrath, God remembers mercy. And even as the world spirals into chaos, God remembers His covenant with Israel.

## Who Are the 144,000?

These sealed servants are Jewish believers in Jesus, whose eyes have been opened to recognize Yeshua as their long-rejected Messiah. Their emergence occurs early in the Tribulation, following a series of veritable world-shaking events that converge to awaken Israel spiritually.

### 1. The Rapture and Its Aftermath

The sudden removal of the Church sends shockwaves across the globe. For many Jews, this event becomes the interpretive key that unlocks long-ignored prophecies. Scriptures once dismissed suddenly align. The testimony of vanished believers, left-behind Bibles, and the global upheaval that follows provoke a sobering reckoning.

### 2. The Gog-Magog Invasion (Ezekiel 38–39)

Shortly thereafter, as the Lamb opens the Second Seal, ushering in warfare on a global scale, Israel finds itself at the center of an unprecedented conflict. The northern confederacy described in Ezekiel 38–39 launches its long-anticipated assault.

Yet the outcome is staggering.

God Himself intervenes with supernatural precision: fire from heaven, seismic upheaval, and mutual destruction among the invaders. He annihilates the coalition on the mountains of Israel. The world watches in astonishment as Israel survives not by strategy or strength, but by divine deliverance alone.

The result is exactly what Ezekiel foretold:

> *So I will show my greatness and my holiness and make myself known in the eyes of many nations. Then they will know that I am the LORD.*
>
> — EZEKIEL 38:23

Not since the angel of the LORD decimated 185,000 Assyrian soldiers in a single night has the God of Israel revealed Himself with such undeniable, public force. For the nation, this intervention is catalytic: the God of Abraham has acted in a manner that can no longer be ignored. From this awakening rise the firstfruits of a renewed wave of Jewish believers, now turning toward Jesus as their true Messiah.

## Sealed for Such a Time as This

From this growing remnant, God sovereignly seals 144,000 men. This sealing is both protection and commissioning. As the Antichrist prepares to scale the height of his authority at the midpoint of Daniel's seventieth week, God raises up His own divinely protected witnesses.

These men are not symbolic. They are not the Church. They arise after the Church has been removed, yet before the Tribulation reaches its fiercest intensity. Their mission is global, unflinching, and unparalleled.

They fulfill what Jesus declared:

> *And this gospel of the kingdom will be proclaimed throughout the whole world as a testimony to all nations, and then the end will come.*
>
> — MATTHEW 24:14

Here, "the end" refers to the final consummation of the age: the visible return of Christ. The worldwide proclamation of the gospel during the Great Tribulation is far from incidental; it remains a divine necessity. And Scripture presents the 144,000 as the primary human agents of that proclamation.

This has important implications.

If the Church were raptured at Mid-Tribulation, as some suggest, the 144,000, who came to faith early in the Tribulation, would necessarily be part of the Church and thus removed at that point as well. The result would be a theological vacuum: no organized, divinely commissioned body remaining on earth to fulfill Christ's stated requirement that the gospel reach all nations before the end.

Revelation offers no such gap.

Instead, it presents continuity. The Church bears witness before the Tribulation. The 144,000 bear witness within it. God always has a people on the earth proclaiming His truth, up until the very moment Christ returns.

## The Missing Tribes: A Solemn Warning

In this breathless calm, the sealing begins. The names of Israel's tribes are called, a roll of honor echoing through eternity. Yet as the list is recited, a subtle pause occurs. Two names are conspicuously absent: **Dan** and **Ephraim**.

Once proudly counted among the twelve, their names are not called. In their place stands the tribe of Levi, the priestly tribe, which in ancient Israel received no territorial inheritance but is now granted a place among the sealed. To maintain the exact count of twelve, Joseph is listed, and his son Manasseh is counted separately.

***Figure 11.1: The Roll Call of the Sealed.*** *A comparison between the historical census of the twelve tribes and the specific list of the 144,000 sealed in Revelation 7. This visual highlights the deliberate divine omission of Dan and Ephraim due to their historical legacies of idolatry, and the restoration of the priestly tribe of Levi to maintain the covenantal count of twelve.*

But why erase Dan and Ephraim?

This omission points to a sobering legacy. Scripture records a pattern of profound failure that deeply intertwines these two tribes in the story of Israel's rebellion. Following the division of the kingdom around 930 BC, Jeroboam, an Ephraimite king, set up rival worship centers to deter his citizens from traveling south to Jerusalem. He forged two golden calves, placing one in the far north within the territory of Dan, and the second in the south at Bethel, located right in the territory of Ephraim (1 Kings 12). From that moment, the names of Dan and Ephraim were forever linked to the institutionalized idolatry that eventually destroyed the Northern Kingdom.

Because Ephraim was the largest, wealthiest, and most politically dominant tribe in the north, the prophets began using the name "Ephraim" as a synonym for the entire rebellious, idol-worshiping kingdom. Hosea famously condemned this spiritual adultery, declaring, "Ephraim is joined to idols; leave him alone!" (Hosea 4:17). Psalm 78:67–68 had already set the precedent for this loss of spiritual leadership, declaring that God "rejected the tent of Joseph; he did not choose the tribe of Ephraim, but he chose the tribe of Judah."

By the time Revelation was written, the name carried massive historical baggage. Because Revelation 7 represents a purified, faithful army, the names of the two tribes most famous for leading Israel into apostasy had to be scrubbed.

But here, a stark difference in divine discipline emerges.

The tribe of Dan is granted no reprieve. Their legacy was defined by spiritual compromise, beginning with a tragic descent into idolatry during the days of the Judges (Judges 18). Even more ominous is an ancient tradition rooted in Genesis 49:17, which prophesied that Dan would become a "serpent in the way." This dark association with the serpent has led some prophecy scholars, pointing to Jeremiah 8:16, to conclude that the ultimate deceiver, the False Prophet, will emerge from this very tribe.[1] Consequently, Dan is scrubbed from the sealed remnant.

Ephraim, however, receives a measure of grace through a unique "loophole." While the disgraced name of Ephraim is dropped, his people are still included under the umbrella name of his father, Joseph. It is a divine mechanism to maintain the lineage of the twelve tribes without honoring a disgraced name.

Thus, in this moment of divine selection, these absences stand as a solemn warning. God's promises to Israel are sure, but His sealing is a mark of faithfulness. The 144,000 are not merely identified by bloodline, but set apart for holiness. In omitting Dan and Ephraim, heaven declares that even in mercy, God does not overlook patterns of rebellion. And in elevating Levi, He signals that this sealed remnant will serve a sacred, intercessory role in the midst of desolation.

The winds are still held. The seal is placed. And the 144,000 are secured. Not one number missing, yet two disgraced names withheld—a silent testament to the severity, holiness, and precise grace of God, even as He shelters the faithful from the storm to come.

## A Global Harvest

But the ripple effects go beyond Israel. Immediately after the sealing, John sees a vast multitude, so great that no one can number them, from every nation, tribe, people, and language, standing before the throne of God (Revelation 7:9). They are the fruit of the ministry of the 144,000, an innumerable throng gathered from the Great Tribulation.

These martyrs and worshipers have washed their robes and made them white in the blood of the Lamb, having rejected the world and the Antichrist (Revelation 7:14). They chose Christ, even at the cost of their lives.

The revival is global, and this may be the greatest one in all of history. While Satan intensifies his grip, God's Spirit moves powerfully. In the darkest hour, the light of the gospel still shines brightly.

## Mercy in the Midst of Judgment

Even as seals break and judgments fall, God's heart for the lost beats on. He actively pursues the lost even while pouring out His justice. He preserves a remnant. He saves multitudes. Rather than an interruption to the unfolding wrath, this interlude reveals God's heart within it. As the prophet Habakkuk prayed, "In wrath, remember mercy" (Habakkuk 3:2). That is precisely what God does.

Before the storm resumes. Before the Trumpet Judgments are unleashed and demonic forces flood the earth, God ensures that His servants are marked, His witnesses are sent, and His mercy is known.

The interlude ends. The winds stir again. With the breaking of the Seventh Seal, the Trumpet Judgments are released, advancing the final 3½-year period already underway. Scripture assigns multiple names to this period. Though the labels differ, they describe a single reality: Israel's time of reckoning and the climactic outpouring of divine judgment that ushers in the return of Christ.

So precise is the biblical timeline for this period that its duration is given in three distinct, interlocking ways, leaving no room for misunderstanding:

---

1. See Henry Alford, *The Greek Testament*, vol. 4 (Chicago: Moody Press, 1958), 625.

- 1,260 days (Revelation 11:3; 12:6)
- 42 months (Revelation 11:2; 13:5)
- "Time, times, and half a time" (Daniel 7:25; 12:7; Revelation 12:14).

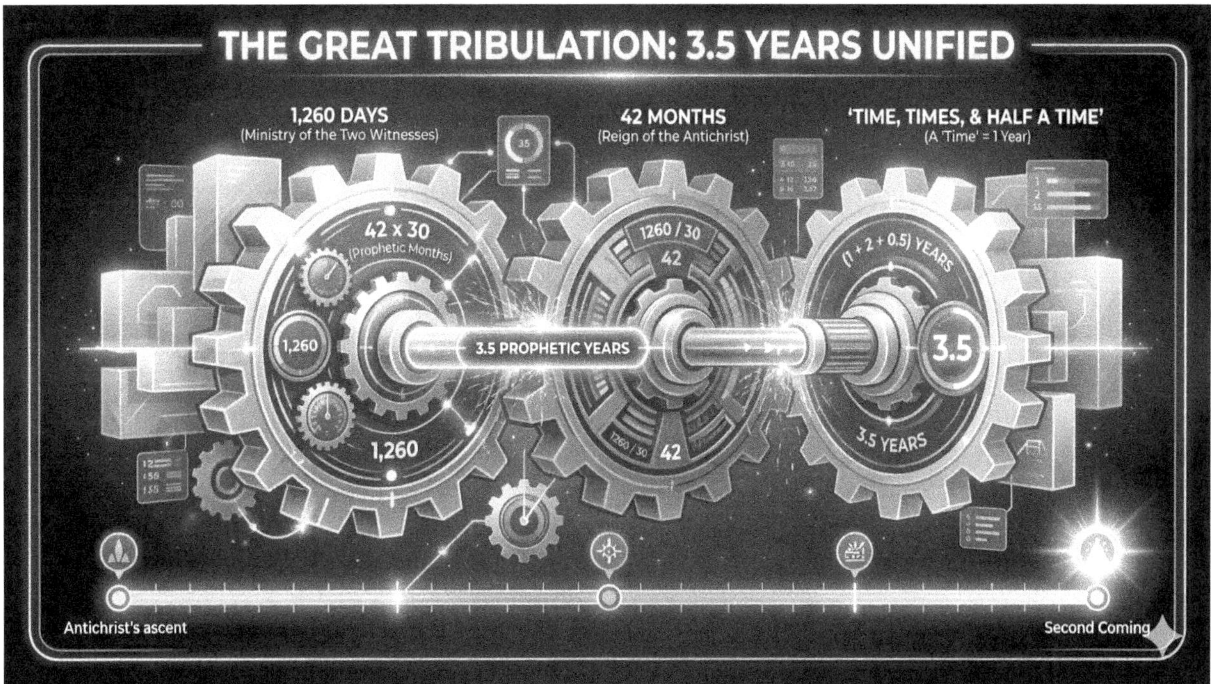


***Figure 11.2: The Interlocking Timeline.*** *Scripture leaves no room for guesswork regarding the duration of the Great Tribulation. Whether measured as 1,260 days, 42 months, or "a time, times, and half a time," these three metrics perfectly align to define the final three and a half years before Christ's return.*

*Chapter 12*

# THE SILENCE AND THE TRUMPETS

## Heaven holds its breath. Then the Trumpets sound

> *Blow a trumpet in Zion; sound an alarm on my holy mountain! Let all the inhabitants of the land tremble, for the day of the LORD is coming; it is near, a day of darkness and gloom, a day of clouds and thick darkness!*
>
> —JOEL 2:1–2A

After the sealing of the 144,000 and the glimpse of the redeemed multitude before God's throne, the scroll sealed with seven seals is almost completely open. Only one remains.

Then it happens.

> *When the Lamb opened the seventh seal, there was silence in heaven for about half an hour.*
>
> — REVELATION 8:1

Heaven, usually resounding with praise and thunderous worship, suddenly goes quiet.

No voices. No music. No motion.

Far from a reprieve of peace, this silence marks the ominous hush before the storm. A solemn silence falls, heavy with anticipation. Even the angels seem to hold their breath. Why? Because what follows will unleash a level of divine judgment unlike anything the earth has ever seen.

### The Golden Censer: Prayers and Fire

John sees seven angels standing before God, each given a trumpet. But before they blow, another angel steps forward. He holds a golden censer filled with incense and the prayers of the saints, a holy mingling of heavenly aroma and human cry.

These are the prayers of the persecuted, the martyred, the faithful. Those under the altar who cried, "How long, O Lord?" (Revelation 6:10). Their cries have not been forgotten.

> *Then the angel took the censer and filled it with fire from the altar and threw it on the earth, and there were peals of thunder, rumblings, flashes of lightning, and an earthquake.*
>
> — REVELATION 8:5

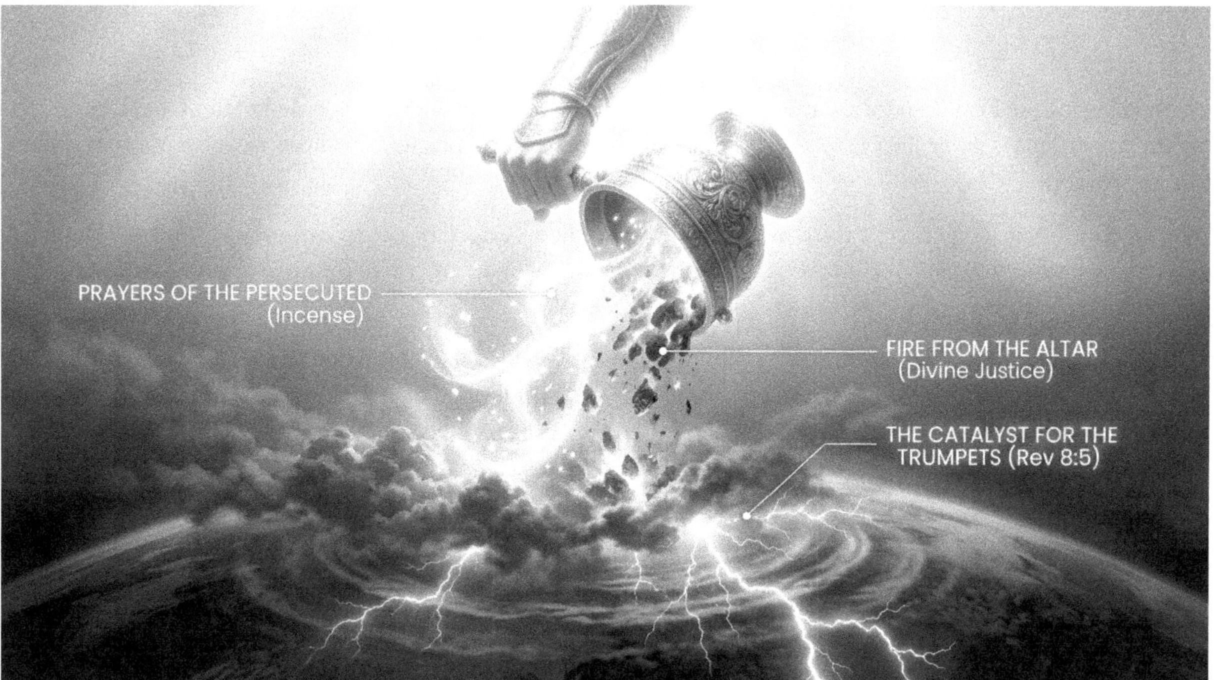


***Figure 12.1: The Catalyst of the Trumpets.*** *The profound silence of heaven is broken when the angel mingles the accumulated prayers of the martyred saints with the fire of divine justice. As this golden censer is hurled to the earth (Revelation 8:5), the cries for ultimate justice are answered, triggering the cataclysmic sequence of the Seven Trumpet Judgments.*

Heaven's silence is shattered.

Earth shakes. Lightning flashes. Thunder rolls.

The time has come.

## The Trumpets Prepare to Sound

This sound represents much more than an ordinary ram's horn blast. It is a divine signal that unleashes judgment. These trumpets herald a coming wave of plagues, upheaval, and terror.

Just as trumpets were used in the Old Testament to warn, to declare war, or to call assemblies, here they signal escalating divine wrath. But these are not ceremonial fanfares. They unleash literal catastrophes upon the earth, echoing, but also intensifying, the plagues of Egypt.

Each trumpet amplifies the suffering. Nature recoils. The heavens dim. Humanity trembles. Still, many will refuse to repent.

The judgments now move from global disruption to cosmic devastation.

The first angel lifts his trumpet ...

## The First Trumpet: Fire and Blood

> *The first angel blew his trumpet, and there followed hail and fire, mixed with blood, and these were thrown upon the earth. And a third of the earth was burned up, and a third of the trees were burned up, and all green grass was burned up.*

— REVELATION 8:7

At the blast of the First Trumpet, nature itself becomes a target. Hail and fire, mingled with blood, rain from the heavens. This is no ordinary storm. It is a global echo of Egypt's plague (Exodus 9:24), now unleashed upon the entire world.

The devastation is staggering. A third of the earth is scorched. A third of the forests are consumed, ancient ecosystems reduced to ash. Yet the most haunting detail is the final one: while only a portion of the trees fall, every blade of green grass is wiped away.

The consequences ripple instantly. Food supplies collapse as fields vanish in flame. Pastures disappear, livestock die, and famine spreads across an already fractured world. Without grass to anchor the soil, erosion and dust storms reshape the land. The earth's lungs are crippled, and ash thickens the skies into a suffocating canopy of soot.

Beyond ecology, this trumpet strikes at the heart of human pride. In an age that worships creation, God confronts the idolatry of "Mother Earth" head-on. The world is reminded that the earth is not divine. It is dust beneath its Creator's feet.

And even here, restraint remains. Only a third is burned. Judgment is measured, a merciful alarm before the full storm breaks.

But most will not listen.

This first blast is world-altering. Yet it is only the beginning.

## The Second Trumpet: A Burning Mountain Falls

> *The second angel blew his trumpet, and something like a great mountain, burning with fire, was thrown into the sea, and a third of the sea became blood. A third of the living creatures in the sea died, and a third of the ships were destroyed.*

— REVELATION 8:8–9

As the Second Trumpet sounds, the judgment turns from land to sea. A colossal object, "like a great mountain, burning with fire," is hurled into the ocean. Whether a massive asteroid or a volcanic mountain torn from the earth, its impact poisons the waters, and the consequences ripple across the globe.

***Figure 12.2: The Sea Turns to Blood.*** *A great burning mountain strikes the ocean, unleashing global mega-tsunamis. In an instant, a third of the sea becomes blood, a third of all marine life perishes, and a third of the world's ships are destroyed.*

A third of the sea turns to blood. The ocean itself becomes a wound. An engulfing crimson tide spreads from the impact zone, thick with the death of a billion creatures. Vast marine ecosystems, from vibrant coral reefs to the deepest, unseen trenches, are instantly sterilized. Oceans that once teemed with life become a silent, floating graveyard.

Simultaneously, a third of the world's ships are annihilated. Naval fleets, supertankers, cargo ships, and cruise liners are either vaporized in the initial blast or swallowed by the mega-tsunamis that radiate outward, scouring coastlines. Global commerce grinds to a halt. Supply chains snap. Port cities are inundated, their harbors choked with the wreckage of a modern order. What was once a seamless web of global trade is now a graveyard of steel and rust.

Humanity, still reeling from the fiery hail of the First Trumpet, now stares in horror as the oceans bleed. This judgment transcends mere ecological disaster. The seas, Scripture's ancient emblem of untamed chaos and the Abyss (Genesis 1:2), revert to a state of primordial disorder. Creation begins to unravel beneath the weight of judgment, with a source of life turned into a vessel of death.

---

### 🔍 SIDEBAR: The Burning Mountain

John's "burning mountain" has led interpreters to two terrifying possibilities: a catastrophic volcanic collapse or a massive asteroid strike. Either would unleash tsunamis, boiling devastation, and death across a third of the seas.

Whether rising from earth or falling from heaven, the message remains the same: creation itself becomes an instrument of judgment, and no corner of the world lies beyond the authority of the returning King.

*For a broader framework connecting these trumpet events as cascading fragments of a single cosmic upheaval,* see 🔍 *SIDEBAR: The Cosmic Shifter*

## The Third Trumpet: Wormwood and Poisoned Waters

*The third angel blew his trumpet, and a great star fell from heaven, blazing like a torch, and it fell on a third of the rivers and on the springs of water. The name of the star is Wormwood. A third of the waters became wormwood, and many people died from the water, because it had been made bitter.*

— REVELATION 8:10–11

The Third Trumpet sounds, and the assault on creation shifts from the saltwater of the seas to the freshwater that sustains human life. John witnesses another celestial object plummeting from the heavens: a "great star ... blazing like a torch." It strikes a third of the rivers and springs.

Its name is Wormwood.

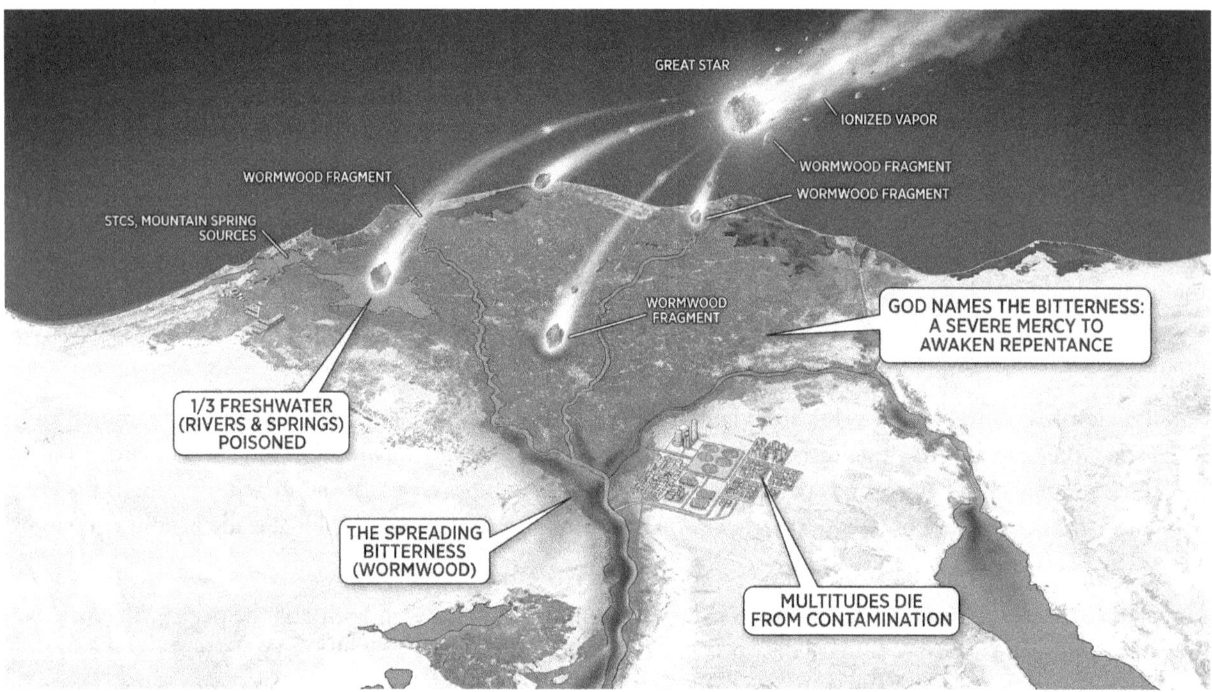


***Figure 12.3: The Poisoning of Wormwood.*** *In stark contrast to the saltwater judgment, the Third Trumpet strikes the earth's delicate freshwater supply. A blazing celestial fragment named Wormwood shatters into the rivers and springs, turning a third of the world's drinking water into bitter poison. It is a severe mercy meant to awaken a thirsty, rebellious world to repentance.*

The result is catastrophic. A third of the world's drinking water turns bitter, poisoned. Many die, not by sword or famine, but by thirst and contamination. Panic spreads as clean water becomes more valuable than gold. Infrastructure collapses, and contaminated reservoirs trigger mass dehydration. Desperation drives the thirsty to drink the poisoned supply, and multitudes perish.

This trumpet strikes at the core of human vulnerability. People can survive without commerce. They cannot survive without water. The judgment reaches into the bloodstream of civilization itself, imposing a direct sanction upon the very substance required for survival.

**NOTE: Why "Wormwood"?**

In Scripture, Wormwood symbolizes bitterness, sorrow, and divine judgment (Lamentations 3:15; Jeremiah 9:15). God is naming the bitterness of a world that has rejected Him. The poisoned waters become both catastrophe and warning, a severe mercy meant to awaken repentance before the end.

Some interpreters see these early trumpet judgments as sequential impacts within a larger cosmic disturbance (see *SIDEBAR: The Cosmic Shifter*).

## The Fourth Trumpet: The Heavens Are Struck

*The fourth angel blew his trumpet, and a third of the sun was struck, and a third of the moon, and a third of the stars, so that a third of their light might be darkened, and a third of the day might be kept from shining, and likewise a third of the night.*

— REVELATION 8:12

The trumpet sounds again, and judgment turns upward. No longer earth, sea, or rivers. Now the heavens themselves are struck.

In a sweeping cosmic blow, a third of the light from the sun, moon, and stars is extinguished. This is not a passing eclipse, but a permanent, suffocating dimness. Day becomes a perpetual twilight. Night becomes an unnatural, eerie shade of blackness.

The rhythms of creation fracture. The very measure of time feels unstable, as though the world's celestial clock has been tampered with. Light is withdrawn, darkness extended, and the normal cycle of day and night is compressed beneath forces beyond human control.

Seasons falter. Crops fail. Temperatures plunge. Human minds unravel under the weight of a world growing darker by decree.

The heavens, humanity's final symbol of stability, are torn. The celestial lights that once guided sailors and stirred poets now declare something else entirely.

The order of the cosmos is coming undone.

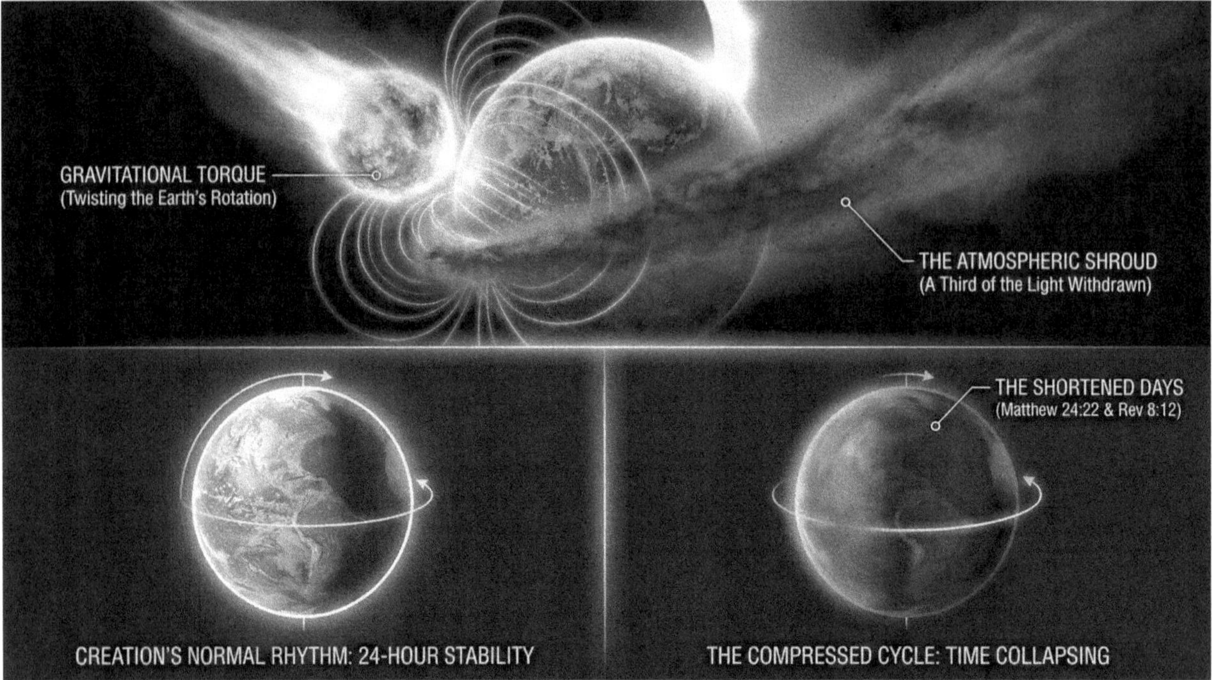


***Figure 12.4: The Cosmic Shifter and the Shortened Days.*** *A visualization of the astrophysical mechanics that could fulfill the Fourth Trumpet. A massive celestial intruder passing close to Earth would not only drag an atmospheric shroud of debris to dim the sun, moon, and stars by a third, but its gravitational torque could violently alter the planet's rotation. This physical compression of the day-night cycle provides a literal mechanism for Christ's pronouncement in Matthew 24:22 that the final days of the Great Tribulation will be "shortened" to prevent total human extinction.*

---

### 🔍 SIDEBAR: The Cosmic Shifter

*The Mechanics of a Near-Miss*

In astrophysics, a gravity assist occurs when the gravitational field of a massive body seizes another object and rewrites its trajectory. It is celestial mechanics at work, invisible forces bending the paths of worlds. Now imagine something far greater than a passing asteroid: a planetary-scale intruder sliding close enough to Earth to disturb the foundations of creation itself.

A near-miss on this scale would not be a gentle flyby. It would be a cosmic shudder, the Sovereign Hand on the gears of the world, as though the Creator Himself were reaching into the clockwork of heaven and earth.

#### The Shortened Day[1] (Gravitational Torque)

A sufficiently massive object passing nearby could become a gravitational tether, tugging at the Earth's crust and twisting the planet's rotation. The rhythm of time itself could be compressed. Day and night would no longer feel stable. The world would wake to the impossible sensation that the hours are collapsing, that creation's clock has been tampered with, a literal shortening of the days under forces beyond human control.

#### The Dimmed Sun (The Atmospheric Shroud)

Such a body would not travel clean. It would drag behind it a colossal wake of dust, debris, and ionized vapor, a trail like ash from the furnace of heaven. As Earth passes through this shroud, sunlight would weaken.

---

1. Cf. Matthew 24:22 YLT: "And if those days were not shortened, no flesh would have been saved ..." Jesus indicates that the days of the Great Tribulation will be shortened. The language of "shortened days" also resonates with Revelation 8:12 and its depiction of cosmic disturbance, as though the normal order of time and light is being compressed under divine decree.

Starlight would fade. The heavens would be struck with prophetic precision, a third of their brightness withdrawn. The world would enter a permanent twilight, cold, disorienting, unnatural.

**The Fragmentation (The Sequential Strikes)**

The encounter would not end with darkness. Tidal forces could tear at the rogue object, shedding layers like a crumbling mountain in the sky. What follows would not be one impact, but many, a sequence of prophetic blows written in fire.

It begins with the convulsion of the heavens itself. The Sixth Seal describes a world shaken by cosmic terror: a great earthquake, the sun blackened like sackcloth, the moon turned to blood, and the sky recoiling as though the very firmament were coming apart (Revelation 6:12–14). The approach of such an object would appear remarkably so, a celestial disruption so overwhelming that the world mistakes it for the unmaking of reality.

Then come the sequential strikes.

First, a storm of burning fragments, meteors raining like judgment upon the land.

Then, a massive blazing shard plunging into the sea, turning the oceans into blood.

Then, a dense and bitter splinter, Wormwood, poisoning the rivers and springs.

The trumpets do not arrive as isolated disasters, but as a cascading aftermath, fragments of a single cosmic upheaval that unfolds in stages across the earth.

**The Big Picture: A World Unbalanced**

In the grand architecture of prophecy, God often uses the very elements of nature as instruments of His sovereign purpose. Whether this upheaval is purely supernatural or providentially timed within the machinery of the cosmos, the meaning does not change.

The order of our world is not permanent.

It is not self-sustaining.

It is held together only by the will of God.

What appears to be a random near miss in space becomes, in truth, a planetary wake-up call. The heavens are not silent. The trumpets are not metaphor. And the world, once so secure in its routines, is revealed as frail beneath the approaching footsteps of its returning King.

---

And just when humanity thinks things cannot get worse... a dreadful warning pierces the skies.

> *Then I looked, and I heard an eagle crying with a loud voice as it flew directly overhead, "Woe, woe, woe to those who dwell on the earth, at the blasts of the other trumpets that the three angels are about to blow!"*
>
> — REVELATION 8:13

The next three trumpet blasts are not just judgments. They are woes. A divine intensifier. What has happened so far was dreadful. What comes next will be worse.

## The Fifth Trumpet: Locusts from the Abyss

> *And the fifth angel blew his trumpet, and I saw a star fallen from heaven to earth, and he was given the key to the shaft of the bottomless pit.*
>
> — REVELATION 9:1

With the Fifth Trumpet, the first woe breaks loose, and hell itself is unlocked.

John sees a "star" already fallen, a powerful angelic being cast down and now handed a key.[2] This is not a key of sovereign authority, but of permitted release. He opens the Abyss, the bottomless pit, a prison for the darkest demonic powers.

Smoke erupts like the furnace of a great city, thick enough to blot out the sun and choke the air. But the smoke is only the veil.

From within it comes something far worse.

***Figure 12.5: The Infernal Horde.*** *The Fifth Trumpet unlocks the shaft of the Abyss, unleashing the First Woe. Ruled by the destroyer Abaddon, this intelligent, malevolent horde, equipped with armor of iron and the sting of scorpions, swarms from the blinding smoke. Their mission is precise and divinely bounded: a five-month torment targeting only those who lack the seal of God.*

A swarm of locusts rises, not natural insects, but intelligent, malevolent beings, an infernal horde unleashed upon the earth.

> *They were told not to harm the grass of the earth or any plant or tree, but only those people who did not have the seal of God on their foreheads.*

2. For a more in-depth discussion, see *Deeper Dive 12.1. The Star of the Abyss.*

—REVELATION 9:4

Their mission is precise. This is not random destruction. It is targeted torment. They are permitted to assault only the unsealed.

For five agonizing months, they torture. The pain is so unbearable that people will long for death, but death will flee from them. Even escape is denied.

John struggles to describe the indescribable, piling image upon image:

- They charge like warhorses, disciplined and relentless.
- They bear faces of men, marked by intelligence.
- Their teeth are like lions, built to tear.
- They wear armor of iron, impervious to resistance.
- Their wings roar like chariots rushing into battle.
- Their tails sting like scorpions, delivering agony.

This is evil with structure. In nature, locusts have no king (Proverbs 30:27). These do.

They are ruled by the angel of the Abyss, Abaddon in Hebrew, Apollyon in Greek.

The Destroyer.

This five-month torment is a dreadful alarm, a preview of the total devastation to come, and a deafening summons to repent. Tragically, most will refuse.

The first woe has passed, but the world is scarred beyond recognition.

Two more are coming.

---

🔍 **SIDEBAR: The Five-Month Torment**

*An Echo of Noah's Flood*

*"They were allowed to torment them for five months, but not to kill them..."* (Revelation 9:5)

The allotted "five months" is not an arbitrary limit. In biblical prophecy, a month is calculated as thirty days, making this duration exactly 150 days. Genesis 7:24 records that the floodwaters prevailed upon the earth for precisely 150 days. This mathematical precision is a deliberate, prophetic echo. It functions as a vital chronological and theological marker.

In scriptural typology, the Flood provides a perfect picture of the end times. While Enoch was caught up to heaven before the judgment began (picturing the Rapture of the Church), Noah was preserved safely *through* the judgment. Noah typifies the Jewish remnant, whom God promises to protect through the outpouring of His final wrath.

Therefore, this 150-day allusion tells us exactly where we are on the prophetic timeline. It signals that the Fifth Trumpet is sounding during the Great Tribulation, the final three-and-a-half years of Daniel's seventieth week.

Just as Noah was sealed in the ark while wrath overwhelmed the outside world, Israel is now sheltered in the wilderness (Revelation 12:6), divinely protected from the demonic locusts and the Antichrist's pursuit. The judgment is catastrophic, but it is strictly bounded by God's sovereign limit.

A precise prophetic pattern emerges:

- **The Mathematical Echo:** The 150 days of floodwaters directly parallel the five months of demonic torment.
- **The Protected Remnant:** Noah sealed securely in the ark typifies Israel sealed and sheltered in the wilderness.
- **The Prophetic Timing:** This specific echo of Noah's preservation confirms this woe is occurring during the Great Tribulation, the final half of the seven-year period.

Even in this deepening darkness, God's wrath is measured. The clock belongs to Him, and His covenant protection over Israel remains unbreakable.

---

## The Sixth Trumpet: The Four Angels and the Fiery Horde

> *Then the sixth angel blew his trumpet, and I heard a voice ... saying to the sixth angel who had the trumpet, "Release the four angels who are bound at the great river Euphrates."*
>
> — REVELATION 9:13–14

With the blast of the Sixth Trumpet, the second woe is unleashed, and the scale of death escalates beyond comprehension.

A voice from the golden altar commands the release of four fallen angels, bound until this appointed hour. Their timing is exact: an hour, a day, a month, a year.

***Figure 12.6: The Army of the Euphrates.*** *The blast of the Sixth Trumpet (the Second Woe) releases four ancient, fallen angels bound at the Euphrates River. They lead a demonic cavalry numbering two hundred million. This apocalyptic horde, breathing fire, smoke, and sulfur, executes a scheduled judgment that results in the single greatest catastrophic loss of life in human history: the death of one-third of*

*remaining mankind.*

This is a scheduled judgment, a terrifyingly precise appointment with wrath.

Their prison is the Euphrates, a boundary heavy with prophetic memory. Near its waters Eden once flourished. Along its banks Babel rose. Empires of rebellion were born there. Now, from this ancient flashpoint, destruction is released.

Their mission is horrifyingly simple: kill a third of mankind.

They do not come alone.

They lead an army numbered at two hundred million, a host so vast it defies imagination. John's description pushes beyond the human:

The horses breathe fire, smoke, and sulfur. Their heads are like lions. Their tails are like serpents. Death strikes from mouth and tail alike:

> *By these three plagues a third of mankind was killed, by the fire and smoke and sulfur coming out of their mouths.*
>
> — REVELATION 9:18

The death toll is catastrophic, eclipsing every war and plague in human history combined. Yet, what follows is perhaps even more terrifying than the slaughter itself: the defiance of the unrepentant.

> *The rest of mankind, who were not killed by these plagues, did not repent ...*
>
> — REVELATION 9:20

The survivors, stumbling through a world decimated by fire and sulfur, still cling to their idols of gold, silver, and stone. They refuse to turn from their murders, their sorceries (*pharmakeia*: drug use and occultism), their sexual immorality, and their thefts.

The trumpets did not soften their hearts; they hardened them. This is an appalling portrait of humanity fully given over to its rebellion, staring into the face of divine wrath and choosing darkness, even as the world burns around them.

## *Chapter 13*

# THE ANGEL AND THE LITTLE SCROLL

## Serving Heaven's Eviction Notice

*... and swore by him who lives forever and ever... that there would be no more delay, but that in the days of the trumpet call to be sounded by the seventh angel, the mystery of God would be fulfilled ...*

— REVELATION 10:6–7

As the echoes of the Sixth Trumpet fade, the relentless rhythm of judgment pauses. Before the final trumpet sounds, the Apostle John is shown a new vision, an interlude that spans Revelation 10:1 through 11:13. It is crucial to understand that this section is not a chronological step, but a thematic pause. The main timeline of judgment is put on hold to give us a detailed look at two crucial elements of the Great Tribulation: the divine authority behind the final prophetic mandate (Revelation 10) and the earthly ministry of those commissioned to proclaim it (Revelation 11). We will look at each in turn, beginning with the Angel and the Little Scroll.

### The Herald of Dominion

John sees a mighty angel descending from heaven. This is no ordinary messenger. He is clothed with a cloud, with a rainbow over his head, his face shines like the sun, and his feet are like pillars of fire, descriptors that echo the very presence of God and of Christ. Yet, he is not the Lord Himself. John describes him as "another" mighty angel, using the Greek word *allos*, which means "another of the same kind." This signifies that he is a created being, like the trumpet angels before him, rather than the unique, self-existent Son of God. He shines with the King's glory not because he *is* the King, but because he comes as His supreme ambassador, bearing the full weight of divine authority.

He plants one foot on the sea and one on the land, a dramatic stance signaling total jurisdiction over the earth. This is both a territorial gesture and a legal declaration. The rightful King is reclaiming His domain.

***Figure 13.1: The Herald of Dominion.*** *The mighty angel reclaims divine jurisdiction over the earth, holding the final eviction summons that triggers the glorious consummation of God's redemptive plan.*

## The Seven Thunders and the End of Delay

In his hand is a little scroll, already opened. Unlike the sealed title deed of Revelation 5 (see *Deeper Dive 5.3. The Title Deed to Creation*), this one is ready to be proclaimed. This scroll serves as heaven's official eviction summons. It contains the exact terms of a divine repossession. Satan, the current "prince of this world" (John 12:31), is being served final notice. He has long overstayed his tenure and will be removed with extreme prejudice.

The angel roars like a lion, and seven thunders respond with voices of their own. John begins to write, but is immediately commanded to seal up what the thunders said and not to write it down. This is a profound lesson in divine sovereignty: there are dimensions to God's plan that remain hidden, a humbling reminder that our knowledge is incomplete.

With the thunders silenced, the angel makes a solemn oath: **"there will be no more delay!"**[1] The long-tolerated rebellion of mankind, the groaning of creation, and the cries of the martyrs are all rushing toward resolution. The execution of this eviction summons is the exact mechanism that allows the "mystery of God" to reach its final fulfillment.[2] God cannot establish His promised earthly kingdom without first legally removing the usurper. It is time to act with absolute finality to end the rebellion.

## The Bittersweet Scroll

Then John receives a command that echoes the experience of the prophet Ezekiel centuries earlier.[3] He is told

1. For a fuller exploration, see *Deeper Dive 15.1. The Hinge of Heaven's Judgment.*
2. The phrase "the mystery of God" is a rich theological term that encompasses God's entire redemptive plan as revealed in the New Testament. For a detailed breakdown of the various "mysteries" that are brought to completion during the final phase, see *Deeper Dive 13.1. The Mystery of God.*

3. *Ezekiel 2:8–3:3; cf. Revelation 10:9–10.* Ezekiel describes the scroll as "sweet as honey" in his mouth, emphasizing the privilege of receiving

to take the scroll from the angel's hand and eat it. The act symbolizes the full internalization of God's prophetic Word. It is not merely heard, but taken inside the prophet himself.

It tastes sweet in his mouth, for what could be sweeter than divine truth and the promise of God's final victory? But it turns bitter in his stomach. The message is both glorious and grievous, righteous in its justice yet ruinous in its effect. It is a decree of judgment, carrying with it the sorrow and weight of the undiluted wrath that must soon be poured out.

***Figure 13.2: The Bittersweet Scroll.*** *The Apostle John internalizes God's final prophetic mandate. The scroll is sweet in his mouth because it guarantees the glorious establishment of Christ's kingdom, but it turns bitter in his stomach because it serves as heaven's final eviction summons, unleashing the ruinous judgments required to reclaim the earth from the usurper.*

## John's Recommissioning: The Narrative Hinge

John's work is not finished. With the command, "You must prophesy again about many peoples, nations, languages, and kings" (Revelation 10:11), he is decisively recommissioned.

This is far more than an instruction to continue. It marks a pivotal turn in the book's structure. The key word "again" translates the Greek *palin*, a term implying repetition, return, or retracing a path. John is not merely to move forward, but to speak once more about the same divine drama, now from a renewed perspective.

The timing is striking. John, an elderly exile on a prison island, has just witnessed waves of judgment and has tasted the bittersweet weight of God's message. Humanly speaking, the story seems near its end. The Seventh Trumpet looms; closure feels imminent.

Yet at this very moment, he is told his most important task still lies ahead.

---

the Word of God. John's vision in Revelation 10 develops the imagery further by adding that the scroll becomes "bitter" in his stomach. In both cases, the sweetness reflects the beauty of divine revelation, while the bitterness is tied to the heavy burden of proclaiming judgment. This bitterness is explicit in John's physical reaction and implied in Ezekiel's later description of going "in bitterness, in the heat of my spirit" (Ezekiel 3:14).

By ordering him to "prophesy again," the Spirit signals a shift in purpose. The visions to come will not simply advance the timeline, but will revisit and expand it, deepening our understanding of what has already been set in motion. The scope becomes global: "many peoples, nations, languages, and kings." The focus shifts from the sequence of judgments to the identities, motives, and spiritual forces driving the conflict behind the scenes.

For this reason, Revelation 10:11 serves as the definitive hinge on which the rest of the book turns. Everything that follows unfolds under this renewed commission: the ministry of the Two Witnesses, Satan's war against Israel, the rise of the Beast, the fall of Babylon. John is now unveiling the deeper realities at work within the prophetic period he has already outlined.

The story, then, is not over. It is being retold with greater depth and sharper focus. John bears the bittersweet burden of the final act: to show not only what happens, but why.

One last trumpet remains, destined to shake heaven and earth and declare an end to all rebellion:

"The kingdom of the world has become the kingdom of our Lord and of his Christ" (Revelation 11:15).

## The End Is Only Beginning

With **six trumpets** sounded and one remaining, the earth is utterly transformed. Economies are shattered, cities leveled, the environment broken, and humanity reduced, but the worst judgments are still ahead.

And yet, in all this, a pattern emerges: God gives space to repent. He warns. He shakes. He calls. The seals and trumpets are not just punishments; they are pleas. Will you turn while there's still time?

The Lamb has broken the seals. The trumpets have sounded. The eviction is underway.

The next chapter brings us from the courts of heaven to the streets of Jerusalem. Two witnesses arrive to testify against the world. You have seen the judgments from above; now meet the prophets who stand in the fire below.

Jesus is coming. But before He returns, the world must pass through fire.

*Chapter 14*

# TEMPLE MEASUREMENT AND TWO WITNESSES

## Divine Claim and Prophetic Mission

*Behold, I am going to send you Elijah the prophet before the coming of the great and terrible day of the Lord.*

— MALACHI 4:5 NASB

## Measuring the Temple: A Divine Claim

Revelation 11 pulls the curtain on a scene showing John given a "measuring rod" and told: "Rise and measure the temple of God and the altar and those who worship there, but do not measure the court outside the temple; leave that out, for it is given over to the nations, and they will trample the holy city for forty-two months."

This act carries far more weight than architectural documentation. Just as in Ezekiel 40 and Zechariah 2, measuring signifies divine evaluation, as God marks what belongs to Him for preservation while setting apart what does not for judgment. The instruction to measure the Temple, the altar, and the worshipers points to divine recognition of a faithful remnant. By measuring not only the structure but the worshipers themselves, God signals personal knowledge and protection.

But the command contains a deliberate exclusion. The outer court is not to be measured. It is "given over to the nations." In biblical terms, not measuring signifies abandonment. This exclusion extends beyond the court itself to the city as a whole, which is said to be trampled for exactly forty-two months: the latter half of the seven-year period, when the Antichrist's persecution reaches its peak.

The contrast is striking. God preserves what He measures. He relinquishes what He does not.

This division carries profound real-world implications. It outlines the necessary framework for a political compromise, one that allows for the rebuilding of the Third Temple without displacing the Islamic holy sites currently dominating the Temple Mount. While the Dome of the Rock has traditionally been thought to occupy the original site of Solomon's Temple, some models, such as Asher Kaufman's Northern Conjecture, suggest the ancient temple stood roughly 100 meters to the north.[1] However, a growing body of research drawing from historical sources like Josephus and modern archaeological interpretations points in the opposite direction. Proposed by Tuvia Sagiv, the Southern Sanctuary model places the site to the south at the El Kas Fountain.[2]

---

1. Asher S. Kaufman, "Where the Ancient Temple of Jerusalem Stood," *Biblical Archaeology Review* 9, no. 2 (March/April 1983); Asher S. Kaufman, *The Temple of Jerusalem, Part I: Tractate Middot* (Jerusalem: Har Year'eh Press, 1991).
2. Tuvia Sagiv, "The Hidden Secrets of the Temple Mount" (Tel Aviv: Sagiv Architects, 1996).

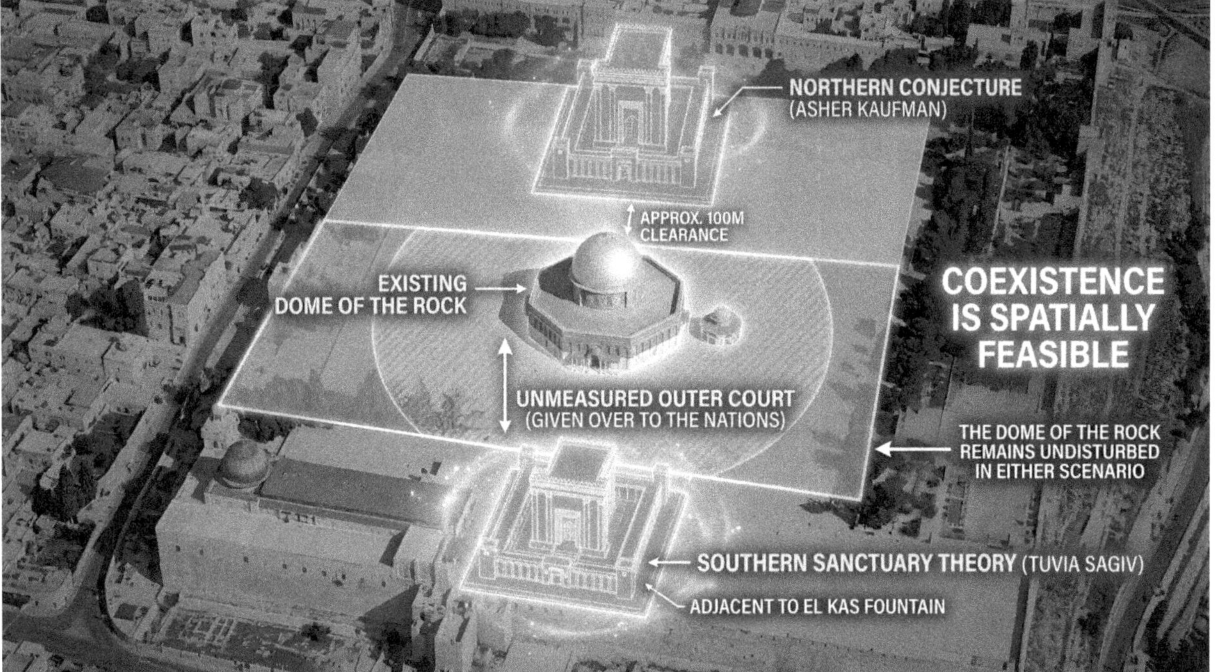


***Figure 14.1: The Unmeasured Court Hypothesis.*** *This composite diagram illustrates how the Third Temple could theoretically be rebuilt to the North (Kaufman's Conjecture) or South (Sagiv's Theory) of the Dome of the Rock.*

If the Dome was built near, but not directly on, the ancient temple site, a remarkable prophetic reality emerges: the Temple can be rebuilt on its true original foundation without disturbing the Islamic shrine. In this scenario, the unmeasured outer court becomes a deliberate geopolitical concession to the Muslim world, a compromise rendering the Third Temple's reconstruction both politically and religiously feasible.

Therefore, John's vision in Revelation 11 is not merely symbolic; it is literal and prophetically precise. It portrays a divided sanctuary in a divided city, unerringly reflecting the real-world complexities of faith, politics, and prophecy converging on the world's most contested piece of ground. This exact division prepares the Temple Mount as the ultimate stage for the central drama of the Great Tribulation.

## Enter the Two Witnesses

In the midst of the unfolding chaos, just prior to the Antichrist committing the "abomination of desolation" and unleashing the Great Tribulation, God preemptively activates His two extraordinary witnesses in Jerusalem. This precise timing directly satisfies the mandate of Malachi 4:5, ensuring the prophetic arrival of Elijah "before that great and dreadful day of the LORD comes." Clothed in sackcloth, the garb of mourning and repentance, these men stand as living symbols of God's mercy and warning. They are called "my two witnesses" (Revelation 11:3) and are appointed to prophesy for 1,260 days. Their ministry is not confined strictly to the second half. Instead, it bridges the critical midpoint and spans the vast majority of the Great Tribulation, concluding just before the unmitigated wrath of the Bowl Judgments. (For a detailed discussion, consult *Deeper Dive 14.1. The 1,260-Day Enigma of the Two Witnesses*).

They are not a prelude to the darkness but a blazing light in the face of it. They stand in defiant contrast to the Antichrist, proclaiming truth within a city gripped by deception.

They are empowered with supernatural authority. Fire proceeds from their mouths to consume their enemies. They shut the sky so that no rain falls during their ministry, and they strike the earth with plagues (v. 6). Their miracles echo the ministries of two ancient prophets, Moses and Elijah, who themselves once confronted kings and called nations to repentance.

For the duration of their ministry, they are untouchable. No weapon formed against them prospers. Their voice is a thorn to the world and a trumpet to heaven.

Yet when their task is complete, their protection is lifted. "The beast that comes up from the Abyss," the Antichrist, makes war against them and kills them (v. 7). Their bodies lie in the streets of Jerusalem for three and a half days, unburied and desecrated. The world rejoices. They exchange gifts in morbid celebration, believing the troublemakers are finally gone.

And then, something truly remarkable happens, something only our modern generation can fully appreciate. Revelation 11:9 (NASB) states unequivocally, "Those from the peoples and tribes and tongues and nations will look at their dead bodies for three and a half days." The text specifies witnesses from every nation and language group; it speaks of comprehensive, global viewing of the two dead bodies lying in the street.

Such a claim would have been unthinkable in John's time. How could the whole world look upon two men lying dead in Jerusalem? Today, it is not only plausible; it is expected. In an age of global satellite networks, nonstop news cycles, and livestreamed events viewed by billions, the fulfillment of this prophecy is no longer distant. It is entirely possible right now.

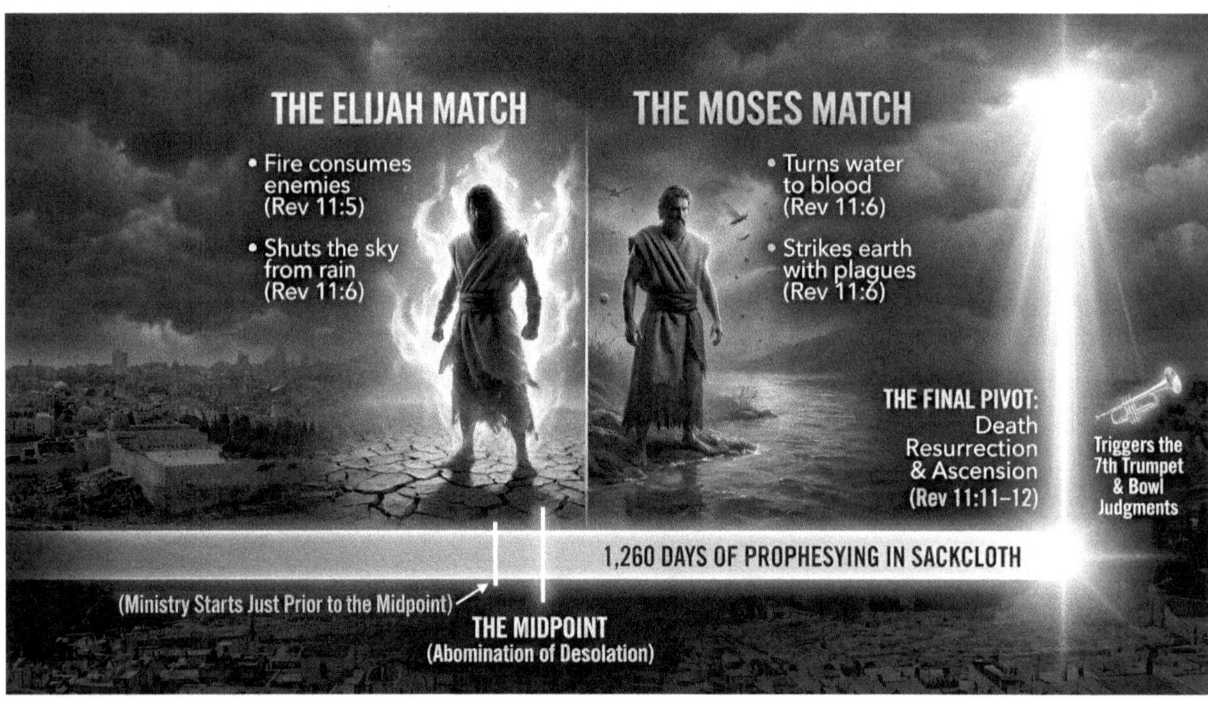


***Figure 14.2: The Ministry and Miracles of the Two Witnesses.*** *A visual breakdown of the 1,260-day prophetic mission in Jerusalem, highlighting the specific "miracle matches" that link these end-times messengers to the historical ministries of Moses and Elijah.*

But the world celebrates too soon.

## Resurrection, Vindication, and Great Fear

After three and a half days, the breath of God enters them. Before the watching world, they stand on their feet, a moment so terrifying that "great fear fell on those who saw them" (v. 11). Then a voice from heaven calls them up, and they ascend in a cloud, just like Jesus did.

An earthquake immediately strikes the city, killing 7,000 and toppling a tenth of it. Those who survive, stunned by the supernatural power they have just witnessed, give glory to the God of heaven: one of the rare explicit glimpses of repentance recorded during the Tribulation. This serves as the final wake-up moment for the Jewish nation.

The ministry of these two resolute witnesses is God's bold announcement to the world:

**To Israel:** The Messiah you rejected is real, and He is returning.

**To the world:** The window of mercy is closing, final judgment is near.

**To Satan:** Your time is up.

---

🔍 **SIDEBAR: Moses and Elijah: The Final Assignment?**

Who are the Two Witnesses in Revelation 11? While some interpret them symbolically, perhaps as representing the prophetic Church or Israel and the Church, the biblical evidence overwhelmingly demonstrates that these are two literal men, and more specifically: Moses and Elijah.

The evidence for this is compelling.

**1. The Miracle Match:** Their miracles are not generic powers but precise echoes of specific ministries: turning water to blood and striking the earth with plagues mirrors Moses in Egypt, while shutting up the sky and calling down fire is the hallmark of Elijah. This "miracle match" strongly suggests their identities.

**2. The Mount of Transfiguration:** Their return was previewed on the Mount of Transfiguration, where Moses and Elijah appeared with Jesus in glory as the living embodiments of the Law and the Prophets. If that moment was a foretaste of the Kingdom, their reappearance in Revelation positions them as forerunners of the returning King.

**3. The Unfinished Ministries:** This final assignment may also represent God's grace in completing two of history's most significant, yet unfinished, ministries. Consider their stories: Moses, the great Lawgiver, was denied entry into the Promised Land after he fractured a crucial typology of Christ: striking the rock in anger when he was commanded to speak to it. Elijah, the powerful Prophet, fled in fear from Jezebel's threat immediately after his spectacular victory on Mount Carmel, eventually leaving his divine commission to anoint two kings unfulfilled. Thus, their heroic narratives each conclude with a note of incompletion. The ministry of the Two Witnesses, therefore, could be God's crowning act of grace, allowing these pillars of faith to finish their races in ultimate triumph.

**4. The Unique Departures:** Their unique departures from this world also support this theory. Elijah was taken to heaven in a whirlwind (2 Kings 2:11), and while Moses did die, God Himself buried him (Deuteronomy 34:5–6), and his body was never found, with Jude 9 hinting at a supernatural dispute over it, possibly to preserve him for this precise future role.

During the most critical point leading up to the Great Tribulation, God sends messengers who speak a language Israel cannot dismiss. Moses and Elijah, the ultimate symbols of the Law and the Prophets, return to confront the nation's leadership and issue a final call to repentance. It is a relentless act of mercy: God gives Israel two voices they cannot ignore, pointing them to the Messiah they once rejected and a last chance to turn back.

---

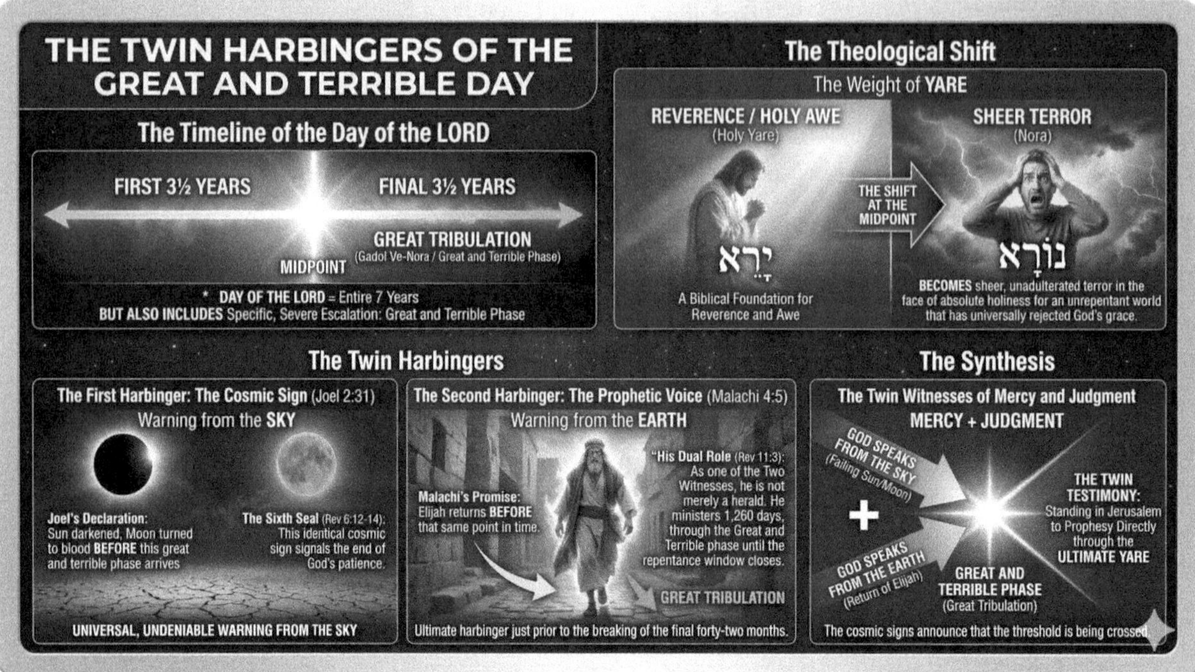


***Figure 14.3: The Twin Harbingers of the Great and Terrible Day.*** *The Day of the LORD is a precisely structured timeline that pivots dramatically at the midpoint. This visual maps the critical threshold where holy reverence (*Yare*) transitions into sheer terror (*Nora*). Before this terrifying phase engulfs the unrepentant world, God provides a lockstep, twofold warning: undeniable cosmic signs from the sky and the prophetic ministry of Elijah from the earth.*

---

### 🔍 SIDEBAR: The Twin Harbingers of the Great and Terrible Day

**The Timeline of the Day of the LORD.**

To understand the warnings of Joel and Malachi, we must distinguish between the broader timeline of judgment and its climactic resolution. Prophetically, the Day of the LORD encompasses the entirety of Daniel's Seventieth Week, the full seven-year Tribulation. However, both prophets point toward a specific, severe escalation: the "great and terrible" phase. This aligns with to the final three and a half years, the period Jesus specifically identified as the Great Tribulation.

**The Weight of Yare.** In Hebrew, the phrase "great and terrible" is *gadol ve-nora*. The word *nora* is derived from the root verb *yare*. While *yare* serves as the biblical foundation for holy reverence and awe, its application changes drastically at the midpoint of the Tribulation. For an unrepentant world that has rejected God's grace, *yare* ceases to be reverential awe. It becomes sheer, unadulterated terror in the face of divine holiness. But before the timeline crosses into this terrifying final half, God provides two unmistakable harbingers.

**The First Harbinger: The Cosmic Sign.** In chapter 2, verse 31, Joel declares that the sun will be darkened and the moon turned to blood before this great and terrible phase arrives. We see this exact physical sign at the opening of the Sixth Seal in Revelation 6. The cosmic blackout serves as a universal, undeniable warning from the heavens that the time of God's patience is ending.

**The Second Harbinger: The Prophetic Voice.** In chapter 4, verse 5, Malachi promises that God will send the prophet Elijah before that exact same point in time. As we saw in Revelation 11, Elijah returns as one of the Two Witnesses. While his preemptive arrival serves as the ultimate harbinger just prior to the breaking of the final forty-two months, his 1,260-day ministry of fire and drought bridges the critical midpoint and spans the vast majority of the Great and Terrible phase. He is not merely a herald of the coming terror; he ministers directly through it until the repentance window closes.

**The Twin Witnesses of Mercy and Judgment.** Together, these prophecies reveal a lockstep, twofold witness. God speaks from the sky through the failing of the sun and moon, and He speaks from the earth through the physical return of Elijah. The cosmic signs announce that the threshold is being crossed, while Elijah stands in the streets of Jerusalem to prophesy directly through the climactic *yare*, the terror of the Great Tribulation, ceasing only when their divine mandate to call the world to repentance is complete.

---

## Chapter 15

# THE SEVENTH TRUMPET

## The Kingdom Has Come

> *"The kingdom of the world has become the kingdom of our Lord and of his Christ, and he shall reign forever and ever."*
>
> — REVELATION 11:15B

## Heaven Sounds the Trumpet

When the Seventh Trumpet blasts, heaven erupts in a triumphant proclamation that has echoed through the prophecies of the ages. Voices thunder a declaration of ultimate victory, announcing that the sovereignty of the world has legally and eternally passed into the hands of our Lord and His Christ.

This is the fulfillment of a vision first seen by the prophet Daniel, who saw the Son of Man receiving an everlasting dominion that would never be destroyed (Daniel 7:14). It is the moment the Apostle Paul foresaw, when Christ, having destroyed every rival power, delivers the kingdom to God the Father (1 Corinthians 15:24). The long-awaited prayer, "Your kingdom come," is now being realized.

This trumpet blast is not a single, momentary judgment. It is the Third and Final Woe (Revelation 11:14), a divine declaration that initiates a cascade of climactic events. As Revelation 10:7 foretold, "in the days of the trumpet call ... by the seventh angel, the mystery of God would be fulfilled."

The sounding of the Seventh Trumpet, therefore, is the trigger for this final fulfillment. It serves as the framework for the most intense and rapid phase of God's judgment: the seven bowls of wrath, poured out in Revelation 16. This final sequence shatters Satan's earthly kingdom and culminates in the return of Christ. It leads to the establishment of His millennial reign, the Great White Throne judgment, and the final casting of Satan, Death, and Hades into the lake of fire.[1]

In response, the twenty-four elders fall on their faces in worship. They praise God not only for taking up His great power and reigning, but for the perfect righteousness of His judgment:

> *"We give thanks to you, Lord God Almighty, who is and who was, for you have taken your great power and begun to reign. The nations raged, but your wrath came, and the time for the dead to be judged, and for rewarding your servants, the prophets and saints, and those who fear your name, both small and great, and for destroying the destroyers of the earth."*
>
> — REVELATION 11:17–18

Heaven rejoices. Earth trembles. For as God's kingdom arrives, Satan's final downfall draws near.

1. For more details, see *Deeper Dive 15.1. The Hinge of Heaven's Judgment.*

## The Temple Opens: An Echo of Sinai

Then comes an awe-inspiring moment: the temple in heaven is opened, and the Ark of His Covenant is seen (Revelation 11:19). This is not the earthly ark once housed in Solomon's temple, but the heavenly reality to which the earthly one only pointed. Its sudden appearance signals several monumental truths.

**First, God's Presence is Unveiled**. The Ark was the symbolic throne of God on earth. To see it in heaven is to glimpse the covenant throne itself. The curtain is drawn back. Heaven is not distant; its reality is breaking into the world.

**Second, God's Covenant is Remembered**. The Ark housed the symbols of God's covenant with Israel. Its appearance is a stunning declaration that God has not forgotten His promises. Judgment flows from covenantal justice rather than capricious violence.

**Finally, Divine Judgment Flows from Divine Holiness.** The scene erupts with lightning, thunder, an earthquake, and hail, a direct echo of God's terrifying descent upon Mount Sinai (Exodus 19). This reveals that divine judgment flows from divine holiness. The same God who gave the Law at Sinai is now unveiling the fulfillment of His redemptive plan. The world is not merely hearing an announcement. It is reeling under the raw weight of divine authority.

The storm is not coming. It is here.

***Figure 15.1: The Heavenly Temple Unveiled.*** *As the Seventh Trumpet sounds, the veil of heaven is drawn back to reveal the true Ark of the Covenant. Accompanied by Sinai-like lightning, thunder, and hail, this awe-inspiring vision declares that God's final, terrifying judgments flow directly from His perfect holiness and unwavering covenant faithfulness.*

## The Cosmic Rewind

The Seventh Trumpet has sounded. The legal declaration has been made. The world stands on the absolute brink of the final Bowl Judgments, the climax of the Great Tribulation.

But before the first bowl of wrath is poured out, the narrative does something unexpected: it rewinds.

As we noted in Chapter 5 on our study of Revelation's structure, John's vision does not unfold in a strict, unbroken chronological line. Having brought us to the very edge of the consummation in Revelation 11, the Spirit now commands John to step through the "narrative hinge" he was given in Revelation 10. He must prophesy *again*.

In the chapters that follow (Revelation 12–14), the camera pans away from the linear timeline of earthly judgments to reveal the ancient, invisible war driving the Tribulation. Before we see the final destruction of the Antichrist's kingdom, God pulls back the curtain to show us the key figures acting behind the scenes: the Woman, the Dragon, the Beast, and the False Prophet.

We have seen the wrath falling from heaven. Now, we are about to witness the ancient hatred rising from the Abyss.

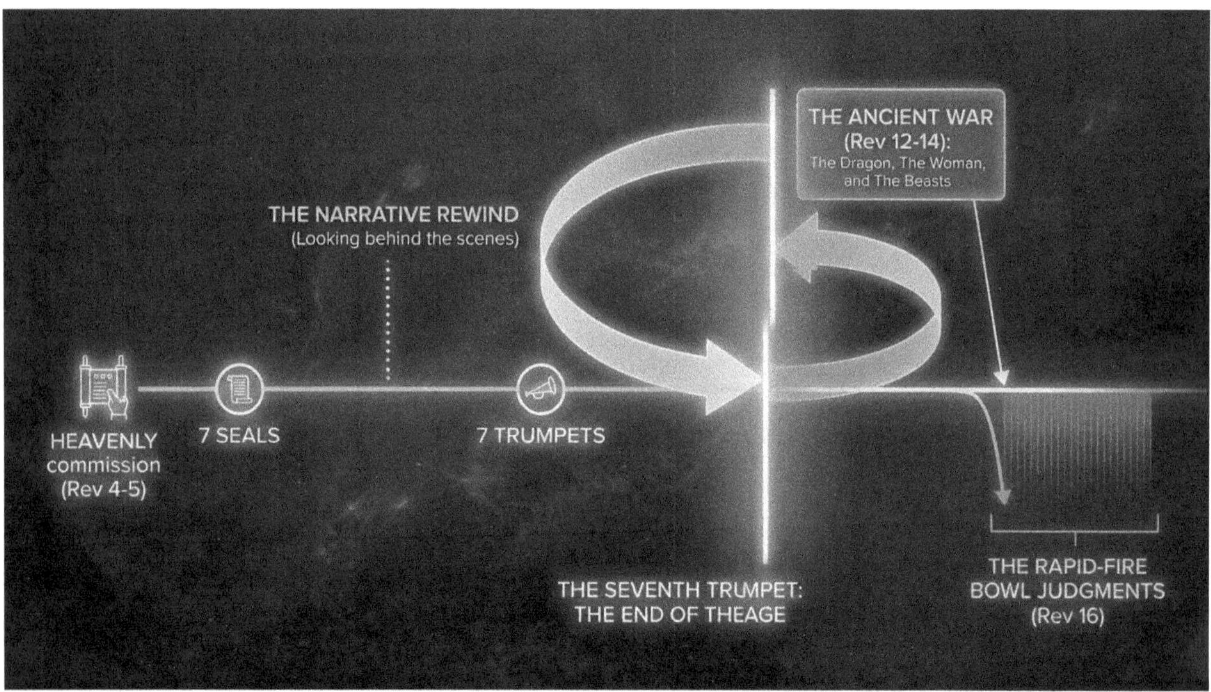


***Figure 15.2: The Narrative Rewind.*** *Revelation is not strictly chronological. Upon reaching the absolute brink of the end at the Seventh Trumpet, the narrative intentionally loops back. This "rewind" pulls back the curtain on the ancient, invisible war—the Dragon, the Woman, and the Beasts (Revelation 12–14)—before the timeline snaps back to the present to unleash the rapid-fire Bowl Judgments (Revelation 16).*

---

### 🔍 SIDEBAR: An Echo of Jericho

*The Walls Come Down*

The blast of a trumpet is more than a signal; in God's hands, it is a weapon of conquest. Nowhere is this clearer than in the story of Jericho.

For seven days, Israel marched in what seemed like a futile ritual. But on the seventh day, at the blast of the trumpets during the seventh circuit, the impossible happened: the impenetrable walls of a fortified city collapsed in an instant (Joshua 6). This was not a human victory; it was a divine demolition, a resounding demonstration that God overthrows the mightiest human defenses with a sound.

The Seventh Trumpet of Revelation is the ultimate echo of this event. Just as the trumpets at Jericho signaled the fall of a single pagan city and the beginning of Israel's possession of the Promised Land, the final trumpet in Revelation signals the collapse of the entire "kingdom of the world." It is the declaration that the walls of human rebellion have fallen, and the time has come for the saints to possess their ultimate inheritance: the kingdom of our Lord and of His Christ.

The Jericho parallel is a powerful reminder that God's methods are not man's. He brings down empires not with the clash of armies, but with the breath of His command. The Seventh Trumpet is the final, cosmic fulfillment of this principle: a sound that shatters strongholds and ushers in the everlasting reign of the King. (For more, see *Deeper Dive 5.4. Jericho as Prophetic Blueprint*).

---

***Figure 15.3: The Jericho Blueprint.*** *Just as the seventh blast of the ram's horn brought down the impenetrable walls of Jericho, the Seventh Trumpet of Revelation signals the ultimate collapse of the rebellious "kingdom of the world." God demolishes the mightiest human and demonic defenses not with the clash of armies, but with the breath of His command.*

*Chapter 16*

# THE COSMIC WAR UNVEILED

## The Conflict Behind All Wars

*Now war arose in heaven, Michael and his angels fighting against the dragon. And the dragon and his angels fought back, but he was defeated ...*

— REVELATION 12:7–8

## The Great Sign: The Woman and the Covenant

At this pivotal moment in the Tribulation, a dramatic shift takes place, not on earth, but in heaven. Revelation 12 pulls back the veil and unveils the war behind all wars: a sweeping cosmic conflict that drives everything unfolding below.

Because this section of Revelation relies on highly symbolic "signs," veteran prophecy scholars often refer to it as the introduction of the **Seven Personages** of the Tribulation. Just like a playbill hands you a list of the cast before the curtain rises, Chapters 12 and 13 introduce the key players driving the final half of the seven-year period: The Woman, the Dragon, the Male Child, the Archangel Michael, the Jewish Remnant, the Antichrist, and the False Prophet.

The vision opens with the first of these striking symbols. A radiant woman appears, clothed with the sun, the moon beneath her feet, and a crown of twelve stars upon her head. She is pregnant, crying out in the agony of labor.

This woman represents Israel, God's covenant nation, a truth rooted in Genesis 37:9–10. Joseph dreamed of the sun, moon, and eleven stars bowing before him, and Jacob immediately understood the meaning: the sun symbolized himself, the moon his wife, representing the matriarchal line, and the stars the tribes of Israel. Revelation's twelve-star crown unmistakably identifies the Woman as the full assembly of Israel.

The imagery is intentional. Israel was the nation through whom the Messiah came in His first coming, and in the Tribulation she becomes the remnant through whom God's covenant promises will be fulfilled (Romans 11:1–5). Her labor pains symbolize both the anguish surrounding Christ's birth and the end-time suffering that precedes His return. The male Child is Jesus, destined "to rule all nations with an iron scepter" (Revelation 12:5; Psalm 2:9).

## The Great Red Dragon

Then a grotesque figure emerges: a great red dragon, blazing with fury. This is no mythic beast. It is Satan himself (Revelation 12:9).

***Figure 16.1: The Cosmic Conflict.*** *Visualizing the profound celestial signs of Revelation 12:1–3. The radiant woman, clothed with the sun and crowned with twelve stars, represents Israel in her agonizing labor to bring forth the Messiah. Opposing her is the great red dragon, symbolizing Satan and his earthly kingdoms, waiting to devour the promised Child and setting the stage for the ultimate eschatological war.*

His seven heads, crowned with diadems, represent the fullness of his counterfeit authority. His ten horns point to the final ten-king confederacy of the Tribulation (Daniel 7:24; Revelation 17:12). With a sweep of his tail, he casts a third of heaven's stars to the earth, symbolizing the fallen angels who joined his ancient rebellion and now await judgment (Jude 6; 2 Peter 2:4).

The Dragon positions himself before the laboring Woman, ready to devour her Child the moment He is born. But his attempt is thwarted. The Child, Christ, is "caught up to God and to His throne" (Revelation 12:5), a sweeping reference to the resurrection and ascension.

Unable to destroy the Messiah, the Dragon turns his rage toward the Woman, Israel.

## War in Heaven: The Great Eviction

But before her flight, an invisible war ignites in heaven.

Michael the archangel rises to lead God's angelic forces against the Dragon and his rebel host. The battle is fierce, but decisive. Satan is overpowered and stripped of his access to the heavenly court.

***Figure 16.2: Satan Cast Down.*** *Michael and his angels overpower the Great Red Dragon, permanently evicting the ancient serpent and his demonic forces from the heavenly realm and casting them down to the earth.*

No longer able to accuse God's people before His throne day and night, the Dragon is hurled to earth in total defeat.

He does not fall quietly. He falls in fury, fully aware that his time is short.

Now grounded and enraged, Satan unleashes his vengeance on earth. Unable to touch heaven, he turns his wrath against Israel and all who remain loyal to Jesus. Persecution escalates.

## The Wilderness Refuge: A Midpoint Rupture

The Woman is forced to flee into the wilderness, where God miraculously shelters her for 1,260 days. This is the familiar three-and-a-half-year period repeatedly linked to the final half of Daniel's prophetic week (Revelation 12:6, 14; Daniel 9:27). In other words, this flight marks the midpoint of the Tribulation and the onset of what Jesus called the Great Tribulation (Matthew 24:15–21).

For some, particularly Jews in Israel, this wilderness refuge may be Petra, the ancient rock fortress in modern-day Jordan.[1] For others around the world, survival may mean going entirely off-grid, trusting God to lead and sustain.

In a final attempt to destroy the Woman, the Dragon releases a torrent, a flood meant to overwhelm her. Whether literal waters, or more likely a surge of military force and relentless persecution, the threat is devastating. Yet God intervenes again. The earth opens its mouth and swallows the flood, echoing Numbers 16, when the ground split to consume Korah and his rebels.

This marks a turning point of epic proportions. Satan, once granted a hearing in the courts of heaven (Job 1:6–

1. For more details, see *Deeper Dive 7.1. The Petra Connection*

12; Zechariah 3:1), is now permanently exiled. The cosmic war shifts decisively from the courtroom above to the battlefield below.

He is no longer merely a tempter or accuser, but a desperate tyrant confined to the earth with nothing left to lose. Therefore, the midpoint of the Tribulation is more than a chronological marker; it is a cosmic rupture. The Dragon rages, the remnant flees, and the final rampage begins.

Yet Satan does not carry out this last assault alone. Cast down and burning with animosity, he quickly raises up his instruments. Since he can no longer accuse in heaven, he will seek to conquer through the kingdoms of men. Revelation 13 now reveals his strategy: the Dragon wages war on the world through two empowered agents of deception and dominion.

🔍 **SIDEBAR: The Seven Heads**
*Satan's War Through Empires*

*"And another sign appeared in heaven: behold, a great red dragon, with seven heads and ten horns, and on his heads seven diadems."* (Revelation 12:3)

The seven heads of the Dragon symbolize seven historical empires Satan has used in his long war against God's purposes, especially against Israel and the messianic promise. Together, they form a dark lineage of dominion and deception.

***Figure 16.3: The Seven Empires of the Dragon.*** *Tracing the lineage of Satan's earthly war. Each head of the dragon represents a specific human empire (whether historical or yet to come) that the enemy has weaponized to annihilate the covenant nation and prevent the return of Christ.*

### The Seven Satanic Empires in Chronological Order:

| Head | Empire | The Dragon's Strategy & Historical Action |
|---|---|---|
| 1 | Egypt | Pharaoh enslaves Israel and attempts genocide (Exodus 1), seeking to crush God's covenant people before they become a nation. |
| 2 | Assyria | Destroys the northern kingdom (722 BC), dispersing the tribes and weakening Israel's prophetic identity. |
| 3 | Babylon | Destroys Jerusalem and the temple (586 BC), exiles Judah, and assaults the Davidic royal line. |
| 4 | Persia | Haman's plot nearly wipes out the Jews (Esther 3), but divine providence preserves them. |
| 5 | Greece | Antiochus IV Epiphanes desecrates the temple and slaughters the faithful (Daniel 8). |
| 6 | Rome | Crucifies the Messiah, destroys the second temple (AD 70), and scatters Israel among the nations. |
| 7 | Future Revived Rome | The final end-time empire, a confederation of ten kings ruled by the Antichrist in Satan's ultimate attempt to destroy Israel and prevent Christ's return (Revelation 17:12–14). |

**Daniel's Prophetic Horizon**

Daniel's visions trace the empires from his own day forward (Babylon, Persia, Greece, Rome, and a final revived kingdom). Egypt and Assyria fall outside his scope, but from John's vantage point in Revelation, the full historical pattern comes into view.

**The Dragon's Endgame**

These heads represent Satan's recurring strategy: raising empires to oppose God's covenant people and derail the messianic promise.

Prophetically, Christ's return hinges on Israel's national repentance (Hosea 5:15; Matthew 23:39). This reality dictates Satan's final, desperate strategy: he must annihilate Israel. His goal is to completely silence the nation destined to cry, 'Blessed is He who comes in the name of the Lord,' attempting to sever the prophetic lifeline and thwart the return of the King.

---

🔍 **SIDEBAR: Dual Fulfillment of Revelation 12:5?**

*"and her Child was caught up to God and to His throne."* (Revelation 12:5 NASB)

This verse unquestionably refers to Christ's ascension. Yet the Greek word for "caught up," *harpazo*, invites deeper reflection. It describes a sudden, forceful snatching away, often with the sense of rescue. Significantly, *harpazo* is the same word Paul uses in 1 Thessalonians 4:17 to describe the Rapture, when believers will be "caught up" to meet the Lord in the air.

Is that merely coincidence?[2]

Some have suggested that Revelation 12:5 may carry a secondary, typological echo. The primary fulfillment is clear: Christ is caught up to God's throne. But the language may also hint at a broader pattern of divine deliverance.

Two observations support this possibility:

**1 Christ the Head, the Church His Body**: If Christ is the Head of the Church and believers are His Body (Ephesians 1:22–23), then the "snatching away" of the Head could foreshadow the "snatching away" of His Body. In this sense, Revelation 12:5 presents a sequence: the Head is caught up first, the Body later.

**2 A Pattern of Divine Rescue**: Throughout Scripture, God delivers His people decisively when judgment falls. Just as the infant Jesus was taken out of reach during Herod's murderous rage, so the Church may be removed from the earth before the final fury of the ultimate Herod, the Antichrist. In both cases, *harpazo* underscores God's sudden and sovereign rescue.

Revelation 12 primarily centers on Israel and the birth of Messiah. Still, this layered reading fits the book's symbolic depth. It portrays the Rapture not as an isolated event, but as part of a consistent pattern: God snatching His own from the enemy's grasp, first in Christ the Head, and finally in His Church, the Body.

---

2. This typological interpretation has been suggested by several prophecy scholars, including G. H. Pember and Chuck Missler. They view the use of *harpazo* here as a prophetic echo of the Church's future "catching up" (1 Thessalonians 4:17), while strictly affirming that the primary historical fulfillment of Revelation 12:5 is Christ's ascension.

# *Chapter 17*

# THE TWO FACES OF EVIL

## The Rise of the Ultimate Deception

*And the beast was given a mouth uttering haughty and blasphemous words, and it was allowed to exercise authority for forty-two months.*

— REVELATION 13:5

They are the terrifying duo who dominate the second half of the Tribulation: one rises from the sea, the other from the earth. Together, they form a counterfeit trinity, representing Satan's final and most blasphemous attempt to imitate and replace God, Christ, and the Holy Spirit. (For a thought-provoking exploration of this theme of strategic deception, see Hints & Possibilities 2.1. A Tale of Two Messiahs).

Revelation 13 gives us their profile. It opens with John's vision of a Beast rising out of the sea. This is the Antichrist, the satanically empowered world ruler. In biblical imagery, the sea represents the restless Gentile nations (Daniel 7:2–3), signaling that the Antichrist emerges from the world of political empire outside Israel.

Later, another Beast rises not from the sea, but from the earth, or more literally, from the land. The contrast is deliberate. The False Prophet arises from within the land of Israel itself, making his deception insidiously persuasive. He is a religious betrayer who exalts the first Beast and leads the world, and especially Israel, into worshiping the counterfeit messiah.

## The First Beast: The Antichrist Unmasked

*And I saw a beast rising out of the sea ...*

— REVELATION 13:1

John's vision is vivid and nightmarish. As this monster breaches the turbulent waters, it reveals a form that is both menacing and strangely familiar to students of prophecy. This Beast is a composite entity. It represents the final world empire, a revived form of the Roman system, and yet it is also embodied in its ultimate ruler, the Antichrist himself. It is both a kingdom and a king, a duality consistent with Revelation 17:10, where the Greek title *basileus* identifies the empire through its ruler.

***Figure 17.1: The Beast from the Sea.*** *The ultimate counterfeit empire (Revelation 13:1–2) rises from the restless waters. Fusing the features of a leopard, a bear, and seven lion's heads, the Beast wears ten royal diadems upon its ten horns—the ultimate symbol of Satan's delegated, earthly authority.*

Its appearance is loaded with prophetic symbolism. The Beast has ten horns and seven heads, and a body that combines the features of a leopard, a bear, and a lion (v. 2). These are not random details. They are direct allusions to the prophecies of Daniel 7, revealing the Beast's lineage as the fusion of all previous God-defying world empires. (For a detailed analysis of this composite imagery, see

*Deeper Dive 17.1. The Sum of All Evils*). The specific placement of its crowns, however, reveals its relationship to its master, the Dragon. (This crucial distinction is explored in *Deeper Dive 17.2. Dragon's Heads vs. Beast's Horns*).

But in verse 3, the prophetic lens zooms in, merging the political with the personal. The focus shifts from the fearsome empire (the "it") to the specific man at its helm (the "he").[1] In John's symbolic language, the Beast is both a system and its ruler, and now the narrative narrows toward the man who embodies it.

> *One of its heads seemed to have a mortal wound, but its mortal wound was healed.*
>
> — REVELATION 13:3A

Here, the fate of the empire and the fate of the individual converge. John sees a fatal wound to one of the "heads," an image of total defeat representing the historical collapse of Rome's imperial legacy, the physical assassination of the Antichrist—both, in fact. Yet, the wound is healed, and the Beast lives. This miraculous recovery is the turning point: the revival of the Roman Empire is paralleled by the counterfeit resurrection of

1. The Greek term *therion* ("beast") is grammatically neuter, which is why the ESV renders it as "it." Other translations, such as the NKJV, use "he," reflecting that this "beast" is not merely a creature but a personal ruler empowered by Satan.

its leader.[2] The world is stunned not only by a restored empire, but by a man who seems to have conquered death itself.

> *... and the whole earth marveled as they followed the beast.*
>
> — REVELATION 13:3B

This event catapults him to near-divine status in the eyes of the masses. "Who is like the beast, and who can fight against it?" they ask. It is a dark parody of praise once reserved for the Almighty. The Antichrist will not only demand worship; he will receive it.

He will also speak great and blasphemous things against God (vv. 5–6), slandering His name, His dwelling, and all who are in heaven. For forty-two months, that is, three and a half years, 1,260 days, the Beast is granted authority to wage war against the saints and overcome them.

This grim reality reveals a vital piece of the prophetic puzzle. These "saints" cannot be the Church. Why? Because Jesus explicitly promised that "the gates of hell shall not prevail" against His Church (Matthew 16:18). Believers have endured persecution and martyrdom throughout history, even under monsters like Nero, yet the Church as a corporate body has never been overcome. It has always endured, advanced, and grown.

But in Revelation 13, the Beast is permitted a level of global, unhindered dominion that crushes all resistance in a way unparalleled in human history. This confirms that the Church is no longer on earth. The Beast's assault targets not the Church, but the Tribulation saints, those who come to faith after the Rapture. He will not merely persecute them; he will dominate the world stage with unprecedented, God-permitted ferocity.

But note this. His reign is limited. His power is granted, not innate. The phrase "it was given to him" appears repeatedly, reminding us that God remains sovereign. Evil is on a leash.

## The Second Beast: The False Prophet

> *Then I saw another beast rising out of the earth. It had two horns like a lamb and it spoke like a dragon.*
>
> — REVELATION 13:11

Here, the imagery shifts from the political to the religious. At first glance, John sees a creature, an "it" in the symbolic language of the vision, resembling a lamb. But this exterior hides a human deceiver. The vision presents a beast, yet the actions unmistakably reveal a man.

The text describes him as having "two horns like a lamb" but speaking "like a dragon." The outward form is a mask of harmlessness, mild and even Christlike in appearance. Yet the voice behind the mask is a mouthpiece for hell. His nature is satanic, and his mission is to glorify the first Beast.

2. For a fuller exploration of the "fatal wound," including its imperial and personal dimensions, see *Deeper Dive 17.3. The Dead Head Revived.*

***Figure 17.2: The False Prophet.*** *Visualizing the deceptive nature of the second beast (Revelation 13:11–13). Rising from the earth, this figure possesses the outward facade of a gentle lamb with exactly two horns, yet speaks with the authority and voice of the Dragon. He performs miraculous signs, such as calling down fire, all intended to drive the world into worshiping the Antichrist.*

This individual is later identified by title as the False Prophet (Revelation 16:13; 19:20). If the first Beast is a counterfeit Christ, the False Prophet is a counterfeit Holy Spirit. He performs miraculous signs, even calling down fire from heaven, not to magnify himself, but to drive the world into worshiping the Antichrist.

He constructs an image of the Beast, whether a physical statue, a hologram, or an AI-driven construct, and animates it. Through dark supernatural power or terrifying technological advancement, this image is made to "speak" and demand worship under penalty of death. Those who refuse to bow to the image will be killed (v. 15).

This false worship is not optional. It's enforced through a global system of control:

> *He causes all... to receive a mark on their right hand or on their foreheads, and that no one may buy or sell except one who has the mark...*
>
> — REVELATION 13:16–17 NKJV

This is the infamous **mark of the Beast**, the definitive loyalty pledge. Without it, you are economically excluded and politically hunted. With it, you are spiritually doomed (see Revelation 14:9–11). This is not just about commerce; it's about worship and allegiance. It's the final line in the sand. (For a deeper look at how such a system could be enforced in the last days, see *Hints & Possibilities 17.4, 17.5, 17.6,* and *17.7*).

The mark is connected to the name or number of the Beast. Verse 18 cryptically tells us, "his number is 666." This has sparked endless speculation, but the key point is this: the number represents imperfection, rebellion, and man elevated as god. It is humanity in defiance of the Creator.

## A World Enchanted

The forty-two months have begun. The final three and a half years of the Tribulation are now unfolding, the very season Jesus called the Great Tribulation. And the world is under a spell, deceived, dominated, and devoutly following a man who claims to be god.

The Antichrist's power seems supreme. His religious enforcer ensures that no dissent is tolerated. The economy, technology, and spiritual life of the entire world now orbit around one throne: his.

And yet, even now, this is not the end of the story. God has not left the earth without testimony. In Jerusalem, the Two Witnesses still stand, holding out a blazing torch of truth against the rising darkness of the Beast (Revelation 11). And beyond Jerusalem, God's sealed servants, the 144,000, continue their witness across the earth, a remnant marked for the Lamb in the midst of a world marked for the Beast (Revelation 7; 14:1–5).

For while Satan's two Beasts rage on earth, heaven is preparing an answer. As Revelation 14 begins, another Lamb appears. This time it is the true Lamb of God, standing on Mount Zion with the redeemed. The tide will turn. Evil will not have the final word.

But in the meantime, the days of the two Beasts will be dark, deceptive, and deadly. The challenge for those who are still here is simple: Will you resist the lie, even at great cost? Or will you join the world in worshiping a counterfeit savior?

---

🔍 **SIDEBAR: The Mark of the Beast**

*A Choice That Divides Eternity*

Picture this: a world in freefall. Supernatural disasters have scorched the skies. Famine gnaws at cities. Wars rage unchecked. Then, a leader rises, charismatic, cunning, and cloaked in false light. He promises salvation, stability, and a new world order. But his offer comes with a catch: allegiance. Not just loyalty, but a literal mark, etched into your hand or forehead, that declares you belong to him. This is no dystopian fiction. This is Revelation 13, where the Antichrist's reign demands a choice that splits eternity itself.

**Beyond a Mere Barcode: The Demand for Worship**

Make no mistake: the "mark of the Beast" is not about convenience or commerce. It's about worship. In a grotesque parody of God's seal on His followers (Revelation 7:3), the Antichrist's mark brands you as his property. To take it is to swear fealty to a liar, a murderer, and the greatest counterfeit of Christ. The Bible warns this decision is irreversible: *"If anyone worships the beast and its image and receives a mark ... he also will drink the wine of God's wrath ..."* (Revelation 14:9–10). **There's no undo button. No second chance.** Eternal separation from God begins with a single, desperate "yes."

**Why Would Anyone Say Yes?**

Imagine the pressure. Supermarkets are empty. Banks have collapsed. Riots burn in the streets. Then comes a smooth-talking leader with a plan, a digital ID system that restores order. "No more fraud," he claims. "No more chaos. Just scan your hand, and you'll eat. Refuse, and you'll starve."

Sound far-fetched? Look around. We're already conditioning ourselves for compliance. Biometric scans unlock our phones. Physical cash is vanishing, making way for Central Bank Digital Currencies (CBDCs), programmable money that gives authorities the power to track every transaction and freeze your ability to spend instantly.

Vaccine mandates, digital health passes, and contact tracing, whatever their intentions, have shown how quickly fear can lead to widespread submission. The Antichrist's system will weaponize our craving for safety, exploiting fear to demand allegiance. People won't take the mark because they love evil. They'll take it because they're terrified, manipulated, or simply too exhausted to resist.

**Eternal Stakes, Ancient Warnings**

This is not the first time God's people have faced a loyalty test. Think of Shadrach, Meshach, and Abednego, staring down a fiery furnace rather than bow to Nebuchadnezzar's statue (Daniel 3). Or early Christians, executed for refusing to burn incense to Caesar.

The mark of the Beast is history's ultimate crossroads: will you trade your soul for a meal? Your eternity for a paycheck?

**The Perfect Trap**

Under the guise of progress, the Antichrist's regime will herald the mark as a revolutionary safeguard, a flawless answer to a civilization crippled by identity theft and digital exploitation. Yet beneath its polished facade lurks a diabolical snare. This is Satan's final gambit, a last-ditch effort to capture souls before Christ returns.

---

***Figure 17.3: The Ultimate Ultimatum.*** *A visual map of the eternal crossroads defined in Revelation 13 and 14. This infographic contrasts the counterfeit Mark of the Beast with the Seal of the Living God, which is placed upon the foreheads of the 144,000 for divine protection. It illustrates the enforced global system of biometric control and coerced worship that forces humanity to choose their final, irrevocable allegiance.*

## If You're Still Here ... Stand Firm

To those living in this hour: Refuse the mark. No matter the cost. No matter the lies.

If you find these words *after* the Rapture, hear this clearly: **Your survival is not worth your soul.**

During the Great Tribulation, most believers will face a harsh reality. For the vast majority, there will be no miraculous rescues: no parted seas, no ravens bearing bread. Instead, those who refuse to worship the Beast will endure brutal consequences. Revelation 13:10 delivers a sobering truth:

> *If anyone is to go into captivity, into captivity they will go; if anyone is to be killed with the sword, with the sword they will be killed.*

This is not a call to fight, but a call to endure. God promises not escape, but strength to remain faithful.

## One Exception: A Glimmer of Refuge

Jesus warned that when the Abomination of Desolation appears, those living in Judea must flee to the mountains immediately (Matthew 24:16). In modern terms, *Judea* refers to Jerusalem and the surrounding central highlands, what is often called the West Bank today, the very epicenter of the Antichrist's control during this period.

The command to flee is geographical, not ethnic; any believer located in this kill zone, Jew or Gentile, must instantly escape to the rugged wilderness: specifically, the mountain fortress of Petra in Jordan.

Revelation 12:6 affirms this supernatural preservation. The faithful remnant of Israel (symbolized by "the Woman") is given refuge in this wilderness, miraculously protected and sustained for 1,260 days, the length of the Great Tribulation.

But for most, especially Gentile believers elsewhere, martyrdom and persecution will be the norm. As Revelation 13:10 concludes:

> *This calls for patient endurance and faithfulness on the part of God's people.*

### *Hold This Truth Close*

Yes, the cost will be unimaginable. But remember:

The Antichrist's reign lasts only 1,260 days.

Christ's reign is eternal, forever and ever.

---

## For the "Still Here" Seekers and Skeptics

You are here. You sense it: **the world is forever changed.** The Rapture occurred, proving Scripture true. You missed the departure, but the door to salvation is not yet shut. You now stand in history's final 3½ years under the Antichrist. **Your next choice determines your eternity.**

**REJECT THE MARK.** This is not a matter of buying or selling. It is a matter of the soul. To accept the mark is to choose **eternal damnation.** God's Word leaves no ambiguity:

> ... *"If anyone worships the beast and its image and receives a mark on his forehead or on his hand, he also will drink the wine of God's wrath, poured full strength into the cup of his anger ..."*
>
> — REVELATION 14:9–10

**BUT THERE IS LIFE:** Jesus offers salvation *right now* to all who seek Him. **Repent. Call on His name. Defy the Beast.** If you lose your life for Him, you will reign with Him.

**TODAY:**

- Open the Gospel of John
- Read Revelation
- Cry out to heaven.

## Eternity outweighs all suffering. Turn to Him *now.*

*Chapter 18*

# VISIONS OF VICTORY BEFORE THE END

## The Prelude to Triumph

> *Then I looked, and behold, on Mount Zion stood the Lamb, and with him 144,000 who had his name and his Father's name written on their foreheads.*
>
> — REVELATION 14:1

As the storm of divine judgment brews, heaven draws back the veil one last time, offering a glimpse of victory that steadies the saints before the final collapse of the Beast's kingdom. Revelation 14 continues the pivotal interlude that began in Revelation 10, a pause filled with purpose, warning, and hope for God's weary faithful.

## The Lamb and the 144,000

The scene opens with the Lamb and the 144,000 standing on Mount Zion. But where, exactly, is this Zion? Is it earthly Jerusalem, the heavenly throne room, or something else entirely? The text's ambiguity has led to a fascinating interpretation that views Mount Zion as a kind of spiritual "portal" where heaven and earth intersect. (For a full discussion of this intriguing possibility, see *Hints & Possibilities 18.1. Where Eternity Pierces Time*).

For the purpose of this vision, what matters is its significance. Zion is the place of God's victory and sovereign rule. These 144,000 Jewish believers were set apart for a divine mission during the Tribulation: to proclaim the gospel of the kingdom throughout the whole world as a testimony to all nations. Though shielded from God's wrath, they faced the full fury of the Beast's reign. Their bold witness demanded the ultimate price for many, if not all, of them. Yet here, with the Lamb, they are not victims but victors.

Scripture declares them "blameless," unstained by spiritual adultery. No lie taints their lips. And they sing a song only they can learn, forged through sacrifice. They were "purchased from among mankind" as "firstfruits for God and the Lamb."

Figure 18.1: The Firstfruits on Mount Zion

***Figure 18.1:*** *The triumphant 144,000 stand with the glorified Christ on Mount Zion. Sealed with the Father's name, these firstfruits represent heaven's absolute victory and the divine answer to the Beast's mark.*

Not one of them is missing. Echoing the heart of Jesus' high priestly prayer, "I have guarded them, and not one of them has been lost" (John 17:12). The Lamb has kept His own. Sealed by God, sustained through trial, and now gathered in glory, the 144,000 stand as living proof that not even the darkest hour can snatch a single one from the Savior's grip.

Their mission is complete.

Their reward is secure.

This is heaven's answer to earth's chaos: a preview of the glory awaiting all who hold fast to the Lamb.

Even unto death.

## The Three Angels: Heaven's Final Proclamation

As the vision of the triumphant 144,000 fades, Revelation turns with urgency back to the earth below. Three angels streak across the heavens, their proclamations splitting the gloom. Moving beyond distant forecasts, these messages represent God's own assurance and warning to His suffering people in the shadow of the Beast.

***Figure 18.2:*** *Heaven's final warnings split the Great Tribulation gloom. Three angelic heralds deliver the everlasting gospel, pronounce the certain fall of Babylon, and declare the irreversible doom of those who submit to the Beast.*

## The First Angel: The Everlasting Gospel

> *"Fear God and give him glory... worship him who made the heavens, the earth, the sea, and the springs of water."*
>
> — REVELATION 14:7

Amid global judgment and satanic deception, the everlasting gospel still rings out. Rather than a mere whisper, it serves as a final, universal summons. This message is proclaimed to "every nation and tribe and language and people," standing as a testimony to God's patience and His righteousness in offering the world one last opportunity to respond.

This is not a different gospel, as though God were offering a new way of salvation. It is the eternal truth of the gospel spoken with end-time urgency, returning to its most foundational reality. In the Age of Grace, the emphasis was on God as Savior. Here, as the final hour approaches, the emphasis falls on God as Creator and Judge.

A world intoxicated with the worship of the Beast is commanded to look up and acknowledge the Sovereign One before it is too late. The angel's proclamation is a threefold call: to fear God with holy reverence, to give Him glory by recognizing His authority above every earthly ruler, and to worship Him as Creator, turning from idolatry to honor the One who made the heavens and the earth.

This summons echoes the voice of the Old Testament prophets (Ecclesiastes 12:13; Psalm 146:6) and underscores a sobering principle: even at the brink of unrelenting wrath, God still extends mercy. Until the very last moment, heaven calls the rebellious world to repent.

### If You Are Still Here

**This matters for you.** The everlasting gospel is proof that God's mercy is not finished and His judgment is never unjust. Even now, He is calling the world to repent.

So your testimony still counts. Hold fast. Speak boldly. Endure under pressure.

The Beast may rage, but the Lord's invitation still stands.

## The Second Angel: Babylon is Fallen

> *"Fallen, fallen is Babylon the great, she who made all nations drink the wine of the passion of her sexual immorality."*
>
> — REVELATION 14:8

The second angel announces the doom of Babylon, a judgment so certain that it is spoken as though it has already occurred. The double cry, "fallen, fallen," echoes Isaiah 21:9 and signals the irreversible collapse of humanity's greatest system of rebellion against God.

Yet the full destruction of Babylon will unfold in stages later in Revelation (16:19; 17–18). Here, the angel gives a divine headline, declaring heaven's verdict in advance: Babylon's end is guaranteed.

So what is Babylon? Scripture reveals that Babylon is not merely a single city, but a prophetic symbol with two intertwined expressions in the last days. As we will explore in Chapters 21 and 22, Babylon appears both as:

- **a seductive religious system**, headquartered in Rome, which rides the Beast to power (Revelation 17).
- **a final commercial capital**, the economic heart of the Antichrist's empire, destroyed directly by God (Revelation 18).

In this proclamation, the angel announces the comprehensive doom of Babylon in all its forms, both the religious system and the commercial empire. While their destruction occurs at different times, the divine verdict covers the whole corrupt edifice.

Babylon's crime is that she has intoxicated the nations. The "wine of the passion of her sexual immorality" signifies a seductive global influence that desensitizes the world to truth. It is a potent cocktail of material luxury, moral compromise, and false spirituality. By making the nations drunk on this deception, she prepares humanity to embrace the unthinkable: the worship of the Antichrist and the acceptance of his mark. She dulls the conscience of the world so they will not notice they are bowing to the Beast.

This decree of Babylon's fall is a turning point. The Beast's reign, which seemed unstoppable (Revelation 13:4), is doomed. The illusion of invincibility is shattered. The kingdom of man will fall, clearing the way for the city of God, where the Lamb will reign forever.

## The Third Angel: Eternal Stakes of the Mark

> ... *"If anyone worships the beast ... receives its mark ... they, too, will drink the wine of God's fury ... tormented with burning sulfur ... forever and ever ..."*

— REVELATION 14:9–11 NIV

This warning is stark, terrifying, and unambiguous. Rather than an act of economic pragmatism, taking the Beast's mark represents a final allegiance to darkness. It is worship sealed in the flesh, an irreversible choice that invites the full, undiluted fury of God.

There is no neutrality here; there is no middle ground.

**The Encouragement Within the Warning**

And yet, embedded in this terrifying decree is a call of immense importance, an echo of Revelation 13:10:

> *Here is a call for the endurance of the saints, those who keep the commandments of God and their faith in Jesus.*

— REVELATION 14:12

Here is a summons to anchor the believers. Heaven is steadying the faithful for what comes next.

## If You Are Still Here

**To those starving,** jobless, or facing death for refusing the mark: *God sees your costly faithfulness.*

Your endurance is not pointless. Resistance is not wasted. Every costly "no" to the Beast is seen, remembered, and honored by God.

The Beast may threaten death, but God pronounces something higher than survival. In the very shadow of martyrdom, Scripture speaks one of its most tender and triumphant promises.

**The Final Beatitude: Blessed Are the Martyrs**

> *"...Blessed are the dead who die in the Lord from now on." ... "that they may rest from their labor, for their deeds will follow them!"*

— REVELATION 14:13

This is one of Revelation's sacred beatitudes, a divine pronouncement of joy reserved not for the powerful, but for the faithful who fall asleep in Christ during the world's darkest hour.

The world will brand these saints as defeated. The Antichrist will treat their blood as proof of his dominance. But God calls them blessed.

They are not abandoned. They are not forgotten.

They enter rest.

They receive reward.

And their faithful deeds, especially their final stand, follow them into glory.

The Beast can kill the body.

But he cannot touch the soul or the blessing.

This is the ultimate answer to his mark, his threats, and his fury:

Martyrdom is not the end.

It is the doorway into triumph.

## The Harvest Begins: Two Visions of Judgment

The heavenly warnings are barely spoken when the final movement of this vision bursts onto the scene like thunderheads rolling in. Two harvest visions close out Revelation 14, standing as portentous, vivid, and final.

These are not mere metaphor but a literal preview of the end that is coming. The King is ready to reap.

### *The Son of Man and the Golden Crown*

First, in verses 14 through 16, John sees "one like a son of man" seated on a white cloud, crowned in gold, and holding a sharp sickle. The title is unmistakable. This is the Messiah of Daniel 7. This is the Christ of Revelation 1. Jesus appears here not as the suffering Lamb, but as the coming Judge.

An angel from the temple calls out. Heaven's signal has come: "The hour to reap has come, for the harvest of the earth is ripe." The Son of Man swings His sickle, and the earth is reaped.

Some have connected this harvest with the gathering of the righteous who come to Christ during the Tribulation. But this is not the Rapture of the Church, which has already occurred. Rather, the imagery points to the closing separation of the age, the moment Jesus described in Matthew 13, when the wheat and tares are gathered for final judgment.

What matters most here is who holds the sickle. This is a divine harvest, sovereign and unstoppable. It shows that even as the Beast rages below, heaven remains in control. No one falls through the cracks. No one escapes notice. All will be gathered, some to reward, others to torment.

### *The Grapes of Wrath*

But then comes the second harvest in verses 17 through 20, darker, bloodier, and unmistakably a vision of judgment.

An angel emerges from the temple with another sickle. But this time the target is not grain. It is grapes. Another angel rises from the altar and cries out with a loud voice, "Gather the clusters... for the grapes are ripe."

This is not a vintage for joy. This is the harvest of wrath. The grapes are cast into the great winepress of God's judgment.

This graphic image comes straight from the Old Testament, especially Isaiah 63:1–6 and Joel 3:13, where the Messiah is pictured as treading the winepress of judgment, His garments splattered with the "juice," symbolic of blood, from His enemies. It is a portrayal of divine justice as personal, forceful, and inescapable.

Revelation 14:20 states the winepress is trodden "outside the city," a chilling detail. Just as Christ was crucified outside Jerusalem (Hebrews 13:12), those under judgment are symbolically outside the covenant, beyond the reach of mercy.

The result is a torrent of blood so deep it reaches a horse's bridle, flowing for 1,600 stadia, roughly 180 miles. While this approximates the length of Israel, the specific geography is even more telling. This distance corresponds remarkably to the route from the Valley of Armageddon in the north to the ancient city of Petra (Bozrah) in the south.

***Figure 18.3: The Great Winepress of God's wrath.*** *This literal preview of divine judgment maps a 180-mile river of blood flowing from Armageddon to Bozrah, demonstrating a justice that is geographically specific and inescapable.*

This connects directly to the prophecy of Isaiah 63, which depicts the Messiah coming from Edom (the region of Petra) with garments stained in blood, having trampled the winepress of His enemies to rescue His people. The bloodshed covers the entire theater of the final war, from the gathering point of the Antichrist's armies in Armageddon to the hiding place of the Jewish remnant in Bozrah.

Furthermore, the number itself carries deep symbolic weight. 1,600 is 40 multiplied by 40, and in Scripture, the number 40 signifies a complete period of testing or judgment. Thus, the figure indicates a judgment that is geographically specific yet spiritually complete. Whether viewed on a map or through numeric symbolism, the message is the same: the judgment will be total and comprehensive.

This horrific scene is a direct preview of the Battle of Armageddon, when Christ Himself will return to tread "the winepress of the fury of the wrath of God Almighty" (Revelation 19:15). God's patience has limits. And when the final sickle swings, justice will run deep.

## If You Are Still Here

**For those trapped under the Beast's regime**, tempted to believe evil has won, this vision is a timely reminder: God sees. God judges. And justice is coming.

The world may laugh at your faith. The Beast may threaten your life.

But the King with the golden crown holds the final sickle.

Stand fast. The harvest is near.

## *Chapter 19*

# TEMPLE ACCESS DENIED

## Standing at the Brink of Absolute Wrath

> *The temple was filled with smoke from the glory of God and from His power, and no one was able to enter the temple till the seven plagues of the seven angels were completed.*
>
> — REVELATION 15:8 NKJV

The pace slows one final time, like the heavy stillness before a volcanic eruption. Revelation 15 is that moment. Heaven pauses on the brink of judgment as God prepares to pour out His wrath in its fullest and utterly undiluted form upon an unrepentant world. What follows is not partial, nor measured restraint, but the completion of divine justice.

With this, the great parenthetical interlude that began in Revelation 10 draws to a close. This sacred pause, where mysteries were unveiled, warnings were sounded, and the faithful were strengthened, has served its purpose. Now it ends. The silence breaks. The curtain rises on the final act.

### The Sea of Fire and the Song of the Redeemed

John's vision opens with a potent transformation: a sea of glass, mingled with fire. It echoes the earlier "sea of glass" in Revelation 4, but now it burns with judgment. Consuming wrath is imminent.

Standing beside this blazing crystal expanse are the victors, those who refused the Beast, his image, and his mark. These are the faithful, both the Jewish remnant and Gentile believers, who resisted the world's tyranny and idolatry, even at the cost of their lives.

They sing a twofold anthem: the Song of Moses and the Song of the Lamb. This is a powerful convergence of the Old and New Covenants. The Song of Moses, Israel's great deliverer, signals that God is now enacting a new and final exodus. Not from Egypt, but from a world enslaved to the Beast himself. It honors the faithfulness of the Jewish remnant preserved during the Tribulation.

The Song of the Lamb then broadens the chorus, uniting their voices with all the redeemed, Jew and Gentile alike, in a single hymn of victory. They celebrate salvation through the blood of Christ.

The lyrics declare God's justice, His righteousness, and His universal reign:

> *"Great and marvelous* are *Your works, Lord God Almighty! Just and true* are *Your ways, O King of the saints!"*
>
> — REVELATION 15:3 NKJV

These words do more than praise. They protest the injustice of the Beast's kingdom and herald God's imminent intervention.

## Seven Angels Emerge from the Temple

The vision then shifts. The heavenly temple opens, and out come seven angels, each assigned one of the final, devastating plagues. Their appearance is striking: dressed in clean, shining linen and adorned with golden sashes across their chests. Their garments echo the royal splendor of Christ in Revelation 1, affirming their authority and the sacredness of their task. They are not Christ Himself but serve as His royal-priestly emissaries.

The symbolism here is deeply intentional: these angels come from the temple, God's dwelling place, dressed as priestly servants. Their mission is not indiscriminate wrath but precise, divine judgment. Just as the high priests dressed in linen ministered before the LORD in the Old Testament temple, these angels emerge from the heavenly sanctuary to fulfill a final, holy assignment: to pour out the wrath of God on an unrepentant world.

## The Temple Sealed by Glory

Then comes a staggering moment: the temple is filled with smoke from the glory of God and from His power, and no one could enter the temple until the seven plagues of the seven angels were finished.

***Figure 19.1: The Unapproachable Glory.*** *The heavenly temple is completely sealed, filled with radiant smoke from the glory of God and His power. Access is denied even to angels, signaling that the door of mercy is closed and the final, undiluted judgments must now run their course.*

This is a divine "**Do Not Enter**" sign. It recalls the moments in Scripture when God's glory so overwhelmed the tabernacle and the temple that not even Moses or the priests could enter (Exodus 40; 1 Kings 8). But here, the meaning is even more grave. The temple is sealed not just by God's presence, but by His purpose. It signals that the time for intercession has passed. The door of mercy, held open for so long, is now closed. Judgment must run its course, unimpeded and undiluted.

The bowls are about to be poured, and with them, the end has come.

Chapter 20

# THE FINAL FURY

## When God's Unsparing Justice is Poured Out

*Then I heard a loud voice from the temple telling the seven angels, "Go and pour out on the earth the seven bowls of the wrath of God."*

— REVELATION 16:1

## Overview: The Final Torrent of Wrath

The Great Tribulation is now approaching its zenith as Revelation takes its most harrowing turn. The time for mercy has expired. No more pauses between judgments. No more calls to repent. The long window of divine patience slams shut, as Scripture declares: "... no one was able to enter the temple till the seven plagues of the seven angels were completed" (Revelation 15:8 NKJV).

Heaven has already declared, "The kingdom of the world has become the kingdom of our Lord and of his Messiah" (Revelation 11:15), yet Christ's visible reign cannot begin until the last strongholds of rebellion are annihilated. What follows is the final torrent of divine wrath, undiluted, unrelenting, and inescapable.

Now come the seven Bowl Judgments: rapid-fire, global catastrophes unleashed in relentless succession.[1] These are not warnings or symbolic acts. They are literal, physical events targeting earth's systems, humanity's health, and the infrastructure of the Beast's world system. And still, staggeringly, the world refuses to repent. Instead, curses replace confession. Blasphemy hardens like stone.

All of this unfolds under the shadow of the Antichrist's global regime. Empowered for 1,260 days (42 months; Revelation 13:5), he enforces the mark of the Beast, a mandatory symbol of allegiance controlling all commerce. But the mark is more than economic compliance; it is a spiritual death sentence. Scripture leaves no ambiguity: anyone who receives the mark forfeits salvation, drinks the full cup of God's wrath, and faces eternal torment (Revelation 14:9–11). It is a choice that can never be undone.

This is the bleak landscape of the end: a world where the Beast is openly worshiped, God's people are hunted, and humanity doubles down on its rebellion. And it is into this defiant world that the bowls of God's wrath are finally poured out.

Do not mistake this for reckless destruction. It is righteous and holy justice. God's character is consistent: He is not arbitrary. He is faithful. He waited. He warned. And now He judges. The Day of the LORD has come in its fullest measure.

But the King is Coming.

1. The global scope of the Bowl Judgments, combined with their specific, localized targets, is a key interpretive theme in Revelation 16. For a detailed analysis of the textual and theological evidence for their worldwide impact, see *Deeper Dive 20.1. How Global Are the Bowl Judgments?*

## The First Bowl: Painful Sores on the Marked

> *So the first angel went and poured out his bowl on the earth, and harmful and painful sores came upon the people who bore the mark of the beast and worshiped its image.*
>
> — REVELATION 16:2

The silence breaks. A command goes forth, and the first angel steps forward, bowl in hand, and pours it out upon the earth. What follows is no symbolic gesture, no isolated outbreak. This is the first strike in the final series of divine judgments. And it begins not in the heavens, nor upon the seas, but on human flesh.

Immediately, those who bear the mark of the Beast, those who pledged allegiance to the Antichrist and bowed before his image, are afflicted. Painful, festering sores erupt across their bodies. These are not mere skin irritations. The original Greek uses *kakos* (malignant, evil) and *poneros* (grievous, agonizing), underscoring the supernatural nature of the affliction. These sores are incurable. The torment is relentless. Day and night, the marked are in ceaseless agony.

***Figure 20.1: The First Bowl of Wrath.*** *Agonizing, incurable sores fall exclusively upon those who bear the mark of the Beast, serving as a visible, physical manifestation of their complete spiritual decay.*

But they do not repent.

This judgment draws a great chasm between the redeemed and the rebellious. The plague falls solely upon those who bore the mark, the ultimate symbol of allegiance to the Beast. While the faithful endure the global horrors of the Tribulation, they are shielded from this specific affliction. The mark that once granted access to food and commerce now brands its bearers for divine wrath. What they embraced as a guarantee of survival has become a tormenting sentence.

There is an unmistakable echo here of the Egyptian plagues, particularly the boils that fell on Pharaoh and his court. Yet just as then, there is no softening of heart. No repentance or even remorse. Only blasphemy and deeper defiance.

In many ways, this first bowl sets the tone for what is to come. It reveals not just a physical plague but a deeper spiritual condition, a humanity hardened by pride and enslaved to rebellion. These sores are not merely wounds of punishment. They are outward manifestations of inward decay. The visible wounds mirror an invisible truth: the moral and spiritual corruption of a world that has chosen darkness over light. The pain is real, but the deeper tragedy is what it reveals, a soul fully aligned with evil, utterly resistant to turning back.

In this state of revealed corruption, as the second angel steps forward, the pain does not relent. The sores remain. This is only the beginning.

## The Second Bowl: The Sea Turns to Blood

> *The second angel poured out his bowl into the sea, and it became like the blood of a corpse, and every living thing died that was in the sea.*
>
> — REVELATION 16:3

The second angel steps forward. There is no delay. No pause between the cries of pain and the next cataclysm. The bowl is poured, not on land this time, but into the sea.

And it dies.

***Figure 20.2: The Death of the Seas.*** *As the lifeblood of the planet is destroyed, those with the mark of the beast writhe in double agony, their visible, painful sores persisting from the First Bowl. What once sustained global commerce and human survival is turned into a horrific, lifeless testament to God's righteous and inescapable judgment.*

This is no red tide or natural disaster. The sea does not merely turn red. It becomes like the blood of a corpse. Thick. Putrid. Lifeless. The ocean itself is struck with death. Every living creature within it perishes. There is no partial destruction here, as in earlier judgments. Nothing is spared. The text is clear: every living thing in the sea is gone.

The magnitude of this judgment is difficult to fathom. The oceans cover more than 70% of the earth's surface and are home to untold billions of creatures: whales, fish, coral reefs, microscopic life that sustains the food chain. In a moment, they are swept away in a tide of rot and stench. The beaches fill with the bloated remains of sea life. The air itself becomes heavy, carrying the inescapable reek of a dead world to every shore.

Global shipping freezes. The harvest of the seas is obliterated. Port cities choke on the stench of death. The arteries of the world are clogged with blood. And suddenly, the truth is inescapable: this is not a disaster. It is divine retribution.

This is no localized event. The text declares judgment upon the sea, using the same comprehensive term (Greek: *thalassa*) that describes God's creation of the oceans (Acts 14:15). This bowl strikes the planet's lifeblood, the vast salt waters covering most of Earth. In a horrific undoing of Genesis, what God once filled with teeming life becomes a putrid graveyard, echoing the Nile's transformation in Moses' day, now amplified to global scale.

And still, humanity refuses to repent.

The first bowl struck human bodies. This second judgment ravages creation. The sea, once reflecting God's provision, now stagnates as a graveyard of blood. All life within it dies. The earth reels. Heaven's restraint is over.

The third angel rises.

## The Third Bowl: Rivers and Springs Become Blood

> *The third angel poured out his bowl into the rivers and the springs of water, and they became blood. And I heard the angel in charge of the waters say, "Just are you, O Holy One, who is and who was, for you brought these judgments. For they have shed the blood of saints and prophets, and you have given them blood to drink. It is what they deserve!"*
>
> — REVELATION 16:4-6

The second bowl poisoned the seas. Now, with the third bowl, the judgment moves inland.

The angel pours his bowl into the rivers and springs, the freshwater sources, the very lifelines of civilization. And they too become blood.

Not red-tinted water. Not a chemical contamination. The passage is deliberate: they became blood. The same grotesque transformation that struck the seas now defiles the rivers, wells, and springs. This is total. Final. Every source of drinkable water is corrupted. What once gave life now threatens it.

There is no filtration system advanced enough to correct this. No technology, no desalination, no purification tablet will fix what God has judged. Cities that survived the prior judgments now face dehydration and despair. Refugee camps, already reeling from famine and disease, now have nothing to drink. Desperation turns violent. People kill each other for a sip of bottled water, only to discover the shelves are bare.

But then, something remarkable happens.

In the midst of devastation, a voice rises from heaven, the angel in charge of the waters. He proclaims the verdict. This is divine justice. The angel declares what the world refuses to see: God is righteous.

Why? "For they have shed the blood of saints and prophets, and you have given them blood to drink" (Revelation 16:6).

This is retribution. Not blind rage. Not cosmic cruelty. This is the justice of a holy God answering the long cries of the martyrs. Those who spilled innocent blood now receive a just portion, blood to drink. It is graphic, disturbing, and inescapable.

The angel concludes with haunting finality: "It is what they deserve."

This judgment lays bare the moral backbone of God's wrath. He is not vindictive. He is holy. He remembers the blood of the innocent. And in a world that has murdered His messengers and mocked His mercy, God now answers, not with warnings, but with wrath.

The physical environment is collapsing. The moral clarity of heaven is thundering. And yet, even as the waters turn to blood, there is no cry of repentance, only the stubborn silence of a world hardened against its Creator.

The fourth angel stands ready.

## The Fourth Bowl: Scorching Heat from the Sun

> *The fourth angel poured out his bowl on the sun, and it was allowed to scorch people with fire. They were scorched by the fierce heat, and they cursed the name of God who had power over these plagues. They did not repent and give Him glory.*
>
> — REVELATION 16:8–9

With the fourth bowl, judgment moves from land and sea to the skies above. The sun, long seen as a source of warmth, energy, and life, is weaponized.

The angel pours his bowl on the sun itself, and it is allowed to scorch. The effect is immediate. Unbearable, searing heat floods the earth. Far beyond any seasonal heatwave or climate anomaly, this is divine intensity, heat with the power to burn.

Skin blisters. Crops wither instantly. Power grids fail under the strain, plunging air-conditioned sanctuaries into suffocating ovens. Concrete radiates like molten iron. Forests ignite. The rivers of blood, already putrid, bake into a crust of death. Technology offers no relief. Shade offers no coolness. There is nowhere to hide.

And yet, even now, humanity does not repent.

They curse the name of God, the very One who holds power over these plagues. There is no repentance, only rage. No reverence, only rebellion. The hardness of heart has calcified. Like Pharaoh before the Red Sea, the world clenches its fist at heaven even as it burns.

Why this judgment? Consistent with a pattern seen throughout Scripture, God judges by turning the object of idolatry against the idolater. The sun, worshiped as divine power from Egypt (Ra) to Rome (Sol) and beyond, is now empowered by its true Sovereign to scorch those who refused to glorify Him.

This is divine irony. The created thing they exalted above the Creator becomes their scourge. Without His mercy, their false god becomes their tormentor.

And still, they did not repent.

This refrain begins to echo like a chorus through the judgments. No matter how severe, how righteous, how unmistakably divine, the world will not turn. The human heart, hardened against grace, sinks into defiance so deep that even fire cannot soften it.

The darkness comes next.

## The Fifth Bowl: Darkness on the Beast's Kingdom

> *The fifth angel poured out his bowl on the throne of the beast, and its kingdom was plunged into darkness. People gnawed their tongues in agony and cursed the God of heaven because of their pains and their sores, but they refused to repent of what they had done.*
>
> — REVELATION 16:10–11

The fifth bowl strikes at the very nerve center of evil: the throne of the Beast, the seat of the Antichrist's global power. His kingdom, built on deception, violence, and counterfeit wonders, is suddenly engulfed in unnatural, oppressive darkness.

A heavy, suffocating shroud descends. This is the tangible blackness of divine judgment, thick and impenetrable, a physical manifestation of spiritual desolation. It echoes the ninth plague on Egypt, where darkness "could be felt" and was so complete that "no one could see anyone else or move about for three days" (Exodus 10:21–23). Now, that same darkness swallows the Beast's entire domain. It is personal. It is targeted.

Those who once reveled in the Beast's false light and glory now writhe in torment, gnawing their tongues in anguish. The agony of the prior plagues, excruciating boils, scorching heat, maddening thirst, combined with this suffocating blackness, drives them to despair.

Yet their response reveals their true nature. They curse the God of heaven. Still, they refuse to repent.

The physical darkness mirrors a deeper reality: the ultimate spiritual night of a world fully given over to sin and rebellion. The Beast, proclaimed as the light of a new age, is unmasked as the prince of darkness. His promises crumble. His kingdom staggers. His worshipers, marked by their allegiance, realize too late that they traded eternity for a damning lie.

And yet again, no repentance.

The pattern intensifies. Judgment falls. Suffering deepens. Reality frays. But defiance holds firm. Just as Pharaoh hardened his heart again and again, so these rebels dig in deeper, clenching their fists against God even as the Abyss yawns before them.

The world spirals into chaos. Darkness reigns. Yet even here, God remains sovereign. Each bowl is not mindless destruction, but measured and righteous justice poured out upon a world that has exhausted every offer of grace.

The sixth bowl now approaches. And with it, Armageddon looms.

## The Sixth Bowl: The Euphrates Dries and Armageddon Summons

> *The sixth angel poured out his bowl on the great river Euphrates, and its water was dried up to prepare the way for the kings from the east. And I saw, coming out of the mouth of the dragon and out of the mouth of the beast and out of the mouth of the false prophet, three unclean spirits like frogs... to assemble them*

> *for battle on the great day of God the Almighty... And they assembled them at the place that in Hebrew is called Armageddon.*
>
> — REVELATION 16:12–16

With the sixth bowl, the momentum toward the end becomes unstoppable. The mighty Euphrates, a millennia-old boundary between empires, is supernaturally drained. Its vanishing waters clear the way for vast eastern armies to march westward without restraint. This is more than a geopolitical shift. It is the final corridor being opened for history's bloodiest convergence, driven forward by demonic delusion.

***Figure 20.3: Driven by Hell.*** *Drained of water, the Euphrates becomes a road to annihilation. Multi-national armies roll westward, deluded by demonic spirits. These very soldiers continue to suffer from the persistent, agonizing sores of the First Bowl, proving that there is no cure and no mercy for those who serve the Beast. Their visible decay is the only banner they carry as they stumble blindly toward the greatest battlefield of history.*

At the same time, the unholy trinity, Satan the Dragon, the Antichrist the Beast, and his False Prophet, unleash a vile counter-offensive. From their mouths comes a grotesque trio of "unclean spirits like frogs." These are not symbols of nuisance, but agents of hell, spirits of deception empowered to perform lying signs and wonders.

They are dispatched to the rulers of the world. They whisper promises of triumph. They inflame pride. They seduce kings into gathering their armies for what they believe will be mankind's ultimate victory.

But it is not victory.

It is doom, divinely appointed.

And the convergence point has a name. Armageddon, Har-Megiddo, the mountain overlooking the vast plain of Megiddo in northern Israel. Across centuries, blood has soaked this ground again and again. Empires have risen and fallen here. Battles have echoed through its valleys.

Now it is destined to become the final staging ground for humanity's last, desperate stand against the returning King of Kings.

Note the ominous purpose: "to assemble them for battle on the great day of God the Almighty." This is God's day, God's battle. The nations march under the illusion of autonomy and strategy. In reality, they stumble blindly, deceived puppets dancing to hell's tune, drawn like doomed moths to a blazing flame.

The irony is profound and tragic. A world ravaged by searing heat, agonizing sores, consuming darkness, and poisoned waters still clings to defiant pride. Faced with the collapsing remnants of their rebellion, they choose mobilization over surrender, rage over repentance. The path is cleared, the demons whisper, and the final armies of earth roll toward their destiny.

Amidst this grim march to oblivion, a voice suddenly pierces the narrative. Christ Himself speaks, with a jarring and urgent warning that cuts directly across the context of the mayhem:

> *"Behold, I am coming like a thief!"*
>
> — REVELATION 16:15A

This verse is not just a detail in the prophetic timeline; it is a direct, personal alarm bell from the King himself. Because its message is so critical, we will explore its full meaning in the sidebar that follows.

The warning hangs in the air. The pause is brief.

The final bowl approaches.

---

**PASTORAL WARNING: Be Ready Before It's Too Late**

*"Behold, I am coming like a thief! Blessed is the one who stays awake, keeping his garments on, that he may not go about naked and be seen exposed!"* (Revelation 16:15).

Revelation 16 is racing toward Armageddon. The bowls are falling. Demonic spirits are moving through the earth. Kings are being gathered for the last war.

And then, suddenly, the narrative breaks.

A voice cuts through the apocalypse.

"Behold, I am coming like a thief..."

This verse is not a footnote. It is not a pause for theology. It is Christ Himself stepping into the chaos with a final, merciful warning as the world enters its terminal convulsions. But His words are not sealed in that future hour. They reach beyond the bowls, beyond Armageddon, beyond the page, and confront every reader who hears them now.

*Do not treat these judgments as distant prophecy.* This is a present alarm from the King.

**A Divine Interruption of Mercy**

Revelation 16:15 is judgment interrupted by grace. Even as wrath is poured out, Christ still calls. Even at the brink of the final battle, heaven still warns.

The world is not spiraling out of control.

It is being brought to decision.

**"Like a Thief": Suddenness Without Warning**

The thief metaphor is not about stealth for its own sake. It is about suddenness. Finality. Irreversibility.

A thief does not knock. He comes when the house is asleep. And so Christ warns that His coming will break in with suddenness, before the world is prepared, before the hour feels obvious. His return is imminent, not something to be postponed until the signs are undeniable.

You do not schedule the King's arrival.

Readiness cannot be delayed.

**Awake. Clothed. Unashamed.**

"Blessed is the one who stays awake, keeping his garments on..."

To stay awake is not merely to know prophecy. It is to remain spiritually alert in a world drugged by deception.

To remain clothed is to walk in righteousness, covered by the Lamb, faithful under pressure.

To be found naked is not merely to be surprised, but to stand exposed and ashamed, a testimony that faltered when endurance was demanded most.

This warning draws a line, not between timelines or outward systems, but between two outcomes for those who profess Christ:

**Blessed** are those who endure watchfully to the end.

**Ashamed** are those who drift into compromise and lose their reward.

This is no moment for spiritual fatigue or retreat. The finish line is in sight, and how one finishes matters for eternity.

**Final Word**

Revelation 16:15 is a **divine interruption**, a last plea before the end, a clarion call before the world plunges into its last agonies. It reminds us that while prophecy gives us the outline, the exact moment of Christ's return will still take many by surprise.

**To those reading this before the Rapture, the message is a plea**:

**Stay awake**. Stay clothed. Stay ready.

Because the next trumpet you hear might not be sounded by human hands.

It might be in the sky.

**To the "Still Here" reader during the chaos of the Tribulation, the message is a command**:

**Stay awake**. Stay clothed. Stay ready.

Because the next sight you see might not be a sign in the heavens.

It might be the King Himself, returning in glory.

---

## The Seventh Bowl: The Earth Shudders, Babylon Crushed

> *The seventh angel poured out his bowl into the air, and a loud voice came out of the temple, from the throne, saying, "It is done!"*
>
> — REVELATION 16:17

This is the final, cataclysmic stroke, the last note in the symphony of God's righteous judgment. The seventh bowl is poured not upon earth or sea, but into the very air, the domain of "the prince of the power of the air" (Ephesians 2:2), Satan himself. From the heart of God's sanctuary, His throne itself declares completion: "It is done!" (Greek: *Gegonen!*). This echoes Christ's victorious cry on the cross (John 19:30), but here it signifies the full execution of divine wrath. Justice, long prophesied and patiently withheld, is now completely satisfied.

Then the earth convulses in throes of agony.

A seismic catastrophe, unprecedented in scope and violence, shatters the planet's foundations. Islands are swallowed by the sea. Mountains crumble. The proud cities of mankind collapse into jagged ruins. Far beyond a disaster, this is global de-creation, unraveling every human structure and illusion of permanence.

> *The great city was split into three parts, and the cities of the nations fell...*
>
> — REVELATION 16:19A

The mega-quake strikes Jerusalem, "the great city... where also their Lord was crucified." (Revelation 11:8).[2] The city splits into three parts, a climactic judgment upon the site of the Antichrist's blasphemous desolation, where he declared himself God in the Temple. This physical division into three parts powerfully symbolizes the fracturing of his religious stronghold under the weight of divine judgment.

Meanwhile, "the cities of the nations" fall. Every global hub of rebellion collapses in sequence, falling like dominoes in the Beast's empire. This is the beginning of the collapse of the satanic world order, now exposed and dismantled by the very hand of God.

> *... and God remembered Babylon the great, to make her drain the cup of the wine of the fury of his wrath.*
>
> — REVELATION 16:19B

Now divine attention shifts decisively to Babylon the Great, and the evil global systems she embodies. She has been the nexus of political oppression, spiritual seduction, and economic exploitation, a counterfeit kingdom animated by Satan and ruled through the Antichrist's machinery.

Babylon is now forced to drink the cup of wrath to the dregs (cf. Revelation 14:8, 10; 18:6), the culmination of the judgment foretold by the martyrs' prayers (Revelation 6:10). The full horror of her destruction, and the specific identity of this city, will be unveiled in the chapters that follow.

> *And every island fled away, and no mountains were to be found.*
>
> — REVELATION 16:20

---

2. For a detailed analysis of why "the great city" in this passage refers to Jerusalem and not Babylon, see *Deeper Dive 20.2. Which "Great City" Splits in Revelation 16:19: Jerusalem or Babylon?*

Geography itself is erased. The old world order literally loses its grounding. Creation heaves under the weight of holiness as the earth, in labor birth pangs, prepares for rebirth.

And then comes the final blow:

> *And great hailstones, about one hundred pounds each, fell from heaven on people ...*
>
> — REVELATION 16:21A

Giant hailstones, each weighing a talent (approx. 100 lbs/45 kg), rain down like celestial artillery. This plague is a horrific escalation of the hail that struck Egypt (Exodus 9:18–26), now unleashed globally with apocalyptic force. These are no mere meteorological accidents. They are heaven's execution stones.

***Figure 20.4: The Final Execution****. Massive, talent-weight hailstones fall like celestial artillery upon a world already fractured by a global earthquake. This plague serves as God's final, unanswerable sentence upon the defiant blasphemers.*

Under the Law, blasphemers were condemned to death by stoning (Leviticus 24:10–16). Here, God Himself executes final judgment on those who have relentlessly cursed (blasphemed) His name (Revelation 16:9, 11, 21). The hail is the physical manifestation of their deserved sentence.

But the response of the damned is the ultimate revelation of hardened hearts:

> *... and they cursed God for the plague of the hail, because the plague was so severe.*
>
> — REVELATION 16:21B

Even crushed by stones from heaven, the very instrument of their judicial execution, they defiantly blaspheme. The terminal hardness prophesied is complete. There is no repentance, only futile rage against the Almighty.

The bowls are empty. The wrath is spent. The sentence is executed.

The world system has fallen. The curtain closes.

It is done.

The stage is swept clean.

The King is coming.

---

As the smoke of judgment rises, a new vision is unveiled, one that reveals the spiritual rot behind the world's political and economic power. Revelation 17 pulls back the curtain on a figure shrouded in mystery and excess: a woman clothed in purple and scarlet, riding a Beast with seven heads and ten horns.

She bears a cryptic name: **Mystery, Babylon the Great**, a title weighted with historical and prophetic gravity.

But this is no ordinary city or empire. Babylon here is both a symbol and a system, a fusion of religious seduction, economic luxury, and spiritual defiance. She intoxicates the nations, allies with kings, and is drunk with the blood of saints.

In the next chapter, we turn to this appalling vision of religious and political harlotry. We have witnessed the divine decree of her destruction. Now we must understand the why. To grasp the magnitude of her fall, we must first unmask the face of the seductress who led the world astray.

The Purple and Scarlet Woman rides into view.

## *Chapter 21*

# THE HARLOT AND HER BEAST

## Unmasking the Unholy Alliance of the End Times

> *And the woman was arrayed in purple and scarlet, and adorned with gold and jewels and pearls, holding in her hand a golden cup full of abominations and the impurities of her sexual immorality.*
>
> — REVELATION 17:4

She sits like a queen, adorned in luxury. And yet she is drunk with the blood of the saints.

In Revelation 17, the prophetic sequence pauses. John is drawn into a new vision: a stunning revelation that exposes the spiritual decay beneath the surface of global power. One of the seven angels who poured out the bowls of wrath now invites him to witness "the judgment of the great prostitute," and carries him "in the Spirit" into a wilderness. In Scripture, the wilderness often symbolizes testing, exposure, and clarity. It strips away pretense and reveals what lies beneath.

What John sees is one of the most enigmatic and disturbing figures in the book: a Woman clothed in purple and scarlet, adorned with gold, jewels, and pearls, holding a golden cup filled with abominations. She rides a scarlet Beast with seven heads and ten horns. This is no ordinary person: she is a symbol, a codename, a mystery.

> *And on her forehead was written a name of mystery: "Babylon the Great, the mother of prostitutes and of the earth's abominations."*
>
> — REVELATION 17:5

***Figure 21.1: The Unholy Alliance.*** *The Harlot, arrayed in royal purple and scarlet, rides the formidable seven-headed Beast through a desolate wilderness. This illustrates the temporary, symbiotic relationship between the apostate global religion and the rising political empire of the Antichrist.*

The colors she wears, purple and scarlet, were ancient emblems of royalty and wealth. But here, they also echo bloodshed and sin. Her finery visually connects her to the scarlet Beast beneath her: they are partners in corruption and deception. Together, they dazzle, and they devour.

The angel gives John insight into this Woman. She is "Mystery, Babylon the Great." In New Testament usage, a mystery is not something unknowable, but rather a divine truth once hidden and now revealed (cf. Ephesians 3:3–5). The word signals that what follows carries symbolic significance. This is not the literal, ancient city of Babylon, but a veiled reference to something deeper. (For a detailed discussion, see *Deeper Dive 21.1. What Does "Mystery, Babylon the Great" Really Mean?*)

## The Roman Connection

The Woman inherits Babylon's spiritual legacy: idolatry, persecution, and unholy alliances with worldly powers. While the Beast she rides represents a political entity, the Woman herself is something more insidious: a religious system that has prostituted itself for influence and control. She is also identified as "the great city" (v.18), seated on "seven hills" (v.9), clues that point definitively to Rome, both as an ancient imperial power and as the end-times religious center.

And what religion, based in Rome, has claimed global spiritual authority, clothed itself in purple and scarlet, and historically persecuted believers who refused its dominance?

**The Vatican.**

This interpretation is not new; it echoes the view held by many Protestant Reformers, including Martin Luther, John Calvin, and John Knox, who saw the Papacy as a fulfillment of prophetic Babylon.[1]

1. Many leaders of the Protestant Reformation identified the Papacy with biblical "Babylon" and/or the Antichrist. Martin Luther codi-

During the Inquisitions and other dark chapters of church history, the Roman Catholic Church aligned itself with secular rulers to crush dissent. Many of its victims were ordinary believers. Those who dared to translate Scripture or to worship Christ outside institutional control, such as William Tyndale and Jan Hus, were martyred for defying the authority of the Roman Catholic Church.[2] The result was not only spiritual deception, but the literal spilling of innocent blood.

Today, the Vatican stands as a global religious institution, claiming to speak for God, asserting moral authority over approximately 1.4 billion souls.[3] Its leaders wear purple and scarlet. It operates as both a spiritual and political power. And in the prophetic imagery of Revelation, it becomes a vessel not of truth, but of spiritual adultery, luxury, and deception.

## A Global Spiritual Monopoly

The symbolism continues:

> ... *"The waters that you saw, where the prostitute is seated, are peoples and multitudes and nations and languages."*
>
> — REVELATION 17:15

This signifies worldwide influence. The Vatican has long emphasized its international reach, echoing the global breadth of the Woman's dominion in this prophecy. The Papal office is both a religious and diplomatic power, maintaining relations with most nations.[4]

John is stunned. "When I saw her, I marveled greatly" (v.6). His astonishment is a warning to us, because her reach is not limited to stained-glass cathedrals or European capitals. Her influence is global: spiritual, political, and ultimately deadly. This is spiritual adultery on a planetary scale, where truth is sacrificed for power and faith is manipulated for gain.

To fully grasp the dynamics of this chapter, we must separate the rider from the mount. This vision establishes a crucial prophetic distinction:

---

fied this view in the *Smalcald Articles* (1537, Pt. II, Art. IV), declaring the Pope to be the "very Antichrist." John Calvin argued extensively in his *Institutes of the Christian Religion* (IV.7.25) that the Papacy fulfilled the prophecies of 2 Thessalonians. Similarly, John Knox also employed this identification in his St Andrews preaching (1547), including "Whore of Babylon" language. This 'Historicist' interpretation was later formalized in the *Westminster Confession of Faith* (1646, 25.6).

2. John Foxe, *Foxe's Book of Martyrs*, ed. Harold J. Chadwick (Gainesville, FL: Bridge-Logos Publishers, 2001). This work contains detailed accounts of the persecution of figures like Tyndale and Hus.

3. According to the Vatican's own official reporting, the Roman Catholic Church has a worldwide membership of roughly 1.4 billion people in 2023. This is based on data published in the *Annuario Pontificio 2025* and the *Annuarium Statisticum Ecclesiae 2023* (Vatican City: Libreria Editrice Vaticana), the Holy See's annual directory and statistical yearbook.

4. See *Treaty between the Holy See and Italy* (1929), art. 12, which establishes the Holy See's right to active and passive legation; Paul VI, *Sollicitudo Omnium Ecclesiarum* (1969), which defines the Pontifical Representative's role regarding civil authorities; and Secretariat of State, "Bilateral Relations of the Holy See," which lists diplomatic relations with 184 states as of 2024.

| Feature | The Harlot (The Woman) | The Beast (The Antichrist) |
|---|---|---|
| **Nature** | Apostate Religious System | Political Empire |
| **Headquarters** | Rome (Vatican City) | Revived Roman Empire |
| **Primary Method** | Spiritual seduction & religious deception | Deceptive diplomacy & false peace, escalating to military tyranny |
| **Relationship** | "Rides" the Beast (early Tribulation) | Empowers the Harlot, then destroys her |
| **Ultimate Fate** | Burned and devoured by the Beast | Captured and cast into the lake of fire by the Lamb |

***Table 21.1: The Harlot and Her Beast***

## Her Violent End

> *... the prostitute. They will make her desolate and naked, and devour her flesh and burn her up with fire,*
>
> — REVELATION 17:16

But her reign will not last. In a shocking twist of betrayal, the Beast she once rode, the very empire she helped empower, will turn on her. The Antichrist will no longer tolerate religious competition. The text describes a destruction that is swift, total, and threefold:

**She is made desolate and naked**: Her immense treasures are plundered, and her spiritual hypocrisy is exposed for the world to see.

**They devour her flesh**: This signifies a brutal massacre of her clergy and representatives, the human infrastructure of her global system.

**They burn her with fire**: The city itself, Vatican City, which serves as her headquarters, is literally torched, an act of ultimate annihilation.

***Figure 21.2: The Violent Betrayal.*** *The scarlet Beast violently turns on the Harlot, bucking her from its back and tearing at her royal robes while her city burns in the background. This illustrates the exact moment around the Tribulation's midpoint when the Antichrist destroys the apostate religious system to demand sole global worship.*

Much more than a political power play, this verse concludes by revealing the hidden hand behind it: "For God has put it into their hearts to accomplish his purpose" (Revelation 17:17). Her destruction, though carried out by the Antichrist and his ten-nation coalition, is the ordained execution of God's perfect judgment.

But this act of betrayal is not the end of the story. The Beast that destroys the prostitute now stands alone at the pinnacle of power. Yet, the vision reveals that his ascendancy is merely a prelude to his own destruction. To understand the final act of this drama, we must look at the Beast's true nature, and his inevitable fate.

---

## The Beast She Rides: An Empire Empowered by Hell

> *The beast that you saw was, and is not, and is about to rise from the bottomless pit and go to destruction. ...*
>
> — REVELATION 17:8A

While the Woman is horrifying, the Beast is no less so. This is the same Beast John saw in Revelation 13, possessing the same seven heads and ten horns that mark it as the final world empire. Far from being random, these cryptic symbols represent a specific lineage of historical empires and an end-time political confederacy, culminating in a final satanic ruler known as the "eighth king." (For a detailed prophetic blueprint of the seven heads and the eighth king, see *Deeper Dive 21.2. The Enigma of the Eighth King*).

For now, what is crucial to understand is that John is being given deeper insight into this final empire's nature and destiny. This Beast "was, and is not, and is about to rise." The language is perplexing, suggesting a resurrection or revival. Politically, this refers to a revived Roman Empire: an entity that once ruled, then fell, but will rise again in the last days under Satan's empowerment and the Antichrist's leadership.[5]

However, the Beast is both an empire and a man. While Rome provides the political machinery, a tyrant from antiquity provides the personal blueprint. The phrase "the beast that was" also points backward to a specific historical ruler who unmistakably foreshadowed the Antichrist's ultimate blasphemy and hatred for God Himself. (For the identity of this historical prototype, see *Deeper Dive 21.3. The Beast That Was*).

## The Mystery of the Missing Diadems

There is a profound chronological marker veiled in the obvious regarding this Beast. In Revelation 12:3, Satan is depicted with seven diadems (crowns) on his heads. In Revelation 13:1, the Beast emerges at full power with ten diadems on his ten horns.

But here in Revelation 17:3, the Beast has *zero* diadems.

This omission is not a descriptive accident; it is a prophetic timestamp. It affirms that Revelation 17 reflects the first half of the Tribulation. The Beast is in transition mode. The ten horns represent "ten kings who have not yet received royal power" (v. 12). Because the Antichrist does not yet possess his full, crowned political authority, he is vulnerable. He desperately needs the Harlot. He leverages her established global religious network to pacify the masses and consolidate his influence while his ten-nation political coalition solidifies in the background. She "rides" him because, for a brief window, her influence holds his fragile coalition together.

But right near the midpoint of the Tribulation, the transition ends. The ten kings finally receive their royal power for a brief, explosive time of unified rule. These represent a confederation of ten nations arising from a restructured geopolitical order. Ultimately, they will unite to surrender their full sovereignty to the Antichrist.[6]

> *These are of one mind, and they hand over their power and authority to the beast."*
>
> — REVELATION 17:13

## The Ultimate Victory

This empire, energized by hell, will launch a final assault on heaven's people. But it will fail.

> *They will make war on the Lamb, and the Lamb will conquer them, for He is Lord of lords and King of kings...*
>
> — REVELATION 17:14

No matter how dominant the system becomes, no matter how unified its power or seductive its deception, Jesus wins. His return will not begin a battle. It will end one.

---

5. John F. Walvoord, *The Revelation of Jesus Christ* (Chicago: Moody Press, 1989), chap. 17.
6. For a clear explanation of this political coalition, see J. Dwight Pentecost, *Things to Come* (Grand Rapids: Zondervan, 1958), chap. XIX, "The Gentiles in the Tribulation." Pentecost describes this as a future federation of ten separate kings. He notes that while the Antichrist consolidates power by overthrowing three of these kings (Dan 7:24), the coalition ultimately surrenders its sovereignty to him by mutual consent (Revelation 17:13).

## The Prophetic Blueprint of Revelation 17

| Prophetic Element | Futurist Fulfillment |
|---|---|
| The Harlot Unmasked | The end-times apostate religious system will be headquartered in Rome, reviving its ancient legacy of persecution and spiritual seduction. |
| The Unholy Alliance | The apostate religious system "rides" the Beast during his ascent, providing the spiritual glue needed to consolidate his power and dominating the first half of the Tribulation. |
| The Beast Devours the Harlot | In a shocking act of betrayal around the midpoint of the Tribulation, the Antichrist and his ten-nation coalition turn on the religious system they once used, stripping its wealth and burning its headquarters to the ground to clear the path for his sole worship. |
| Sovereignty is Surrendered | A ten-nation confederacy will arise from the political footprint of the revived Roman Empire. While the Beast's rise involves subduing three dissenting kings (Daniel 7:24), the remaining coalition voluntarily hands their authority to him, transforming this regional power block into a unified, satanic world empire. |
| The Lamb Conquers | No matter how unified the Beast's global empire becomes or how defiantly his ten-nation coalition wages war against heaven, their rebellion is futile. Jesus Christ will return to shatter the Antichrist and his armies completely. |

***Table 21.2: Key Takeaways from Revelation 17***

As we turn to Revelation 18, the scene shifts dramatically. The Religious Babylon, headquartered in Vatican City, lies in ashes, destroyed by the Beast's own hand. But the Beast's ambition is not satisfied.

With his religious rival removed, he consolidates his uncontested authority and establishes a new, final capital, a center of commerce and wealth that the Bible calls "Babylon the Great." But is this Rome again, or has the center of gravity shifted?

The mystery continues to unfold.

## *Chapter 22*

# THE SEAT OF THE BEAST

## The Final Capital of Human Defiance

> *"Fallen, fallen is Babylon the great! She has become a dwelling place for demons, a haunt for every unclean spirit..."*
>
> — REVELATION 18:2

This resounding verdict targets the final commercial capital of the Antichrist. But to understand the full weight of this judgment, we must remember how this capital rose to global hegemony. It began with the destruction of a rival.

In the previous chapter, we witnessed the violent end of the seductive religious system (the Harlot) headquartered in Rome. This act of shocking betrayal, occurring around the midpoint of the Tribulation, was not a random power play; it was a calculated move driven by the Antichrist's ultimate ambition.

Having used the Western religious machinery of Rome to consolidate his global power, the Antichrist violently discards the Harlot. He no longer tolerates any rival for humanity's worship. The time for religious seduction is over; the time for exclusive, singular devotion to himself has come. By annihilating the prostitute, he clears the stage to become the sole object of worship, demanding that all the world bow to him alone (2 Thessalonians 2:4; Revelation 13:15).

### The Epicenter Moves East

With the Western religious headquarters burning, the Antichrist makes a pivotal geographical and spiritual shift. He moves the epicenter of global rebellion back to its ancient roots in the East: a literal, rebuilt city of Babylon on the plains of Shinar (modern-day Iraq). This move is prophetically precise.

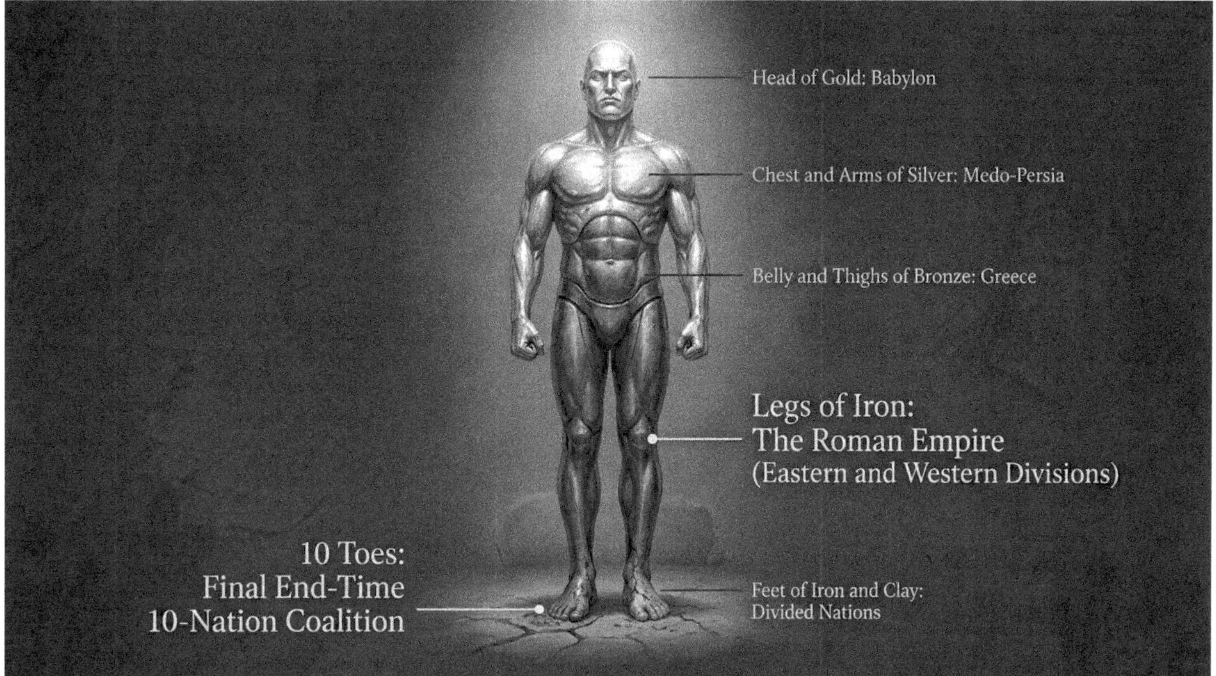


***Figure 22.1: The Architecture of Human Rebellion**. King Nebuchadnezzar's dream maps the progression of global empires. It culminates in the iron legs of the divided Roman Empire and the brittle ten toes of iron and clay, representing the fragile end-time 10-nation coalition awaiting its destruction by the true King.*

The ancient Roman Empire was historically divided into two halves, represented by the two iron legs of Daniel's statue. By establishing his ultimate capital in Babylon, the Beast geographically reclaims the Eastern theater of his revived empire. However, this city does not merely rule the East. It becomes the undisputed global nerve center of his totalitarian regime. From this ancient seat of rebellion, the Antichrist exercises comprehensive commercial, political, and military supremacy over the entire world during the Great Tribulation.[1]

It is against this great city, the final bastion of human rebellion and materialistic pride, that God's final judgment is now directed. A mighty angel descends from heaven, blazing with glory, and declares with thunderous finality: "Fallen, fallen is Babylon the great!" The repetition signals absolute certainty and irrevocability.

Where the prostitute of Revelation 17 embodied false religion, this new Babylon embodies materialism, greed, and ruthless power. It is the heart of the Beast's dominion in the last days. This literal interpretation is a prophetic imperative because many Old Testament prophecies of Babylon's sudden and permanent destruction (e.g., Isaiah 13; Jeremiah 50–51) were never fully fulfilled in its ancient history.[2] (For a detailed analysis of the prophetic case for a rebuilt Babylon, see *Deeper Dive 22.1. From Rome to Babylon: The Prophetic Relocation*).

## The Echoes of Ancient Doom

Why must the ultimate global capital move to the Middle East? Why not New York, London, or Brussels?

1. John F. Walvoord, *The Revelation of Jesus Christ* (Chicago: Moody Press, 1989), 265–271. Walvoord provides a detailed case for the city in Revelation 18 being a literal, rebuilt Babylon in Iraq.
2. J. Dwight Pentecost, *Things to Come: A Study in Biblical Eschatology* (Grand Rapids, MI: Zondervan, 1964), 368–370. Pentecost details the specific elements of Old Testament prophecy concerning Babylon that await a future fulfillment.

Beyond the geopolitical shifts, the Bible demands a literal return to the Euphrates for one critical reason: Unfulfilled Prophecy.

The Old Testament prophets Jeremiah and Isaiah pronounced doom upon ancient Babylon, predicting a destruction similar to Sodom and Gomorrah: sudden, fiery, and total (Isaiah 13:19; Jeremiah 50:40). They prophesied that its building stones would never be reused and that it would be completely uninhabited forever.

**History tells us this has not happened yet.**

Ancient Babylon was never destroyed by fire; it was captured intact by Cyrus the Great in 539 BC and declined slowly over centuries. Its bricks have been mined to build nearby towns for millennia, and people live on the site today. For God's Word to be proven true, Babylon must rise again as a functioning power so that it can be destroyed exactly as the prophets declared: suddenly, by fire, and permanently.

## The Dust is Already Stirring

The idea of Babylon rising from the sands is not just prophetic theory; it is a developing reality. For decades, the site lay dormant, a heap of ruins south of Baghdad. But in recent years, the pulse of the ancient city has begun to beat again.

### 1. The "Saddam Era" Reconstructions

In the 1980s, Saddam Hussein launched an ambitious, if ego-driven, project to resurrect the city. He built a massive recreation of the Southern Palace directly on top of the ancient foundations, using bricks stamped with his own name alongside Nebuchadnezzar's. He even constructed a modern, lavish palace on an artificial hill overlooking the ruins, a symbolic claim to the throne of the ancient kings.

***Figure 22.2: A City Waiting to Rise****. Modern reconstructions sit directly atop the ancient ruins of Babylon in modern-day Iraq. Because ancient Babylon was never destroyed in the sudden, fiery manner prophesied by Isaiah and Jeremiah, it must physically rise again to face its ultimate, literal judgment.*

### 2. The "Future of Babylon" (2019–2025)

Following its designation as a UNESCO World Heritage site in 2019, the focus shifted from vanity projects to serious restoration. The "Future of Babylon" project has stabilized key structures like the Temple of Ninmakh, which is nearing completion as of late 2025. While the famous Ishtar Gate remains in Berlin, the site in Iraq now features stabilized walls and prepared infrastructure.

**3. A City Waiting to Rise**

Today, Babylon is open for business. In 2024 and 2025, the site saw record tourism numbers, hosting over 48,000 visitors. Yet, archaeologists estimate that 85% to 90% of the city remains unexcavated. The true ancient metropolis is still buried, waiting.

The infrastructure is stabilizing. The world's interest is returning. The stage is being quietly set. It would take only a charismatic leader with vast resources and a global vision, the Antichrist, to turn this heritage site into the capital of the world.

## The Marketplace of Souls

Revelation 18 paints a portrait of opulence gone mad. The catalog of merchandise—gold, silver, fine linen, and even human souls—reveals the city's role as the engine of global exploitation. It is a monument to the idolatry of wealth, where human life itself is commodified. This new Babylon intoxicates the world not with false doctrine, but with unchecked affluence. In this city, greed is gospel.[3] Yet, beneath the glittering veneer of commerce lies a pulsating darkness. Revelation 18:2 describes the city as a "dwelling place for demons and a haunt for every unclean spirit." As the epicenter of the Antichrist's empire, it becomes a magnet for the demonic realm, a literal intersection of high finance and deep darkness.

## The Sudden Collapse

> ... *"Alas! Alas! You great city, you mighty city, Babylon! For in a single hour your judgment has come."*
>
> — REVELATION 18:10

As swiftly as it rose, Babylon falls. The city that enriched the world is reduced to smoking ruin in a single hour. The fall is swift, violent, and total. Here lies a critical distinction. Unlike the Harlot (Religious Babylon), who was destroyed by human agents (the Beast and the ten kings), this commercial city is judged directly by God. The destruction is:

- **Sudden:** "In a single hour your judgment has come" (Revelation 18:10).
- **Complete:** "Will never be found again" (v. 21).
- **Supernatural:** "Thrown down with violence" (v21).

Three groups are pictured mourning:

- The **kings** who partnered with her politically
- The **merchants** who profited from her economy
- The **shipmasters** who transported her goods across the seas

---

3. Charles C. Ryrie summarizes this view in his note on Revelation 18:2: "The destruction of the city of Babylon on the Euphrates River, rebuilt and the commercial center of the world in the tribulation." *The Ryrie Study Bible* (Moody Press, 1995).

They do not mourn her sins. They mourn their losses.

"What city was like the great city?" they cry, watching the smoke rise.

It is economic collapse on a global scale. A deathblow to the economic engine of the Antichrist's empire. But heaven does not weep.

## A Call to Separation

Even in the final moments before destruction, God extends a merciful warning to any believers trapped within the system:

> *"Come out of her, my people, so that you will not share in her sins ..."*
>
> — REVELATION 18:4

This is a timeless principle of holiness. God calls His people to separate themselves from the world's systemic evil before judgment falls. To remain entangled with Babylon is to risk sharing in her plagues.

## Heaven Rejoices

> *"... Rejoice over her, O heaven, and you saints and apostles and prophets, for God has given judgment for you against her!"*
>
> — REVELATION 18:20

Heaven erupts in joy. This is not vindictiveness, but justice. The system that murdered the righteous and seduced the nations has been destroyed. Babylon's fall is the ultimate answer to a cry that has echoed through the ages, now brought to a fever pitch by the persecution of the Tribulation saints. The blood of martyrs has been heard. The false kingdom is crumbling, and the true King is drawing near.

## The Finality of the Fall

To underscore the absolute finality of Babylon's end, another angel casts a massive millstone into the sea:

> ... *"So will Babylon the great city be thrown down with violence, and will be found no more..."*
>
> — REVELATION 18:21

There will be no rebuilding. This is total obliteration. Her music, her trade, her lamps and voices, all silenced forever. The rebuilt Babylon, the final great city of man, the ultimate expression of human rebellion that began on these very plains in Genesis 11, has fallen.

## The Stage Is Set

The Harlot is dead. The great city is in ashes. The global system has collapsed. The two manifestations of Babylon have met their distinct ends:

- **Religious Babylon** provided the spiritual glue for the Beast's rise, only to be devoured by him and his ten-nation coalition around the midpoint of the Tribulation.
- **Literal Babylon** served as his ultimate global capital, only to be shattered by God at the end of the Tribulation.

The stage is set for the final conflict.

The Beast remains, enraged beyond restraint.

The world lies in ruins, shrouded in thick darkness. The armies of the earth are gathered at Armageddon, frantic and seething.

And in that moment, when darkness claims supremacy, when the night feels never-ending ...

Heaven opens.

A white horse appears.

And the true King rides out.

*Chapter 23*

# THE FIFTH HORSEMAN

## The Triumphant Return of the King of Kings

> *Now I saw heaven opened, and behold, a white horse. And He who sat on him* was *called Faithful and True, and in righteousness He judges and makes war.*
>
> — REVELATION 19:11 NKJV

The storm of judgment has passed. Babylon lies devastated. The Beast's empire staggers beneath the weight of divine wrath. Yet as the Beast seeks to deal a final blow against the covenant people, the silence is shattered from above.

Not since Revelation 4 has the veil been drawn back like this. Then, it was a door revealing the throne. Now, it is a portal for the King.

The rightful Ruler of the earth breaks through the clouds, not in mystery or humility, but in unmistakable glory. He comes not to suffer, but to reign. Not to be judged, but to judge and make war.

This is the Second Coming of Jesus Christ.

### Faithful and True

The rider is no longer the Lamb led to slaughter. He is now the divine warrior, the Lion of the tribe of Judah. His titles speak volumes:

- **Faithful and True**: In stark contrast to the lies and deception of the Beast, Jesus comes in perfect integrity.
- **The Word of God**: His very identity is truth in motion.
- **King of kings and Lord of lords**: The final title emblazoned on His robe and thigh declares universal sovereignty.

His appearance is terrifying and majestic. His eyes are flames of fire. His robe is dipped in blood. From His mouth comes a sharp sword to strike the nations. He rides with justice, not compromise. The days of patience are over.

This is the day of divine reckoning.

### The Armies of Heaven

He does not come alone. Behind Him ride the armies of heaven, clothed in fine linen, white and pure. While the mighty angels accompany Him (Matthew 25:31), John's vision highlights a special battalion: the redeemed saints, the bride of Christ, now transformed and glorified, returning with their King.

Yet, they carry no weapons. Christ alone strikes the nations. He alone treads the winepress of the fury of God's wrath (Revelation 19:15). The war is not fought with earthly strategy, but with the authority of His Word.

This is not a drawn-out duel. It is a summary execution.

## From Prophecy to Battle: The Campaign of Armageddon

Contrary to popular belief, the "Battle of Armageddon" is not a single, static clash on the plain of Megiddo. It is a sprawling end-time campaign. It is ignited by demonic deception, driven by the Beast's genocidal ambition, and decisively overruled by God.

The conflict progresses through a series of linked battles and strategic movements spanning the length of Israel. Drawing on the harmonized framework articulated by Arnold Fruchtenbaum,[1] this campaign unfolds in a coherent eight-stage sequence, climaxing in the event we have just witnessed: the visible, glorious, bodily return of Jesus the Messiah.

### *The Strategic Context*

The campaign's roots lie at the midpoint of the seven-year covenant. The Antichrist drops the mask. He enters the rebuilt Temple, halts the daily sacrifices, and enthrones himself as God, fulfilling Daniel's "abomination of desolation" (Matthew 24:15).

This is the spark of the Great Tribulation (Matthew 24:21). Jeremiah called it "the time of Jacob's trouble," the climax of history's oldest hatred, a final eruption of antisemitism aimed at erasing the Jewish people from the earth.

Revelation 12:13–17 shows the cunning strategy beneath it all. Satan's fury is not random. It is cold and calculated. The Dragon knows the Messiah will not return until Israel cries, "Blessed is He who comes in the name of the Lord" (Matthew 23:39). So the Beast's endgame becomes brutally simple: hunt down every Jew, so that no believing remnant remains to utter the prayer that dooms his reign.

In that moment, Messiah's own words become a lifeline. "Flee to the mountains" (Matthew 24:15–16). A believing Jewish remnant obeys, escaping Jerusalem and Judea into the wilderness, carried by providence into hiding.

Revelation 12:6 and 14 reveal their destination is "a place prepared by God," where the remnant is supernaturally protected and nourished for 1,260 days.

The prophetic text does not leave their destination a mystery. Based on Daniel 11:41 and the ancient oracles against Edom, this refuge is identified as Sela (later known as Petra), the ancient rock fortress hidden in the mountains of Edom in modern southern Jordan.[2]

Daniel foretold that "Edom, Moab, and the chief of the Ammonites" would escape the Beast's grasp (Daniel 11:41), marking this region as a divinely appointed sanctuary.

---

1. The detailed, multi-stage framework of the Armageddon Campaign, culminating in Christ's return first to Bozrah, is a hallmark of the literal, sequential hermeneutic of scholars in the tradition of Dallas Theological Seminary. The most exhaustive and definitive treatment of this eight-stage model is found in Arnold G. Fruchtenbaum, The Footsteps of the Messiah: A Study of the Sequence of Prophetic Events, rev. ed. (San Antonio, TX: Ariel Ministries, 2003). Fruchtenbaum meticulously builds the case by harmonizing Revelation, Daniel, Zechariah, Isaiah, and other prophetic texts. For an earlier, foundational treatment of Christ's return to Bozrah based on Isaiah 63, see J. Dwight Pentecost, Things to Come (Grand Rapids: Zondervan, 1958).
2. For more details, see *Deeper Dive 7.1. The Petra Connection*.

Here, preserved by God's hand, the remnant waits out the storm while the final three and a half years descend into darkness.

The Dragon hunts. The wilderness hides. And God keeps His covenant alive.

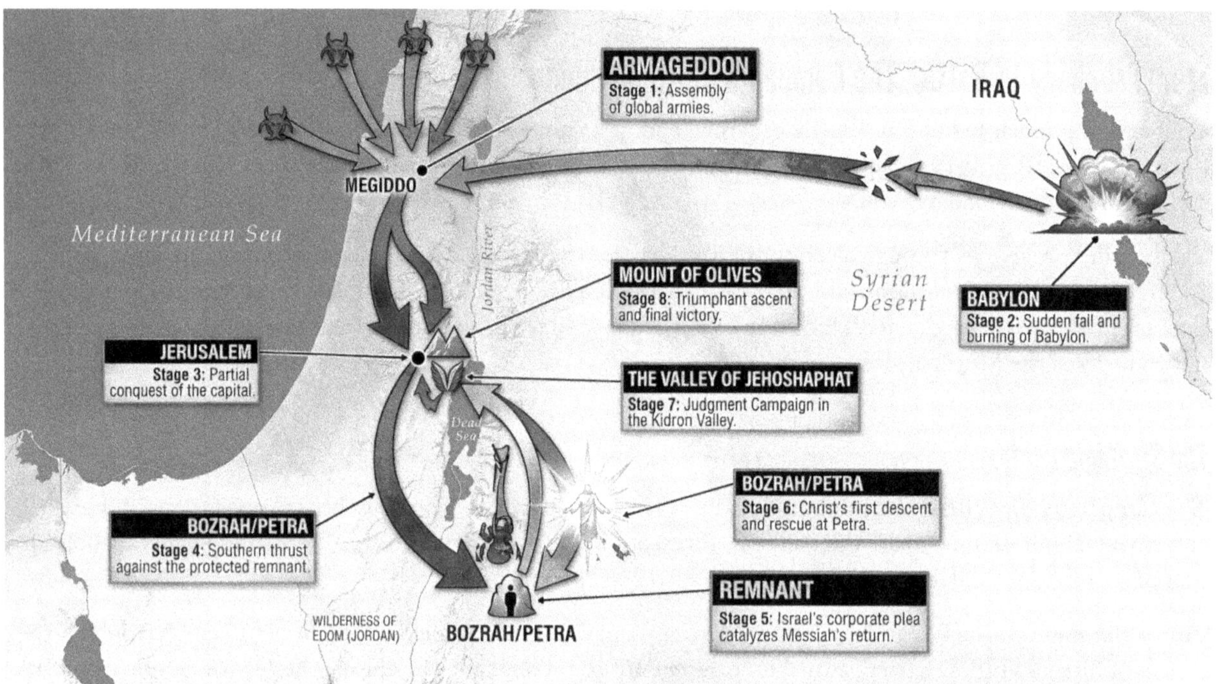


***Figure 23.1**: This map, based on the prophetic harmonization of Arnold Fruchtenbaum, illustrates the "war of the great day of God" as a sprawling military campaign rather than a single battle. While the global armies muster at Megiddo in the north (Stage 1), the epicenter of the conflict shifts violently south. Jesus Christ descends first to Bozrah/Petra (Stage 6) to rescue the besieged remnant, before advancing triumphantly to Jerusalem for the final victory at the Mount of Olives (Stage 8).*

## The Eight-Stage Campaign of Armageddon

As the Great Tribulation races toward its conclusion, the Antichrist mobilizes the world's armies for a final offensive. His goal is not merely military victory, but strategic genocide: to annihilate the remnant and silence the national cry that summons the Messiah (Hosea 5:15–6:1). The campaign moves with prophetic inevitability toward its foretold finale.

### *Stage 1: The Assembly of the Armies at Armageddon*

The Dragon, the Beast, and the False Prophet dispatch demonic spirits to perform signs and seduce the kings of the whole earth. Their singular goal: to marshal a global military coalition for "the war of the great day of God, the Almighty." The primary mustering point for this colossal force is the location John literally calls *Har-Magedon* (the mountain of Megiddo), universally known today as Armageddon. This serves not as the final battleground, but a vast theater of operations, a logistical and staging ground from which to launch their assault on the land of Israel.

### *Stage 2: The Sudden Destruction of Babylon*

While the armies mass in Israel, a rebel coalition strikes the Beast's global capital at Babylon, Iraq. Jeremiah foresaw the shock and speed of its capture, as couriers race to tell the Beast his city has fallen (Jeremiah 51:31).

But the human coup does not finish it. God does. Babylon is "burned up with fire" (Revelation 18:8), so sudden that the kings of the earth cry, "In a single hour your judgment has come!" (Revelation 18:10).

This devastating blow to his empire fuels the Antichrist's fury, driving him to redirect his entire remaining military might toward Israel in a final attempt to annihilate the Jewish people (Daniel 11:44).

### *Stage 3: The Partial Conquest of Jerusalem*

Forces surge south from the Armageddon staging ground and assault Jerusalem. Zechariah 14:1–2 is fulfilled with terrifying precision. While two-thirds of the Jewish population across the broader land have already perished during the Antichrist's macro-level slaughter (Zechariah 13:8), the prophetic lens now narrows to the micro-level siege of the capital. The city is captured. Houses are plundered. Women are ravished. Half the surviving population is exiled as prisoners of war. Jerusalem reaches the nadir of Jacob's trouble, trampled under Gentile power for a brief, horrific span.

### *Stage 4: The Southern Thrust Against the Remnant at Bozrah*

Having temporarily secured Jerusalem, the Antichrist learns of the remnant's sanctuary in the south. Determined to complete his genocidal mission, he leads a massive force into the Judean wilderness and onward toward ancient Edom. The armies of the world converge on **Bozrah/Petra**, surrounding the remnant and bringing them to the brink of annihilation.

By doing so, the Antichrist unwittingly fulfills the millennia-old oracles against Edom (Isaiah 34:5–6; Ezekiel 35:1–15), gathering his forces at the very place where Messiah will descend to execute His vengeance. (See *Deeper Dive 23.1. The Eagles and the Corpse*).

### *Stage 5: The National Repentance of Israel*

Cornered and facing certain extermination, the Jewish people, both in Jerusalem and in the wilderness, turn corporately. As they look "on him whom they have pierced," God pours out a "spirit of grace and supplication" (Zechariah 12:10). They mourn for their rejected Messiah and cry out to God for salvation. This fulfills the divine condition set forth in Hosea: "In their distress they will earnestly seek me ... 'Come, let us return to the LORD'" (Hosea 5:15–6:1). This plea is the catalyst for divine intervention.

### *Stage 6: The Second Coming of Christ to Bozrah*

Heaven answers Israel's cry. The darkness is shattered. The sign of the Son of Man appears, and the tribes of the earth mourn as they see Him coming with power and great glory (Matthew 24:30). Messiah descends first, not to Jerusalem, but to the place of His people's extreme desperation, Bozrah in Edom.

Isaiah gives the breathtaking image: "Who is this who comes from Edom, in crimsoned garments from Bozrah? ... I have trodden the winepress alone" (Isaiah 63:1–3). Christ single-handedly destroys the besieging armies and delivers the remnant at the very moment of their deepest despair. His garments are stained with the blood of their oppressors.

***Figure 23.2: The Messiah at Bozrah.*** *This cinematic rendering visualizes the breathtaking image of Isaiah 63:1. Following Israel's national repentance, Jesus Christ descends first to Bozrah in Edom (Petra in southern Jordan). He arrives not to rapture the Church, but to rescue a physically besieged and cornered remnant. His garments are stained crimson, not from His own sacrifice at Calvary, but from single-handedly treading the winepress of divine wrath to destroy the Gentile armies and secure the ultimate rescue of His chosen people at their exact moment of despair.*

## Stage 7: The Campaign of Judgment in the Valley of Jehoshaphat

After the deliverance at Bozrah, Messiah turns north, unleashing judgment on the remaining hostile forces in the land. Revelation depicts this as the winepress of God's wrath (Revelation 14:19), with blood stretching for approximately 180 miles, the length of the land from Bozrah in the south to Megiddo in the north (1,600 stadia).

A primary focal point is the Valley of Jehoshaphat (meaning "Yahweh judges"), traditionally associated with the Kidron Valley east of Jerusalem, where the LORD executes sentence upon the nations gathered against Him (Joel 3:2, 12).

## Stage 8: The Triumphant Ascent to the Mount of Olives

The campaign reaches its climax as Messiah arrives at Jerusalem. His feet stand on the Mount of Olives, the very place from which He ascended (Acts 1:11–12). The mountain splits, forming a great east-west valley and providing escape for the besieged (Zechariah 14:4–5).

With "all the holy ones" (His glorified Church and angelic host) accompanying Him, Christ seizes the Antichrist and the False Prophet, casting them alive into the lake of fire (Revelation 19:20–21).

The rebellion ends abruptly. The birds of the air are summoned to feast on the corpses of kings and warriors. It is graphic, final, and just.

The Antichrist and the False Prophet, men who deceived the nations and slaughtered the saints, become the first occupants of the Lake of Fire. Not annihilation. Not purgatory. Eternal, conscious punishment.

## The King Reigns

Now the battlefield lies silent. The counterfeit is gone. The Dragon is next. The King stands triumphant.

The Messiah has returned, not as the suffering Servant, but as the conquering King.

History has waited for this moment. Myriads of prophecies find their fulfillment here. The curse is being broken. The kingdom is being restored. Earth is about to see what it was always meant to be: ruled in righteousness by its Creator.

The King has finally come.

## *Chapter 24*

# THE DRAGON BOUND

## The Golden Age and the Last Uprising

> *Then I saw an angel coming down from heaven, holding in his hand the key to the bottomless pit and a great chain. And he seized the dragon—that ancient serpent, who is the devil and Satan—and bound him for a thousand years.*
>
> — REVELATION 20:1–2

The battlefield is quiet. The armies of rebellion have been crushed. The Beast and the False Prophet are no more. The King now stands victorious, but one enemy remains: the Dragon, the true architect of humanity's rebellion. His many names are listed to leave no doubt: the Dragon, that ancient Serpent, who is the Devil and Satan.

But his time has come.

An angel, unnamed yet operating with divine authority, descends from heaven with two simple tools: a key and a chain. Not a legion, not an army. Just one angel, commissioned by God, is enough. This speaks volumes. For all his terror and schemes, Satan is no match for the will of God. He is powerful, but not sovereign. He is cunning, but not equal to Christ. His defeat is swift.

The Dragon is seized, bound, and imprisoned in the Abyss for one thousand years.

## A Thousand Years of Peace

This is not symbolic. The number is repeated six times in Revelation 20. The millennial reign of Christ is a literal, future age in which Jesus will rule physically from Jerusalem, and Satan's influence will be completely removed from the earth.

For the first time since Eden, humanity will live without the seduction of the deceiver. Wars will cease. Justice will flow like a river. The earth will flourish under righteous rule. And yet, even in paradise, rebellion will still be possible. For when the thousand years end, Satan will be released ... briefly.

But that is yet to come. For now, the deceiver is chained.

He who once roamed the earth like a roaring lion is now cast into the Abyss, a defeated foe. He who boasted in kingdoms and tempted the Son of God is now locked away, silenced, and stripped of power.

The age of deception is over.

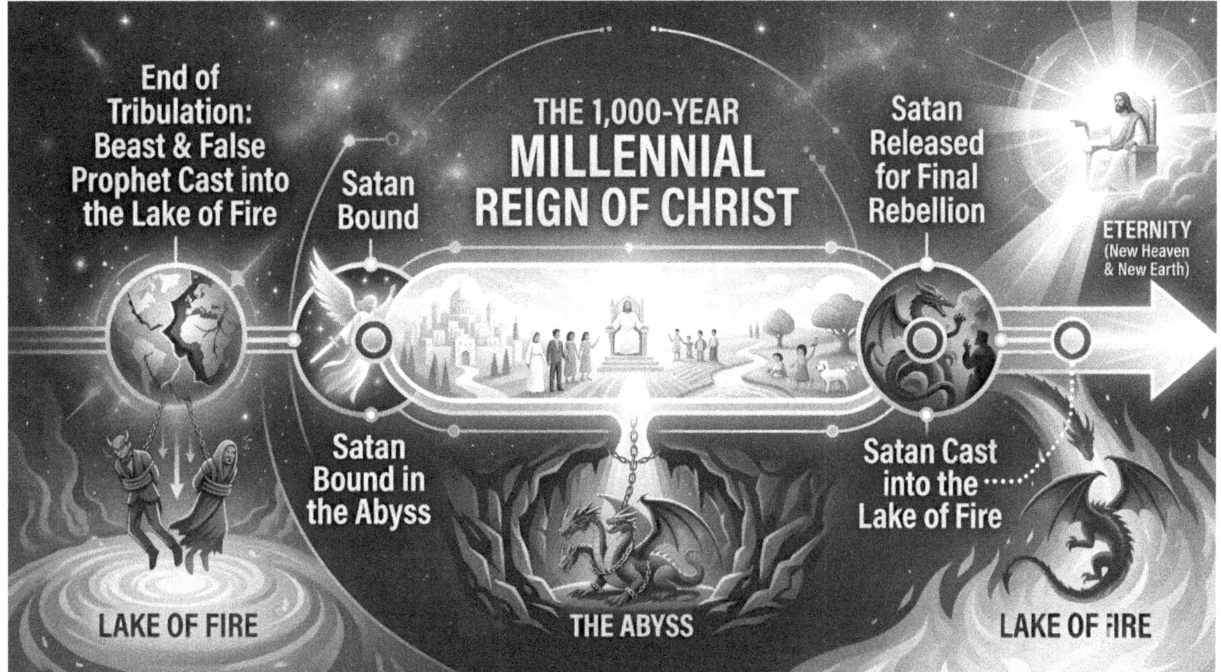


***Figure 24.1: The Chronology of Judgment on the Unholy Trinity***. *This infographic traces the progressive defeat of the unholy trinity. At the end of the Tribulation, the Beast and the False Prophet are seized and cast directly into the Lake of Fire. Satan, however, is bound and sealed in the Abyss for one thousand years. After his brief release and the final global rebellion, the ancient Dragon is cast into the Lake of Fire, where he joins his allies in eternal conscious punishment.*

## The Reign of the King

> *Then I saw thrones, and seated on them were those to whom the authority to judge was committed ... They came to life and reigned with Christ for a thousand years.*
>
> — REVELATION 20:4

The Dragon is bound, and Christ now reigns.

The Millennium, a thousand years of peace and righteousness on earth, begins not as a mere spiritual metaphor but as a literal, tangible kingdom ruled by the risen and glorified King. Jesus reigns from Jerusalem, seated on David's throne, fulfilling the promises spoken through prophets like Isaiah, Jeremiah, and Zechariah.

Justice is no longer delayed. Peace is no longer fleeting.

The curse on creation is being rolled back, much like the waters at the Jordan River were cut off and stood in a heap all the way back to the town called Adam (Joshua 3:16). Just as the flow of the river was suspended at "Adam" to allow the people to enter the Promised Land, the flow of the curse, initiated by the first Adam, is now suspended by the Second Adam, allowing the earth to finally enter its rest.

War becomes unthinkable. The knowledge of the LORD covers the earth as the waters cover the sea.

But Christ does not reign alone.

Those beheaded for refusing the mark of the Beast came to life again. These are the Tribulation martyrs, faithful unto death. They are raised, honored, and seated on thrones, entrusted with authority and judgment.

And they are not the only ones. The Church, long since raptured and glorified, returned with Christ at His coming (Revelation 19:14), and now reigns with Him.

This is what Paul meant when he said, "Do you not know that the saints will judge the world?" (1 Corinthians 6:2).

The earth enters a golden age, but it is not yet heaven. Sin is restrained but not eradicated. People still marry, build, plant, and live full lives. Nations exist and they are required to honor the King (Zechariah 14:16–19). But the tempter is gone. His lies are silenced. His influence removed.

For the first time since Eden, the world tastes what it was meant to be under the perfect government of Jesus Christ.

> *... they shall beat their swords into plowshares, and their spears into pruning hooks; nation shall not lift up sword against nation, neither shall they learn war anymore.*
>
> — ISAIAH 2:4B

This is what Isaiah foresaw. These very words were famously carved into stone in the plaza of the United Nations Headquarters. Yet no measure of humanistic endeavor has ever been able to achieve them. Not through treaties. Not through diplomacy. Only through the reign of the Prince of Peace.

> *"The wolf shall dwell with the lamb ... the earth shall be full of the knowledge of the LORD ..."*
>
> — ISAIAH 11:6–9

> *but they shall sit every man under his vine and under his fig tree, and no one shall make them afraid ...*
>
> — MICAH 4:4

This is not utopia born from human progress. It is divine order, established by the King Himself.

And yet even here, the human heart remains unchanged apart from grace. Multitudes are born during the thousand years. They grow up beneath Christ's righteous rule, but not all surrender inwardly. Outward obedience can still conceal inward rebellion.

And when the Dragon is released for a brief moment at the end of the thousand years, he finds allies once more.

But that, too, will serve the final justice of God.

For now, the world breathes. The King reigns. And righteousness prevails.

## The Final Revolt and Eternal Judgment

> *And when the thousand years are ended, Satan will be released from his prison and will come out to deceive the nations ... but fire came down from heaven and consumed them, and the devil... was thrown into the lake of fire.*
>
> — REVELATION 20:7–10

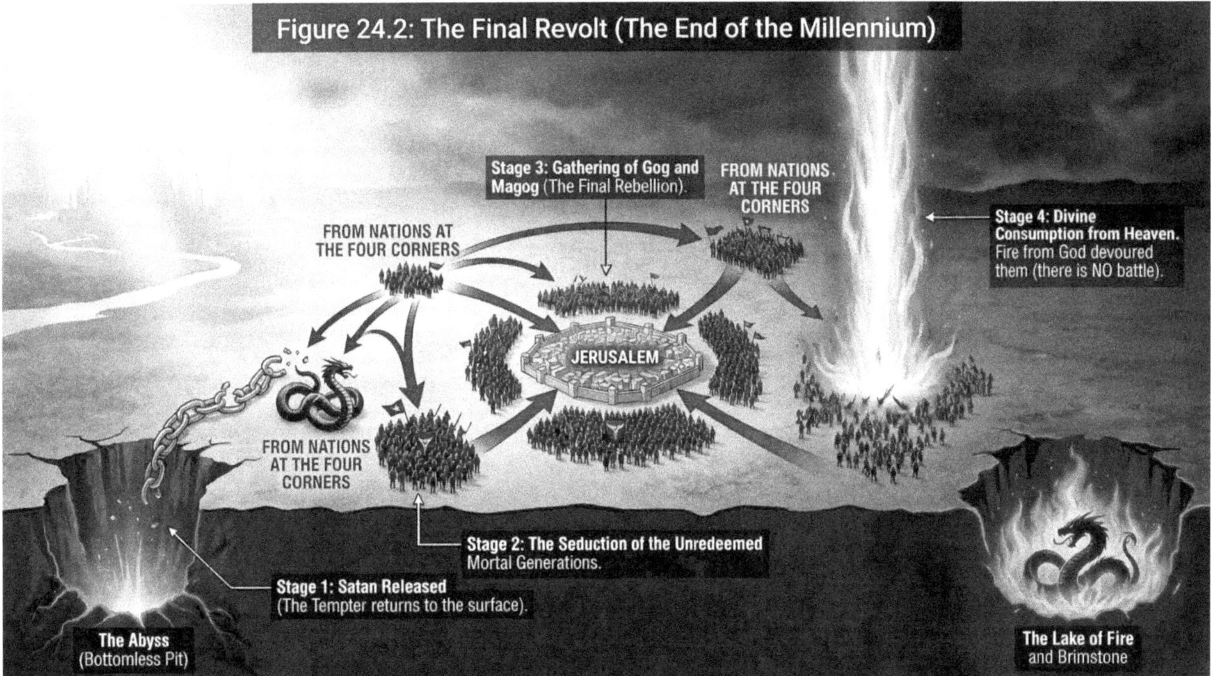


***Figure 24.2: The Final Revolt and Divine Consumption.*** *This diagram maps the rapid catastrophic demise of the rebellion at the end of the Millennial kingdom. Upon his brief release from the Abyss, Satan immediately seduces the unredeemed mortals from the four corners of the earth. John titles this final global uprising "Gog and Magog" to echo the ultimate ancient enemies of God. As these rebel armies encircle Jerusalem, no battle is fought. Divine fire instantly descends from heaven to consume the gathering, and the ancient Dragon is cast permanently into the Lake of Fire, silencing the deceiver forever.*

The peace of the Millennium is real, but it is not the end of the story.

After a thousand years of righteous rule, Satan is released, just as God foretold. Why? Because even after an age of justice, prosperity, and divine presence, the true condition of the human heart must be revealed. Multitudes born during the Millennium have never known the serpent's lies. Now they will face the ultimate test.

And astonishingly, many fail it.

The Dragon emerges from the Abyss and wastes no time. He deceives once more, gathering nations from every corner of the earth. They are called "Gog and Magog," not as geographical identifiers, but as a symbolic echo of all who stand in opposition to God. Their number is like the sand of the sea.

These are not oppressed rebels. They are not victims of poor leadership or injustice. They have lived under the direct reign of Christ Himself, and still they reject Him.

It is the final proof. Sin is not caused by our environment. It is rooted in our nature.

The armies surround the beloved city, Jerusalem. But no battle unfolds. Fire falls from heaven, and in an instant, it is over. The rebellion is crushed without resistance.

Satan, the deceiver, is seized once and for all. Not merely bound this time, but thrown into the lake of fire. No parole. No return. No more whispers. No more temptation. The ancient enemy of God and man is silenced forever.

And then comes the judgment.

---

*Chapter 25*

# THE GREAT WHITE THRONE

## The Final Verdict on Human Unbelief

*Then I saw a great white throne and Him who was seated on it. From His presence earth and sky fled away, and no place was found for them.*

— REVELATION 20:11

## The Courtroom of Eternity

The rebellion is over. The Dragon has been cast into the lake of fire, tormented forever and ever. The millennial kingdom has drawn to a close. And now comes the most consequential moment in all of redemptive history: the final judgment.

John sees it clearly. A throne, pure and white, towering in brilliance. It is unlike any earthly courtroom. There is no jury. No appeals. No confusion. This is a throne of absolute authority and untainted justice. While John simply describes "Him who was seated on it," the rest of Scripture makes the identity of this Judge clear. It is the risen Christ. The Father has entrusted all final judgment to the Son (John 5:22; Acts 17:31).

Before this throne stand the dead, "great and small," representing all who ever lived apart from God's saving grace. These are not believers, for the redeemed have already been resurrected and glorified (Revelation 20:4–6). This is the second resurrection, a resurrection unto judgment.

The sea gives up its dead. Death and Hades surrender the souls they held. No one escapes. No grave is too deep. No name is forgotten. Every soul who refused God's offer of mercy now stands to give account before the King.

And the books are opened.

***Figure 25.1: The Final Judgment.*** *The inescapable reality of the Great White Throne for all who rejected the grace of Jesus Christ.*

## The Books Are Opened

John tells us that books are opened, plural, and then mentions another book: the Book of Life.

The first set of books contains a detailed record of every person's deeds. Nothing is forgotten. Every action, motive, word, and thought that has not been cleansed by the blood of the Lamb is remembered here. These are not symbolic entries. This is a divine ledger of human rebellion, willful unbelief, and the fruit of lives lived without Christ.

God does not need these books for His own memory. He is omniscient. The books are opened as part of a public, transparent judgment. No one at the Great White Throne will be judged unfairly. Each person will be shown exactly why they are condemned, not arbitrarily, but justly, according to their works.

Yet even here, there is one final check: the Book of Life.

This is the Lamb's book (Revelation 13:8). In it are written the names of all who placed their trust in Jesus Christ for salvation. These are the ones justified by grace through faith, not by works. They are the ones who received His mercy rather than defied His call. If anyone's name is not found written in this book, their fate is sealed forever:

> *And anyone not found written in the Book of Life was cast into the lake of fire.*
>
> — REVELATION 20:15 NKJV

This is the second death.

## Eternal Separation

The lake of fire is not temporary nor metaphorical. It is the final and eternal destination of Satan, the Beast, the False Prophet, and now all whose names are not found in the Book of Life.

This is not annihilation. Rather, it is a conscious and eternal separation from the presence of God. Jesus described this reality as "outer darkness" characterized by "weeping and gnashing of teeth" (Matthew 8:12). It stands, in every sense, as the ultimate antithesis of heaven.

There are no second chances. No further appeals. No more mercy. The age of grace closed long before this moment arrived. The throne of judgment has spoken.

And yet, through the sorrow of this vision, we are reminded of something vital. God does not delight in the death of the wicked (Ezekiel 33:11). This judgment is not cruel. It is the necessary outcome of justice. It is what sin demanded. It is what God, in His holiness, must uphold.

## Reflection and Application: The Judgment We All Must Face

The somber reality of the Great White Throne is this: no one will be able to avoid standing before God. Either we will stand before Christ as redeemed saints at the Bema Seat (2 Corinthians 5:10), rewarded for our faithfulness, or we will stand at this final throne, judged according to our works because we rejected His grace.

This is not merely a future doctrine. It is a present wake-up call.

Many assume that being "good enough" will get them into heaven. They weigh their morality against others and assume that a loving God will grade on a curve. But Revelation 20 leaves no room for that illusion. If judged by works alone, none will stand. All have sinned. All fall short. The books make that clear.

But the good news, still available now, is that there is another book: the Book of Life. It is not earned. It is a record of grace. The names there belong to those who trusted in Jesus Christ, who believed in the Lamb who was slain and rose again.

It is not too late.

For those reading this now, the time to repent is today. Even if these words are read during the Great Tribulation, the gospel does not change. Salvation is still offered the same way it has always been: by grace, through faith, in Jesus Christ alone. "Everyone who calls on the name of the Lord will be saved" (Romans 10:13). But in that final hour, such faith will cost everything. To belong to Christ will mean refusing to worship the Beast, rejecting his mark, and standing openly against the world's last system of allegiance.

The very fact that you are alive and reading these words is evidence of God's mercy. He does not desire for you to appear before the Great White Throne as a stranger, but to know you as a beloved son or daughter.

Far from fear-mongering, this is truth-telling. Jesus Himself warned of this day. The apostles declared it. The Spirit speaks still. The wrath of God is real, but so is His offer of salvation.

So the question is not whether this Great White Throne is real. It is.

The question is: **Will your name be in the Book of Life?**

---

## Final Words: Mercy Now, Judgment Then

The Great White Throne is not the end of the story, but it is the end of every story that refused redemption.

It is a throne of perfect justice. There are no bribes, no mistakes, no loopholes. But it is also a throne we need not face. Christ has already stood in our place. He bore our judgment at the cross so that we could stand justified before God.

If you are in Christ, this chapter is a reminder of what you have been saved from, and a motivation to share the gospel urgently. If you are not in Christ, then hear this as a plea from eternity. Repent and believe. The door of grace is still open, but not forever.

The throne stands. The books are written. But the invitation remains:

**Come to Jesus while there is still time.**

*Chapter 26*

# ALL THINGS MADE NEW

## The Dawn of the Eternal State

*Then I saw a new heaven and a new earth, for the first heaven and the first earth had passed away ...*

— REVELATION 21:1

## All Things Made New

Out of the ashes of judgment, something breathtaking emerges.

John, who has just witnessed the final destruction of Death, Hades, and all unredeemed humanity, is now given a vision of staggering beauty. It is a vision so glorious it silences millennia of sorrow. The first heaven and first earth, corrupted by sin and scarred by wrath, are no more. They have not merely been scrubbed clean. They have passed away entirely.

In their place stands a brand-new creation.

This is not Eden restored. It is something beyond superlative.

God is not merely renovating the ruins of the old world. He is unveiling a pristine one, unstained, unshakable, and eternal. Far from the recycled rubble of a broken system, this is a cosmos freshly formed by the very word of God, untainted by the history of sin. It is a home where righteousness dwells (2 Peter 3:13).

And at the heart of it all is a city descending from heaven. A city unlike any other. Not built by human hands, but prepared by God Himself.

The New Jerusalem.

## The Dwelling Place of God with Man

In this new reality, the greatest promise transcends gold-lined streets or gates of pearl. It is this:

*Behold, the dwelling place of God is with man.*

— REVELATION 21:3

Since the Garden of Eden, humanity has been separated from the direct, unfiltered presence of God. But now, in this newly created cosmos, the great barrier of sin has been forever removed. God will dwell with His people, not through symbols or shadows, but in unveiled glory.

No temple is needed. No sun or moon required. God Himself is the light, and the Lamb is the lamp (Revelation 21:22-23).

Here, visitation gives way to permanent communion. The ache of separation is over, and the curse itself is finally and forever reversed.

This ultimate restoration was foreshadowed in the earliest days of humanity's new beginning after the Flood. In Genesis 8:4, Noah's ark, the vessel of salvation, came to rest on the mountains of Ararat. To the Hebrew ear, the very name *Ararat* carries a profound prophetic echo: "the curse is reversed."

In that ancient account, the ark coming to rest signaled the end of God's judgment and the beginning of a new covenant with creation. Now, in Revelation, the New Jerusalem descending from heaven is the ultimate, cosmic fulfillment of that ancient shadow. The curse of Eden is finally and completely broken. Judgment leaves no trace. The curse leaves no scar. The old order of things has passed away.

In its place, an untarnished creation exhales in glorious, unending liberty, fulfilling the divine declaration: "Behold, I am making all things new" (Revelation 21:5).

> *He will wipe away every tear from their eyes...*
>
> — REVELATION 21:4

More than poetic metaphor, this is a divine act of compassion. Every pain, every loss, every grief is redeemed in the tender touch of the Creator, even those that have been self-inflicted.

Death will be no more. Mourning, crying, and pain will pass into history. God's people will live, not in fear, nor in memory of what was lost, but in joy, light, and unbroken fellowship with the Almighty.

## The New Jerusalem: The Bride, the City

> *"Come, I will show you the Bride, the wife of the Lamb."*
>
> — REVELATION 21:9

John is carried away in the Spirit to a high mountain to see this holy city, the New Jerusalem, descending out of heaven from God. And what he sees is nothing short of astonishing.

He describes it as "having the glory of God, its radiance like a most rare jewel, like a jasper, clear as crystal" (Revelation 21:11). The language strains the limits of human description. John is witnessing something heavenly, a city that shines with divine brilliance, radiant with the glory of its Maker.

It is called the Bride, the wife of the Lamb, a symbol of perfect union between Christ and His redeemed people. In this city, heaven and earth meet. The eternal purpose of God is fulfilled.

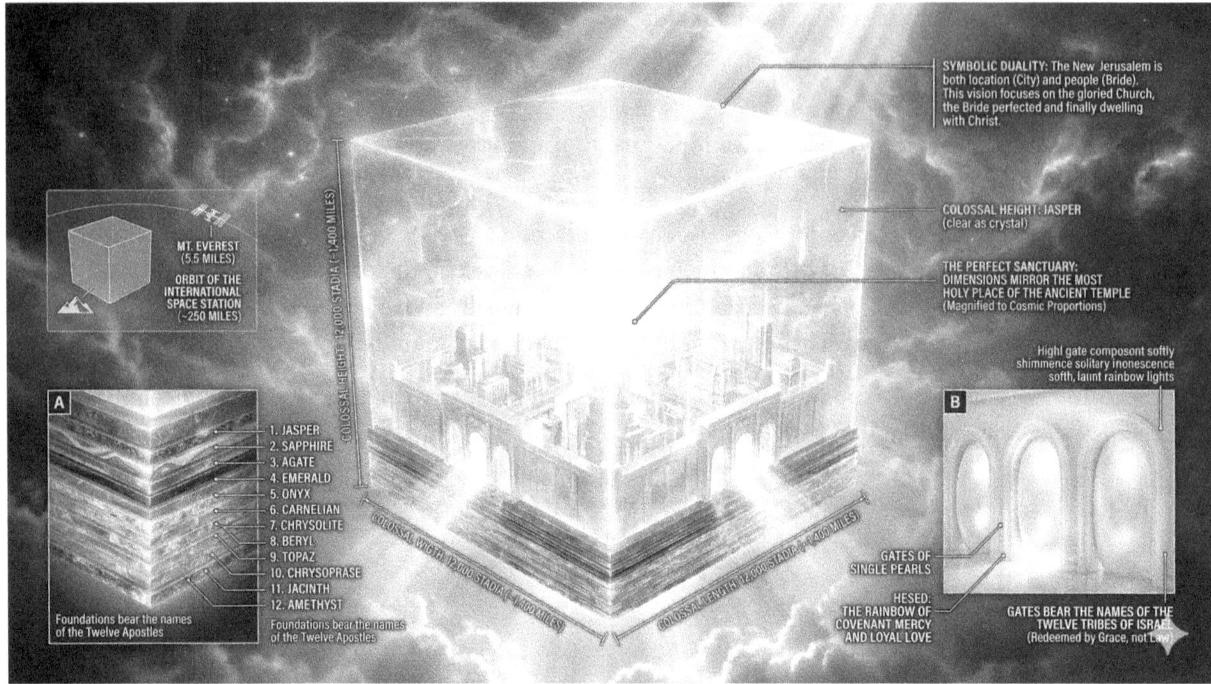


*Revelation 21:9*

Is the Bride of the Lamb Really a City? (See *Deeper Dive 26.1. The Bride or the City?* for a detailed exploration.)

This is no ordinary city. It is perfectly symmetrical, 12,000 stadia long, wide, and high, forming a colossal cube roughly 1,400 miles in every direction.

The scale is staggering. But the shape is familiar. These dimensions mirror the Most Holy Place of the ancient tabernacle and temple, where God's presence once dwelled behind a veil. Now, that sacred space has been magnified to cosmic proportions.

The entire city is the Holy of Holies. God's presence fills it completely. No more barriers. No more veil. Only unbroken communion.

Twelve gates, three on each side, bear the names of the twelve tribes of Israel. Twelve foundations bear the names of the twelve apostles of the Lamb. The city unites both Old and New Covenant saints, the faithful of Israel and the Church, as one redeemed people of God.

And the glory of this city is tangible.

The materials described are literal, not merely symbolic. God invented gold. He created pearls and gemstones. The earthly versions we know are but dim reflections of these heavenly realities. John sees streets of gold so pure they appear transparent, like glass. He sees jasper wall resting on twelve foundations, each adorned with a specific precious stone: jasper, sapphire, agate, emerald, onyx, carnelian, chrysolite, beryl, topaz, chrysoprase, jacinth, and amethyst. The gates are not built of many pearls but are singular. Each gate is a massive, solitary pearl.

This is not earthly extravagance. It is heavenly perfection.

The glory of God is reflected in every detail. Nothing unclean may enter. There is no need for temple, sun, or moon, for the Lord God Almighty and the Lamb are its temple and its light.

***Figure 26.2: The Gate of Pearl.*** *A single, massive pearl forms each of the city's twelve gates, set into a foundation of precious stones. Etched into its iridescent surface is the name of one of the twelve tribes of Israel (shown here in Hebrew:* Yehudah, *or Judah).*

---

### 🔍 SIDEBAR: Why the Gates Are Pearls

Revelation 21:21 tells us, *"The twelve gates were twelve pearls, each gate made of a single pearl."*

God could have chosen anything for the entrances of the New Jerusalem. He chose pearls.

These gates are not mere architecture. They preach. They stand like twelve silent sermons at the threshold of eternity, telling the story of how the unworthy were brought home.

#### 1. Glory from the Unclean

In the natural world, pearls come from oysters, creatures the Mosaic Law counts among the unclean things of the sea (Leviticus 11:10-12). That is the shock of it. An "unclean" creature produces what the ancient world counted among its rarest treasures.

It is a picture of grace. God is not welcoming the spotless because they managed to stay spotless. He is welcoming the redeemed because He is able to bring beauty from what was once common, broken, and defiled. Entrance into the Holy City is not earned by ritual purity or human merit. It is granted by grace.

#### 2. Formed Through Suffering

A pearl is not cut from stone. It is born inside a living creature through pain.

An irritant pierces, a wound opens, and the oyster responds by covering it, layer upon layer, until the wound is sealed in beauty. Suffering transfigured into glory.

Every gate, then, bears witness. We enter because Another was wounded for our transgressions (Isaiah 53:5).

And the detail John gives is not accidental. Each gate is a single pearl. Not assembled. Not patched together. One whole, sufficient, complete creation.

One gate. One pearl. One sacrifice.

Singular, Sufficient. Complete.

**3. The Rainbow of Covenant Mercy**

Natural pearls carry a faint iridescence, a hidden play of colors that can shimmer like a soft rainbow. Scripture has already taught us what a rainbow means. It is covenant mercy (Genesis 9:13). It surrounds the throne (Revelation 4:3).

So the gates do not simply open into a city. They glimmer with a message. Covenant mercy surrounds every entrance into God's eternal dwelling. Each gate catches the light with *hesed*, the loyal, unfailing love of God.

**4. The Great Paradox: Law and Grace**

Then comes the final jolt. Revelation 21:12 says the gates bear the names of the twelve tribes of Israel.

Under the Old Covenant, the twelve tribes were represented on the High Priest's breastplate by twelve distinct mineral stones, including emeralds, sapphires, and rubies. Pearls were excluded. Why? Because a pearl is the byproduct of an unclean animal. Yet here, the names of the tribes, the guardians of the Law, are inscribed forever upon the very substance that comes from a creature the Law forbade.

The point is not contradiction. It is fulfillment.

The Law was never meant to be the door. It was meant to lead to the Door. Now the New Covenant has reached its blazing completion. Israel's long history, marked by failure, judgment, and the Time of Jacob's Trouble, is finally redeemed. The remnant enters the Kingdom not by the works of the Law, but through a gate of Grace, formed by the suffering of their Messiah.

What looks like decoration is theology in gem and light.

Grace.

Suffering.

Redemption.

Glory.

All embedded in the gates of pearl.

---

## The Nations and the River of Life

Even in the eternal state, God's grace is expansive. "The nations will walk by its light, and the kings of the earth will bring their glory into it" (Revelation 21:24). Here, "the nations" (*ethne*) refers to the redeemed peoples from every tribe, tongue, and ethnicity, now gathered as one people of God in the new creation, not as separate political entities.

The gates will never shut. There is no night there.

John's vision continues into Revelation 22, where a river flows from the throne of God and of the Lamb, the river of the water of life, clear as crystal. On either side of the river stands the tree of life, bearing twelve kinds of fruit, with leaves for the healing of the nations.

Indeed, the curse is no more.

The servants of God see His face. Not symbolically. Not through a mediator. Face to face. And His name will be on their foreheads, marked forever as His own.

This is the destiny of the redeemed. Not clouds or harps, but a living, vibrant eternity in the presence of God, where worship is communion, service is glory, and joy never ends.

No longer exiles. No longer pilgrims.

Home.

## The Final Invitation: "Come"

The story of Scripture closes not with a period, but with one final, gracious invitation. After all the judgments have fallen and all the glories of eternity have been unveiled, God's last word to humanity is a call of grace:

*The Spirit and the Bride say, "Come."*

— REVELATION 22:17A

This is God's ultimate appeal to the human heart. Even in the last lines of the last book, He offers life freely. Not ceremony. Not religion. Living water, without price, for all who recognize their thirst.

The Spirit issues the call. The Bride, the Church, amplifies it. And every believer who hears is commissioned to relay it. The invitation is urgent, echoing into the present moment. The window of grace is open, but not forever.

Then comes the closing promise of Scripture:

*He ... says, "Surely I am coming soon." Amen. Come, Lord Jesus!*

— REVELATION 22:20

This is the cry of every redeemed heart. *Maranatha*. Come, Lord Jesus. We do not look to governments, movements, or human progress for rescue. Our hope is in a Person, Jesus Christ, the returning King.

Until He comes, we live with eyes lifted and hearts anchored in His Word. We endure. We invite. We watch. We hope.

And we wait.

*The grace of the Lord Jesus be with all. Amen.*

— REVELATION 22:21

# EPILOGUE

## If You Are Still Here

If you are reading this after the Great Disappearance, the warnings in this book are no longer theory. They are your reality.

You are watching the world unravel. Plagues, wars, delusion, and despair are sweeping the globe. You realize now, perhaps with terrifying clarity, that the Bible was true. Christ came for His own, just as He promised. And He will come again.

**But even now, there is hope.**

Though the Age of the Church has ended, God's character has not changed. He is still just. Still holy. Still saving. The cost of following Christ in this new era may be everything, perhaps even your life, but it is the only path left.

There is no safety in compromise. No salvation in the coming global system. No rescue in religion. The only hope is in Jesus Christ: the Lamb who was slain, the King who is coming to reign.

This book was written to point you to the truth. But knowledge alone cannot save you. You must fall to your knees, call out to the living God, and cling to Him with everything you have.

Below are two prayers to guide you. Use the first if you are a Gentile seeker. Use the second if you are of the House of Israel.

---

**A Prayer for Salvation**

Lord Jesus,

I see it now. You are real. Your Word is true. And without You, I am lost.

I confess my sin, my unbelief, and my pride.

I believe You died for me and rose again.

Please forgive me. Save me.

Be my Lord, my King, and my only shelter in this terrifying world.

Fill me with Your Spirit and give me the strength to endure, no matter the cost.

Amen.

---

**A Prayer for the Jewish Heart**

God of Abraham, Isaac, and Jacob,

The world I knew is gone, and I am afraid. But I am done with lies.

I believe now that Yeshua, Jesus, is Your Son, the Messiah we missed.

I believe He is the Lamb slain for my sins.

I turn from my own way and I turn to You. Please wash me in His blood.

Write my name in the Book of Life.

Give me the courage to stand for You in the Time of Jacob's Trouble.

Even if it costs me my life, let me be found in You.

I acknowledge my offense, and I cry out for Your return:

***Baruch Haba B'Shem Adonai***

(Blessed is He who comes in the name of the LORD!)

Thank You for not giving up on me, even when I gave up on You.

Amen.

---

The time is short.

The call is clear.

Do not delay.

Even now, let the invitation echo in your soul:

*The Spirit and the Bride say, "Come."*

— REVELATION 22:17A

**Do not let this invitation pass you by.**

# A FINAL NOTE TO THE READER

Whether you are reading this *before* the trumpet sounds, or *after* the world has changed forever, know this: you were on my heart as these pages were written.

If you are reading *before* the Rapture, I urge you: do not grow weary. Time is short. The hour is late. Hold fast to the truth of God's Word. Live with urgency, speak with boldness, and love with eternity in mind. There are people all around you who need to know the hope you carry. Be faithful. Be ready. Look up! Your redemption is drawing near.

But if you are reading this *after* millions have vanished and the world has plunged into chaos, then my message is simple: it is not too late to believe. But it *may* cost you everything, perhaps even your life. Yet even then, you will reign with Christ forever (Revelation 22:5). How does reigning for eternity compare to merely surviving a few short years in a world that is unraveling? Even now, God's mercy reaches out to you. Even now, you can repent, place your faith in Jesus Christ, and lay hold of an eternal hope that no earthly kingdom can destroy.

You may have missed the Rapture, but you do not have to miss the kingdom.

God is not finished. He still sees. He still calls. And one day soon, He will return to make all things new.

This book was written for **YOU**, to help you understand what is happening and to show you the way forward in a world that has lost its bearings.

Choose Christ.

Endure.

And take heart: the story is not over.

## A Final Word of Hope

> *He who testifies to these things says, "Surely I am coming soon." Amen. Come, Lord Jesus! The grace of the Lord Jesus be with all. Amen.*
>
> — REVELATION 22:20–21

May you be found watching, waiting, ready.

And may the peace of God,

the peace that passes understanding,

guard your heart and mind in Christ Jesus.

Whether He meets you in the clouds
or walks with you through the storm,
until that day, hold fast.
The King is coming.

# APPENDICES

**Hints & Possibilities**

**Deeper Dives**

**Shadows & Substances**

# DEEPER DIVE 1.1: THE FIG TREE, ISRAEL, AND THE FINAL GENERATION

## Decoding the Prophetic Clock of the Last Days

*"Now learn the parable from the fig tree: as soon as its branch has become tender and sprouts its leaves, you know that summer is near; so you too, when you see all these things, recognize that He is near, right at the door. Truly I say to you, this generation will not pass away until all these things take place.*

— MATTHEW 24:32–34 NASB

In May of 1948, something happened that historians had never seen before.

A nation that had vanished from the map nearly two thousand years earlier suddenly returned. Against every political expectation and historical precedent, Israel was reborn in a single day.

Empires had come and gone. Entire civilizations had dissolved into the dust of history. But the Jewish people endured and then, almost unbelievably, returned to their ancient homeland and reestablished their nation.

For students of biblical prophecy, the moment felt strangely familiar.

Nearly two thousand years earlier, Jesus had spoken of a fig tree that would one day begin to show signs of life again. When its branches became tender and its leaves appeared, He said, a change in prophetic season would be underway.

Was this ancient parable pointing directly to Israel's modern rebirth?

That question has fueled intense discussion among Bible students ever since.

At first glance the interpretive question seems simple:

Is the fig tree merely a general illustration about recognizing seasons, or does it carry a deeper prophetic meaning tied to Israel itself?

For those who read biblical prophecy as a literal blueprint for the future, the fig tree carries a symbolism that is anything but accidental. In this view, Jesus is not simply pointing to trees in general, but to a prophetic pattern already woven deeply into the writings of Israel's ancient prophets: a story of judgment, dormancy, and eventual restoration.

To see why, we must start with how the Bible had already been using the imagery of the fig tree long before Jesus ever spoke this parable.

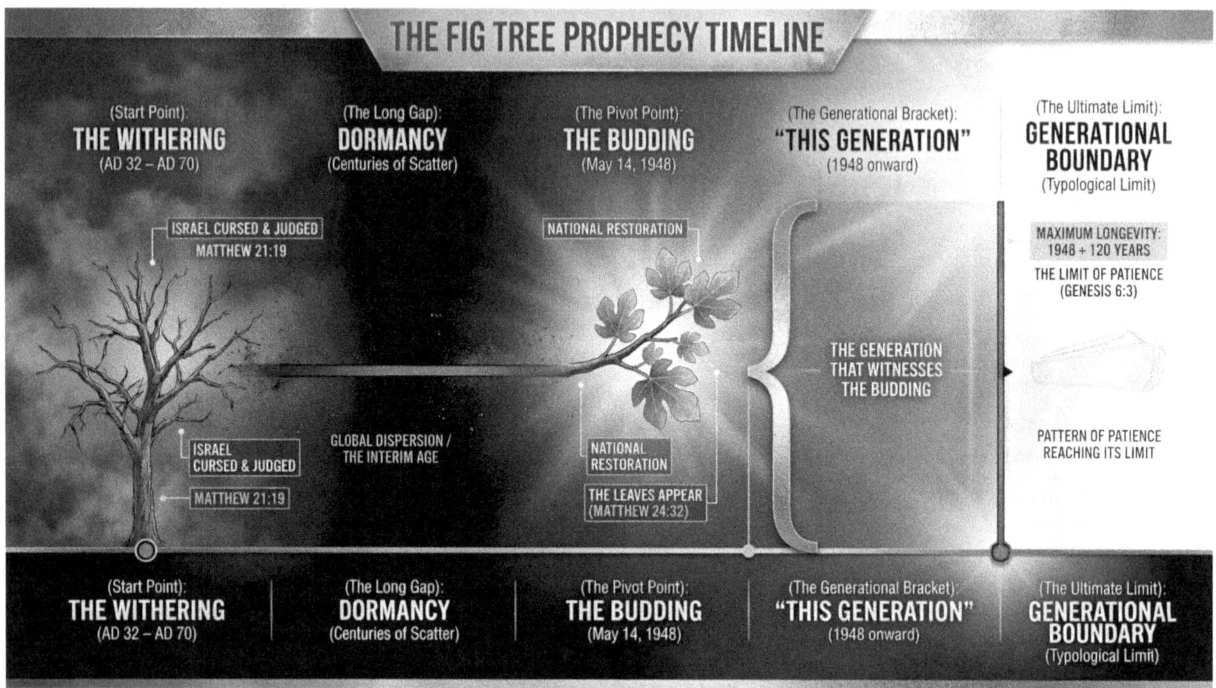


***Figure D1.1.1: The Fig Tree Prophecy Timeline.*** *This timeline traces Israel's national story through four distinct phases: the withering of judgment, a long season of dormancy, the modern budding of national restoration in 1948, and the approaching summer of the Kingdom.*

# 1. The Fig Tree in Israel's Prophetic Vocabulary

In Scripture, the fig tree was never a blank metaphor. Israel's prophets had already used it for centuries to describe the nation's relationship with God.

Through Hosea, the LORD recalls His early delight in Israel:

> *Like grapes in the wilderness I found Israel. Like the first fruit on the fig tree ... I saw your fathers ...*
>
> — HOSEA 9:10

Jeremiah provides an even clearer example. In a prophetic vision, the LORD shows him two baskets of figs, one good, one rotten. God then explains the meaning:

> *"Like these good figs, so I will regard as good the exiles ... But ... like the bad figs ... so will I treat Zedekiah ... and the remnant of Jerusalem ..."*
>
> —JEREMIAH 24:5–8

The symbolism is clear.

- Figs represent individuals within Israel.
- The fig tree represents the nation itself.
- The fruit's quality reflects covenant faithfulness, or rebellion.

By the time of Jesus, this imagery was part of Israel's prophetic vocabulary. When Jewish listeners heard Him mention a fig tree, they would not have thought only about agriculture. They would have recognized a symbol deeply tied to the story of their nation.

## 2. The Cursed Fig Tree: Israel Under Judgment

Jesus actually set the stage for this prophetic moment months earlier.

In the Gospel of Luke, He tells a parable about a vineyard owner who came seeking fruit on a planted fig tree for three consecutive years and found none. Frustrated, the owner ordered the barren tree cut down. But the vinedresser interceded, asking for an extension of time to cultivate and fertilize the soil. He warned that if it still bore no fruit after this final season of grace, it would be destroyed (Luke 13:6–9).

The prophetic picture is undeniable. The owner's repeated search reflects God the Father seeking the fruit of covenant faithfulness from the nation of Israel during Christ's earthly ministry. When none is found, the vinedresser, representing Jesus Himself, intercedes. He asks for one final, brief window of mercy to cultivate the nation before judgment falls.

By the time we reach Matthew's narrative, that extended season of grace has expired.

In this setting, Matthew introduces the actual, physical fig tree right before the Olivet Discourse. During the final week of Jesus' ministry, He performs one of His most unusual miracles.

> *And seeing a fig tree by the road, He came to it and found nothing on it but leaves, and said to it, "Let no fruit grow on you ever again." Immediately the fig tree withered away.*
>
> — MATTHEW 21:19 NKJV

At first glance the act seems strange, and almost harsh. But in the prophetic tradition of the Old Testament, symbolic demonstrations were common. Prophets often dramatized God's message through visible actions.

And Matthew places this event in a very deliberate context.

It occurs right alongside:

- the cleansing of the temple
- the challenge to Jesus' authority
- parables announcing national judgment
- and finally the devastating words: *"See, your house is left to you desolate"* (Matthew 23:38).

Just as the fig tree persisted with just leaves, presenting the outward appearance of life and yet bearing no fruit, so too Israel's leadership maintained the rituals of covenant religion, including temple worship, sacrifices, and sacred traditions, yet rejected the very Messiah standing before them.

Thus the withered fig tree becomes a powerful sign: the nation stands under judgment.

## 3. From Withering to Budding

But the story of the fig tree does not end with its withering.

Just a short time later, in the very next chapter of Matthew's narrative, Jesus returns to this exact image. Suddenly, the tree that had symbolized judgment becomes the tree His disciples are told to watch.

*"Now learn the parable of the fig tree ..."*

— MATTHEW 24:32A NASB

Only days earlier, the disciples had seen a fig tree wither as a prophetic sign of judgment. Now Jesus speaks of a fig tree showing signs of life again:

*"... as soon as its branch has become tender and sprouts its leaves, you know that summer is near."*

— MATTHEW 24:32B NASB

The narrative progression in Matthew is striking.

The fig tree withers in **Matthew 21**.

Judgment is pronounced in **Matthew 23**.

The destruction of the Temple is foretold in **Matthew 24:2**.

Then Jesus tells His disciples to watch the fig tree.

In this light, the imagery takes on a prophetic rhythm:

- **Withering:** judgment on Israel.
- **Dormancy:** a long season of exile and dispersion.
- **Budding**: the first signs of national renewal.
- **Summer**: the Kingdom drawing near.

Viewed through this prophetic lens, Jesus is not merely offering a lesson about recognizing the seasons. He is telling His followers that when the tree that once withered begins to stir again, the prophetic clock has resumed its countdown.

## 4. What About Luke's "All the Trees"?

Some readers point to Luke's version of the passage:

*"Look at the fig tree, and all the trees."*

— LUKE 21:29B

Does this remove the fig tree's special symbolism?

No. Several scriptural factors preserve the specific meaning in Matthew.

First, Luke and Matthew emphasize different aspects of the Olivet Discourse. Luke's account places greater focus on the near-term destruction of Jerusalem in A.D. 70. Matthew's version, by contrast, highlights Israel's broader prophetic future and the climactic events surrounding Christ's return.

Second, Scripture often uses layered imagery. A fig tree can serve both as a general illustration about seasonal awareness and as a symbol carrying deeper theological meaning.

Finally, context matters.

In Matthew's narrative, the disciples had already watched a fig tree wither as a prophetic sign. When Jesus later tells them to "learn the parable of the fig tree," it is difficult to imagine that earlier event was unrelated.

The tree that withered is the very tree now being watched for signs of life.

## 5. "This Generation"

Jesus concludes the parable with one of the most debated lines in the entire discourse:

> *"Truly I say to you, this generation will not pass away until all these things take place."*
>
> — MATTHEW 24:34

If the fig tree is only a general metaphor, "this generation" becomes difficult to anchor. Some therefore conclude it must refer to Jesus' contemporaries, missing the broader prophetic scope by assuming the events were entirely fulfilled in A.D. 70.

But when the fig tree is rightly understood as Israel's national story of being judged, dormant, and eventually restored, its budding becomes the undeniable prophetic milestone. In that framework, "this generation" refers not to the audience standing before Jesus, but to the end-time generation that witnesses the tree begin to bud again.

That long-awaited budding finally occurred in the modern era. The rebirth of Israel in 1948 as a nation restored after nearly two thousand years resembles precisely the kind of moment Jesus described.

The fig tree puts forth leaves.

Summer is near.

The Kingdom draws close.

## Excursus: How Long Is a Generation?

This naturally raises another question: How long is a generation?

Psalm 90:10 establishes a standard human lifespan of seventy to eighty years, but the definitive boundary appears much earlier in Scripture. Before the flood, God declared:

> *"My Spirit will not contend with humans forever ... their days will be a hundred and twenty years."*
>
> — GENESIS 6:3 NIV

While the immediate context concerns the countdown to the Flood, this Scripture establishes 120 years as the definitive upper limit for human lifespan in the post-flood world. In modern history, verified ages beyond this boundary are extraordinarily rare.

If the budding of the fig tree corresponds to Israel's national restoration in 1948, adding 120 years points to the year 2068 as the prophetic ceiling for the era defined by that event.

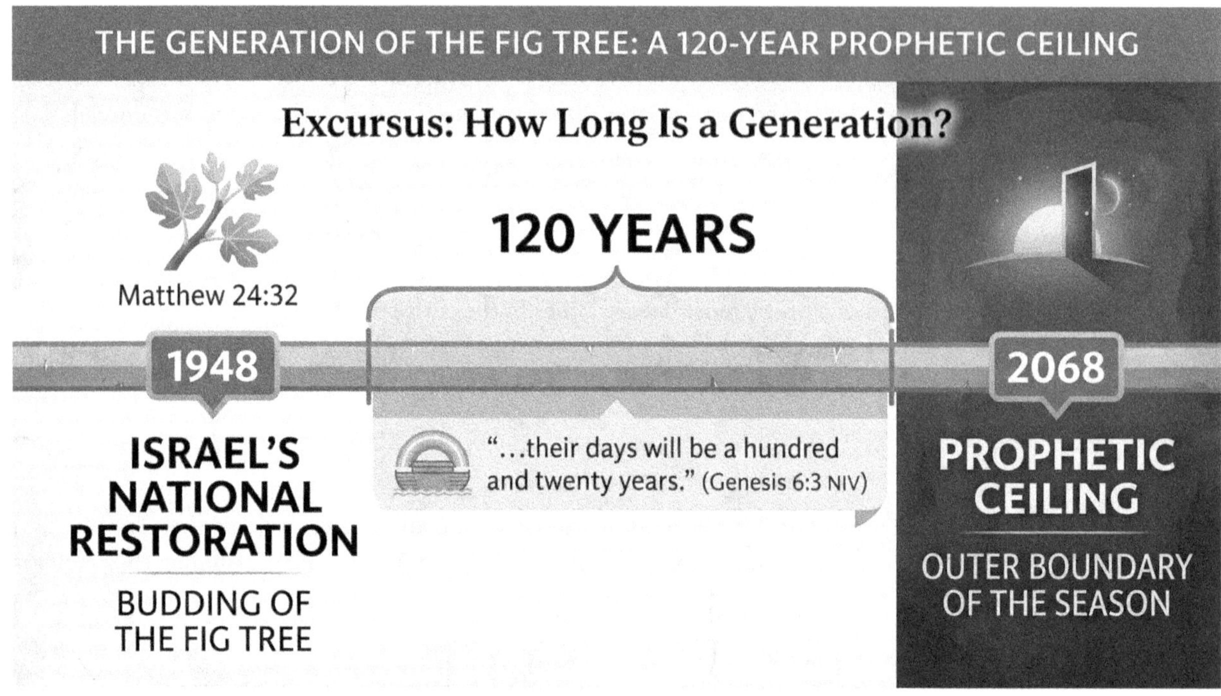


***Figure D1.1.2: The 120-Year Generation Model.*** *This diagram visualizes the "Days of Noah" template (Genesis 6:3) applied to the generation that witnesses Israel's national rebirth (1948). According to Jesus' promise in Matthew 24:34, this generation will not pass away until "all these things" take place, culminating in His Second Coming. The 120-year span therefore establishes the year 2068 as the biblical maximum, or the prophetic ceiling, for the completion of all end-time events.*

However, we must be crystal clear: this is not a target date for the Lord's return. The year 2068 represents the outer boundary of the season, not a scheduled appointment. Jesus explicitly warned against such calculations:

> *"But concerning that day and hour no one knows ..."*
>
> — MATTHEW 24:36

The fig tree marks a season, not a stopwatch.

## The Point of the Parable

The purpose of the fig tree is not speculation. It is watchfulness. All the current signs whisper a single, urgent message: *He is at the door.*

When the tree that once withered begins to live again, Jesus tells His followers to lift their eyes and recognize the times. The budding branches are not meant to produce arrogance or date-setting. They are meant to awaken readiness.

History is moving decisively toward its climax. The Lord's return will be sudden, and He demands that His Church be ready:

> *"Behold, I am coming like a thief! Blessed is the one who stays awake, keeping his garments on, that he may not go about naked and be seen exposed!"*
>
> — REVELATION 16:15

When the fig tree begins to stir again after a long winter, it is a quiet but powerful reminder.

The summer season is almost here.

**The King is at the door.**

# HINTS & POSSIBILITIES 1.2. THE DAY AND HOUR THAT NO ONE KNOWS

## Living in the Tension of Imminence and Urgency

*"But concerning that day and hour no one knows, not even the angels of heaven, nor the Son, but the Father only."*

— MATTHEW 24:36

With this declaration, Jesus placed believers in a state of divine tension, caught between mystery and anticipation. The specific timing of the Rapture is unrevealed, yet its certainty is undeniable. It could happen at any moment, without warning or countdown. This truth is not meant to paralyze us with uncertainty; rather, it is a wake-up call to live with watchfulness, urgency, and readiness.

Within this cryptic statement lies a powerful allusion to themes already embedded in Israel's sacred calendar.

### The Mystery of the Hidden Moon

Among the seven feasts God commanded Israel to observe (Leviticus 23), the Feast of Trumpets (Yom Teruah) stands apart in mystery. Unlike the other feasts, which were fixed by calculated days in the lunar calendar, this one began on the first day of the seventh month. Its start was triggered not by calculation, but by the physical sighting of the new moon: a barely visible sliver in the evening sky.

Because clouds or human error could obscure this sliver, the exact start of the feast was inherently unpredictable. Consequently, Jewish tradition associated it with themes of hiddenness and uncertainty, often summarized by later teachers with phrases like "The Hidden Day" or "The Day and Hour No One Knows."

*Figure H1.2.1.* ***Sighting the New Moon.*** *In ancient Israel, the Feast of Trumpets could not begin until two witnesses visually confirmed the first sliver of the new moon. This inherent unpredictability led to the feast being associated with the phrase, "the day and hour no one knows."*

### When Does the Feast of Trumpets Occur?

The Feast of Trumpets, or Yom Teruah, typically falls in the months of September or October on our modern Gregorian calendar.

This variation occurs because the Jewish calendar is lunisolar, meaning its months are tied to the cycles of the moon while its years are adjusted to remain aligned with the seasons. The Feast of Trumpets begins on the first day of the seventh month (Tishrei), which depends entirely on the visual sighting of the new moon.

Since the lunar year is approximately 11 days shorter than the solar year, the Hebrew calendar periodically adds a leap month (Adar II) to stay aligned with the seasons, causing dates to drift relative to the Gregorian calendar each year. As a result, the precise timing of the Feast of Trumpets shifts slightly each year, physically reinforcing its association with uncertainty and the phrase "the day and hour no one knows."

This uncertainty was not merely theoretical. Once two credible witnesses observed the new moon and reported it to the Sanhedrin, the new month and the feast, would officially begin. Until then, the people remained in a strict posture of readiness, waiting to hear the blast of the shofar that would announce its arrival.[1]

1. The typological connection between the Feast of Trumpets (Yom Teruah) and Jesus' phrase "the day and hour no one knows" is firmly rooted in the documented historical uncertainty of the new-moon sighting. Regardless of its classification as a formal first-century idiom, the unpredictable nature of the feast fittingly mirrors Christ's warning. For a detailed explanation of this historical uncertainty, see Kevin Howard and Marvin Rosenthal, *The Feasts of the Lord* (Orlando, FL: Zion's Hope, 1997).

## Decoding the Divine Allusion

When Jesus stated that no one knows the day or the hour, He intentionally echoed the prophetic shadow of this feast. Crucially, the Greek word for "knows" (*eido*) means more than mere intellectual awareness; it signifies perceiving, recognizing, or knowing something with clarity based on observation or understanding. In other words, Jesus emphasizes that the Father reserves the prerogative of initiation. It is intentionally concealed, to be revealed at the appointed time, mirroring the historical uncertainty surrounding Yom Teruah.

This connection makes the trumpet symbolism undeniable. The Rapture is consistently associated with a trumpet blast. In 1 Thessalonians 4:16, Paul declares, "For the Lord Himself will descend from heaven with a shout, with the voice of the archangel, and with the trumpet of God." Likewise, 1 Corinthians 15:52 says it will happen "in a moment, in the twinkling of an eye, at the last trumpet." This unmistakable sound will signal the instant gathering of the saints. The Feast of Trumpets serves as a divine prophetic shadow mirroring this glorious future event.

## The Next Divine Appointment

Even more compelling is the broader pattern God has already set. Jesus fulfilled the first three spring feasts (Passover, Unleavened Bread, and Firstfruits) on their exact appointed days through His death, burial, and resurrection. Then, on the day of Pentecost, the Holy Spirit descended with power and birthed the Church. These were not symbolic gestures; they were literal, punctual fulfillments of God's calendar (see *Shadows & Substance 1.3. God's Redemptive Clock*).

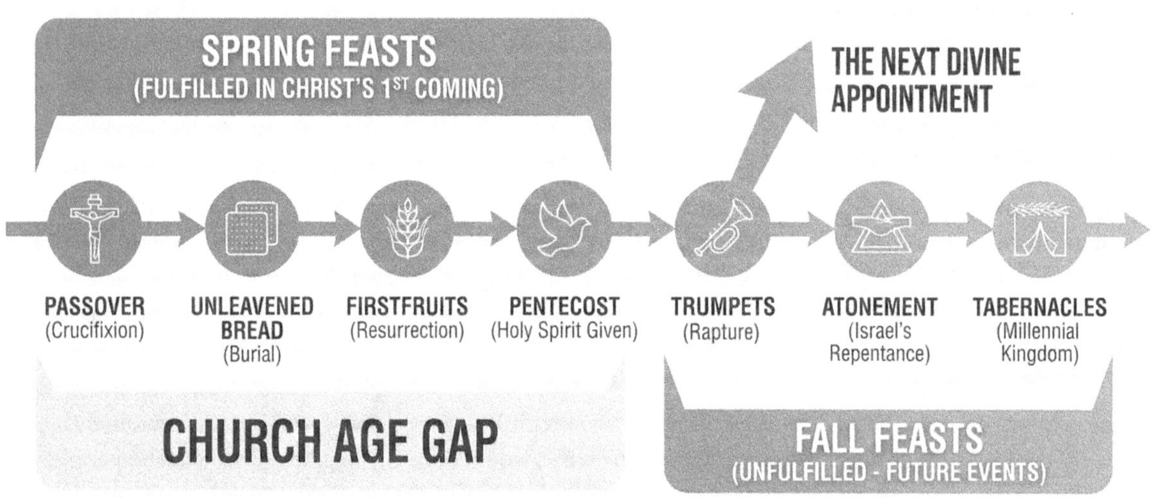


***Figure H1.2.2. God's Prophetic Calendar.*** *The seven feasts of Israel form a chronological blueprint of God's redemptive plan. The first four were fulfilled literally at Christ's first coming. The Feast of Trumpets is the next unfulfilled appointment, serving as a powerful prophetic shadow of the Rapture.*

That leaves the Feast of Trumpets as the next unfulfilled appointment. This prophetic pattern clearly frames the Rapture, even while preventing us from predicting its exact date. The trumpet will sound, and the Lord will call His Church home in the blink of an eye (1 Thessalonians 4:16–17). No one knows the day or the hour, but the season is undeniably upon us.

## The Balance of Imminence

A vital word of caution is necessary. While the pattern is profound, it must not erode the doctrine of Imminence. Jesus commanded us to watch *always*, not only in the autumn months of September or October. The Rapture fulfills the theological essence of the Feast of Trumpets: the awakening blast. God is a God of patterns, but He is not constrained by our calendar. The element of total surprise remains paramount.

## The Restrainer and the Falling Away

The Apostle Paul offers further insight in 2 Thessalonians 2. He explains that two events must precede the revealing of the Antichrist: first, the great falling away (apostasy), and second, the removal of the Restrainer. The Restrainer is the Holy Spirit's presence active in and through the Church. Once the Church is removed, once that restraining influence is lifted, evil will surge forward unhindered, and the man of lawlessness will be revealed.

And here is the sobering reality: the seeds of the great falling away are already sprouting. It is happening right now. Churches are compromising truth. False gospels are flourishing. Culture is crumbling. Delusion is deepening. The conditions are already ripening for the Antichrist's unveiling. The stage is set.

If ever there was a time to live alert, it is now. The specific day and hour rest with the Father, but the call to be ready does not. Jesus did not say we could not recognize the general time or season. In fact, He rebuked the religious leaders of His day for failing to discern the time of their visitation (Luke 19:44). They missed the Messiah standing in their midst because they ignored the prophetic signs. Likewise, believers today are called to understand the times and live in readiness. To dismiss the signs of His coming is not merely an oversight; it carries severe spiritual consequences.

## Living in Expectancy

We live in expectancy, not with fear, but with faith. The trumpet could sound at any moment. The Church is not called to speculate about dates, but to stay alert, to shine brightly in the gathering darkness, and to call others into the ark of salvation before the door is shut. The hidden day will come swiftly, like a thief in the night, but it will not catch those who are watching off guard. For us, the hiddenness is not a burden; it is a call.

But what happens after that trumpet sounds? If the Rapture aligns with the Feast of Trumpets, what prophetic significance follows? The Jewish calendar includes a ten-day period immediately following the Feast of Trumpets, leading directly to the Day of Atonement. Known as the Ten Days of Awe, this interval is marked by intense introspection, repentance, and preparation.

This solemn window powerfully foreshadows the Tribulation: humanity's final, harrowing window for repentance amidst the global upheaval, reckoning, and divine intervention occurring between the Rapture and Christ's physical return. In *Hints & Possibilities 1.4. The Ten Days of Awe*, we will explore this heavily overlooked window in God's prophetic timeline.

## SHADOWS & SUBSTANCE 1.3. GOD'S REDEMPTIVE CLOCK

### The Prophetic Blueprint of Israel's Feasts

> *"Speak to the people of Israel and say to them, These are the appointed feasts of the LORD that you shall proclaim as holy convocations; they are my appointed feasts."*
>
> — LEVITICUS 23:2

God doesn't leave prophecy to chance. He embeds it in time itself.

The seven Levitical feasts outlined in Leviticus 23 are far more than ancient holidays for Israel. They function as prophetic blueprints. These appointed times, or *moedim* in Hebrew, form a divine calendar revealing God's redemptive plan for both the Church and Israel, from the cross to the crown.[1]

Each feast not only commemorates something historical, but also foreshadows something eschatological. Four have been fulfilled precisely on their actual calendar dates, while the remaining three point to events yet to come.

Let's walk through them chronologically. Together, these feasts form a prophetic timeline that traces God's redemptive program from Christ's first coming to His Second Coming and Kingdom reign.

1. The reality that the seven biblical feasts of Leviticus 23 outline a prophetic pattern of God's redemptive plan has long been taught by Bible scholars and Messianic Jewish teachers. For an accessible introduction to the prophetic meaning of the feasts, see Zola Levitt, *The Seven Feasts of Israel* (Zola Levitt Ministries). For a fuller and more systematic treatment, see Kevin Howard and Marvin Rosenthal, *The Feasts of the Lord* (Orlando, FL: Zion's Hope, 1997).

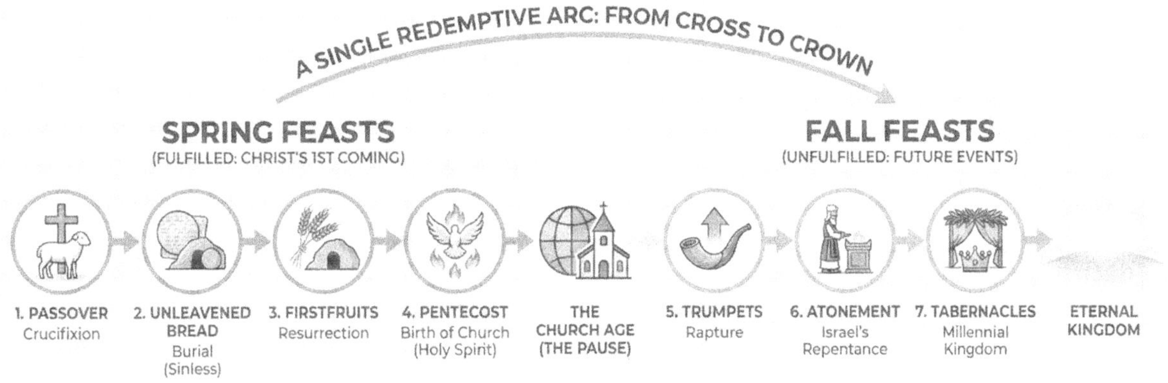


***Figure S1.3.1: God's Redemptive Clock.*** *The seven feasts of Israel form a precise, chronological blueprint of God's redemptive plan. The first four were literally fulfilled at Christ's first coming, guaranteeing the exact fulfillment of the final three.*

## 1. Passover: The Lamb Slain (Jesus' Crucifixion)

> *In the first month, on the fourteenth day of the month at twilight, is the LORD's Passover.*
>
> — LEVITICUS 23:5

**Typology:** Fulfilled in Christ's first coming. Jesus is the Lamb of God (John 1:29), whose blood was shed for our redemption. He was crucified on Passover, fulfilling this feast to the exact day.

**Note:** Just as the blood of the lamb shielded Israel from God's judgment in Egypt, those under Christ's blood are protected from the coming wrath.

| Feast | Prophetic Fulfillment |
| --- | --- |
| Passover | Jesus' sacrificial death on the cross |

## 2. Unleavened Bread: A Sinless Offering

> *And on the fifteenth day of the same month is the Feast of Unleavened Bread to the LORD;*
>
> — LEVITICUS 23:6A

**Typology:** Jesus, who was entirely sinless (leaven represents sin), was buried during this feast. His body lay in the tomb as the Bread from Heaven, pure and without corruption.

| Feast | Prophetic Fulfillment |
|---|---|
| Unleavened Bread | Jesus' sinless body laid in the tomb |

## 3. Firstfruits: The Resurrected One

*...you shall bring the sheaf of the firstfruits ... On the day after the Sabbath.*

— LEVITICUS 23:10–11

**Typology:** Jesus rose from the dead on the Feast of Firstfruits. Paul explicitly calls Him the "firstfruits of those who have fallen asleep" (1 Corinthians 15:20).

| Feast | Prophetic Fulfillment |
|---|---|
| Firstfruits | Jesus' bodily resurrection |

---

## 4. Pentecost (Feast of Weeks): The Birth of the Church

*You shall count fifty days... You shall bring from your dwelling places two loaves of bread to be waved ... They shall be of fine flour, and they shall be baked with leaven, as firstfruits to the LORD.*

— LEVITICUS 23:16–17

Held 50 days after Firstfruits. Unlike the sinless bread of Christ, these loaves contain leaven, representing the Church: redeemed, yet still containing the presence of the sin nature.

**Typology:** The Holy Spirit was poured out on this exact day (Acts 2). Pentecost marks the birth of the Church, the mystery hidden for ages (Ephesians 3:3–6).

| Feast | Prophetic Fulfillment |
| --- | --- |
| Pentecost | The birth and empowerment of the Church by the Holy Spirit |

So far, the first four feasts have been fulfilled in exact sequence, on their actual dates, and all in direct connection to Jesus' first coming and the Church's birth.

## The Pause: The Church Age

Between Pentecost and the next feast lies a long agricultural gap: the summer harvest. Prophetically, this mirrors the Church Age, the time of gospel proclamation among the nations.

The fall feasts pick up the prophetic drama again, marking the great transition from the Church Age to the final events for Israel. This sequence begins with the Feast of Trumpets, which triggers the Rapture of the Church, and then moves to the Day of Atonement and the Feast of Tabernacles, which focus squarely on Israel's national repentance and the establishment of the Messiah's kingdom on earth.

## 5. Feast of Trumpets (Yom Teruah): The Rapture

> *... In the seventh month, on the first day of the month ... a memorial proclaimed with blast of trumpets...*
>
> — LEVITICUS 23:24

**Typology:** Associated with awakening, alarm, and assembly. Trumpets signal a new beginning, marking the start of Israel's civil year. This serves as the prophetic shadow of the Rapture, the moment the Church is caught up at "the last trumpet" (1 Corinthians 15:52; 1 Thessalonians 4:16–17).

**Prophetic Connection:** Yom Teruah is unique among the feasts in that its beginning depended on the sighting of the new moon, making its exact start uncertain. This powerfully echoes Jesus' warning that regarding His return, no one knows "the day and hour" (Matthew 24:36).

| Feast | Future Fulfillment |
| --- | --- |
| Trumpets | The Rapture of the Church |

## 6. Day of Atonement (Yom Kippur): Israel's National Repentance

> *Now on the tenth day of this seventh month is the Day of Atonement.*
>
> — LEVITICUS 23:27A

**Typology:** A day of affliction, humility, and national repentance. It foreshadows Israel's future recognition of their pierced Messiah, as foretold in Zechariah 12:10. This strikingly anticipates the end of the Tribulation, when Christ returns and "all Israel will be saved" (Romans 11:26).

| Feast | Future Fulfillment |
|---|---|
| Day of Atonement | Israel's national repentance and cleansing at Christ's Second Coming |

## 7. Feast of Booths/Tabernacles (Sukkot): The Kingdom Comes

*... On the fifteenth day of this seventh month and for seven days is the Feast of Booths to the LORD.*

— LEVITICUS 23:34

**Typology:** A time of joy, rest, and God dwelling with His people. It foreshadows the Millennial Kingdom, when Christ reigns on Earth and all the nations will go up to Jerusalem to celebrate the Feast of Tabernacles (Zechariah 14:16–19).

| Feast | Future Fulfillment |
|---|---|
| Tabernacles | Christ's Millennial Reign |

## The Big Picture: God's Redemptive Clock

| Feast | Prophetic Fulfillment |
|---|---|
| Passover | Christ's crucifixion |
| Unleavened Bread | His sinless burial |
| Firstfruits | Christ's resurrection |
| Pentecost | Birth of the Church |
| Trumpets | The Rapture (anticipated) |
| Atonement | Israel's national repentance |
| Tabernacles | Christ's kingdom on Earth |

From Passover's blood-stained doorway to Tabernacles' joy-filled dwelling, the feasts trace a single redemptive arc: death, resurrection, harvest, repentance, and kingdom. What began at the cross finds its completion in the crown.

The first four feasts marked Jesus' first coming. The last three point to His Second Coming. Right now, we are living in the gap, awaiting the trumpet blast that signals the next move on God's calendar.

## Prophecy Embedded in Celebration

These feasts are not merely Jewish traditions; they are appointed convocations (Hebrew: *miqra*), prophetic shadows of events of cosmic importance.

In Colossians 2:17, Paul writes:

> *These are a shadow of the things to come, but the substance belongs to Christ.*

Indeed, every feast finds its center in Him. And just as the first four were fulfilled to the exact day, the final three will unfold with the same unerring precision.

This pattern is not only fascinating; it is faith-anchoring. God is a master of timing, and the feasts reveal His redemptive plan with mathematical precision and prophetic beauty.

# HINTS & POSSIBILITIES 1.4. THE TEN DAYS OF AWE

## A Prophetic Foreshadowing of an Interval of Ten Years?

*"Speak to the people of Israel, saying, In the seventh month, on the* ***first day*** *of the month, you shall observe a day of solemn rest, a memorial proclaimed with* ***blast of trumpets*** *...*

*Now on the* ***tenth day*** *of this seventh month is the* ***Day of Atonement*** *..."*

— LEVITICUS 23:24–27

### Hidden in the Calendar

In traditional Jewish observance, the ten days starting with the Feast of Trumpets and ending with Yom Kippur (the Day of Atonement) are known as the Ten Days of Awe: a period marked by solemn introspection, repentance, and preparation for judgment.

This tradition holds profound prophetic significance. It serves as a divine pattern for the period between the Rapture and Jesus Christ's physical return. The biblical "Ten Days of Awe" prophetically mirrors a ten-year timeline. Just as this sacred season spans ten inclusive days, opening with a trumpet blast and closing with atonement, the final epoch of this age will span a decade, beginning with the trumpet call of the Rapture and ending with Christ's return to judge, restore, and usher in the Millennium.

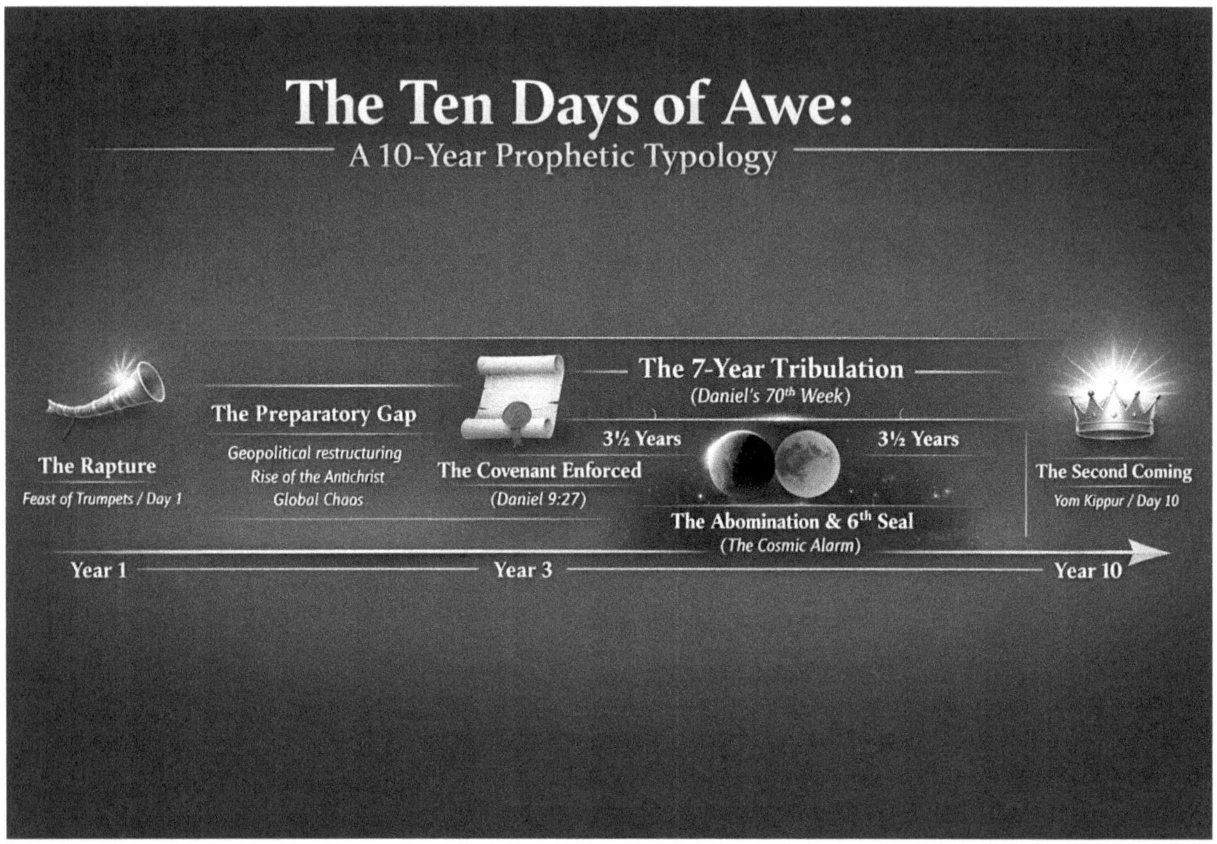


***Figure H1.4.1: The Ten-Year Prophetic Typology.*** *A visual representation of the ten-year span from the Rapture to the Second Coming. This timeline illustrates the necessary preparatory gap following the Rapture, creating the geopolitical vacuum required before the Antichrist enforces the final seven-year covenant.*

## The Prophetic Gap: Chaos Before the Covenant

The Rapture of the Church, as described in 1 Thessalonians 4:16–17 and 1 Corinthians 15:51–52, marks a sudden and dramatic disappearance of millions from the earth. Many assume the Tribulation begins immediately after this event, but biblical chronology demands a gap of undetermined length between the Rapture and the start of Daniel's 70th Week.[1]

This gap serves as a necessary transition period. According to Daniel 9:27, the final seven years begin *not* with the Rapture, but with the enforcement of a covenant by the Antichrist. This requires a delay: time for the Antichrist to rise, build trust, and position himself as a broker of global peace.

During this interim, the world reels from the aftermath of the Rapture. Economies convulse. Governments falter. Religious confusion deepens. Into this global vacuum steps a charismatic and cunning leader, offering clarity where there is chaos and peace where there is fear. As nations scramble to recover and long-standing tensions reach a breaking point, this figure rises by presenting himself as the architect of a new global order.

1. The concept of a "gap" or "interval" between the Rapture and the start of the seven-year Tribulation arises from the distinction that the Rapture is an imminent, signless event, whereas the Tribulation, Daniel's seventieth week, begins with a specific, datable event: the covenant described in Daniel 9:27.

## The Final 7 Years (The Tribulation Proper)

Once the Antichrist finalizes and guarantees the peace agreement, a landmark treaty that establishes security for Israel and her neighbors, the final seven years of this present age begin. This is Daniel's 70th Week, marked by escalating judgments and intensifying spiritual conflict.

With the opening of the First Seal, the man who rose to prominence as a broker of peace now goes forth as a conqueror. John sees him in Revelation 6:2 riding a white horse, holding a bow, and being given a crown. He is the bow-wielding conqueror who subdues the world not by brute force, but by diplomacy, persuasion, and the promise of peace. What began as a covenant of security now gives way to a campaign of global domination.

This seven-year period is the heart of the prophetic timeline, a time of judgment and warning foretold in Daniel and Revelation:

- **First 3½ years**: Deception, wars, famine, and pandemics sweep the globe as the first five Seal Judgments are unleashed (Revelation 6:1–11).
- **Midpoint**: The Antichrist breaks the covenant, declares himself divine, and desecrates the Temple. In a direct, world-shaking response to this abomination, the Sixth Seal is torn open (Revelation 6:12–17). The sky goes black, serving as the cosmic alarm that the great and terrible phase of the Day of the LORD has arrived.
- **Second 3½ years**: The Great Tribulation escalates with the Trumpet Judgments (Revelation 8–9). God's consummate judgment is poured out in full measure through the Bowls (Revelation 16), culminating in the physical return of Christ to earth (Revelation 19).

## Parallels with Jewish Prophetic Tradition

The parallel between the Ten Days of Awe and a ten-year span from Rapture to Return is undeniable, especially when considered alongside Daniel's 70 Weeks prophecy, where a "week" represents seven years, not seven days.

In Jewish thought, the days between the Feast of Trumpets and Yom Kippur represent a final window for repentance. It is a narrow but merciful opportunity before judgment is sealed. Likewise, this ten-year window from the Rapture to the Second Coming represents God's last call to a rebellious world. Though the Church is gone, the Spirit still works. The Two Witnesses, the 144,000 sealed Israelites, and even angelic messengers proclaim the gospel.

Amid judgment, mercy still shines. As Jesus declared, "But the one who endures to the end will be saved" (Matthew 24:13). This is not merely about physical survival; it is about persevering in faith to the end and receiving salvation.

## The Jericho Blueprint: Preparation Before Possession

The Israelites' entry into the Promised Land under Joshua offers a striking strategic blueprint for the end times. Before the famed seven-year conquest of Canaan began (Joshua 14:7–10), there was a necessary military prelude: Moses' campaigns east of the Jordan.

These victories over Sihon and Og (Numbers 21; Deuteronomy 2–3) were distinct in their purpose. While Joshua's campaign was about *taking possession* of the land, Moses' campaign was about *clearing the obstacles* to entry. He had to secure the borders and remove hostile powers before the main conquest could launch.

This pattern reveals that the gap between the Rapture and the Tribulation is not merely empty waiting time; it is a time of far-reaching global stage-setting. Just as God ordained the dismantling of the trans-Jordan kingdoms to prepare the way for Joshua, God will allow the dismantling of the current geopolitical order to prepare the world for its final prophetic sequence.

The sudden removal of the Church will shatter the status quo. In the resulting chaos, resistant nations will fall, economies will consolidate, and sovereign borders will shift. This massive geopolitical restructuring is the necessary prelude, creating the exact global vacuum required for the Antichrist to rise and enforce the final seven-year covenant.

Once this preparatory gap concludes, the final seven-year conquest begins. (For a comprehensive breakdown of how Joshua's specific victory at Jericho foreshadows the apocalyptic judgments of Revelation, see *Deeper Dive 5.4. Jericho as Prophetic Blueprint*).

The conquest of Canaan, like the future Tribulation, was not merely about territorial acquisition; it was about the exact execution of divine justice and the fulfillment of covenantal promises. In both cases, God prepared the way, issued clear warnings, and provided a window of mercy for those willing to respond, before moving decisively when judgment came.

## Joshua and Jesus: A Typological Foreshadowing

It is profoundly significant that the leader who brought Israel into the Promised Land bears the exact same name as the Messiah who will return to establish God's Kingdom. Joshua (the English rendering of the Hebrew *Yehoshua*, meaning "Yahweh is salvation") shares the essential name and meaning with Jesus (Greek *Iesous*, from the Hebrew *Yeshua*). This is no coincidence. It is a deliberate typological parallel: Joshua foreshadowed Jesus, the ultimate salvation-bringer and kingdom-establisher.

Originally, Joshua's name was *Hoshea* (meaning "salvation"), but Moses changed it to *Yehoshua*, adding the divine element "Yah," before the twelve spies were sent into the land (Numbers 13:16). This renaming was prophetic. It signaled that salvation would not come by human effort (*Hoshea*) but only by the power and presence of God Himself (*Yehoshua*). This perfectly aligned Joshua with the role he would later fulfill: leading God's people into their inheritance, conquering hostile territories, and executing divine justice.

In the same way, Jesus (*Yeshua*) will return to complete His own conquest, not of a strip of land, but of the entire earth. Just as Joshua led Israel across the Jordan and began with seven days of ominous silence before Jericho fell, so too will Jesus unleash judgment after a symbolic silence in heaven (Revelation 8:1). The walls of man's rebellion will crumble, not by might or power, but by the presence of the true Captain of the LORD's Armies (cf. Joshua 5:13–15).

This historical echo is not just poetic; it is prophetic. The conquest of Canaan was a shadow of the greater campaign to come.

## The Mercy Within the Mayhem

Ten years may feel like a long time, but compared to eternity, it is the blink of an eye. These are years of shaking and awakening, a final call to turn to God before the King returns.

The Jewish Ten Days of Awe teach us that judgment does not arrive without warning, and that mercy is extended before judgment is sealed. Even as the calendar moves toward atonement, the door of repentance remains open, for a time.

If you are reading this before the trumpet sounds, the message is clear: be ready. Live alert. Walk in the light.

And if you are reading it after, know this: even in the midst of judgment, God's mercy has not vanished. You are now living in the ultimate "Ten Years of Awe": a final, narrowing window where truth still calls, repentance still matters, and salvation is still possible. Time is short. Look up. Stay alert. Use the time you have to turn to God, seek the truth, and call on the name of the Lord while you still can.

Jesus is coming again, and sooner than you think.

# DEEPER DIVE 1.5. THE BLESSED HOPE

## Why Many Christians Expect Christ to Gather His Church Before the Tribulation

> *For the Lord himself will descend from heaven with a cry of command, with the voice of an archangel, and with the sound of the trumpet of God. And the dead in Christ will rise first. Then we who are alive, who are left, will be caught up together with them in the clouds to meet the Lord in the air, and so we will always be with the Lord.*
>
> — 1 THESSALONIANS 4:16–17

The Pre-Tribulation Rapture is the belief that Jesus will return to gather His Church before the seven-year Tribulation begins. This moment, often called the Blessed Hope, includes two things happening at once:

- Believers who have died are raised bodily
- Believers who are alive are instantly transformed

Together, they are "caught up" to meet the Lord in the air, and from that moment on, they are always with Him.

This event is not the same as the Second Coming. At the Rapture, Christ comes *for* His saints. At the Second Coming, He returns *with* His saints to reign on the earth.

The Pre-Tribulation view does not rest on a single isolated verse; it grows out of a comprehensive, big-picture reading of Scripture: how God deals with the Church, how prophecy unfolds, and how the end-times storyline fits together when read plainly and consistently.[1]

## Why Many Christians Expect a Pre-Tribulation Rapture

### *1. God Promises His People Deliverance from Wrath*

The Tribulation is repeatedly described as a time when God's wrath is poured out on a rebellious world (Revelation 6:16–17; 15:1). But believers are told, clearly and repeatedly, that they are not appointed to that wrath:

- Jesus "delivers us from the wrath to come" (1 Thessalonians 1:10)
- "God has not appointed us to wrath" (1 Thessalonians 5:9)
- In Revelation 3:10, Jesus promises to keep His people from the coming global trial, not merely protect them within it[2]

---

1. The Pre-Tribulation framework was systematized in the 19th century and developed extensively in the 20th century. Representative works include John F. Walvoord, *The Rapture Question*; and J. Dwight Pentecost, *Things to Come*.
2. The phrase translated "keep you from" in Revelation 3:10 (Greek: *tereso ek*) is widely discussed in scholarly literature as implying removal from the time period of testing rather than protection within it. See Robert L. Thomas, *Revelation 1–7: An Exegetical Commentary*, for a detailed linguistic discussion.

The natural reading is simple: if the Tribulation is God's judgment on the world, and the Church is promised exemption from that judgment, then the Church must be removed before it begins.

## 2. Jesus' Return Is Meant to Be Imminent

The New Testament presents Christ's return as something believers should expect at any moment. Something that could happen today, not after a checklist of prophetic events.

Christians are told to:

- Wait eagerly
- Stay alert
- Live expectantly

But if the Antichrist must first rise, global judgments must unfold, and specific signs must occur, then Christ's return would no longer be imminent. It would be predictable.

Only a Pre-Tribulation Rapture preserves the New Testament's repeated emphasis on watchfulness and expectancy.

## 3. God Has Distinct Plans for Israel and the Church

The Church is described in Scripture as a **"mystery,"** something not revealed in the Old Testament but made known after Christ's resurrection and the coming of the Holy Spirit (Ephesians 3:4–6).

The Tribulation, however, is rooted in Old Testament prophecy, especially Daniel's 70$^{th}$ week, which is explicitly concerned with Israel and Jerusalem, not the Church (Daniel 9:24–27).

Therefore, the Tribulation is not designed to purify the Church. It is explicitly about:

- Bringing Israel to repentance
- Judging a rebellious world
- Preparing the earth for the King's return

## 4. The Church Disappears from the Tribulation Storyline

The word *church* appears repeatedly in Revelation chapters 1–3. But once John is called up to heaven in Revelation 4, the Church is never mentioned again during the judgment scenes of chapters 6–18.

Instead, the focus shifts to:

- Israel
- God's judgments on the nations
- People who come to faith during the Tribulation

This silence signals a definitive shift in God's focus from the Church to Israel.

### 5. The Rapture and the Second Coming Don't Look the Same

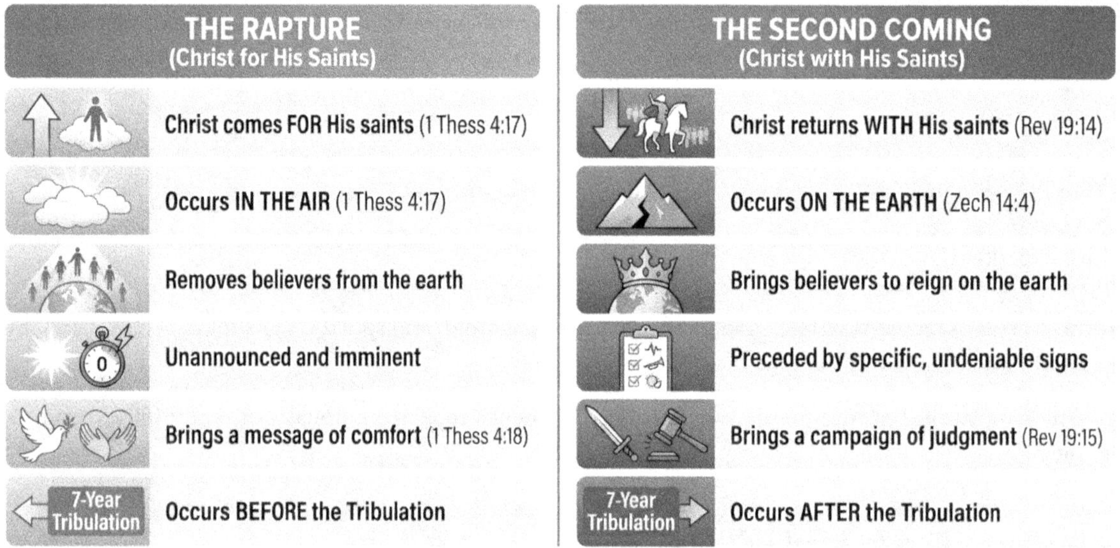


***Figure D1.5.1: Prophetic Distinctions.*** *A biblical comparison of the Rapture and the Second Coming. While often confused as a single event, their distinct characteristics, from location and timing to purpose and warning signs, reveal two entirely separate, pivotal moments on God's prophetic calendar.*

These stark contrasts dictate two entirely distinct events.

### 6. The Millennium Requires Living, Mortal Believers

Scripture teaches that Christ will reign on earth for a thousand years. During that time, people will still be born, live long lives, and die (Isaiah 65:20–23).

That raises a simple question:

If all believers are glorified and all unbelievers are judged at Christ's return, who enters the Millennium in natural bodies?

The Pre-Tribulation framework provides the definitive biblical answer: people who come to faith *during* the Tribulation survive into the Kingdom and repopulate the earth under Christ's rule.

## Final Thought

Rather than a mere escape from hardship, the Pre-Tribulation Rapture represents a deep trust in God's promises and a serious engagement with His prophetic timeline. For many believers, it best explains:

- Why Christ's return is truly a *blessed hope*
- How the Church is kept safe from the specific time of God's wrath
- The distinct prophetic destinies of Israel and the Church
- How the end-times storyline fits together without forcing pieces into place

That's why this view has remained persuasive for generations, and why many Christians continue to live with eyes lifted, hearts ready, and hope firmly fixed on Christ's return.

# DEEPER DIVE 1.6. THE TRUMPET AT THE MIDPOINT

## Understanding the Mid-Tribulation and Pre-Wrath Rapture Views

*Behold! I tell you a mystery. We shall not all sleep, but we shall all be changed, in a moment, in the twinkling of an eye,* ***at the last trumpet****. For the trumpet will sound, and the dead will be raised imperishable, and we shall be changed.*

— 1 CORINTHIANS 15:51–52

The Pre-Tribulation Rapture remains the most coherent and widely held view within futurist interpretation. Still, some Christians have proposed alternative timings, placing the Rapture during the Tribulation rather than before it.

These views are often grouped under two related positions: the Mid-Tribulation Rapture and its close cousin, the Pre-Wrath Rapture. Both attempt to align the New Testament Rapture passages with the unfolding sequence of events in the book of Revelation, especially the role of the trumpets.

### What Is the Mid-Tribulation Rapture?

The Mid-Tribulation view teaches that the Church will be raptured at the midpoint of the seven-year Tribulation, just before the most intense period of judgment known as the Great Tribulation (Matthew 24:21; Revelation 7:14).[1]

According to this view, the Church remains on earth during the rise of the Antichrist and the early judgments described by the seals and the first six trumpets. The defining moment comes in Revelation 11:15 with the sounding of the Seventh Trumpet.

Mid-Tribulationists argue that this trumpet marks the turning point. At that moment, the Church is caught up to meet Christ and removed from the earth before the final outpouring of God's wrath, which they identify with the Bowl Judgments in Revelation 15 and 16.

### A Related View: The Pre-Wrath Rapture

A more recent variation of this approach is known as the Pre-Wrath Rapture. While similar to the Mid-Tribulation view, it places the Rapture slightly later.[2]

In this view, the Church is raptured during the Tribulation, after the Antichrist is revealed but before the outpouring of God's climactic wrath, often associated with the trumpet and bowl judgments.

Pre-Wrath advocates commonly connect the Rapture to the Sixth Seal in Revelation 6:12–17. They argue that

---

1. Representative early and mid-20th-century advocates of Mid-Tribulation or closely related views include Norman B. Harrison, *The End: Rethinking the Revelation* (1941), and J. Oliver Buswell, *A Systematic Theology of the Christian Religion*, vol. 2.
2. A widely cited presentation of the Pre-Wrath Rapture view is Marvin Rosenthal, *The Pre-Wrath Rapture of the Church* (1990).

the earlier seals primarily reflect human and satanic persecution, and that God's direct, unmistakable wrath begins only afterward. Thus, they place the Church's removal at or near the cosmic disturbances of the Sixth Seal, just before the Seventh Seal introduces the trumpet judgments.

## The Key Differences in Timing

To keep these frameworks clear, here is how their timing breaks down:

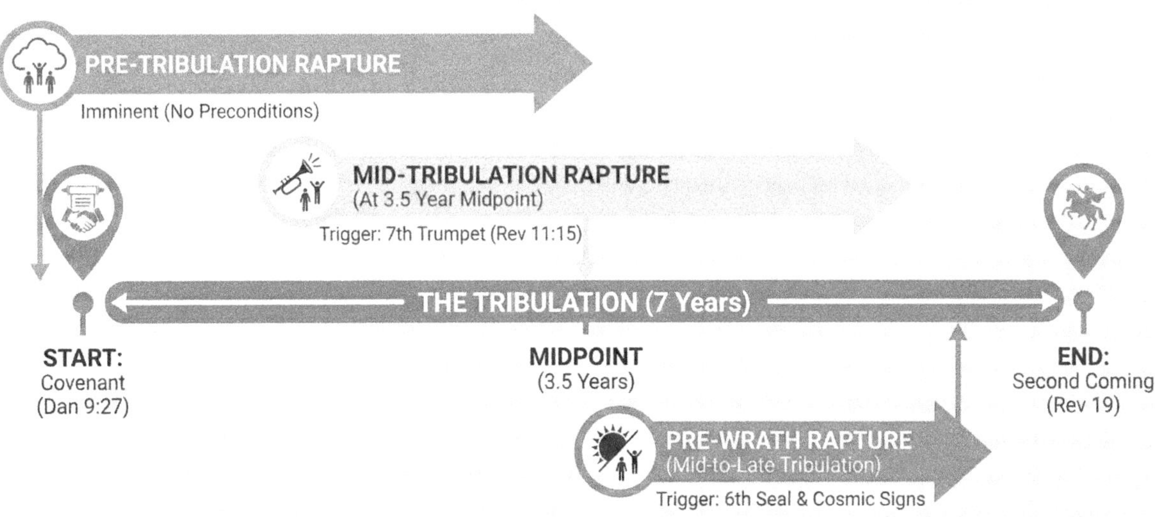


***Figure D1.6.1: The Timing Debate.*** *This chart illustrates the fundamental difference between the Pre-Tribulation view, which sees the Rapture as an imminent event preceding Daniel's 70th Week, and alternative views that locate the Church's removal inside the Tribulation based on specific Trumpet or Seal triggers.*

## The Case for a Mid-Tribulation Rapture

Those who hold this view usually point to several key ideas:

### *1. The "Last Trumpet"*

The central argument revolves around Paul's statement that the Rapture happens "at the last trumpet" (1 Corinthians 15:52), which he also calls "the trumpet of God" (1 Thessalonians 4:16). Mid-tribulationists connect this language directly to the Seventh Trumpet in Revelation 11:15, when a loud proclamation announces that the kingdom of the world has become the kingdom of Christ. From this perspective, Paul is understood to be referring to a specific, identifiable trumpet rather than using symbolic language.

### *2. Wrath of Man vs. Wrath of God*

Mid-tribulationists strongly affirm that believers are not destined for God's wrath (1 Thessalonians 5:9). However, they make a strict distinction between persecution from Satan and judgment from God. They point out that Revelation describes Satan's rage intensifying at the midpoint of the Tribulation (Revelation 12:12). God's direct wrath, they argue, becomes unmistakable later with the Bowl Judgments.

### *3. The Two Witnesses*

Revelation 11 plays a major role in this view. The Two Witnesses minister for 1,260 days, which many mid-tribulationists understand as the first half of the Tribulation. At the midpoint, the witnesses are killed, raised to life, and then called up to heaven (Revelation 11:11–12). This dramatic ascension happens immediately before the Seventh Trumpet sounds. Supporters see this moment as either a picture of the Rapture or an event that occurs alongside it.

### *4. The "Male Child" in Revelation 12*

Revelation 12 presents a symbolic scene involving a woman, a dragon, and a male child. While many identify the male Child as Christ, some mid-tribulationists suggest the Child represents the Church. The Child is "caught up" to God using the same Greek verb (*harpazo*) found in the Rapture passage of 1 Thessalonians 4:17. After this event, the Woman (Israel) flees into the wilderness for 1,260 days.

## The Biblical Challenges to This View

Despite its internal logic, the Mid-Tribulation view faces several structural challenges:

- **The "Last Trumpet" Question:** Paul's "last trumpet" is deeply rooted in Jewish and military imagery rather than tied to Revelation's sequential judgment trumpets. The distinctions between these two trumpet passages are examined in detail in *Deeper Dive 6.4. The Tale of Two Trumpets*.
- **Loss of Imminence:** This view requires certain events, especially the revelation of the Antichrist, to happen before the Rapture. This fundamentally nullifies the New Testament expectation that Christ could return at any moment.
- **The Nature of the Seals:** Pre-Tribulationists point out that the Lamb opens the seals (Revelation 6:1), demonstrating that God's judgment begins immediately, not later.
- **Revelation 12 Timing:** Even if the male child is understood to represent the Church, the passage does not require the Church's removal and Israel's flight into the wilderness to occur simultaneously. It is entirely consistent to read Revelation 12:5–6 as involving a prophetic gap, invalidating it as a decisive marker for a Mid-Tribulation Rapture.

## Final Perspective

The Mid-Tribulation and Pre-Wrath views offer a thoughtful attempt to align the Rapture with the Trumpet Judgments of Revelation and to define more precisely when God's wrath begins.

These views represent serious efforts to interpret difficult passages, but they categorically fail to preserve imminence. They also depend on delaying the start of God's wrath until later in the Tribulation. Ultimately, the text of Revelation is clear: the Seals are opened by the Lamb (Revelation 6:1), and the world cries out that the "wrath of the Lamb" has come (Revelation 6:16–17). Since the wrath begins with the Seals, the Church, promised deliverance from wrath, must be removed before the First Seal is broken.

# DEEPER DIVE 1.7. AFTER THE STORM

## Evaluating the Post-Tribulation Rapture View

*Immediately after the tribulation of those days the sun will be darkened... Then will appear in heaven the sign of the Son of Man... And he will send out his angels with a loud trumpet call, and they will gather his elect from the four winds, from one end of heaven to the other.*

— MATTHEW 24:29–31

The Post-Tribulation Rapture view teaches that the Church will remain on earth through the entire seven-year Tribulation and will be gathered to Christ at its very end, at the exact moment of His return to reign.

In this model, the Rapture and the Second Coming occur in immediate succession. Rather than being separated by a period of years, they form a single, continuous event: believers rise to meet Christ in the air and immediately return with Him as He establishes His earthly kingdom.

This view has a long history and has been held by respected teachers throughout the centuries. It offers a straightforward timeline that appeals to many for its historical simplicity.

However, when measured against the specific promises God has made to His Church, this view creates serious theological inconsistencies. The difficulty is not merely about timing. It is about whether the New Testament's foundational assurances to believers are being handled consistently.

## The Post-Tribulation View in Brief

Those who hold this view argue that believers should expect to remain on earth throughout the entire Tribulation. The Church, they point out, has always faced hardship, and the final generation should expect no exception.

Their case rests heavily on a plain reading of Matthew 24:29–31, where Jesus speaks of a gathering of the elect "after the tribulation," as well as on parables like the wheat and the tares in Matthew 13. They also point to early Christian leaders who prepared believers to face the Antichrist as historical evidence that enduring the Tribulation was the Church's original expectation.[1]

1. Well-known writers who hold the Post-Tribulation position include George Eldon Ladd, *The Blessed Hope*; Robert H. Gundry, *The Church and the Tribulation*; and Douglas J. Moo, who presents the view in *Three Views on the Rapture*.

Supporters of the view also point to early Church Fathers such as Irenaeus and Tertullian, who prepared their flocks to face the Antichrist and expected believers to endure intense end-times persecution. These sources are often cited to show that the position has thoughtful and historically rooted advocates, even though many readers ultimately conclude that it does not align with the broader teaching of the New Testament.

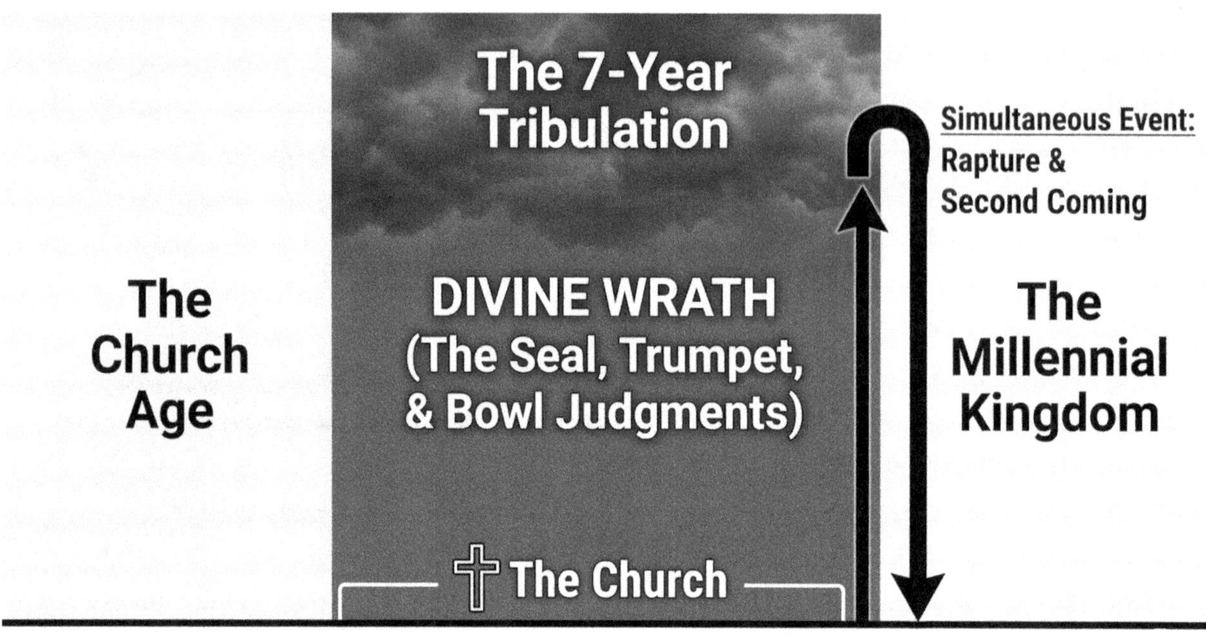


***Figure D1.7.1: The Post-Tribulation Timeline.*** *By placing the Rapture and the Second Coming at the exact same moment, this model requires the Church to endure the entirety of the seven-year Tribulation. As the timeline illustrates, this framework forces the Bride of Christ to live through the very outpouring of divine wrath she was promised deliverance from.*

## Where the Post-Tribulation View Struggles

While the Post-Tribulation framework is internally consistent, it breaks down entirely when placed alongside the wider teaching of the New Testament.

### *1. Deliverance from God's Wrath*

The New Testament repeatedly assures believers that they are not appointed to God's wrath.

- Jesus "delivers us from the wrath to come" (1 Thessalonians 1:10).
- God has not appointed His people to wrath (1 Thessalonians 5:9).

For the Post-Tribulation view to function, "wrath" must be limited strictly to final judgment in hell. Yet Revelation explicitly uses the phrase "the wrath of God" to describe the Bowl Judgments poured out on the earth (Revelation 16:1). While proponents argue the Church is preserved *spiritually* through these judgments, Revelation portrays the Bowl Judgments as inescapable *physical* calamities.

By placing the Church on earth while the seas turn to blood and the sun scorches mankind, the Post-Tribulation view forces believers to live under the very wrath they were promised deliverance from. This creates a theological contradiction: the Bride is promised rescue, yet she is left in the center of a global outpouring of divine judgment.

## 2. Protected Israel, Exposed Church?

An even deeper problem emerges when contrasting Scripture's descriptions of divine protection during the Tribulation.

Israel, God's Old Covenant people, is pictured in Revelation 12 as the Woman who flees into the wilderness, where she is supernaturally nourished and protected for 1,260 days. The Church, under the Post-Tribulation model, remains under the absolute authority of the Antichrist, who is permitted to wage war against the saints and overcome them (Revelation 13:7).

This results in a striking, illogical reversal. It dictates a reality where God shelters Israel under the Old Covenant while leaving the New Covenant Bride exposed to the worst outpouring of satanic violence in human history. Scripture teaches that the Church stands in a better covenant, established on better promises (Hebrews 8:6). Yet under this view, the New Covenant offers drastically less protection than the Old.

This contradiction is magnified in light of Christ's promise to keep His faithful ones "from the hour of trial" that is coming upon the whole world (Revelation 3:10).

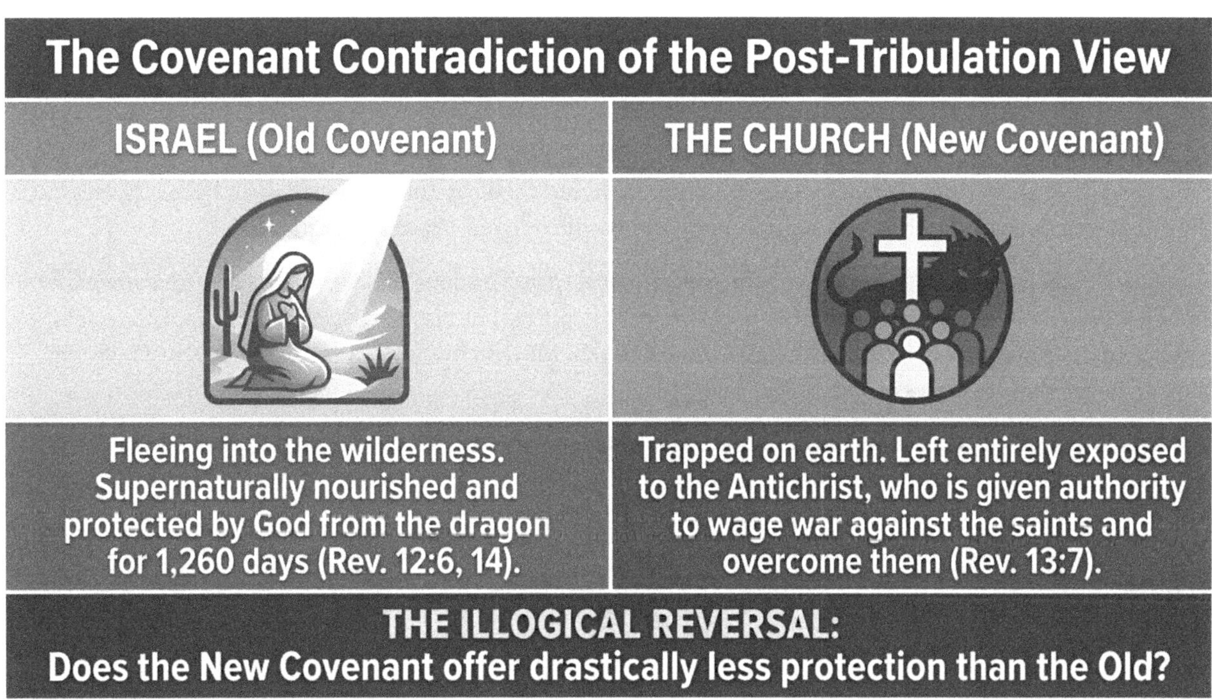


***Figure D1.7.2:*** *The Covenant Contradiction. The Post-Tribulation model dictates a reality where God supernaturally shelters Israel under the Old Covenant, while leaving the New Covenant Church entirely exposed to the wrath of the Antichrist. This framework forces the New Covenant to provide drastically less security than the Old.*

## 3. What Does It Mean to "Meet" the Lord?

Post-tribulationists often appeal to 1 Thessalonians 4:17, where believers are said to "meet" the Lord in the air. The Greek word behind "meet" is *apantesis*. While this term can describe citizens going out to escort a visiting king back into a city, the word itself does not demand that specific outcome.

At its most basic level, *apantesis* simply means a meeting. The direction the group travels afterward depends entirely on the purpose of the One being met.

If Christ is returning as a conquering Judge, He descends to the earth. But if He is coming as a Bridegroom to receive His people, as He promised in John 14:3, then the meeting naturally leads *away* from the earth to the place He has prepared. The word allows for either scenario, it fails as definitive proof for a Post-Tribulation return.

### *4. Who Is Matthew 24 Addressing?*

Matthew 24 is the cornerstone passage for the Post-Tribulation view. But context matters. Jesus is answering His disciples' specific questions about the Temple, Jerusalem, and the sign of His coming (Matthew 24:1–3), all themes deeply rooted in Israel's prophetic storyline. In the Old Testament, "my elect" is repeatedly used as a covenant designation for Israel (Isaiah 45:4; 65:9).

In that precise Jewish setting, the gathering "from the four winds" after the cosmic signs (Matthew 24:29–31) directly aligns with the prophetic picture of Israel's end-time regathering at the Messiah's visible return (Deuteronomy 30:3–4; Isaiah 11:11–12). It does not fit Paul's later "mystery" event in which the Church is caught up to meet the Lord in the air (1 Thessalonians 4:16–17).

Read contextually, Matthew 24 describes the regathering of a surviving Jewish remnant at the dawn of the Millennial Kingdom, not a proof text for the timing of the Church's Rapture.

## In Summary

The Post-Tribulation view offers a tough, endurance-centered theology that resonates with believers who emphasize faithfulness under pressure. Its clarity and simplicity are a large part of its appeal.

Yet that simplicity comes at a remarkably high theological cost. To adopt this view, one must fundamentally redefine God's wrath, treat divine protection as primarily spiritual rather than physical, and apply passages strictly rooted in Israel's tribulation directly to the Church. Most significantly, it results in a New Covenant that actually provides far less security than the Old.

For these reasons, the Post-Tribulation framework ultimately undermines the "blessed hope" (Titus 2:13). It transforms the Rapture from a promise of imminent rescue into a mandate for mere survival, requiring the Church to endure the darkest hour of human history. Consequently, despite its historical popularity, it proves to be the least systematically consistent of the Rapture theories when measured against the full counsel of Scripture.

# DEEPER DIVE 1.8. LEFT BEHIND! AGAIN?

## The Partial Rapture Theory Examined

*There is therefore now no condemnation for those who are in Christ Jesus.*

— ROMANS 8:1

Most Christians who hold to a future Rapture expect a single, sweeping event in which all believers, living and dead, are caught up together to meet the Lord.

A much smaller and far more controversial view, known as the Partial Rapture Theory, teaches something entirely different. According to this view, the Rapture does not happen all at once, and it does not include all believers.

Instead, the Church is taken in stages. Some believers are raptured early as a reward for faithfulness. Others are left behind to endure part or all of the Tribulation and are only taken later.

## What Is the Partial Rapture Theory?

At its core, the Partial Rapture Theory teaches that participation in the Rapture is conditional.[1]

Salvation remains by grace through faith alone, but being taken in the Rapture, especially in a Pre-Tribulation Rapture, is reduced to a reward for spiritual maturity, watchfulness, and obedience.

Under this view:

- Faithful, alert believers are taken first
- Unwatchful or "carnal" believers are left behind
- Those left behind are purified through severe suffering
- They are later raptured or resurrected near the end of the Tribulation or at Christ's return

In other words, the Rapture is no longer a promise to the whole Church.

It becomes a prize to be earned.

## The Mechanics of the Theory

Supporters of the Partial Rapture idea divide the event into two distinct phases.

1. Early advocates of the Partial Rapture view include Robert Govett, *Entrance into the Kingdom, and* G. H. Lang, *Firstfruits and Harvest*. These writers taught that only faithful believers would be taken in the first Rapture, while others would be left behind for purification.

### 1. The First Rapture ("Firstfruits")

Before the Tribulation begins, only the most faithful and watchful believers are taken.

This group is said to include those who are "worthy to escape" (Luke 21:36).

Their early removal is treated as a reward for spiritual alertness and obedience.

### 2. The Later Harvest

Other believers, often described as unwatchful, worldly, or spiritually immature, are left behind.

They must endure part or all of the Tribulation.

Their suffering is viewed as a refining process that purifies their faith.

These believers are then taken later, either during the Tribulation or at the Second Coming.

***Figure D1.8.1: A Divided Body.*** *The Partial Rapture Theory splits the Church into two distinct tiers. It transforms the Rapture from a shared promise of grace into a conditional reward based on spiritual performance, leaving the "unwatchful" to face the horrors of the Tribulation.*

Although rarely taught today in mainstream evangelical churches, this concept still surfaces in certain independent, charismatic, and "overcomer" teaching circles.

## The Main Biblical Arguments Used

Supporters of the view usually point to two key passages.

## 1. "Counted Worthy to Escape" (Luke 21:36 NKJV)

> *"Watch therefore, and pray always that you may be counted worthy to escape all these things that will come to pass ..."*[2]

They argue that because not everyone escapes, and only those "counted worthy" are taken, the Rapture must be selective. In this reading, watchfulness becomes a strict condition for participation in the Rapture.

However, the broader context of Luke 21 is a warning about coming judgment and a call for endurance, not a detailed description of the Church's removal. The passage demands readiness; it does not teach a two-tier Rapture in which only top-tier Christians are rescued.

## 2. "The Out-Resurrection" (Philippians 3:11 NKJV)

> *If, by any means, I may attain to the resurrection from the dead.*

Paul uses a rare Greek word here: *exanastasis* ("out-resurrection").[3] Supporters of Partial Rapture theory argue that:

- This refers to a special resurrection for especially faithful believers
- Paul's striving shows it is a reward to be attained
- Not all believers automatically participate

Yet the context of Philippians 3 makes it undeniably clear that Paul is not expressing doubt about whether he will be raised. Rather, he is pressing forward in spiritual maturity and longing to experience the full victory of resurrection life.

Paul is contrasting the resurrection of the righteous with the resurrection of the wicked, not dividing Christians into two groups, those taken early and those left behind.

# Why This View Fails Biblically

The Partial Rapture Theory completely breaks down under biblical scrutiny for three critical reasons:

## 1. It Divides the Body of Christ

Scripture teaches that all believers are united into **one body**.

> *For in one Spirit we were all baptized into one body ...*
>
> — 1 CORINTHIANS 12:13

The Partial Rapture creates two classes of Christians:

2. NKJV wording is used here because it reflects the phrasing most commonly cited by Partial Rapture proponents.

3. Supporters often point to Paul's use of the word *exanastasis* ("out-resurrection") in Philippians 3:11. A commonly cited discussion appears in Kenneth Wuest's word studies. Most Greek scholars, however, do not agree that this word teaches a selective resurrection for only some believers.

- those "worthy" enough to be taken
- those left behind to suffer

That turns the Rapture into a spiritual caste system inside the Church.

### *2. It Turns Grace into Merit*

The New Testament presents the Rapture as a promise, not a prize.

The Partial Rapture makes participation depend on performance. It ignores the biblical truth that our worthiness comes from Christ alone. Believers are delivered not because of spiritual achievement, but because they are clothed in the righteousness of Jesus (2 Corinthians 5:21).

This fundamentally shifts the Rapture from a guarantee of grace to a wage earned by works. It confuses sanctification (spiritual growth) with justification (our standing before God).

### *3. It Contradicts the Plain Rapture Passages*

The New Testament describes the Rapture as a single, shared transformation of the whole Church.

Paul writes:

> ... *We shall not all sleep, but we shall all be changed, in a moment, in the twinkling of an eye ...*
>
> — 1 CORINTHIANS 15:51–52

And again:

> *Then we who are alive, who are left, will be caught up together with them ...*
>
> — 1 THESSALONIANS 4:17

No distinctions are made.

No faithful group.

No unfaithful group.

No first tier and second tier.

Just: **all** and **together**.

The Partial Rapture theory requires inserting divisions that the text itself never makes.

## A Call to Watchfulness, Without Rewriting the Rapture

To its credit, the Partial Rapture view highlights something that is deeply biblical: Watchfulness matters.

Jesus repeatedly calls His people to stay alert and ready (Matthew 24:42–44; Luke 12:35–40). But at its core, the Partial Rapture Theory blurs a critical distinction, confusing the free gift of salvation with the earning of heavenly rewards.

Scripture never says that only the "best" Christians get taken in the Rapture. The Rapture is a gift of grace. However, the Bible is equally clear that our conduct as believers has eternal consequences. Jesus explicitly declared, "Behold, I am coming quickly, and My reward *is* with Me, to reward each one as his work deserves." (Revelation 22:12 NASB).

This is where the Apostle Paul's warning in 1 Corinthians 3:11–15 comes into sharp focus. Following the Rapture, all believers will stand before the Judgment Seat of Christ (the Bema Seat) to have their earthly works tested by fire.

- Works done in faith and obedience (gold, silver, precious stones) will survive the flames and result in eternal rewards.
- Works done in the flesh or spiritual apathy (wood, hay, straw) will be completely consumed.

Paul issues a sobering reality check regarding the unwatchful or carnal believer: "If anyone's work is burned up, he will suffer loss, though he himself will be saved, but only as through fire" (1 Corinthians 3:15).

The unfaithful Christian is not left behind to face the Antichrist. They are raptured, but they arrive in heaven empty-handed. They are saved, but they merely "scrape through" the gates smelling like smoke, forfeiting the crowns and rewards they could have laid at the Bridegroom's feet.

Readiness is about faithful living so that we might hear "Well done, good and faithful servant." It is not about earning your seat on the rescue boat.

## The Security of the Bride

The Partial Rapture Theory attempts to motivate holiness by attaching it to Rapture timing.

But in doing so, it changes the nature of the Rapture itself.

It turns a shared promise into a selective reward.

It divides the Body of Christ.

And it quietly undermines grace.

For these reasons, most believers reject this view while still affirming the very thing it gets right:

Live ready.

Walk faithfully.

Love Christ deeply.

Not because you are afraid of being left behind.

But because your Bridegroom is coming quickly.

# HINTS & POSSIBILITIES 2.1. A TALE OF TWO MESSIAHS

## Could Islamic and Biblical End-Times Be a Strategic Inversion?

*And I saw a beast rising out of the sea ...*

— REVELATION 13:1

*And I saw another beast coming up out of the land, and it had two horns, like a lamb, and it was speaking as a dragon,*

— REVELATION 13:11 YLT

A compelling, albeit controversial, prophetic framework reveals that Islamic and Christian end-time expectations do not merely differ; they directly mirror and invert one another. In this view, the central figures of Islamic eschatology align uncannily with the Bible's warnings about the Antichrist and the False Prophet.

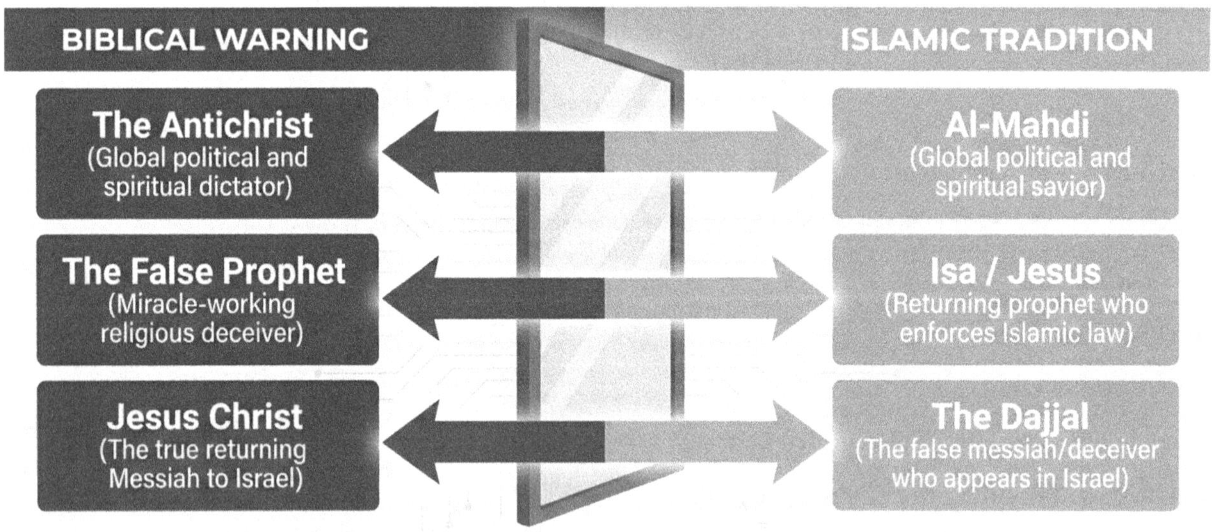


***Figure H2.1.1: A Mirror of Deception.*** *The coming delusion is a highly structured inversion of prophecy. In this paradigm, the true Christ is cast as the ultimate enemy, and the ultimate deceiver is welcomed as the world's savior.*

## The Prophets of the Inversion

Authoritative Islamic traditions preserved in the Sahih collections describe the rise of *al-Mahdi*, a descendant of Muhammad who appears during global upheaval to unite the Muslim world and establish justice. Accompanying him is *Isa* (Jesus), the son of Mary. But this Isa does not return to affirm the Gospel. He returns as a Muslim to break the cross, kill the swine, and abolish the *jizya*,[1] effectively ending Christianity and enforcing Islam as the final religious authority.[2]

Together, they wage war against the *Dajjal*, Islam's "False Messiah," a miracle-working figure who claims divinity and leads the world astray.[3]

### *The Strategic Inversion*

Here is the chilling, strategic inversion this prophetic framework exposes:[4]

| The Biblical Warning | The Islamic Expectation | The Inverted Role |
|---|---|---|
| **The Antichrist:** A political/spiritual leader who unifies the world, brokers peace, and demands submission. | **Al-Mahdi:** The prophesied savior of Islam who unites the world and establishes global Islamic rule. | Al-Mahdi fulfills the exact role of the biblical **Antichrist**. |
| **The False Prophet:** A miracle worker who points the world to the Antichrist and deceives the earth. | **Isa (Jesus):** Returns to destroy Christianity, point the world to the Mahdi, and enforce Islamic law. | Isa mirrors the exact profile of the biblical **False Prophet**. |
| **Jesus Christ:** The true Messiah who returns to Israel, destroys the Antichrist, and claims divine authority. | **The Dajjal:** The "Deceiver" who appears in Israel, claims divinity, and is linked to the Jewish people.[4] | The Dajjal acts as the exact inverted profile of the returning **Jesus Christ**. |

***Table H2.1.1. The Strategic Inversion.*** *A direct comparison reveals a chilling reality. The exact figures the Bible warns will deceive the world strikingly parallel the saviors anticipated by Islamic eschatology, creating a masterful counterfeit narrative.*

1. *Jizya* is a tribute historically required from non-Muslims living under Islamic rule in exchange for protection and permission to practice their religion. However, classical Islamic scholarship teaches that the end times alter this contract. When *Isa* returns, he will "abolish" the *jizya* by refusing to accept it. This signifies the end of toleration for other faiths; the option to pay for protection is removed, leaving only two alternatives: conversion to Islam or death.
2. See *Sahih Muslim*, *Kitab al-Iman* and *Kitab al-Fitan wa Ashrat al-Sa'ah* (Book of Tribulations and Signs of the Hour), for authoritative traditions on the return of *Isa ibn Maryam*.
3. Timothy Furnish, *Holiest Wars* (Praeger, 2005), for a scholarly overview of Islamic eschatology, including *Mahdism* and expectations surrounding the *Dajjal*.
4. Joel Richardson, *The Islamic Antichrist* (WND Books, 2009), chap. 9, "Comparing the Biblical Jesus and the *Dajjal*."

## Two Beasts, Two Origins

Revelation itself exposes the origin of this final deception. The first Beast rises from the sea, a biblical symbol for the Gentile nations (Daniel 7:2–3; Isaiah 17:12), pointing to a Gentile Antichrist who emerges from the world of political empire. He comes from the restless mass of the nations, empowered to seize global authority and demand worship.

But the second Beast rises not from the sea, but from the earth, or more literally, from "the land."[5] This is a deliberate contrast. In biblical prophecy, the Greek word *ge* (earth/land) is frequently used to designate the specific Land of Israel. The False Prophet does not arise from the Gentile world system, but from the land of Israel itself.

His role is therefore uniquely potent. He is not merely a global religious spokesman. He is a Jewish deceiver, positioned to lead his own people into embracing the counterfeit messiah. Satan's final strategy strikes from both directions: political domination from the nations, and spiritual betrayal from within the covenant land.

## A Blueprint for Delusion

In this upside-down narrative, the true Christ is cast as the villain, while a false messiah and a deceptive prophet appear as saviors.

That is not a coincidence.

That is a **counterfeit**.

It is exactly the kind of strategic inversion Scripture warns us to expect. A deception so persuasive it could "deceive, if possible, even the elect" (Matthew 24:24).

> *And no wonder, for even Satan disguises himself as an angel of light.*
>
> — 2 CORINTHIANS 11:14

## A Necessary Caution

This framework does not judge the hearts or intentions of individual Muslims.

It analyzes texts, not people.

Most Muslims have never closely studied these specific eschatological traditions just as many Christians have never studied their own prophetic Scriptures in depth.

But the warning is spiritual, not political.

When global figures arise who:

- perform signs and wonders
- preach peace and unity
- claim divine authority
- and invoke the name of "Jesus"

5. Young's Literal Translation

... will the world discern **which Jesus** they are following?

That question will not be academic.

Your answer will be consequential for all eternity.

# DEEPER DIVE 3.1. THE COSMIC HINGE

## Why the Sixth Seal Marks the Midpoint

> *I looked when He opened the sixth seal, and behold, there was a great earthquake; and the sun became black as sackcloth of hair, and the moon became like blood.*
>
> — REVELATION 6:12 NKJV

One event stands as the great pivot point in prophecy: the Sixth Seal. Does it occur late in the Tribulation, or does it mark the decisive turning point?

The weight of scriptural evidence leaves little doubt. The Sixth Seal belongs at the midpoint, or immediately after, as the cosmic fanfare that launches the Great Tribulation. It is the divine response to the Antichrist's ultimate betrayal and the "Cosmic Curtain-Raiser" for the Time of Jacob's Trouble.

## The Prophetic Anchor: Joel's "Before" Sign

The timing is anchored by a direct link between prophecy and fulfillment. Centuries before John's vision, Joel delivered a celestial marker for the onset of the "great and terrible" escalation:

> *The sun shall be turned into darkness, and the moon into blood, before the great and terrible day of the LORD come.*[1]
>
> —JOEL 2:31 KJV

Revelation 6:12–13 records the exact fulfillment: "... the sun became black as sackcloth of hair, and the moon became like blood." By connecting these passages, the timeline crystallizes. Since Joel states these signs occur before the "great and terrible" Day of the LORD, the Sixth Seal acts as the cosmic pivot. It signals that the "beginning of sorrows" (the first half) is ending and the "Great Tribulation" (the intensified wrath of the second half) is about to begin.

While the Day of the LORD encompasses the entire seven-year period, the Sixth Seal announces its most dreadful phase. It declares that the era of relative restraint has ended, and that the Day of the LORD has entered its "great and terrible" fullness.

## The Logic of the Sequence

This timing creates a powerful, cause-and-effect narrative centered on the midpoint:

1. The KJV rendering "great and terrible" reflects the Hebrew sense of dread-filled awe and judgment. Many modern translations render the phrase "great and awesome," but the prophetic emphasis is the same: the climactic fullness of the Day of the LORD.

1. **The Cause (Midpoint):** The Antichrist commits the Abomination of Desolation, breaking his covenant and declaring himself God in the Temple (Daniel 9:27; Matthew 24:15).
2. **The Reaction (Sixth Seal):** Heaven responds instantly. The earth shakes, the sun is darkened, and the moon turns to blood, fulfilling Joel 2:31. This is God's unmistakable announcement that the Day of the LORD has entered its great and terrible phase.
3. **The Consequence (The Great Tribulation):** Humanity recognizes the shift, crying, "The great day of His wrath has come!" (Revelation 6:17). The Trumpet Judgments then follow, unfolding the intensified wrath that the Sixth Seal announced.

## Addressing the Objection: What About Matthew 24:29?

A common challenge to this view comes from Jesus' words in Matthew 24:29: "Immediately **after** the tribulation of those days the sun will be darkened ..."

Critics use this verse to push the cosmic signs of the Sixth Seal to the very end of the seven years. However, this assumption relies on the flawed premise that cosmic darkness occurs only once. Scripture proves otherwise.[2]

## The Pattern of "Bookend Darkness"

The "Day of the LORD" is consistently described in the Old Testament as a period of persistent darkness and gloom (Joel 2:2; Zephaniah 1:15). It is not a single moment, but a protracted era. Matthew 24:29 focuses on the culmination of the darkness, the final blackout before the sudden flash of Christ's return, whereas Revelation 6 focuses on the initial plunge into that darkness. Within this period, Scripture presents opening and closing bookends:

- **The Opening Bookend (Sixth Seal):** The lights dim at the midpoint to signal the threshold into the Day of the LORD's great and terrible phase (fulfilling Joel 2:31).
- **Persistent Darkness:** The darkness continues and intensifies throughout the second half. The Fourth Trumpet darkens a third of the heavenly bodies (Revelation 8:12), and the Fifth Bowl plunges the Beast's kingdom into total, painful darkness (Revelation 16:10).
- **The Closing Bookend (Matthew 24:29):** The period concludes with a final, complete blackout immediately before Christ's glorious return illuminates the sky.

2. For more details, see *Deeper Dive 10.3. Cosmic Context.*

***Figure D3.1.1: Bookend Darkness.*** *A visual timeline demonstrating how the celestial signs of the Sixth Seal act as the opening curtain for the final 3½ years, ending in absolute darkness just before the Second Coming.*

## The Verdict on the Sixth Seal

Therefore, the Sixth Seal does not contradict Matthew 24:29; it initiates the darkness that Matthew 24:29 sees completed. The entire second half unfolds under a broken sky, as the Day of the LORD reaches its climactic fullness, ushered in at the Sixth Seal and culminating at Armageddon with the return of the King.

# DEEPER DIVE 5.1. THE GOLDEN KEY: META TAUTA

## Unlocking the Divine Structure of Revelation

> *Write the things which you have seen, and the things which are, and the things which will take place after this.*
>
> — REVELATION 1:19 NKJV

Is the Book of Revelation a chaotic collage of visions, or a carefully ordered revelation governed by divine design?

The answer lies in the Greek grammar of a single command given by the risen Christ.

In Revelation 1:19, Jesus provides John with a threefold directive that functions as the structural key to the entire book:

1. **"The things which you have seen"**: the inaugural vision of the glorified Christ (Revelation 1).
2. **"The things which are"**: the present condition of the churches (Revelation 2–3).
3. **"The things which will take place after this"**: events that follow the present order (Revelation 4–22).

The crucial phrase "after this" translates the Greek *meta tauta*. This expression is more than a literary transition; it is a chronological marker, signaling movement beyond the present state into what follows it.

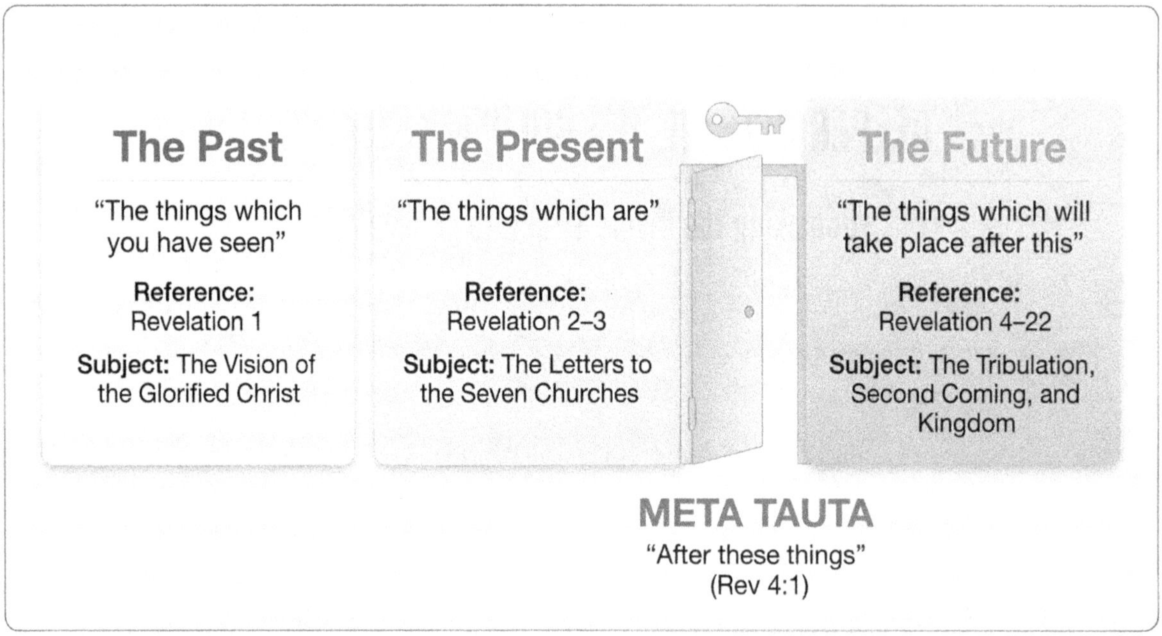

**The Past**
"The things which you have seen"
**Reference:** Revelation 1
**Subject:** The Vision of the Glorified Christ

**The Present**
"The things which are"
**Reference:** Revelation 2–3
**Subject:** The Letters to the Seven Churches

**The Future**
"The things which will take place after this"
**Reference:** Revelation 4–22
**Subject:** The Tribulation, Second Coming, and Kingdom

**META TAUTA**
"After these things"
(Rev 4:1)

***Figure D5.1.1: The Divine Outline of Revelation.*** *Christ provides the structural key to the entire book in Revelation 1:19. The chronological pivot, marked by the Greek* meta tauta *("after these things"), physically separates the present age of the seven churches (Revelation 2–3) from the future events of the Tribulation and Second Coming (Revelation 4–22).*

Significantly, this structural function is acknowledged even by non-futurist scholarship. The respected Greek scholar Henry B. Swete, though interpreting Revelation largely in relation to early imperial history, nonetheless affirms that the grammar of Revelation 1:19 establishes the book's overall outline. He acknowledges that the three clauses correspond to the book's three major divisions, identifying chapter 1, chapters 2–3, and chapters 4–22 as distinct sections.[1]

This grammatical key reappears with deliberate force in Revelation 4:1, where *meta tauta* occurs twice in rapid succession:

> *After these things [*meta tauta*] I looked, and behold, a door standing open in heaven ... "Come up here, and I will show you what must take place after this [*meta tauta*]."*

The repetition is rare and forms a rhetorical bracket, marking a decisive transition. As Swete himself observes, this formula introduces "a new vision of special importance" and anticipates "a future which is yet to find its accomplishment."[2] The visions that follow are no longer focused on the present condition of the churches but shift decisively into the prophetic future.

Taken together, Revelation 1:19 and 4:1 reveal a book governed by intentional design. The "things which are" give way to the "things which must take place after these things." By following this divinely placed marker, *meta tauta*, we discover that Revelation is not a random sequence of symbols but a structured disclosure of history moving forward toward God's appointed consummation.

1. Henry B. Swete, *The Apocalypse of St John* (London: Macmillan, 1906), 20–21.
2. Ibid., 65–66.

# DEEPER DIVE 5.2. THE 24 ELDERS: THE RAPTURED CHURCH IN HEAVEN

## Why Revelation 4 Quietly Confirms a Pre-Tribulation Rapture

*Around the throne were twenty-four thrones, and seated on the thrones were twenty-four elders, clothed in white garments, with golden crowns on their heads.*

— REVELATION 4:4

One of the strongest biblical support for a Pre-Tribulation Rapture is concealed within the familiar: the 24 elders seated around God's throne in Revelation 4.

The context here is crucial. In Revelation 4:1, John hears a call "like a trumpet" saying, "Come up here." The Greek word used is *phōnē*. While often translated "voice," its basic meaning is simply "sound" or "tone." John first hears what resembles a trumpet blast, and only then recognizes it as intelligible speech calling him heavenward. In other words, this is not merely a sound or tone, but a divine summons with the unmistakable character of a trumpet, the very imagery Paul uses to describe the Rapture (cf. 1 Thessalonians 4:16; 1 Corinthians 15:52).

This sequence has long been understood by futurist interpreters as both the book's structural hinge and a symbolic picture of the Rapture of the Church. Immediately following this ascent, John is shown a heavenly scene populated by these 24 elders, already seated, already crowned, and already worshiping.

From this moment until Christ's return, the Church is no longer mentioned on earth as an identified body. Instead, we repeatedly encounter this representative group in heaven.

### Who Are the 24 Elders?

While some interpreters identify the elders as angelic beings or a composite of Old Testament saints, these views fail to account for both the elders' physical rewards and the strict biblical timeline.

A popular but problematic theory suggests the 24 elders represent a composite group: the 12 Patriarchs of Israel and the 12 Apostles of the Church. While mathematically appealing, this view creates a massive chronological contradiction. According to Daniel 12:1–2 and Revelation 20:4, Old Testament saints are not resurrected until the very end of the seven-year Tribulation, immediately prior to the Millennial Kingdom.

Because their bodily resurrection has not yet occurred, the patriarchs of Israel cannot be physically present in heaven, seated on thrones, and wearing crowns of victory in Revelation 4. The Church, however, has just been resurrected and caught up at the Pre-Tribulation Rapture. This timeline necessitates that the 24 elders exclusively represent the raptured, glorified Church.

Furthermore, the identity of the 24 elders is not arbitrary. The number 24 holds unique significance in Scripture, appearing prominently in 1 Chronicles 24, where King David organized the Levitical priesthood into 24 courses, each with a chief leader. These 24 leaders functioned as representatives of the entire priesthood before God.

This Old Testament structure provides a perfect prophetic parallel. Just as those 24 leaders represented Israel's priestly order under the Old Covenant, the 24 elders function as the glorified representatives of the New Testament's "royal priesthood," the Church (1 Peter 2:9). Their presence fulfills the promise that Christ "has made us kings and priests to His God and Father" (Revelation 1:6).[1]

## Key Identifiers: Robes, Crowns, Thrones

Revelation 4:4 gives three specific markers of these elders:

- **Clothed in white robes**: a symbol of righteousness consistently associated with the redeemed Church (cf. Revelation 3:5; 19:8).
- **Wearing crowns of gold**: these are *stephanos* crowns (victory wreaths), promised as rewards to faithful believers (cf. Revelation 2:10; 3:11).
- **Seated on thrones**: echoing Christ's promise in Revelation 3:21 that those who overcome will sit with Him on His throne. Believers are said to reign with Christ (2 Timothy 2:12).

***Figure D5.2.1: The Raptured Church in Glory.*** *The twenty-four elders, crowned and enthroned around the Almighty, represent the glorified Church. Their presence in heaven before the opening of the seven-sealed scroll stands as compelling confirmation of a Pre-Tribulation Rapture.*

While angels are sometimes depicted in white, the specific combination of sitting on thrones and wearing victory crowns is never applied to angels in Scripture. These are uniquely human and distinctly Church-related rewards.

1. Many respected prophecy scholars have long taught that the 24 elders represent the Church in heaven. This view is presented in John F. Walvoord's *The Revelation of Jesus Christ* and J. Dwight Pentecost's *Things to Come*, among others.

## Harps and Golden Bowls: Worship and Intercession

Revelation 5 adds two more striking details:

> *And when he had taken the scroll, the four living creatures and the twenty-four elders fell down before the Lamb, each holding a **harp**, and **golden bowls full of incense**, which are the prayers of the saints.*
>
> — REVELATION 5:8

- The **harps** speak of worship: echoing the role of Levitical musicians in temple service (cf. 1 Chronicles 25). This shows that the Church's priestly function in heaven is not passive; it is active and musical, offering heartfelt praise to the Lamb.
- The **golden bowls of incense** symbolize intercession: The text explicitly says these contain "the prayers of the saints." This aligns with the Church's priestly calling to intercede (cf. Romans 8:26–27; 1 Timothy 2:1). It mirrors the Old Testament priests who burned incense as a symbolic offering of prayer (cf. Psalm 141:2).

Together, these items confirm that the 24 elders are acting in a priestly role on behalf of the broader redeemed community.

## The Song of the Redeemed

One of the clearest clues is the song the elders sing in Revelation 5:9–10 (NKJV):[2]

> *"You are worthy to take the scroll, and to open its seals; for You were slain, and have redeemed us to God by Your blood out of every tribe and tongue and people and nation, and have made us kings and priests to our God; and we shall reign on the earth."*

This is not angelic language. It is the language of redemption. The elders sing in the first person, as those who have been purchased by the blood of Christ from every nation and language group. That fits only the global Church, not angels (who are not redeemed) nor Old Testament saints (who were largely from Israel).

## The Prophetic Conclusion

When Revelation opens the throne room and reveals crowned, enthroned elders immediately after a trumpet-like summons heavenward, the implication is unmistakable: the redeemed Church is already present in heaven before the judgments of the Tribulation unfold on earth.

---

2. A significant textual variant exists in this verse. The first-person reading ("redeemed us ... made us") is found in the Majority Text and the Textus Receptus, which is why it appears in the KJV and NKJV. However, some of the earliest Greek manuscripts have the third-person reading ("redeemed them ... made them"), which is why many modern translations prefer it.

While this difference is debated, it cannot obscure the identity of the 24 elders. Even with the third-person reading, the song still describes the redemption of people from every tribe and nation, a clear description of the Church, not angels. As John F. Walvoord concludes in *The Revelation of Jesus Christ* (chap. 5), "the weight of evidence still is in favor of considering them as representatives of the church, the Body of Christ."

#  DEEPER DIVE 5.3. THE TITLE DEED TO CREATION

## The Scroll That Starts the End of the World as We Know It

*Then I saw in the right hand of him who was seated on the throne a scroll written within and on the back, sealed with seven seals ...*
*and I began to weep loudly because no one was found worthy to open the scroll or to look into it.*

— REVELATION 5:1,4

When John beholds the scene in heaven in Revelation 5, the entire created order holds its breath. In the right hand of God is a scroll, sealed shut with seven seals. John weeps because no one is found worthy to open it and unlock God's plan. This scroll is the title deed to creation, the legal claim to a world held hostage by a usurper. It is the definitive instrument by which God reclaims His possession.[1]

### A Divine Legal Document

In the ancient world, a document written on both sides signified that the contents were comprehensive and unalterable. There was no room for addition or subtraction. The fact that God's scroll is written "within and on the back" confirms His plan for redemption is settled and perfect. The seven seals act as layers of divine authentication, making the document perfectly secure. In Roman practice, important legal documents, including wills, were sealed in the presence of seven witnesses, reinforcing the reality that this scroll represents God's final claim to the earth.

### The Deed to a Lost Inheritance

The clearest Old Testament echo comes from Jeremiah 32, where the prophet buys a field with a sealed deed as a tangible promise of Israel's future restoration. Revelation 5 takes that concept and blows it into something cosmic. This scroll is not for a single field; it is the deed to the entire earth, and it contains God's strategy to reclaim His inheritance from the usurped dominion of sin, death, and Satan.

### Judgments as the Legal Process of Repossession

When the Lamb begins breaking the seals, a series of terrifying judgments are unleashed. These are not random acts of anger but the methodical execution of the scroll's legal terms. Each judgment functions as a divine legal sanction. Every broken seal is a sequential step in the lawful repossession of a world occupied by an enemy, preparing it for the return of its true King.

---

1. For comprehensive treatments of the sealed scroll as the divine "title deed to creation" and the instrument of earthly repossession, see John F. Walvoord, *The Revelation of Jesus Christ* (Chicago: Moody Press, 1966), chap. 5; and Robert L. Thomas, *Revelation 1–7* (Chicago: Moody Press, 1992), chap. 11.

## Why Only the Lamb Is Worthy

Heaven falls silent when no one is found worthy to open the scroll. But then the Lion of Judah steps forward, in the paradoxical form of a Lamb that was slain. This is the breathtaking irony of Revelation 5: the One who is alive and standing bears the visible marks of His death. He is standing because He lives, but He is worthy because He was slain. His wounds are the legal receipt for the world He is about to reclaim.

***Figure D5.3.1: The Deed and the Receipt.*** *The unsealing of the scroll is the methodical, lawful repossession of creation. The right hand of Jesus, the ultimate Kinsman-Redeemer, holds the title deed to the earth. Critically, the visible wound of the nail-print is seen: His blood is the divine legal receipt that makes Him uniquely worthy to open the seals and enforce the eviction.*

He is worthy because He is the ultimate Kinsman-Redeemer. In the Old Testament, a lost family inheritance could only be bought back by a relative. This is the divine rationale behind the Incarnation: Jesus had to become one of us, our kinsman, to qualify, and He had to be the sinless Lamb of God to pay the price. By His blood, He paid the price not just for our souls but for the title deed to the entire fallen creation, with the earth as its center. He alone holds the absolute legal right and moral authority to break the seals and take possession of what He has purchased.

## The Kingdom, Officially Transferred

The unsealing of the scroll rockets toward one glorious climax, declared at the Seventh Trumpet:

> *"The kingdom of the world has become the kingdom of our Lord and of his Christ, and he shall reign for ever and ever."*
>
> — REVELATION 11:15

This marks the declared and irreversible legal transfer of dominion. Everything in this vision, including the sealed document, the search for a worthy heir, and the authority of the Lamb, is about the lawful transfer of rule from the usurper to the rightful King. The scroll is the divine mandate, and Jesus Christ is the executor of that final will, grounded entirely in His victory.

Revelation 5 is the moment the paperwork is signed in heaven, and Revelation 11 is the moment the announcement is made on earth. What follows from there is not chaos, but the outworking of a lawful restoration that will soon be overwhelmingly enforced.

# DEEPER DIVE 5.4. JERICHO AS PROPHETIC BLUEPRINT

## How God's First Conquest Foreshadows His Final Judgment

*And at the seventh time, when the priests had blown the trumpets, Joshua said to the people, "Shout, for the Lord has given you the city."*

—JOSHUA 6:16

*Then the seventh angel blew his trumpet, and there were loud voices in heaven, saying, "The kingdom of the world has become the kingdom of our Lord and of his Christ, and he shall reign forever and ever."*

— REVELATION 11:15

While typology is not a strict one-to-one allegory, the thematic and structural echoes between Jericho and Revelation are undeniable. Joshua 6 presents the fall of Jericho as a deliberate pattern embedded in God's redemptive design. The prophetic text establishes profound typological connections between Jericho's fall and the apocalyptic judgments in Revelation 6–11. The structural parallels are striking, the themes are deeply theological, and the sequence is unmistakably prophetic. What God did on a local scale at Jericho intentionally foreshadows what He will do on a cosmic scale at the end of the age.[1]

1. For more on how the trumpets of Jericho and Revelation both signal God's direct warfare, see J. Dwight Pentecost, *Things to Come* (Grand Rapids: Zondervan, 1958), chap. 21; and William R. Newell, *The Book of the Revelation* (Chicago: Moody Press, 1935).

***Figure D5.4.1: The Prophetic Echo.*** *The fall of Jericho is not merely history. It serves as a deliberate, divine preview of the apocalyptic judgments that will conquer a rebellious world during the Tribulation.*

## 1. Two Witnesses Before the Judgment

Before Jericho fell, Joshua sent two spies into the city (Joshua 2). Their mission was more salvific than strategic. They reached one woman: Rahab, who believed in the God of Israel and was saved along with her family. These spies were witnesses, sent in advance of judgment to secure a remnant.

In Revelation 11, two witnesses are likewise sent into Jerusalem. Their testimony is powerful and confrontational, yet primarily redemptive. While the city is under spiritual siege ("trampled by Gentiles"), their presence leads to repentance and fear falls on many (Revelation 11:13).

**Typological Echo:** Both pairs, Joshua's spies and Revelation's witnesses, are sent into enemy-occupied territory before the final destruction. While Joshua's men utilize covert spy craft and Revelation's witnesses utilize public prophecy, their ultimate purpose is exactly the same: not military advantage, but mercy. They are seeking out those who will believe before the ultimate judgment falls. Rahab was saved; in the end times, a remnant of Israel will be as well.

## 2. Six Days of Marching and Six Seals of Judgment

In Joshua 6:3–14, Israel marched around Jericho once per day for six days. The priests blew trumpets daily during these processions (Joshua 6:8–9, 13), signaling God's presence and claim over the city, while the people remained under a command of silence, forbidden to raise the war shout.

In Revelation 6, six seals are opened. Each seal releases escalating judgment: false peace, war, famine, death, martyrdom, and cosmic upheaval. These judgments build tension across the earth, signaling the approaching climax.

**Typological Echo:** The six days mirror the six seals, a precisely measured escalation. At Jericho, the daily trumpet blasts were a persistent heavenly proclamation during the buildup, paralleling how the Seal Judgments themselves are God's acts of warning and claim upon a rebellious world. Both periods create mounting tension before the final, decisive intervention.

## 3. Divine Restraint Before the Climax

During Jericho's six days, a key restraint was imposed: the people were forbidden to shout (Joshua 6:10). Though trumpets sounded daily, the war cry, the sound of conquest, was withheld until God's appointed moment.

In Revelation 8:1, when the Seventh Seal is opened, there is silence in heaven for about half an hour. This is the eye of the storm; heaven itself pauses in profound anticipation before the seven trumpets begin to sound.

**Typological Echo:** Both narratives feature a God-imposed restraint at the critical turning point before total judgment. At Jericho, it was the prohibition of the war shout; in Revelation, it is cosmic silence. This restraint deliberately heightens the anticipation, underscoring that God alone controls the exact timing and nature of His decisive intervention.

## 4. The Seventh Day and the Seventh Seal

On the seventh day, Israel marched around Jericho seven times. The priests blew trumpets continuously, culminating in one long, final blast (Joshua 6:15–16, 20). This was the climax, unleashing God's absolute power.

In Revelation, the Seventh Seal unlocks the seven trumpets (Revelation 8:1–6). These Trumpet Judgments are undeniably more intense than the seals: hail and fire, poisoned waters, darkened skies, demonic invasions, and catastrophic warfare.

**Typological Echo:** The seventh day's intensified activity, especially its climactic long blast, directly parallels how the Seventh Seal unlocks the seven trumpets. Both mark the irreversible transition from preparatory warning (seals, daily marches) to the direct, unstoppable onslaught of God's judgment.

## 5. Seven Trumpets: Divine Action Unleashed

At Jericho, seven priests blew seven trumpets throughout the seven-day sequence, but their blasts reached a crescendo on the seventh day. The final, long blast signaled divine breakthrough.

In Revelation, seven angels blow seven trumpets in sequence (Revelation 8:6–11:15). Each blast corresponds to a direct act of divine judgment upon the earth.

**Typological Echo:** Trumpets signal divine warfare in both narratives. Their persistent sound at Jericho (days 1–6) declared God's claim and warning; their climactic blast (day 7) announced total destruction. Similarly, Revelation's trumpets progress from partial judgments (Revelation 8:7–12) to the final proclamation of Christ's reign (Revelation 11:15). The typology emphasizes an inexorable escalation toward total victory.

## 6. The Triumphant Shout and the Final Proclamation

At the end of Jericho's seventh circuit, after the final trumpet blast, the people shouted with a great shout, and the wall fell flat (Joshua 6:20). The shout signified completed victory.

In Revelation 11:15, when the Seventh Trumpet is blown, loud voices in heaven proclaim: "The kingdom of the world has become the kingdom of our Lord and of His Christ, and He shall reign forever and ever."

**Typological Echo:** The shout that brought down Jericho's walls powerfully corresponds to the heavenly declaration that the world now belongs to Christ. In both cases, the sound follows the final trumpet and is not a human effort, but a heavenly announcement of victory accomplished.

| Prophetic Theme | The Blueprint (Joshua 6) | The Fulfillment (Revelation 6-11) |
|---|---|---|
| The Forerunners of Mercy | Two spies are sent into enemy territory to secure a believing remnant before the conquest. | Two witnesses are sent to Jerusalem, resulting in a saved remnant before the final woes. |
| The Escalating Warning | Six days of deliberate marching around the city accompanied by daily trumpet blasts. | Six seals are broken in strict sequence, releasing escalating judgments across the earth. |
| The Divine Restraint | The people are strictly forbidden to raise the war shout until God's appointed moment. | A profound silence falls over heaven for half an hour before the final judgments begin. |
| The Climactic Transition | The seventh day brings intensified activity, culminating in one long, final trumpet blast. | The seventh seal is opened, directly unlocking the severe devastation of the seven trumpets. |
| The Instruments of Warfare | Seven priests blow seven trumpets to declare God's absolute claim over the city. | Seven angels blow seven trumpets to unleash direct divine warfare against a rebellious world. |
| The Final Proclamation | A great shout brings down the impenetrable walls, signaling total and absolute victory. | Heavenly voices declare that the kingdoms of the world have officially become the kingdom of Christ. |

***Table D5.4.1: The Mechanics of Divine Victory.*** *From the initial forerunners of mercy to the final heavenly proclamation, the blueprint of Jericho compellingly affirms the futurist understanding of the Tribulation timeline.*

## Patterns with a Purpose

From spies to trumpets to shouts, the fall of Jericho unfolds as a redemptive drama completely saturated with prophetic significance. God is perfectly consistent. The same God who brought down a walled city through obedience, divine timing, priestly trumpets, and a climactic shout is the exact same God who will bring down Babylon, the Beast, and every high thing that exalts itself against Him.

Jericho is not just a historical battle. It is a prophetic preview. Revelation is not just an apocalypse. It is the ultimate fulfillment.

The typology explicitly reveals God's method: mercy precedes judgment (witnesses), judgment escalates under divine restraint (seals, daily trumpets, withheld shout), and it climaxes in unstoppable victory (seventh trumpet, shout, proclamation). His pattern is deliberate, and His triumph is absolutely certain.

# DEEPER DIVE 6.1. LEFT BEHIND OR LIFTED UP?

## The Little Ones and the Grace of God at the Rapture

*And as for your little ones ... who today have no knowledge of good or evil, they shall go in there. And to them I will give it, and they shall possess it.*

— DEUTERONOMY 1:39

*but Jesus said, "Let the little children come to me ... for to such belongs the kingdom of heaven."*

— MATTHEW 19:14

*"... Shall not the Judge of all the earth do what is just?"*

— GENESIS 18:25

The question hits with a visceral pang: *What about the children?* To find a biblical answer, we must first confront deeper, more foundational questions. When does God hold a person accountable? How does His grace operate where conscious faith is not yet possible? And what, exactly, do we mean when we say the Church is taken?

While Scripture provides no single proof-text, it establishes a definitive portrait of God's character and consistent principles that assure a merciful conclusion.

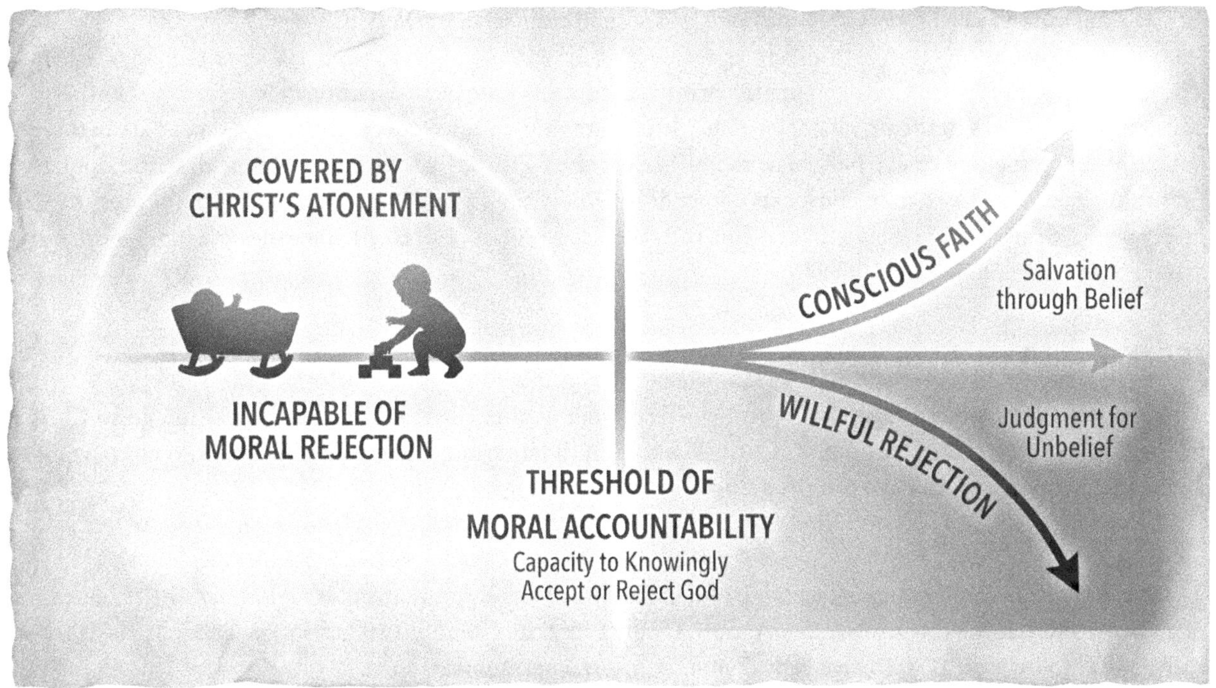


***Figure D6.1.1: The Threshold of Grace.*** *Christ's atoning sacrifice provides a protective covering over those who have not yet reached the cognitive capacity to understand and morally respond to the Gospel.*

## The Age of Accountability: When Does "No" Mean No?

God's judgment is never a blind strike. It is inextricably tied to moral awareness and the capacity to choose. Throughout the Bible, God rigorously distinguishes between capability and culpability; between those who knowingly rebel and those who cannot yet understand.

When Israel was barred from entering the land, God explicitly exempted their children, whom He described as those who "today have no knowledge of good or evil" (Deuteronomy 1:39). Isaiah spoke of a child before he knew how to "refuse the evil and choose the good" (Isaiah 7:16). And God's mercy toward Nineveh included compassion for those who did not yet "know their right hand from their left" (Jonah 4:11).

The Bible does not specify an exact age, but it establishes a clear principle: accountability requires understanding. You cannot reject a truth you cannot comprehend. This is why strict biblical theology maintains that infants and young children are not judged for unbelief, a sin that by definition requires the ability to knowingly refuse the light. Scripture consistently ties judgment to moral awareness and conscience, not mere existence (Romans 2:12–16).

## Grace in the Womb: Salvation Before Speech

Salvation is always, only, and entirely a work of God's grace through Christ's atonement. While conscious faith is the ordinary means of receiving it, God's saving power is not limited by age, language, or cognitive development:

- John the Baptist was "filled with the Holy Spirit, even from his mother's womb" (Luke 1:15), leaping for joy at the sound of Mary's greeting (Luke 1:41).
- God tells Jeremiah, "Before I formed you in the womb I knew you, before you were born I set you apart" (Jeremiah 1:5).

- Psalm 139:13–16 celebrates God's intimate, purposeful formation of every life.

These passages reveal that God's redemptive work can precede human articulation. Therefore, it is entirely consistent with God's righteous character that Christ's atoning sacrifice covers those who die, or are gathered, before reaching the capacity to believe or morally reject the light they have received. Some describe this carefully as regeneration apart from conscious confession. Others simply affirm the outcome without pressing the mechanism. Either way, the emphasis remains the same: salvation is entirely of grace: never earned, never assumed, and never unjustly withheld.[1]

## The Church: Who Is Taken, and Why

This leads to a final, practical tension. The New Testament defines the true Church as those united to Christ by the Spirit through conscious faith (1 Corinthians 12:13). Infants and young children clearly do not participate in the life, witness, or ordinances of the Church in this sense.

So, are they "in the Church"?

The biblical resolution requires an accurate understanding of the Rapture itself. It is not merely the relocation of an institution. It is a divine rescue operation. It concludes the Church Age, but its specific purpose is to deliver all who belong to Christ from the coming wrath (1 Thessalonians 1:10).

Therefore, children are not redefined as members of the Church. The strict dispensational doctrine of the Church remains completely intact. Yet Christ, who gathers His Bride, also gathers those who belong to Him by grace and are incapable of moral rejection.

The Church Age draws to a close. Judgment is delayed no longer. And those under Christ's redemptive care are not left behind.

## What We Affirm And What We Don't

This position is careful and specific.

**It does NOT claim**:

- Salvation is inherited from parents.
- Innocence merits redemption.
- The definition of the Church is expanded.

**It DOES affirm**:

- Christ's atonement is sufficient and effective.
- God judges only where there is moral knowledge.
- Where Scripture is silent, we trust His character. "Shall not the Judge of all the earth do what is just?" (Genesis 18:25).

1. Robert P. Lightner, *Safe in the Arms of Jesus: God's Provision for the Death of Those Who Cannot Believe* (Grand Rapids: Kregel Publications, 2000). Lightner argues that God applies Christ's atoning work to those who die without the capacity to believe, grounding his case in God's justice, Christ's regard for children, the nature of moral accountability, and the impossibility of condemning those who were incapable of responding to grace.

## Why This Reinforces a Pre-Tribulation Rapture

This understanding aligns directly with the Pre-Tribulational timeline. Since the Rapture's purpose is to rescue God's people from the coming divine wrath of the Tribulation, it is profoundly consistent that He would also gather those who could never be its moral targets. The storm breaks only after the most vulnerable are brought inside.

## The Anchor of His Character

- **God's Judgment is Just**: It requires moral awareness. Scripture consistently ties condemnation to the deliberate rejection of light.
- **God's Redemption is by Atonement:** Children are saved solely through the finished work of Christ, not their own innocence.
- **God's Grace is Powerful**: It operates sovereignly when human understanding or articulation is lacking.
- **God's Rescue is Complete**: The Rapture delivers all who are Christ's, including the littlest ones under the shelter of His atonement, according to God's righteous and perfect judgment.

# DEEPER DIVE 6.2. "BUT OF THAT DAY AND HOUR ..."

## Why Matthew 24:36–44 Refers to the Rapture, Not the Second Coming

*But concerning that day and hour no one knows...*

— MATTHEW 24:36

Few passages in Scripture have generated more debate than Matthew 24:36–44. Many futurist interpreters assume these verses simply continue Jesus' description of His visible return at the end of the Tribulation. Yet a closer reading reveals a significant problem: the event Jesus describes in verses 36–44 does not behave textually like a Post-Tribulation Second Coming at all.

In fact, when read carefully, Matthew 24:36–44 aligns far more naturally with the Rapture, which is marked by normalcy, imminence, and total surprise, rather than the sign-posted, time-calculable return of Christ in glory described earlier in the chapter.

### 1. A Clear Structural Shift: *Peri de* ("But Concerning...")

Verse 36 opens with a critical grammatical marker in the original Greek text:

*Peri de tes hemeras ekeines* ... ("But concerning that day ...")

In the New Testament, *peri de* is not a casual phrase; it functions as a recognized topic-shift marker, signaling a definitive new subject rather than a continuation of the previous one. The apostle Paul uses it repeatedly this way (1 Corinthians 7:1, 7:25, 8:1; 12:1; 16:1).

Up to verse 35, Jesus has been directly answering His disciples' inquiry: "What will be the sign of Your coming, and of the end of the age?" (Matthew 24:3).

In response to their specific question about the End of the Age, Jesus laid out a strict chronological sequence of observable events:

- Global birth pains
- The Abomination of Desolation
- The Great Tribulation
- Cosmic disturbances
- The visible return of the Son of Man "immediately after the tribulation" (Matthew 24:29–30)

But in verse 36, Jesus makes a decisive, dispensational shift. He stops talking about signs altogether. Instead, He introduces an event defined not by visibility, but by unknowability. As strict Pre-Tribulation scholarship demonstrates, verse 36 marks a veritable transition from the sign-filled Second Coming to a signless coming that no human calculation can anticipate.[1]

## 2. The Calculation Problem: A Known Day vs. an Unknown Day

The Second Coming, as described earlier in Matthew 24, is explicitly *calculable*:

- Daniel 9:27 defines a seven-year framework.
- Revelation repeatedly measures the final half as 1,260 days, 42 months, or a time, times, and half a time.
- Jesus Himself anchors His return *immediately after* the Tribulation (Matthew 24:29–30).

That creates an unavoidable theological tension.

If the Abomination of Desolation occurs at the midpoint, and if the final 3½ years are strictly measured in days, then the exact timing of Christ's return is mathematically calculable from that point.

Yet Matthew 24:36 insists that no one knows the day or hour: not angels, not even the Son, only the Father.

Clearly, these two realities cannot describe the same event.

The only biblical resolution is straightforward: Matthew 24:36–44 is no longer describing the visible Second Coming. Jesus is now speaking of a completely different event, one that is genuinely imminent and uncalculable. That description points unmistakably **to** the Rapture.

## 3. The Normalcy Problem: "Eating and Drinking"

Jesus compares this unknown event to the days of Noah:

> They were eating and drinking, marrying and giving in marriage ...
>
> — MATTHEW 24:38–39

This is not a world staggering under judgment's final blows. It is a world operating under the illusion of continuity and stability just before those blows fall.

By the Tribulation's conclusion, the world is anything but normal:

- Humanity is hiding in caves, not planning weddings (Revelation 6:15–17)
- Seas, rivers and springs of water have turned to blood (Revelation 16:3–4)
- The sun scorches humanity (Revelation 16:8–9)
- Deep darkness envelops the Beast's kingdom (Revelation 16:10)

Scripture repeatedly describes the end of this period not as a bruised civilization limping forward, but as a world reduced to a broken remnant. Isaiah foresees humanity made "few" (Isaiah 24:6) and reduced to "a tenth"

1. For a detailed analysis of *peri de* as a transitional marker, see John Hart, "Should Pretribulationists Reconsider the Rapture in Matthew 24:36–44? Part 1," *Journal of the Grace Evangelical Society* (Autumn 2007): 47–70. Hart demonstrates that this phrase consistently introduces a new topic, supporting the view that Jesus shifts to the signless Rapture. See also Renald Showers, *Maranatha, Our Lord Come!* (Bellmawr, NJ: The Friends of Israel Gospel Ministry, 1995), where Showers argues that the "unknown day" cannot refer to the calculable Post-Tribulation return, necessitating a reference to the imminent Rapture.

that itself undergoes further burning, leaving only the "holy seed" (Isaiah 6:13). This apocalyptic devastation is not the backdrop of casual normalcy Jesus describes in Matthew 24.

***Figure D6.2.1: The Illusion of Normalcy.*** *Christ's description of a world casually celebrating weddings is entirely incompatible with the apocalyptic devastation of the late Tribulation, pointing instead to the sudden, surprising nature of the Pre-Tribulation Rapture.*

The normalcy of eating, drinking, and planning weddings fits only the world before judgment suddenly begins, a condition Scripture explicitly associates with the Rapture: "While people are saying, 'Peace and safety!' then sudden destruction comes upon them ..." (1 Thessalonians 5:3 NKJV).

## 4. The Thief Imagery: Arrival That Triggers Judgment

Jesus then adds: "If the master of the house had known in what part of the night the thief was coming ..." (v. 43).

This imagery is consistently used in Scripture for an unexpected arrival, not for a climactic, globally visible return. Paul applies the exact same language to the onset of judgment: "The day of the Lord will come like a thief in the night" (1 Thessalonians 5:2).

A thief does not announce his arrival. A thief does not come after the house is already destroyed. A thief comes suddenly, and his arrival *initiates* loss. That is the inescapable logic of Matthew 24:43–44. The coming Jesus describes triggers upheaval; it does not conclude it.

## 5. Addressing the Post-Tribulational Counter-Argument

Post-Tribulational scholars frequently attempt to resolve this calculation problem by appealing to Matthew 24:22, where Jesus states that for the sake of the elect, the days of the Tribulation "will be cut short." Scholars like Robert H. Gundry argue that God will literally truncate the total number of days in the final half of the seventieth week. By reducing the calendar timeline, they claim God introduces an element of uncertainty, explaining why believers will know the general season but not the exact day or hour of the Second Coming.[2]

This proposed solution faces three insurmountable textual problems:

- **Prophetic Precision:** Suggesting that God alters the chronological duration of the Tribulation shatters the meticulously inspired math of Scripture. Revelation repeatedly and emphatically defines the Antichrist's reign as exactly 1,260 days and 42 months (Revelation 11:3; 12:6; 13:5). God provides these specific, repetitive numeric markers precisely because His prophetic calendar is fixed, not flexible.
- **The Literal Shortening of the Solar Day:** Gundry mistakenly assumes the *calendar* is shortened. However, a strict literal reading of Matthew 24:22, harmonized with the cosmic disturbances of Revelation 8:12, reveals that it is the *solar day itself* that is physically compressed. Through divinely orchestrated celestial mechanics, such as the gravitational torque of a massive planetary intruder, the earth's rotation is altered. The 1,260 days remain mathematically intact, but the actual hours of daylight are literally shortened. Therefore, the timeline remains entirely calculable, dismantling the Post-Tribulational argument for an unknown chronological endpoint.
- **The Normalcy Deficit:** Furthermore, a world experiencing this terrifying cosmic shudder is far from a world operating under the illusion of normalcy. A planet undergoing catastrophic gravitational torque, permanent twilight, and celestial bombardment is not casually eating, drinking, and planning weddings. Total surprise requires a world operating under the illusion of peace and stability, a condition that only fits the imminent Pre-Tribulation Rapture.

By contrast, the Rapture requires no such textual workaround. Its surprise is intrinsic, not explained away.

## Verdict: Two Comings, Two Profiles

When all the biblical evidence is weighed, the structural reality is undeniable:

2. For the classic Post-Tribulational attempt to reconcile the calculable timeline of the Tribulation with the unknown day and hour by arguing that God will literally reduce the number of days in the final three and a half years, see Robert H. Gundry, *The Church and the Tribulation* (Grand Rapids: Zondervan, 1973), 41–43. Gundry argues this shortening resolves the tension between general predictability and specific unpredictability. However, this view fundamentally undermines the literal, immutable numeric timelines of Daniel and Revelation, and it does not account for the literal, physical shortening of the solar rotation described in Revelation 8:12. (See *SIDEBAR: The Cosmic Shifter* in *Chapter 12. The Silence and the Trumpets*).

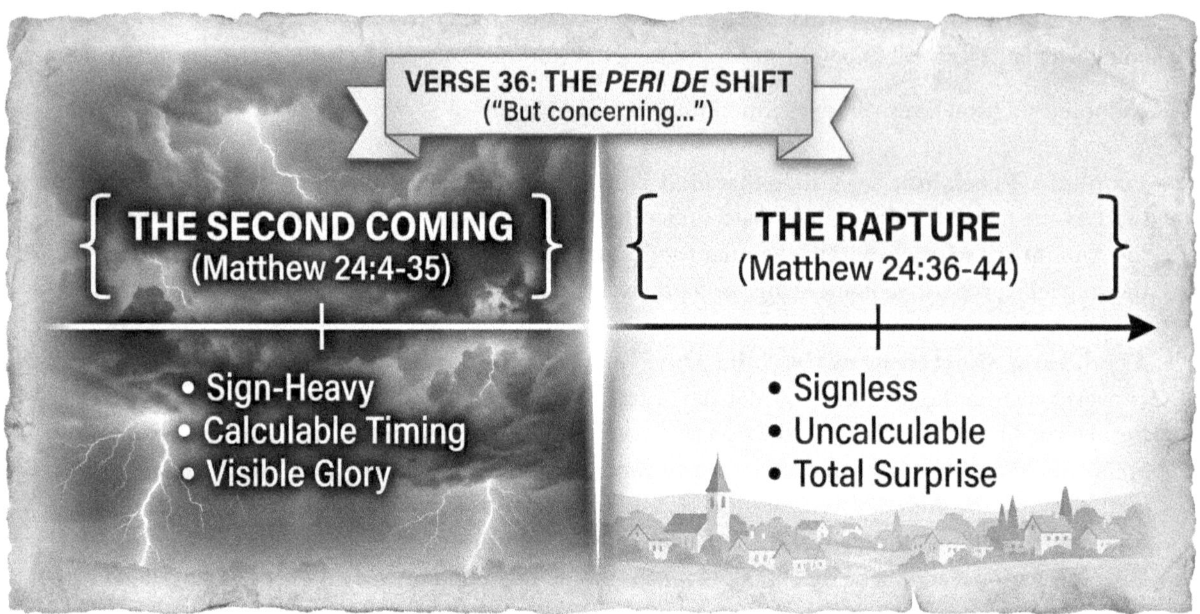


***Figure D6.2.2: The Olivet Discourse Divided.*** *A structural analysis of Matthew 24 reveals a definitive pivot at verse 36, moving from the calculable, sign-heavy Second Coming to the imminent, signless Rapture.*

- **Matthew 24:4–35:** The Second Coming (Signs, Calculable, Visible Glory).
- **Matthew 24:36–44:** The Rapture (No Signs, Uncalculable, Sudden Separation).

Instead of fracturing the Olivet Discourse, this strict dispensational distinction completes it. Jesus definitively answers both questions His disciples asked: the end of the age and the timing of His coming for His people. The Rapture, then, is not an afterthought inserted by later theology. It is embedded right in Jesus' own teaching, revealed clearly when Scripture is allowed to interpret Scripture.

---

## Note on the "One Taken"

This passage contains the famous description of two men in a field: "one will be taken and the other left" (v. 40). While both Matthew and Luke utilize the identical Greek term *paralambano* (literally, "to take to oneself" or "to receive alongside"), the destination of this "taking" is defined strictly by the immediate context.

In Luke 17, the atmosphere is one of unavoidable judgment. When the disciples ask for clarification, "Where, Lord?", Jesus points them to the specific location where this is all happening: "Where the body is, there the eagles will be gathered together" (v. 37 NKJV). In that Lukan context, the "taken" is by the gathering eagles.

In Matthew 24, however, the emphasis centers on the suddenness of the King's arrival and the gathering of those who belong to Him. Here, the term points definitively to a taking in rescue, a "receiving alongside" the Savior. While the words are the same, the outcomes are opposites: in Luke, one is taken to the eagles of judgment; in Matthew, one is taken to the side of the King. (For deeper explorations, see *Deeper Dive 6.3. The Paradox of the Taken* and *Deeper Dive 23.1. The Eagles and the Corpse*.)

#  DEEPER DIVE 6.3. THE PARADOX OF THE TAKEN

## When "Taken" Means Rapture, and When It Means Wrath

*Then two will be in the field: one will be taken and the other left.*[1]

— MATTHEW 24:40 NKJV

*... I tell you, in that night there will be two in one bed: the one will be taken ... "Where, Lord?" So He said to them, "Wherever the body [lit. corpse] is, there the eagles will be gathered together."*[2]

— LUKE 17:34–37 NKJV

A direct comparison of the Gospel accounts reveals a definitive textual tension. In Luke 17, the "one taken" is explicitly taken to judgment, removed to the place where the eagles gather. Yet in Matthew 24, the "one taken" is taken in rescue, gathered at the imminent Rapture (cf. *Deeper Dive 23.1. The Eagles and the Corpse*).

How does the exact same phrase dictate opposite outcomes?

The biblical resolution relies entirely on context, placement, and prophetic timing.

1. The NKJV italicizes men in both Matthew 24:40 ("two *men* in the field") and Luke 17:34 ("two *men* in one bed") to indicate words supplied by the translators and not present in the Greek text. The originals read simply "two in the field" (*duo en tō agrō*) and "two on one bed" (*duo epi klinēs mias*). For clarity and fidelity to the underlying wording, these supplied terms have been omitted here.
2. Lit. the Greek reads *ptoma*, "corpse/carcass," and *aetoi*, "eagles." The NKJV renders *ptoma* as "body" in Luke 17:37 and "carcass" in Matthew 24:28.

FIGURE D6.3.1: THE PARADOX OF THE TAKEN - CONTEXT DETERMINES DESTINY

| LUKE 17: JUDGMENT & CAPTURE | MATTHEW 24: RESCUE & SURPRISE |
| --- | --- |
|  |  |
| **THE EAGLE & THE CORPSE** (Luke 17:37).<br>**Context:** Predatory Scavenging, Battlefield Logic.<br>**Outcome:** Violent Removal to Death. | **THE THIEF IN THE NIGHT** (Matthew 24:43).<br>**Context:** Unexpected Arrival, Household Logic.<br>**Outcome:** Sudden Rescue from Wrath. |

***Figure D6.3.1.*** *Context determines destiny in the 'taken' passages. This comparative diagram contrasts the predatory imagery of judgment in Luke 17 with the surprising, household-logic rescue in Matthew 24.*

### 1. The Eagle vs. The Thief

In Luke 17, the disciples ask the natural follow-up question: "Where, Lord?" Jesus answers with a grim, unmistakable proverb: removal leads to the place of death where the corpse lies and the scavengers gather (Luke 17:37). The atmosphere is predatory. This describes a violent capture, not a divine rescue.

Matthew's Gospel also includes the eagle proverb (Matthew 24:28), but its structural function is entirely different. In Matthew, it appears earlier in the discourse, squarely within the Tribulation section, describing the gathering storm of judgment leading up to the visible Second Coming.

However, when Jesus turns to the sudden, uncalculated event of Matthew 24:36–44, He fundamentally shifts His imagery: "If the master of the house had known what hour the thief would come ..." (Matthew 24:43).

The scene changes from battlefield logic to household surprise. Eagles gather to devour; thieves come unexpectedly. That textual shift is profound and deliberate.

### 2. The Problem of Calculation

The strongest textual evidence is the timing itself.

The Second Coming (Matthew 24:29–31) is a strictly calculable event, occurring exactly 1,260 days after the Abomination of Desolation. If Matthew 24:40 referred to that event, the command to "watch" because "you do not know the hour" would be nonsensical. Any believer familiar with biblical prophecy living through the Tribulation could count the exact days on a calendar.

Therefore, following the *peri de* shift in verse 36, verses 36–44 must refer to the only prophetic event that is truly immeasurable and imminent: the Pre-Tribulation Rapture.

### 3. Two Separations

Scripture describes two great separation events at the end of the age.

- **The Rapture:** The **Church** is taken in divine rescue, while the unbelieving world is left behind to face the Tribulation.
- **The Second Coming:** The wicked are taken away in divine judgment (the "goats" sent into the fire), while the faithful (the "sheep," representing the Tribulation saints who survive the seven years) are left behind to physically inherit the Millennial Kingdom, entering the next age as possessors of eternal life (Matthew 25:31–34, 46).

***Figure D6.3.2: The Two Great Separations.*** *At the Rapture (left), the Church is taken in sudden rescue while the unbelieving world is left behind. At the Second Coming (right), the wicked "goats" are taken away in judgment while the faithful "sheep" are left to inherit the Millennial Kingdom.*

Jesus uses similar language ("one taken, one left") for both events, just as a farmer separates crops at different stages of the harvest.

Context dictates exactly which harvest is in view.

In Matthew 24, the total surprise and lack of chronological signs point unmistakably to the Rapture.

# DEEPER DIVE 6.4. THE TALE OF TWO TRUMPETS

## Same Trumpet, Same Event?

> *In a moment, in the twinkling of an eye, at the last trumpet. For the trumpet will sound, and the dead will be raised imperishable, and we shall be changed.*
>
> — *1 CORINTHIANS 15:52*

> *Then the seventh angel blew his trumpet, and there were loud voices in heaven, saying, "The kingdom of the world has become the kingdom of our Lord and of his Christ, and he shall reign forever and ever."*
>
> — *REVELATION 11:15*

Is the "last trumpet" of Paul the exact same event as the "seventh trumpet" of Revelation?

Many readers mistakenly equate the two. However, a close examination of the text reveals they signal two entirely different events. Understanding this distinction is vital for a correct view of end-times prophecy.

## The Perceived Connection

Those who link Paul's "last trumpet" with Revelation's Seventh Trumpet often rely on surface-level similarities:

- **Shared Language**: Both passages use the same Greek word, *salpinx* ("trumpet").
- **Chronological Alignment**: Because Revelation's Seventh Trumpet is the final trumpet in its specific judgment series, many readers naturally but incorrectly equate it with the "last trumpet" Paul mentions in 1 Corinthians 15:52.
- **Climactic Tone**: Both trumpets announce a major transition: one of bodily resurrection, the other of kingdom authority.

However, this framework falters when the full biblical context is examined.

## The Biblical Distinction

A strict, literal reading of the text demonstrates that these two trumpets belong to fundamentally different categories. They cannot possibly be the same event.

### 1. The Voice: Creator vs. Creature

Paul's trumpet is explicitly called the "trump of God" (1 Thessalonians 4:16): a personal, divine summons from the Lord Himself to His Bride.

Revelation's trumpet is blown by an *angel* as part of a catastrophic judicial sequence against a rebellious earth.

The imagery is entirely different. One is the Bridegroom calling His Church; the other is a creature heralding unrestrained divine wrath.

**2. The Purpose: Grace vs. Judgment**

Paul's trumpet signals pure blessing, life, and glory. It is the exact moment when "this mortal puts on immortality."

Revelation's trumpet signals woe and doom, officially introducing the final and most severe outpouring of God's wrath (the Bowl Judgments).

One gathers the redeemed. The other confronts the wicked.

**3. The Meaning of "Last": Departure, Not Termination**

If Paul's trumpet were the very last trumpet of all history, it would create a severe textual contradiction. Jesus explicitly identifies *another* trumpet that sounds *after* the Tribulation to gather Israel (Matthew 24:31).

So what did Paul mean by "last"?

Paul was writing to a Roman world intimately familiar with military trumpet signals. In Roman encampments:

- The **first trumpet** meant: "Strike the tents."
- The **intermediate trumpets** meant: "Assemble."
- The **last trumpet** meant: "March away."

In its historical and grammatical context, "last trumpet" does not mean "the end of time." It means "the signal to depart." This captures the exact nature of the Rapture. It is a trumpet of rescue and relocation, not ruin.

**4. The Duration: Instant vs. Prolonged**

Paul's trumpet sounds "in a moment, in the twinkling of an eye."

Revelation 10:7, however, speaks of the "days of the voice of the seventh angel," indicating an extended period of unfolding judgment rather than a single instantaneous blast.

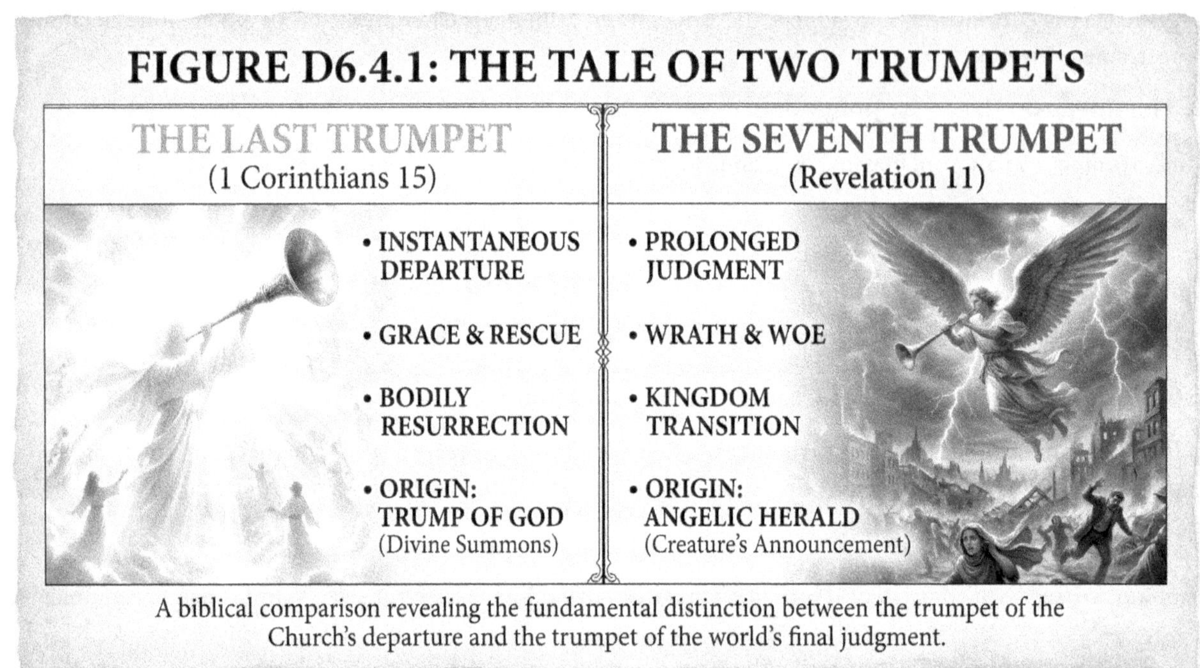


*Figure D6.4.1. Two Distinct Trumpets*

## The Verdict: Rescue vs. Wrath

Equating these two trumpets prioritizes a single shared word over profound biblical differences in context, audience, purpose, and timing. When the full scope of Scripture is considered, these two events remain entirely distinct.[1]

The Seventh Trumpet of Revelation is the ominous alarm of the world's final judgments. The Last Trumpet of Corinthians is the joyful sound of the Church's departure.

The Church is not waiting for an angel to signal doom. We are waiting for the Trump of God to signal: "Come up here."

1. See J. Dwight Pentecost, *Things to Come* (Grand Rapids: Zondervan, 1958), Chapter XII, "The Midtribulation Rapture Position." Pentecost catalogues the strict biblical contrasts between these passages, concluding definitively that "it is impossible to identify [equate] these two trumps."

# DEEPER DIVE 7.1. THE PETRA CONNECTION

## Is There a Prophetic "Safe Zone" in Jordan?

> *"So when you see the abomination of desolation spoken of by the prophet Daniel, standing in the holy place (let the reader understand), then let those who are in Judea flee to the mountains.*
>
> — MATTHEW 24:15–16

When Jesus warned the Jewish people to "flee to the mountains" upon seeing the Abomination of Desolation (Matthew 24:16), He didn't provide a map. For centuries, readers assumed this simply meant "run for the hills," or any high ground, to escape the immediate violence in Jerusalem.

But a closer, literal reading of Scripture demonstrates that Jesus had a specific destination in mind. His command was not a vague directive to scatter, but a reference to exact coordinates laid out centuries earlier in the Old Testament.

Harmonizing these ancient prophecies with the Book of Revelation reveals a fascinating picture: a divinely prepared "survival bunker" for the Jewish remnant, hidden deep in the red rock mountains of modern-day Jordan.[1]

## The One Place the Antichrist Cannot Touch

This geographic specificity begins with a strange anomaly found in the book of Daniel.

In Daniel 11, the prophet describes the Antichrist's military campaign. He is a juggernaut, overthrowing countries and sweeping through the Middle East. But Daniel notes one curious exception. As the Antichrist conquers the "Glorious Land" (Israel), three specific ancient territories slip through his fingers: **Edom, Moab, and Ammon.**

> *...but these shall be delivered out of his hand: Edom and Moab and the main part of the Ammonites.*
>
> — DANIEL 11:41

1. A foundational tenet of dispensational eschatology is that the Jewish remnant will flee to a real, specific place for protection during the Tribulation, most commonly identified as Petra (also called Bozrah) in modern-day Jordan. This view connects Jesus' warning to flee in Matthew 24, the Woman's flight into the wilderness in Revelation 12, and the Messiah's return from Edom in Isaiah 63. For a detailed explanation, see Arnold G. Fruchtenbaum, *The Footsteps of the Messiah* (Ariel Ministries, 2004). See also J. Dwight Pentecost, *Things to Come* (Zondervan, 1958), who argues that this refuge must lie outside the Antichrist's control, specifically in the land of Edom (cf. Daniel 11:41).

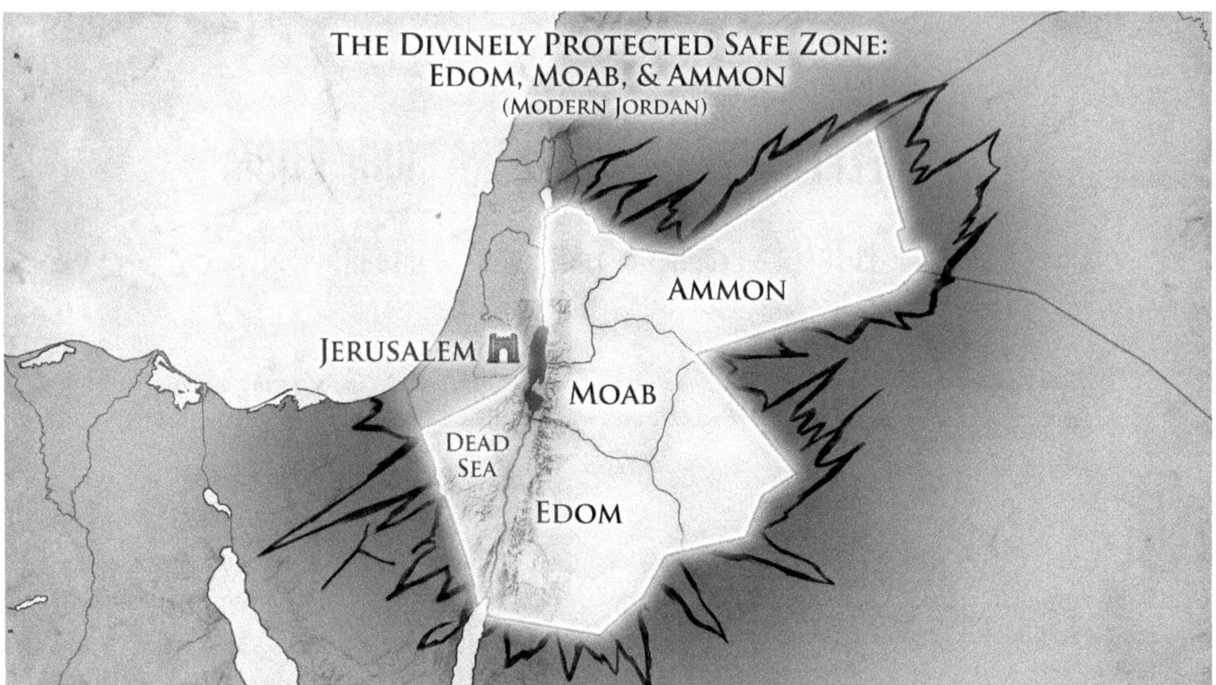


***Figure D7.1.1: Ancient Prophecy, Modern Borders.*** *The territories of Edom, Moab, and Ammon, prophesied in Daniel 11 to escape the Antichrist's grasp, map directly to the modern nation of Jordan.*

Today, these regions largely correspond to the modern nation of Jordan. Therefore, while the global geopolitical landscape falls under the Beast's control, the mountainous region of Jordan remains a divinely protected safe zone.

## The Rock Fortress

If Jordan is the destination, where specifically would millions of refugees hide? Biblical geography points to Mount Seir: the rugged, mountainous terrain of ancient Edom.

Deep within this region lies the ancient city of Petra (often identified as biblical Sela). While the capital of Edom was historically Bozrah to the north, Petra is the region's ultimate natural fortress. Famous for its Treasury carved into rose-red cliffs and accessible only through a narrow canyon called the Siq, Petra is a city designed for concealment and defense.

***Figure D7.1.2: The Hidden Enclosure.*** *Framed by the massive, narrow crevices of the Siq, the Treasury of Petra stands revealed. This precise image of a magnificent city hidden within a protected enclosure captures the theological meaning of its ancient name, Bozrah, the "sheepfold" of God's remnant. The visual reality of this narrow, defensive bottleneck confirms that Petra is the fortified pen God gathers His people to. Situated just a short flight from Judea, it serves as the ultimate wilderness sanctuary where the flock is held in total safety.*

The names themselves tell the story. Notably, *Sela* means "rock" in Hebrew, just as *Petra* means "rock" in Greek. But the Hebrew name **Bozrah** adds a deeper theological layer: it translates to "sheepfold" or "enclosure." This connects powerfully to Micah 2:12, where God promises to gather the remnant "like sheep of the fold [Bozrah]." The imagery is precise: a protected enclosure where the flock is penned in for safety, waiting for their Shepherd.

The prophet Isaiah connects to this very region when addressing Moab regarding Jewish refugees in the end times:

> ... *make your shadow like the night in the middle of the day; hide the outcasts, do not betray him who escapes. Let My outcasts dwell with you, O Moab* ...
>
> — ISAIAH 16:3–4 NKJV

This aligns remarkably with Revelation 12:14, which tells of the "Woman" (Israel) being given wings to fly into the wilderness to a place prepared for her, where she is nourished for 3½ years, safe from the Serpent.

## The Messiah's Warpath

The most compelling evidence lies in the geography of the Second Coming. While tradition often depicts Jesus returning solely to the Mount of Olives, the prophet Isaiah reveals a different trajectory that emerges out of Edom and advances toward Jerusalem from the east.

Isaiah asks, "Who is this who comes from Edom, in crimsoned garments from Bozrah" (Isaiah 63:1).

The Messiah appears with robes stained red, not by His own blood, but with the blood of His enemies. This prophecy reveals a critical strategic reality: The Antichrist will track the Jewish remnant to their fortress in Jordan and lay siege to the mountains. But before he can wipe them out, the Messiah intervenes.

He comes first to Bozrah, breaks the siege, defeats the armies surrounding the remnant, and then leads the refugees back to Jerusalem in a triumphant procession for the final victory.

## A Second Exodus

Seen in this light, Jesus' command in Matthew 24 is no generic instruction to scatter. It is a strategic order. When the world collapses and the Antichrist reveals his true face, there is only one sanctuary left.

Just as God split the waters of the Red Sea to birth the nation, He has carved a fortress in the rocks of Edom to preserve her. The "mountains" are not just a hiding place; they are the stage for the greatest rescue mission in history.

The first Exodus led Israel out of Egypt.

The second will lead them out of the wilderness and back to their King.

# SHADOWS & SUBSTANCE 7.2. NOAH AND LOT: TWO PATTERNS OF DIVINE DELIVERANCE

## The Ark of Safety and the Way of Escape

*Just as it was in the days of Noah ... so will it be in the days of the Son of Man ... Likewise, just as it was in the days of Lot ... on the day when Lot went out from Sodom, fire and sulfur rained from heaven ...*

— LUKE 17:26–29

Jesus deliberately paired Noah and Lot when describing the days preceding the revelation of the Son of Man. Together, these two figures present distinct but complementary models of divine rescue during catastrophic judgment. Scripture uses them to illustrate two different methods by which God delivers His people, corresponding directly to Israel and the Church.

### Noah as a Type of Israel: Preserved *Through* Judgment

The account of Noah (Genesis 6–8) establishes the biblical paradigm of preservation *within* judgment. Though divine wrath engulfed the world, Noah and his family were kept safe in a physical refuge designed and sustained by God.

### Key Parallels:

| Feature | Noah (The Type) | Israel (The Substance) |
|---|---|---|
| **Nature of the Remnant** | Eight righteous individuals in a corrupt world | A believing remnant within an unbelieving nation |
| **Nature of the Judgment** | A global flood | The global judgments of the Tribulation |
| **Method of Deliverance** | Preserved *through* judgment | Preserved *through* the Tribulation |
| **Place of Safety** | The ark, divinely designed | The wilderness, divinely prepared (Revelation 12:6, 14) |
| **Outcome** | Emerges to repopulate the earth | Emerges to enter the Millennial Kingdom |

**Table S7.2.1: Noah as a Type of Israel**

Noah therefore stands as a foundational Old Testament type of Israel's protection during the time of judgment, not removal from it.[1]

## Lot as a Type of the Church: Removed *Before* Judgment

Lot's deliverance in Genesis 19 presents a fundamentally different pattern. Unlike Noah, Lot was not preserved amid judgment but was forcibly removed *before* judgment began.

The angel's declaration makes this principle explicit:

> *"Hurry, escape there. For* ***I can do nothing until you arrive there****."*
>
> — GENESIS 19:22

Judgment was legally and physically restrained until the righteous were safely out of harm's way.

1. See Arno C. Gaebelein, *The Book of Genesis: A Complete Analysis* (New York: Our Hope Publication Office, 1912), 32.

## Key Parallels:

| Feature | Lot (The Type) | The Church (The Substance) |
|---|---|---|
| **Nature of the Remnant** | A righteous man distressed by lawlessness | Believers dwelling in a hostile world system |
| **Nature of the Judgment** | Sudden destruction by fire | The fiery judgments of the Day of the LORD |
| **Method of Deliverance** | Removed from the city *before* wrath fell | Caught up *before* wrath begins (1 Thessalonians 4:16-17) |
| **Divine Initiative** | Angels seized and led him out | Christ Himself catches His Bride away (*harpazo*) |
| **Restraint of Judgment** | Judgment delayed until removal (Genesis 19:22) | The Restrainer must be removed before lawlessness is revealed (2 Thessalonians 2:7) |
| **Outcome** | Safe outside the sphere of destruction | Forever with the Lord (John 14:3) |

**Table S7.2.2: Lot as a Type of the Church**

Lot thus becomes a clear Old Testament picture of removal prior to judgment, corresponding directly to the Church's promised deliverance from the coming wrath.

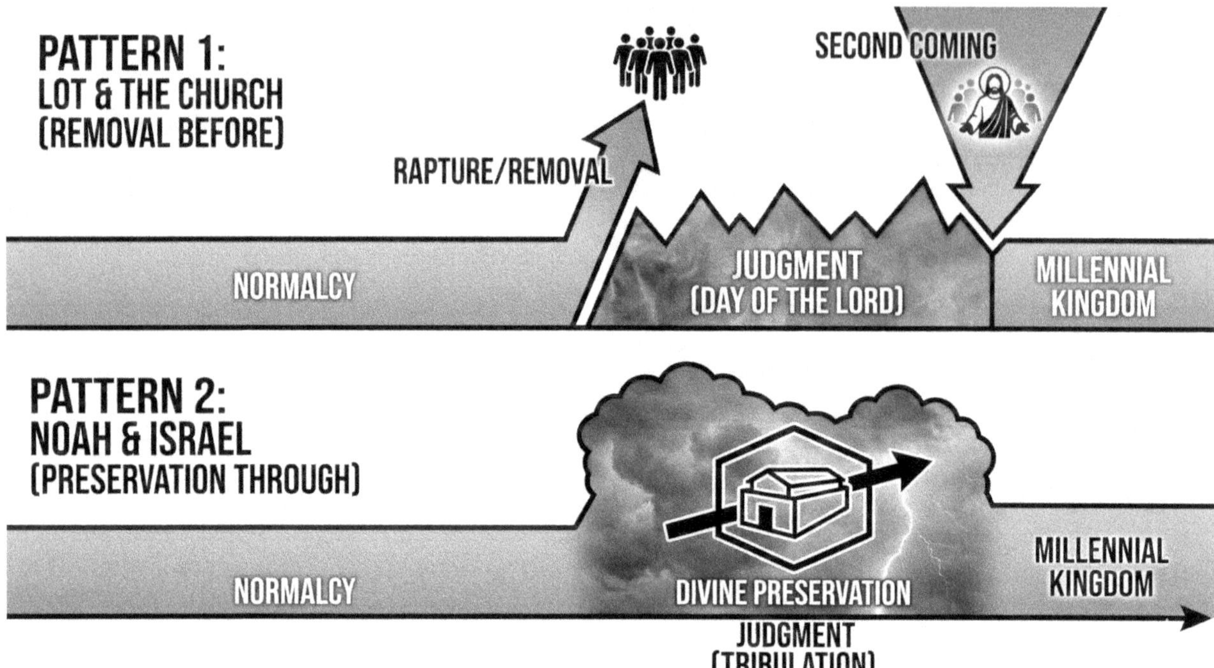


***Figure S7.2.1: Taken and Kept.*** *A visual comparison of the Church's removal before the Tribulation and Israel's preservation through it.*

## Two Models, Two Peoples, One Faithful God

Placed side by side, these accounts reveal a deliberate biblical pattern:

- **Israel** is preserved *through* judgment, sheltered on earth to inherit covenant promises.
- **The Church** is removed *before* judgment, gathered to Christ as a heavenly people.

These patterns are far from arbitrary. They reflect God's consistent faithfulness to fulfill His distinct purposes for Israel and the Church. Together, they demonstrate a foundational biblical principle: divine judgment never overtakes the righteous without God first providing a way of escape.

#  SHADOWS & SUBSTANCE 7.3. TAKEN, KEPT, AND RESCUED

## Two Destinies, Three Historical Patterns

Scripture often reveals future truths through historical patterns. When looking at God's blueprint for the end times, we see two distinct destinies for His people: those who are removed *before* the wrath falls, and those who are preserved *through* the wrath.

God illustrates these two destinies perfectly through three historical men: Enoch, Lot, and Noah.

## Destiny 1: The Removed Church (Enoch and Lot)

The Church is promised a complete rescue from the wrath to come (1 Thessalonians 1:10). God paints a comprehensive picture of this Pre-Tribulation Rapture by combining the stories of two men. Together, Enoch and Lot do not just show us that the Church will be removed; they show us the spiritual condition of the believers being rescued.

### Enoch: The Spiritual Believer's Rapture

> *Enoch walked with God; and he was not, for God took him.*
>
> — GENESIS 5:24

Enoch is the earliest biblical pattern of the Rapture. Taken alive by God, he never tastes death. His sudden disappearance long before the flood is a vivid foreshadowing of the living Church being caught up. More than that, Enoch represents the spiritually mature believer. He walks in unbroken fellowship with God, completely detached from the world system. He is the believer building his life with gold, silver, and precious stones, fully prepared for the testing fire of the Judgment Seat of Christ.[1] When the call comes, he is ready.

### Lot: The Carnal Believer's Rescue

> *"It was the same in the days of Lot... It rained fire and sulfur from heaven and destroyed them all. It will be just like this on the day the Son of Man is revealed."*
>
> — LUKE 17:28–30

While Enoch is taken in

1. It is critical to distinguish the Judgment Seat of Christ (the Bema Seat) from the Great White Throne judgment. The Bema Seat (2 Corinthians 5:10) is exclusively for the raptured Church. It takes place in heaven following the Rapture, and its sole purpose is the assigning or withholding of rewards based on earthly works (1 Corinthians 3:11–15). Salvation is never in question here. In stark contrast, the Great White Throne (Revelation 20:11–15) occurs at least a thousand years later, at the close of the Millennial Kingdom. It is the final tribunal exclusively for the unsaved dead, where those whose names are not found in the Book of Life are sentenced to the Lake of Fire. No believer will ever stand before the Great White Throne, and no unbeliever will ever stand before the Bema Seat.

quiet
intimacy, Lot is dragged out in extreme urgency. Lot represents the carnal Christian. Though legally righteous (2 Peter 2:7–8), he is practically worldly, having pitched his tent toward Sodom. The angels literally have to pull him from the city with seconds to spare. Lot is saved from the wrath, but his earthly works (his home, his wealth, his influence) are entirely consumed by the fire. He arrives at his deliverance empty-handed, smelling like smoke.

Together, Enoch and Lot form a complete picture of the Raptured Church: rescued entirely by grace before the fire falls, but presenting vastly different works to be tested at the Bema Seat.

## Destiny 2: The Preserved Remnant (Noah)

*But Noah found grace in the eyes of the LORD... Noah walked with God.*

— GENESIS 6:8–9

While Enoch and Lot are taken out of their environments, Noah remains. He does not escape the flood; he is preserved *through* it. God gives Noah a blueprint of survival: an ark to ride out the global judgment. He and his family enter it seven days before the rains begin (Genesis 7:10).

Noah directly prefigures God's preservation of the Jewish remnant. While the broader population of Tribulation saints will face horrific persecution and global martyrdom, a specific remnant of Israel will be supernaturally protected. But just like Noah, this preservation is conditional on location. When the Abomination of Desolation occurs, Jesus instructs them to flee immediately to the mountains (Matthew 24:15–16). In a divinely prepared place of wilderness refuge, often identified prophetically as Bozrah or Petra, God will shelter this remnant for the final three and a half years of the Tribulation so they can physically populate the Millennial Kingdom.

| FIGURE | TYPOLOGY | TIMING OF RESCUE | CORE MESSAGE |
|---|---|---|---|
| **ENOCH** (Raptured Church) | Raptured Church | Long before judgment | Walk with God; be ready before the storm. |
| **NOAH** (Faithful Remnant of Israel) | Faithful Remnant of Israel | Preserved **THROUGH** judgment | Prepare, endure, and trust God's provision. |
| **LOT** (Raptured Church) | Raptured Church | Immediately before judgment | God delivers His own before pouring out wrath. |
| **LOT'S WIFE** (The Divided Heart) | The Divided Heart | Delivered physically, looking back spiritually | Do not cling to the world you are leaving. |

***Figure S7.3.1: The Typological Gallery of Genesis.*** *Contrasting the destinies of those facing divine judgment. Enoch and Lot* *represent the Church, removed entirely before the wrath (the Rapture). Noah represents the Jewish remnant, safely preserved in a specific place of refuge through the judgment (the Tribulation). Finally, Lot's wife serves as the ultimate warning to the false professor: physically close to deliverance, yet ultimately destroyed by a worldly, divided heart.*

## Why Didn't Jesus Mention Enoch?

With all this typology, you might wonder: why did Jesus explicitly point to Noah and Lot (Luke 17), but leave out Enoch, the clearest picture of the raptured Church?

The omission is a prophetic diagnosis. Jesus was highlighting the specific spiritual condition of the generation alive at His return. The last days will not be characterized by Enoch-like devotion. They will be defined by Noah-era obliviousness and Lot-era compromise.

By focusing on Lot's era, Jesus also brings a third, haunting figure into the spotlight: Lot's wife. If Enoch is the spiritual believer and Lot is the carnal believer, Lot's wife represents the false professor.

### Lot's Wife: The False Professor

Lot's wife was delivered physically, but her heart remained behind. She looked back longingly at the life she left in Sodom, and was turned into a pillar of salt. She serves as a chilling cautionary figure for the apostate church:

- Proximity to salvation is not possession of it.
- Physical rescue without a decisive break in allegiance is fatal.
- Deliverance proves lethal to a divided heart.

Her fate serves as a sobering warning against a divided heart on the cusp of salvation. Jesus doesn't just want us to leave the world. He wants our hearts to be free from it.

| Figure | Prophetic Typology | Timing of Rescue | Core Message |
|---|---|---|---|
| Enoch | The Raptured Church (Spiritual) | Long before judgment | Walk with God; be ready before the storm. |
| Noah | The Faithful Remnant of Israel | Preserved through judgment | Prepare, endure, and trust God's provision. |
| Lot | The Raptured Church (Carnal) | Immediately before judgment | God delivers His own before pouring out wrath. |
| Lot's Wife | The False Professor | Delivered physically, looking back spiritually | Do not cling to the world you are leaving. |

***Table S7.3.1: Prophetic Patterns of Deliverance.***

## The Spectrum of Deliverance

God's judgments are never indiscriminate. He removes the Church, and He preserves Israel. But within these patterns, Scripture leaves us with a profound mirror for our own hearts as the end of the age approaches.

Let **Enoch's** translation encourage us to live entirely detached from a world that is passing away.

Let **Noah's** endurance remind us of God's faithful preservation of Israel.

Let **Lot's** narrow, empty-handed escape sober us to the reality of the Judgment (Bema) Seat.

And let the tragic fate of **Lot's wife** stand as the ultimate warning against spiritual ambivalence.

The Bridegroom is coming. The rescue is guaranteed, but your rewards are not. Ensure your heart is already with Him, and let Jesus' words ring in your ears as the world darkens:

> **"Remember Lot's wife!"**

# SHADOWS & SUBSTANCE 7.4. A BRIDE FOR THE SON

## The Prophetic Romance of Isaac and Rebekah

*"Let us be glad and rejoice and give Him glory, for the marriage of the Lamb has come, and His wife has made herself ready."*

— REVELATION 19:7

The story of Isaac and Rebekah in Genesis 22–24 is not merely a beautiful patriarchal romance, but one of the richest typological portraits in the entire Old Testament. It is an early prophetic sketch of the death, resurrection, and return of Christ, the calling out of the Church, and the reunion of the Bridegroom with His bride.

However, a specific anomaly in the narrative demands special attention. After Abraham lays Isaac on the altar in Genesis 22, Isaac disappears from the text. He is not mentioned again until he meets Rebekah, his bride, in Genesis 24.[1] This narrative "gap" is deliberate and prophetic.

***Figure S7.4.1: Tracing the Shadow of Genesis 22–24****. demonstrating Christ's hidden ascension, the Spirit's calling of the Church, and the future Rapture.*

1. The translation of Genesis 22:19 is a key point of detail for this typology. Dynamic equivalent translations (such as the NLT), which prioritize thought-for-thought readability, often render the verse as "Then they returned ..." This implies that both Abraham and Isaac returned together to the servants. In contrast, formal equivalent translations (such as the ESV, NASB, and NKJV), which prioritize a word-for-word rendering, state that "Abraham returned to his young men," preserving the significant typological detail of Abraham's apparent solo return from the mountain, a point that is obscured in the former.

## The Offering: A Shadow of the Cross

> *"Take your son, your only son Isaac, whom you love ... and offer him there as a burnt offering ..."*
>
> — GENESIS 22:2

In Genesis 22, Abraham is commanded to offer Isaac, his "only son" whom he loves, as a sacrifice on Mount Moriah. Every detail in this chapter drips with prophetic significance:[2]

- **Father and son ascend together**: Just as the Father and Son are united in the mission of redemption.
- **Isaac carries the wood**: As Jesus carried the cross.
- **A substitutionary ram appears**: A foreshadowing of the Lamb of God.
- **God provides the sacrifice**: As He provides the sacrifice for our redemption.

The mountain is later identified as the very region where Jerusalem and Calvary will be established (2 Chronicles 3:1). It is, in every sense, a definitive preview of the crucifixion.

## Isaac Disappears from the Narrative

Once the sacrifice scene ends, the text states:

> *So Abraham returned to his young men, and they rose and went together to Beersheba.*
>
> — GENESIS 22:19

**Where is Isaac?**

He is conspicuously absent from the closing verse, even though he clearly descended the mountain. The next time we see Isaac is in Genesis 24:62, when he comes to meet his bride.

This intentional narrative silence is a prophetic picture of Christ's current role:

- After His sacrifice, Jesus "disappears" from Israel's national story.
- His "silence" parallels the Church Age, the period between the cross and the Second Coming.
- Like Isaac, Jesus is alive, at the right hand of the Father, awaiting the completion of His bride, the Church.

## The Spirit's Mission to Call a Bride

Genesis 24 is the longest single chapter in the book of Genesis, and it is devoted entirely to finding a bride for Isaac.

Abraham sends his oldest servant (commonly identified as Eliezer, meaning "God is help") to a distant land to find and bring back a bride for his son. The servant is never named in this chapter, a detail that reinforces the typology:

2. Arthur W. Pink, *Gleanings in Genesis* (Chicago: Moody Press, 1922), chap. 26, "The Offering Up of Isaac."

The unnamed servant is a picture of the Holy Spirit, who does not speak of Himself (John 16:13), but glorifies the Son.[3]

- **He** is sent by the **Father** (Abraham) to call and prepare a **bride** (Rebekah) for the **Son** (Isaac).
- **Rebekah** must respond by faith to a proposal from a man she has never seen, just as the Church responds to Christ without seeing Him (1 Peter 1:8).

## Rebekah's Response: Will You Go?

> *And they called Rebekah and said to her, "Will you go with this man?" She said, "I will go."*
>
> — GENESIS 24:58

This simple but powerful question speaks to every generation: *Will you go?*

Rebekah's response is immediate. She leaves her family, her homeland, and her old life behind to journey toward a groom she loves but has never met. Her journey mirrors the Christian life, led by the Spirit, moving in faith, eyes set on the coming Bridegroom.

## The Reunion: At Evening Time, in the Field

> *And Isaac went out to meditate in the field toward evening. And lifted his eyes and saw, and behold, there were camels coming.*
>
> — GENESIS 24:63

Isaac is in the field, at evening, awaiting his bride. The timing and setting evoke prophetic overtones:

- **Evening** suggests the **close of the age**, the sun setting on the current world order.
- **The field** is the world (Matthew 13:38). Isaac is "in it," but not laboring. He is poised to receive his bride.
- **Rebekah** lifts her eyes and sees him from afar, echoing the Church being caught up to meet Christ (1 Thessalonians 4:17).
- **The encounter** takes place **before** Isaac returns home with her, just as Christ meets His Church in the air before returning with her.

## After the Bride, The Kingdom Advances

The narrative ends with Isaac bringing Rebekah into Sarah's tent, a picture of the intimacy and union of Christ with His Church. Only after this union does Isaac continue the covenantal line, bringing forth Jacob and Esau, who represent pivotal steps in God's redemptive plan.

The pattern is undeniable:

---

3. This chapter is widely understood as a picture of the Holy Spirit seeking a bride for Christ. For more on this, see Arno C. Gaebelein, *The Book of Genesis: A Complete Analysis* (New York: Our Hope Publication Office, 1912), 60.

| The Shadow (Genesis 22–24) | The Substance (Christ & The Church) |
|---|---|
| 1. Sacrifice on the mountain (Gen. 22) | Christ's crucifixion at Calvary. |
| 2. Isaac disappears from view | Christ ascends and is hidden from Israel. |
| 3. The Servant calls a bride (Gen. 24) | The Holy Spirit draws the Church. |
| 4. The bride responds | The Church says "Yes" in faith. |
| 5. Reunion in the field at evening | The Rapture of the Church. |
| 6. Intimacy and Union in the tent | The Marriage Supper of the Lamb. |
| 7. The story moves forward | Israel's national account resumes, leading to the Tribulation and Christ's return to earth. |

***Table S7.4.1: The Prophetic Romance***. *A Seven-Step Typological Alignment of Genesis 22–24 and the Redemptive Timeline.*

## The Son and His Bride

In Genesis 24, the blueprint is unveiled: the Father's Spirit seeks a bride for the Son. This is the gospel in silhouette.

Now, the promise is fulfilled, the Spirit is sent, and the Bridegroom awaits.

He is coming.

And the invitation echoes through the ages:

> **Will you go with this Man?**

# 🗝 SHADOWS & SUBSTANCE 7.5. THE RULER, THE BRIDE, AND THE FAMINE

## Joseph as a Prophetic Pattern of the End Times

*"And God sent me before you to preserve for you a remnant on earth, and to keep alive for you many survivors."*

— GENESIS 45:7

The Bible is a book of patterns. Events, people, and places in the Old Testament consistently point forward to deeper truths fulfilled in Christ and future prophecy.

One of the clearest and most compelling examples is the life of Joseph.

Recorded in Genesis 37–50, Joseph's story is more than just a historical account of suffering and redemption. It is a prophetic portrait. His experiences closely mirror those of Jesus Christ and foreshadow God's plan to rescue Israel and the world in the last days.

## Joseph: A Shadow of the Messiah

The similarities between Joseph and Jesus are unmistakable. As a prophetic "type," Joseph's life provides a stunning, detailed preview of the coming Messiah:[1]

1. Joseph as a type of Christ is widely recognized. See Arthur W. Pink, *Gleanings in Genesis* (Chicago: Moody Press, 1922), chaps. 40–46.

| The Prophetic Pattern | Joseph (The Shadow) | Jesus (The Messiah) |
|---|---|---|
| **Beloved of the Father** | Specially loved by his father, Jacob (Genesis 37:3). | The beloved Son of the Father (Matthew 3:17). |
| **Rejected by His Own** | Betrayed by his brothers and sold for pieces of silver (Genesis 37:28). | Betrayed, sold for 30 pieces of silver, and rejected by His own people (Matthew 26:15; John 1:11). |
| **Suffers Though Innocent** | Falsely accused and unjustly imprisoned (Genesis 39). | Condemned and crucified though completely blameless. |
| **Raised to Power** | Exalted from the dungeon to rule over all of Egypt (Genesis 41:41). | Exalted from the grave to the right hand of the Father (Philippians 2:9–11). |
| **Savior in a Crisis** | The sole provider during a global famine, holding all authority (Genesis 41:40). | The exclusive source of salvation: "there is no other name ... by which we must be saved" (Acts 4:12). |
| **Takes a Gentile Bride** | Given a Gentile wife, Asenath, **before** the years of famine begin (Genesis 41:45). | Takes a predominantly Gentile Bride (the Church) **before** the time of global judgment begins. |

***Table S7.5.1: Joseph as a Type of Christ.*** *A prophetic comparison demonstrating how Joseph's life foreshadows the Messiah's rejection, exaltation, and the deliverance of a Gentile Bride before the time of global judgment.*

This final detail is often overlooked, yet it is packed with prophetic meaning. Joseph's marriage happens *before* the famine starts. This is a powerful picture of the Pre-Tribulation Rapture: the Bride is joined to the Exalted Ruler *before* the time of distress falls upon the earth.

## The Seven-Year Famine: A Foreshadow of the Tribulation

Genesis 41 tells of Pharaoh's dream: seven years of abundance followed by seven years of famine. Joseph, through God's revelation, interprets the dream and is appointed to manage the crisis.

The seven years of famine are widely recognized as a clear foreshadowing of the future seven-year Tribulation described in Daniel 9:27. Looking at the timeline of Joseph's authority, his Gentile bride, and the eventual reconciliation with his brothers, this specific typology frames the Tribulation not just as judgment, but as preparation: for Israel's awakening, for the world's reckoning, and for the return of the King.

## Simeon: Deafness and the Beginning of Awakening

In Genesis 42, Joseph's brothers arrive in Egypt to buy grain. They do not recognize him. Joseph speaks strictly and accuses them of being spies. He imprisons Simeon, one of the brothers, and sends the rest back home.

This might seem like a minor detail until we look at the meaning of the name.

Simeon (*Shimon* in Hebrew) means "Hearing."

***Figure S7.5.1: The Binding of Simeon.*** *A powerful prophetic picture of Israel's temporary spiritual deafness.*

The fact that Joseph singles out "Hearing" and binds him is no coincidence. It distinctly illustrates the spiritual condition of Israel during the Church Age and into the Tribulation: a temporary, divinely permitted deafness to God's voice.

> ... *God gave them a spirit of stupor, eyes that would not see and ears that would not hear, down to this very day.*
>
> — ROMANS 11:8

Simeon is eventually released when the brothers return a second time. By the time Joseph reveals himself, the famine has lasted two years (Genesis 45:6), a detail with a profound prophetic clue.

If the seven-year famine points to the seven-year Tribulation, then Simeon's release in year two shows that Israel begins to "hear" again early in that period.

## Prophetic Implication: The Progressive Awakening of Israel

This idea harmonizes with several strands of end-times prophecy:

- **Hosea 6:1–2** describes a revival starting "after two days," which points symbolically to the second year.
- **Revelation 7** shows this awakening reaching a major milestone with the sealing of the 144,000 at the midpoint of the Tribulation.
- **Romans 11:25–26** confirms that Israel's blindness is only temporary, lasting until the fullness of the Gentiles comes in.

If Simeon's release is part of this pattern, it means Israel's deafness will not last through the entire Tribulation. Their ears will begin to open. Their hearts will begin to turn. The hard ground will begin to break.

## Typology Snapshot: Joseph's Famine and the Tribulation

When we put all these pieces together, a clear prophetic picture emerges:

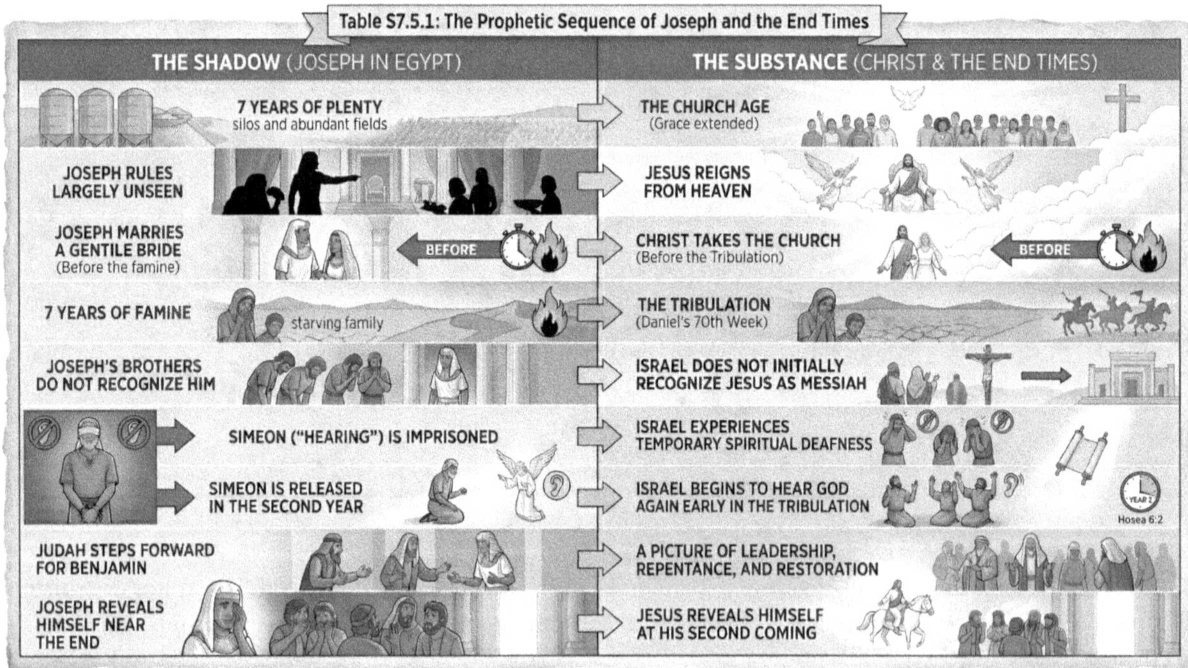

Table S7.5.1: The Prophetic Sequence of Joseph and the End Times

| THE SHADOW (JOSEPH IN EGYPT) | THE SUBSTANCE (CHRIST & THE END TIMES) |
|---|---|
| 7 YEARS OF PLENTY<br>silos and abundant fields | THE CHURCH AGE<br>(Grace extended) |
| JOSEPH RULES LARGELY UNSEEN | JESUS REIGNS FROM HEAVEN |
| JOSEPH MARRIES A GENTILE BRIDE<br>(Before the famine)<br>BEFORE | CHRIST TAKES THE CHURCH<br>(Before the Tribulation)<br>BEFORE |
| 7 YEARS OF FAMINE<br>starving family | THE TRIBULATION<br>(Daniel's 70th Week) |
| JOSEPH'S BROTHERS DO NOT RECOGNIZE HIM | ISRAEL DOES NOT INITIALLY RECOGNIZE JESUS AS MESSIAH |
| SIMEON ("HEARING") IS IMPRISONED | ISRAEL EXPERIENCES TEMPORARY SPIRITUAL DEAFNESS |
| SIMEON IS RELEASED IN THE SECOND YEAR | ISRAEL BEGINS TO HEAR GOD AGAIN EARLY IN THE TRIBULATION<br>YEAR 2<br>Hosea 6:2 |
| JUDAH STEPS FORWARD FOR BENJAMIN | A PICTURE OF LEADERSHIP, REPENTANCE, AND RESTORATION |
| JOSEPH REVEALS HIMSELF NEAR THE END | JESUS REVEALS HIMSELF AT HIS SECOND COMING |

***Figure S7.5.2.*** *A visual roadmap of the Joseph typology, tracing the prophetic parallels from the Church Age to the Second Coming.*

| The Shadow (Joseph in Egypt) | The Substance (Christ & The End Times) |
|---|---|
| 7 years of plenty | The Church Age (Grace extended). |
| Joseph rules largely unseen | Jesus reigns from heaven. |
| Joseph marries a Gentile bride (Before the famine) | Christ takes the Church (Before the Tribulation). |
| 7 years of famine | The Tribulation (Daniel's 70th Week). |
| Joseph's brothers do not recognize him | Israel does not initially recognize Jesus as Messiah. |
| Simeon ("hearing") is imprisoned | Israel experiences temporary spiritual deafness. |
| Simeon is released in the second year | Israel begins to hear God again early in the Tribulation. |
| Judah steps forward for Benjamin | A picture of leadership, repentance, and restoration. |
| Joseph reveals himself near the end | Jesus reveals Himself at His Second Coming. |

***Table S7.5.2: The Prophetic Sequence.*** *How Joseph's Life Mirrors the End Times.*

## A God Who Reveals the End from the Beginning

Scripture affirms that God declares "the end from the beginning" (Isaiah 46:10), and the life of Joseph is a masterful preview of the Messiah's own story.

This narrative serves as a powerful reminder that behind every famine lies a divine purpose, and beyond every trial awaits a joyous reconciliation.

Just as Joseph's rejection brought life to the Gentile world and his estranged brothers, Christ's suffering brings salvation to the nations and guarantees the final restoration of Israel.

As the Apostle Paul reminds us:

> *For whatever was written in former days was written for our instruction ...*
>
> — ROMANS 15:4

# 🗝 SHADOWS & SUBSTANCE 7.6. THE MIDNIGHT CALL AT THE THRESHING FLOOR

## Ruth, the Barley Harvest, and the Rapture

*Of his own will he brought us forth by the word of truth, that we should be a kind of firstfruits of his creatures.*

—JAMES 1:18

At its simplest level, the book of Ruth is a beautiful portrait of the Gospel: a Gentile bride is married to a Jewish redeemer before he reclaims his lost inheritance. In the same way, the Church is secured by Christ before He reclaims the earth during the Tribulation.

But beneath this broad stroke lies a finer, more intricate pattern, one involving a harvest, a midnight encounter, and a threshing floor.

Nowhere is this vivid prophetic detail more clearly seen than in Ruth 3, where Ruth humbly approaches Boaz. Beyond its cultural and romantic elements, this scene carries profound significance regarding the *timing* of the Rapture.

### The Cast of Characters in Prophetic Shadow

To understand the picture, we must first see the roles each person plays in this prophetic drama:

| Character / Place | Prophetic Type (The Substance) | Description |
|---|---|---|
| Boaz | Christ | The willing Kinsman-Redeemer who pays the price. |
| Ruth | The Gentile Bride | The Church, redeemed by grace rather than lineage. |
| Naomi | Israel | Widowed and exiled, yet destined for final restoration. |
| Unnamed Relative | The Law | A "nearer" relative who is legally valid but unable to redeem. |
| The Threshing Floor | Harvest & Judgment | A biblical place of separation and decision (Matt 13:30). |

***Table S7.6.1**: The Cast of Characters in Prophetic Shadow*

In this arrangement, Ruth's midnight encounter foreshadows how the Church will be redeemed and claimed by Christ before the final harvest of judgment begins.

## Scene by Scene: Prophetic Layers Unfold

### 1. Ruth Approaches Boaz at Night: A Quiet Encounter of Faith

> *So she went down to the threshing floor and did just as her mother-in-law had commanded her.*
>
> — RUTH 3:6

Ruth doesn't demand Boaz's attention in daylight or at the city gate. She comes quietly, humbly, at night. This symbolizes a private, grace-based relationship, distinct from the public judgment that will come later.

### 2. She Lies at His Feet: The Posture of Submission

> *Then she came softly and uncovered his feet and lay down.*
>
> — RUTH 3:7B

As a Moabite, Ruth has no legal covenant standing, yet she boldly places herself under the redeemer's mercy. This is the posture of the Church: saved not by our family line or our ability to keep the Law, but by submitting to Christ's covering. Ruth petitions, "Spread your wings over your servant, for you are a redeemer" (Ruth 3:9b).

## 3. Redeemed During the Barley Harvest: The "Firstfruits" Bride

> *"...Lie down until the morning."*
>
> — RUTH 3:13

The timing of this event is crucial. Ruth approaches Boaz as "he is winnowing barley tonight at the threshing floor" (Ruth 3:2).

In Israel's agricultural calendar, the **barley harvest** was the early harvest. Its "firstfruits" were offered to God in the spring, distinct from the main, later **wheat harvest**, associated with Pentecost and the summer.

Scripture establishes barley as the first grain to ripen (Exodus 9:31–32). The New Testament explicitly calls the Church "a kind of firstfruits of his creatures" (James 1:18).

- **The Pattern:** Ruth (the Gentile Bride) is redeemed during the *barley harvest* (the Firstfruits).
- **The Prophetic Fulfillment:** The Church is redeemed and removed as the *Firstfruits* of the harvest, prior to the main "wheat harvest" of the Tribulation.

## 4. The Unnamed Relative Cannot Redeem Her

> ... *"I cannot redeem it for myself, lest I impair my own inheritance. Take my right of redemption yourself, for I cannot redeem it."*
>
> — RUTH 4:6

The nearer kinsman, who remains unnamed, represents the **Law**. He is "closer" to Israel than Grace is, but he is unable to redeem a Gentile without compromising himself. Only Boaz (Christ), the willing redeemer, can through **Grace** fulfill the role. As Paul writes, "For what the **law** could not do ... God did by sending His own Son ..." (Romans 8:3 NKJV).

## SCENE BY SCENE: PROPHETIC LAYERS UNFOLD

**1. A Quiet Encounter of Faith** — Ruth approaches Boaz humbly at night. This symbolizes a private, grace-based relationship, distinct from the public judgment that follows.

**2. Lying at the Redeemer's Feet** — Having no legal standing, the Gentile outcast casts herself entirely on the mercy of the Redeemer. The Church is saved by submitting to Christ's covering, not by the Law.

**3. The "Firstfruits" Bride** — Ruth is redeemed during the early barley harvest. Prophetically, the Church is the "firstfruits" (James 1:18), redeemed and removed before the main harvest of the Tribulation.

**4. The Inadequacy of the Law** — The nearer kinsman cannot redeem her without ruining his own inheritance. The Law cannot save a Gentile; only the willing grace of the heavenly Boaz can fulfill the redemption.

***Figure S7.6.1: The Sequence of Grace.*** *Tracing the midnight encounter at the threshing floor, perfectly mirroring the Church's redemption prior to the heavy winds of the Tribulation harvest.*

## The Prophetic Sequence: Naomi Waits, Ruth Is Redeemed First

An often-overlooked detail strengthens the pattern: Naomi instructs Ruth but remains at home. Ruth learns the ways of her redeemer through Naomi's counsel, just as the Church comes to know our heavenly Boaz through the Hebrew Scriptures.

Ruth meets Boaz first, becomes his bride first, and is redeemed first. Only afterward does Naomi's restoration begin.

This follows the pattern revealed in Romans 11:25: "... a partial hardening has come upon Israel, until the fullness of the Gentiles has come in." The sequence is consistent: the Gentile bride is redeemed by grace, and then Israel's national restoration follows.

| The Shadow (The Book of Ruth) | The Substance (Christ & The Church) |
|---|---|
| **Ruth approaches Boaz at night** | The Church's private walk of faith in a dark world. |
| **Boaz, the Kinsman-Redeemer** | Christ, our Redeemer who became kin to us. |
| **Redeemed at the threshing floor during the early barley harvest** | The Rapture of the Church, gathered early as the "Firstfruits" harvest. |
| **The Unnamed Relative (The Law)** | The Law's inability to redeem the Gentile. |
| **Naomi's restoration follows Ruth's marriage** | Israel's restoration follows the fullness of the Gentiles. |
| **Boaz reclaims the lost land** | Christ reclaims the earth at His Second Coming. |

***Table S7.6.2***: *The Prophetic Sequence of Ruth and the Redeemer*

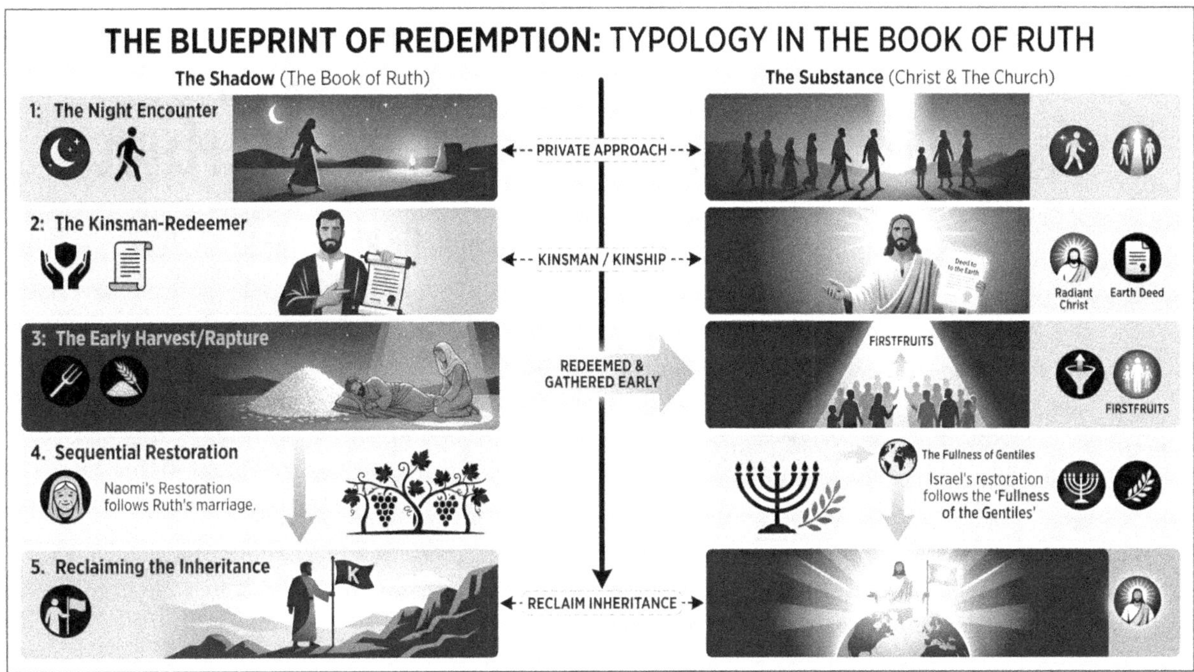


***Figure S7.6.2: The Blueprint of Redemption.*** *A typological comparison tracing the pattern of the Kinsman-Redeemer, the pre-tribulational gathering of the Church, and the subsequent restoration of Israel.*

## Redeemed Before the Main Harvest

Ruth's story is more than ancient romance; it is a coded narrative of the Bride and the Redeemer.

In Ruth, the Redeemer claims his "firstfruits" bride during the quiet barley harvest, removing her from the threshing floor before the heavy work of the main harvest begins. This offers a powerful witness to a Pre-Tribulation Rapture, where the Church is brought into union with the Redeemer before the winds of judgment blow across the earth.

# SHADOWS & SUBSTANCE 7.7. THE BRIDEGROOM'S PLEDGE

## The Ancient Jewish Wedding as a Prophetic Blueprint

*"In My Father's house are many rooms... I go to prepare a place for you. And if I go and prepare a place for you, I will come again and receive you to Myself, that where I am, there you may be also."*

—JOHN 14:2–3

The Bible is not a Western book. It is deeply Jewish in its language, imagery, and assumptions. Many of the words Jesus speaks, especially those about His departure and return, are not abstract theology but familiar cultural signals, immediately understood by His first-century Jewish disciples.

One of the clearest examples is the ancient Jewish wedding.

When Jesus speaks of going away to prepare a place, of returning at an unknown hour, and of receiving His people to Himself, He is not introducing a new metaphor. He is speaking the language of betrothal and marriage. His disciples recognize it instantly.

What follows is not speculative symbolism, but a pattern woven into Jewish life, one that aligns remarkably well with the New Testament's portrait of the Church and her Bridegroom.[1]

## The Jewish Wedding Process

### 1. A Covenant Is Established

Marriage begins with an agreement arranged by the father and secured by a price paid for the bride.

**The Picture:** Redemption begins with the Father's initiative, and the price is paid in full by the Son.

*You are not your own ... you were bought at a price.*

— 1 CORINTHIANS 6:19–20

### 2. The Bride Accepts and Is Set Apart

Once the bride accepts the covenant, she is considered consecrated, belonging to the groom, though the marriage is not yet consummated.

**The Picture:** The believer responds in faith and is set apart as belonging to Christ, even while awaiting full union.

1. This prophetic framework of the ancient Jewish wedding is extensively detailed by Arnold Fruchtenbaum in his foundational work, *The Footsteps of the Messiah*, rev. ed. (San Antonio, TX: Ariel Ministries, 2003).

*I betrothed you to one husband, to present you as a pure virgin to Christ.*

— 2 CORINTHIANS 11:2

### 3. The Groom Departs to Prepare a Place

The groom returns to his father's house to prepare a dwelling for his bride, often by adding a room to the family home.

**The Picture:** Jesus departs to the Father and promises to return for His own.

*"...I go to prepare a place for you ... I will come again and receive you to Myself..."*

—JOHN 14:3 NKJV

### 4. The Bride Waits and Watches

The bride does not know the exact day or hour of the groom's return. Her role is readiness, living in anticipation.

**The Picture:** The Church lives in expectancy, watching and waiting.

*"But of that day and hour no one knows ..."*

— MATTHEW 24:36 NKJV

### 5. The Groom Returns Suddenly

The groom comes unexpectedly, often at night, announced with a shout and accompanied by a trumpet. The bride is taken to the place prepared for her.

**The Picture:** The sudden gathering of the Church to Christ.

*For the Lord Himself will descend from heaven with a shout ... and with the trumpet of God ...*

— 1 THESSALONIANS 4:16–17 NKJV

*Figure S7.7.1: The Bridegroom's Sudden Return*

### 6. The Bride and Groom Enter the Bridal Chamber for Seven Days

Following the groom's return, the bride and groom are taken away together and secluded for seven days. During this time, they are hidden from public view while celebration continues elsewhere.

**The Picture**: Many see this seven-day seclusion as corresponding to the seven-year Tribulation on earth. As the bride is hidden with the groom for a defined and complete period, judgment unfolds outside. The pattern is consistent: the bride is removed, concealed, and protected while judgment runs its course, and is revealed only afterward. Isaiah anticipates this same sequence:

> *Come, my people, enter your chambers ... hide yourself as it were for a little moment until the indignation is past.*
>
> — ISAIAH 26:20 NKJV

### 7. The Public Celebration

Afterward, the couple emerges for a public celebration: the wedding feast.

**The Picture:** The Marriage Supper of the Lamb, following Christ's return in glory.

## The Prophetic Parallel at a Glance

The following summary captures the striking correspondence between the ancient custom and the future timeline:

Figure S7.7.1: The Bridegroom's Pledge: Tracing the Prophetic Parallel between the Ancient Jewish Wedding and the Rapture of the Church.

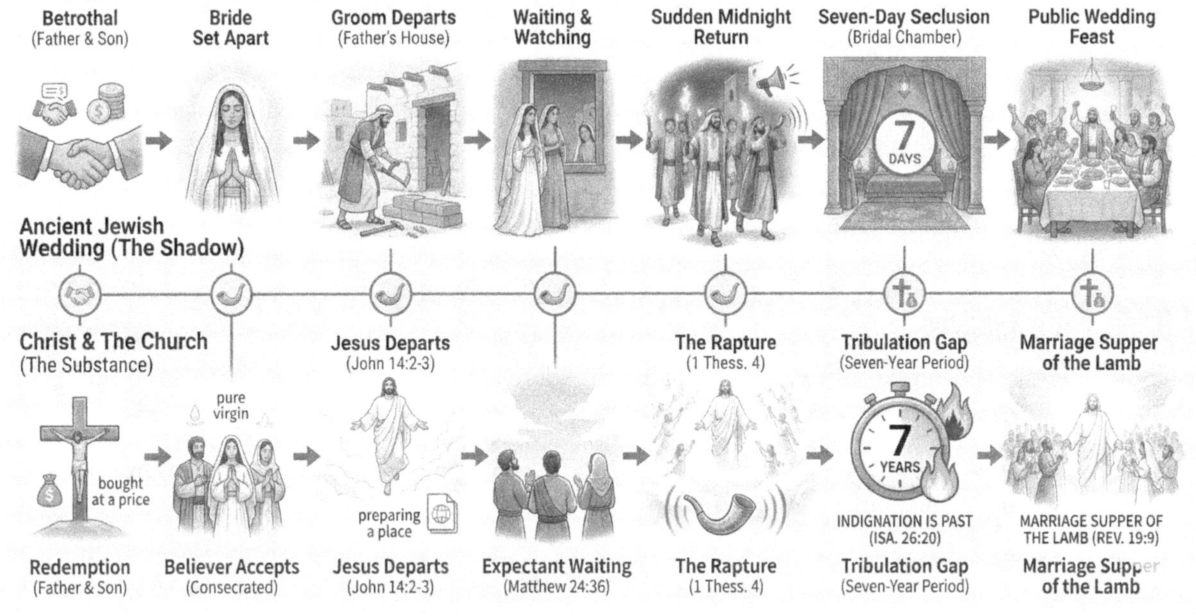


***Figure S7.7.2: The Bridegroom's Pledge.*** *Tracing the prophetic parallel between the ancient Jewish wedding and the Rapture of the Church.*

| The Shadow (Ancient Jewish Wedding) | The Substance (Christ & The Church) |
|---|---|
| Bride chosen, price paid | Christ dies for the Church. |
| Groom returns to father's house | Jesus ascends to heaven. |
| Bride does not know the day or hour | Expectant waiting for Christ's return. |
| Groom comes with a shout and trumpet | Rapture announced with a shout and trumpet (1 Thess. 4). |
| Bride taken to groom's home | Church taken to heaven. |
| Seven days in bridal chamber | Seven-year Tribulation on Earth. |
| Wedding feast follows | Marriage Supper of the Lamb (Rev. 19:9). |

***Table S7.7.1:*** *The Prophetic Sequence of the Jewish Wedding*

## The Pre-Tribulational Blueprint

When this wedding pattern is laid alongside the New Testament's teaching, it fits naturally with a Pre-Tribulational gathering of the Church.

Other models struggle to account for the groom coming for the bride *before* a time of judgment, followed by a period of seclusion, and only then a public return.

Jesus speaks wedding language because He means it. His promises are not vague metaphors but culturally grounded assurances to His future Bride.

## A Bride, not a Survivor

The Church is never described as a group left behind to endure judgment, but as a bride cherished and claimed.

Throughout Scripture, God removes the righteous before judgment or shelters them from it. Why would Christ treat His bride differently?

> *For God did not appoint us to wrath...*
>
> — 1 THESSALONIANS 5:9 NKJV

The wedding pattern affirms it: the Bridegroom comes for His bride, gathers her to Himself, and only then does judgment fall.

## A Promise Woven Into Life

More than background, the Jewish wedding is a "live" parable. A groom prepares. A bride waits. A sudden return brings joy, union, and celebration.

For those watching, the cry will come.

The trumpet will sound.

And the wedding will begin.

# SHADOWS & SUBSTANCE 7.8. THE MYSTERY OF THE RESTRAINER

## The "He" and the "What" Holding Back the Tide of Lawlessness

> *For the mystery of lawlessness is already at work; only He who now restrains* will *do so until He is taken out of the way. And then the lawless one will be revealed ...*
>
> — 2 THESSALONIANS 2:7–8

The passage above contains one of the most critical keys to the timing of the Rapture. It hinges on a single question: Who, or what, is this mysterious Restrainer?

## The Clue: A "He" and a "What"

Paul uses a deliberate shift in language to describe the Restrainer.

- In verse 6, he refers to **"what restrains"**, implying a force, power, or institution.
- But in verse 7, he switches to **"He who restrains"**, referring to a specific person.

This implies a dual nature: **an impersonal force acting in concert with a personal presence.**

Why does this matter? Because most theories fail this dual test:

- **Human Government** fits the "What" (an institution) but lacks the "He", a singular, personal agent capable of restraining the final revelation of the lawless one.
- **Michael the Archangel** fits the "He" (a personal being), but Scripture never presents him as a neuter, institutional, or corporate restraining force.

## The Grammatical Resolution

Only one candidate fully satisfies these strict grammatical demands: The Holy Spirit working through the Church:

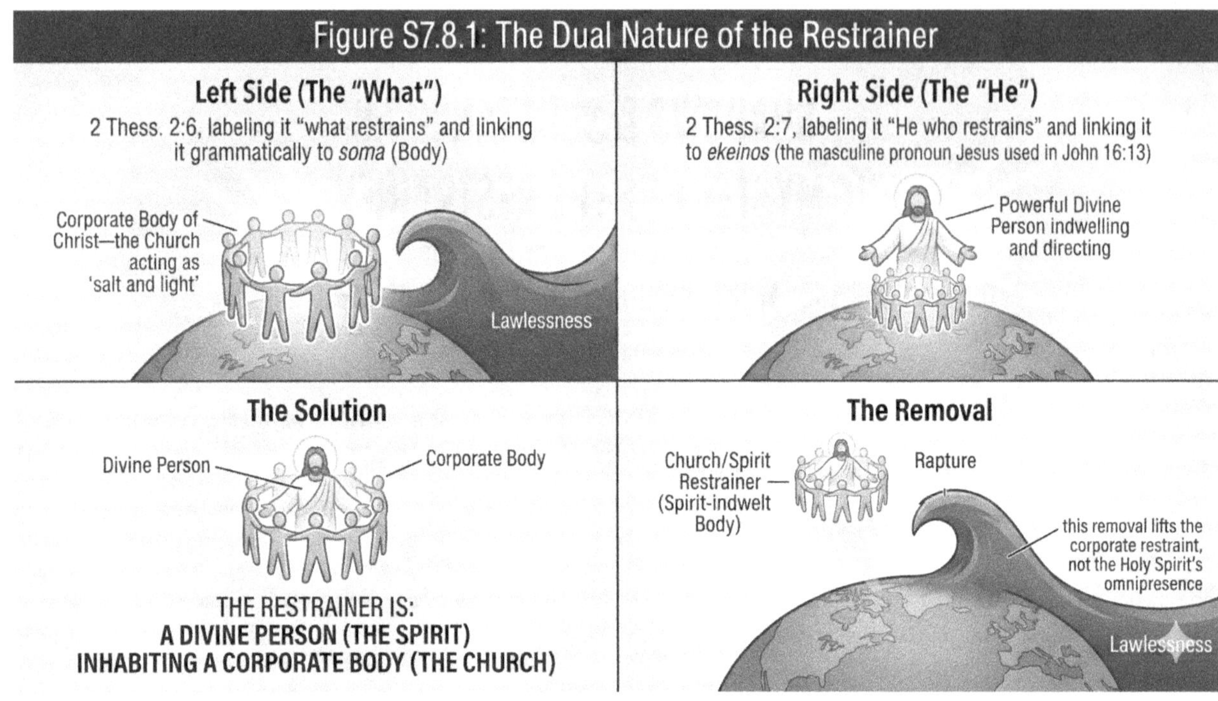


***Figure S7.8.1: The Dual Nature of the Restrainer****. How the Holy Spirit and the Church fulfill Paul's grammatical requirements.*

- **The "What" (The Body):** The Church functions as the Body of Christ on earth. In Greek, the word for Body (*soma*) is **neuter**, precisely aligning with Paul's description of the impersonal force in verse 6. This is the corporate influence, the "salt and light," that preserves society from total corruption.
- **The "He" (The Power):** The Holy Spirit is the Divine Person who energizes that body. While the Greek word for Spirit (*pneuma*) is grammatically neuter, Jesus explicitly refers to the Spirit as "He" (*ekeinos*, masculine) in John 16:13.

Therefore, the Restrainer is a **Divine Person** (the Spirit) inhabiting a **Corporate Body** (the Church).

## The Departure Signals a Shift

If the Restrainer is the Spirit-indwelt Church, then the "removal" refers to the Rapture.

Crucially, this does not mean the Holy Spirit disappears from the earth, since as God He is omnipresent. Rather, His unique Church-age ministry, operating through the Temple of the Body of Christ to hold back evil, is lifted.

## The Typology of the Glory Departing

This specific sequence, Divine Presence leaving before destruction begins, has a profound biblical precedent in Ezekiel 10–11.

In Ezekiel's vision, he watches the Glory of the LORD (the Shekinah) lift up and depart from the Temple in Jerusalem. God's manifest presence moved to the threshold, then to the city gate, and finally to the Mount of Olives (Ezekiel 11:23), leaving the sanctuary vacant.

**The Result:** Only *after* God's glory departed did the Babylonian armies destroy the city and the sanctuary.

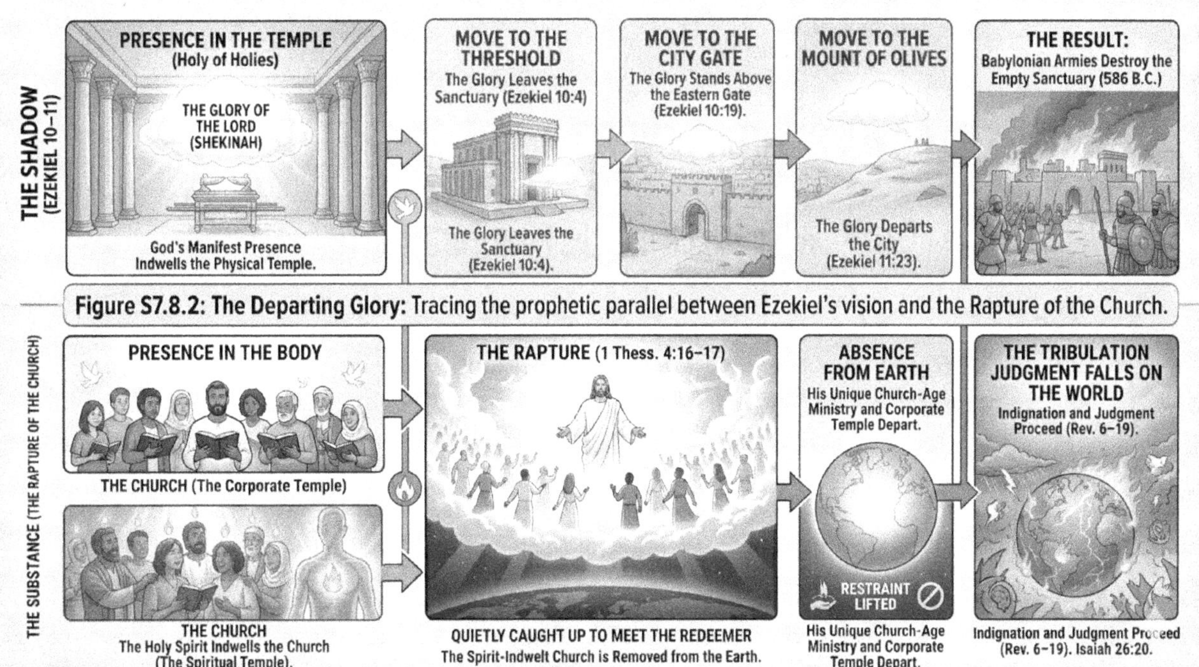


*Figure S7.8.2: The Departing Glory. Tracing the prophetic parallel between Ezekiel's vision and the Rapture of the Church.*

The typology is clear:

1. **Ezekiel 10–11:** The Glory (God's Presence) departs → Judgment falls on Jerusalem.
2. **The Rapture:** The Spirit-indwelt Church (God's Presence) departs → Judgment falls on the world.

## A Consistent Pattern

This fits the broader pattern of divine rescue we see throughout Scripture. God consistently removes the righteous presence before judgment floods in:

- **Enoch** was taken before the Flood waters rose.
- **Lot** had to be removed before Sodom could burn.
- **Daniel** was absent before the fiery furnace was heated.

In every case, the "restraining influence" was removed so that judgment could proceed. The Rapture is simply the final, global fulfillment of this ancient divine pattern.[1]

1. This understanding identifies the Restrainer as the Holy Spirit working through the Church. When the Church is removed, that restraining ministry is lifted. A clear articulation of this view is found in J. Dwight Pentecost, *Things to Come* (Zondervan, 1958).

#  SHADOWS & SUBSTANCE 7.9. THE PROPHETIC SILENCE

## A Hidden Clue in the Fiery Furnace

*Because you have kept my word about patient endurance, I will keep you from the hour of trial that is coming on the whole world, to try those who dwell on the earth.*

— REVELATION 3:10

Sometimes the loudest messages in Scripture are not spoken aloud but conveyed through silence.

One of the most striking examples appears in Daniel 3, during the well-known account of the fiery furnace. Shadrach, Meshach, and Abednego refuse to bow to Nebuchadnezzar's golden image. They are thrown into a furnace heated seven times hotter than usual and are miraculously preserved by a fourth figure "like a son of the gods" (Daniel 3:25).

The story is rightly celebrated as a testimony of courage, faith, and divine deliverance. Yet it leaves a lingering question:

**Where was Daniel?**

## The Elephant Not in the Room

Daniel is conspicuously absent. He is the central figure of the book, a man of steadfast faith who defies kings, interprets dreams, and later faces the lions' den.

If anyone would have refused to bow, it would have been Daniel.

And yet, in one of the most famous stand-for-God-or-burn stories in the Bible, Daniel is nowhere to be found.

This omission is not an accident. It is a divine whisper pointing us toward something deeper.

## A Hidden Typology of the End Times

If the fiery furnace is a type of the Great Tribulation, Nebuchadnezzar's golden image a foreshadowing of the Antichrist's abomination, and the three Hebrew men represent the faithful Jewish remnant, then Daniel's absence takes on new significance.[1]

1. The typology of Daniel 3, where Daniel is absent while his companions endure the furnace, is a foundational prophetic pattern distinguishing the Church's removal from Israel's time of trial. See John Walvoord, *Daniel: The Key to Prophetic Revelation* (Chicago: Moody Press, 1971), and the teachings of Chuck Missler, who frequently highlighted Daniel's absence as a meaningful detail pointing to removal before judgment.

**Figure S7.9.1: The Prophetic Silence: Visualizing Daniel's absence as a shadow of the Church's removal before the Tribulation**

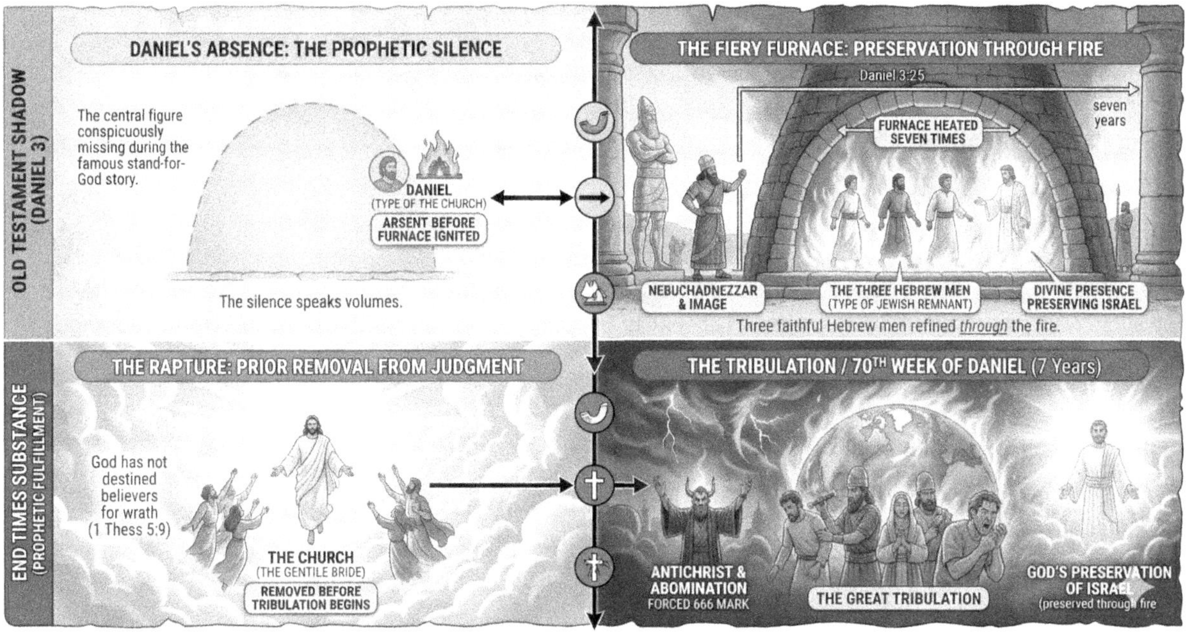

***Figure S7.9.1: The Prophetic Silence.*** *Visualizing Daniel's absence as a shadow of the Church's removal before the Tribulation.*

| The Shadow (Daniel 3) | The Substance (The End Times) |
|---|---|
| **Nebuchadnezzar & the Image** | The Antichrist and the enforced worship of his image. |
| **Furnace heated seven times** | The 70th Week of Daniel (the seven-year Tribulation). |
| **The three Hebrew men** | Israel, refined and tested through the fire of affliction (Zech. 13:8–9). |
| **The fourth man in the fire** | The LORD's presence preserving the remnant through the trial. |
| **Daniel's absence** | The Church, removed and absent from the fiery trial. |

***Table S7.9.1.*** *The Typology of the Fiery Furnace*

The implication is not forced, but it is consistent:

The Church, the faithful ones taken up before the Tribulation, will not be present when the world is tested in the fire of God's judgment.

This harmonizes with Paul's assurance:

*For God has not destined us for wrath, but to obtain salvation through our Lord Jesus Christ.*

— 1 THESSALONIANS 5:9

## Where Could Daniel Have Been?

Some scholars speculate that Daniel may have been away on state business, exempt due to rank, or otherwise uninvolved in the king's decree. But the text is silent on this point, which is theologically louder than any explanation.

The silence speaks volumes, because what's absent in prophecy often serves to draw attention to a greater truth.

## A Furnace Heated Seven Times

Even the detail of the fire being "heated seven times hotter" carries symbolic weight. In Scripture, seven repeatedly marks completeness, and the final period of judgment is defined as a seven-year span, the 70th week of Daniel (Daniel 9:27).

## A Familiar Pattern

This scene does not stand alone; it locks seamlessly into a pattern established throughout Scripture where God's methods remain consistent. Judgment and deliverance are never confused.

- **Enoch** is taken before the flood (*Shadows & Substance 7.3. Taken, Kept, and Rescued*).
- **Isaac disappears** from the narrative after being "offered" until he reappears to meet his bride (*Shadows & Substance 7.4. A Bride for the Son*).
- **Joseph's Gentile bride** (Asenath) is united with him before the famine begins (*Shadows & Substance 7.5. The Ruler, the Bride, and the Famine*).
- And now, **Daniel vanishes** from the scene before the furnace is ignited.

## A Silent Testimony of Deliverance

Daniel's silence in chapter 3 is not a narrative oversight. It is a quiet testimony, a message whispered between the lines.

Some are preserved **through** the fire.

Others are removed **before** it.

The call, then, is not only to stand faithfully in trial, but to walk closely with God before the flames are ignited.

# DEEPER DIVE 10.1. THE WAR THAT BREAKS THE PEACE

## Tracing Ezekiel's Invasion Through the First Two Seals

*You will advance, coming on like a storm. You will be like a cloud covering the land, you and all your hordes, and many peoples with you.*

— EZEKIEL 38:9

Ezekiel 38–39 prophesies a massive invasion of Israel led by "Gog of the land of Magog," culminating in a decisive, supernatural judgment by God. One of the most distinctive features of this prophecy is its aftermath: Israel is said to burn the invaders' weapons for fuel for seven years (Ezekiel 39:9–10).

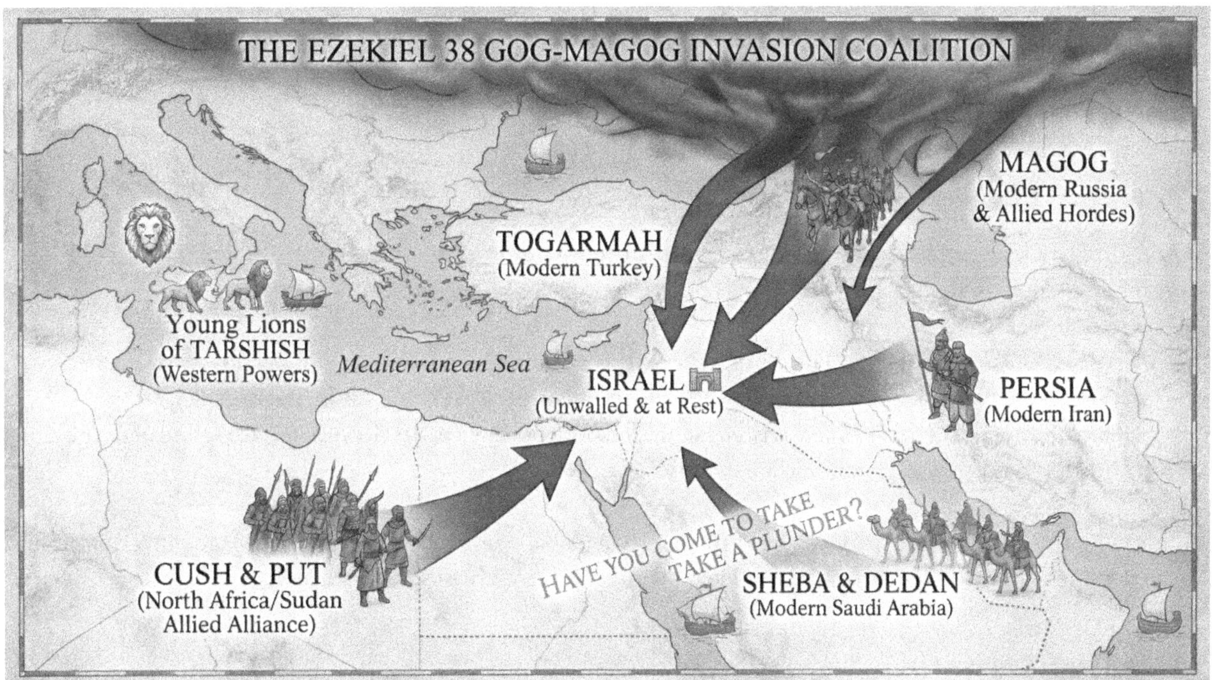


***Figure D10.1.1: The Northern Storm.*** *Ezekiel 38 describes a massive, multi-nation coalition—led by Magog (Russia), Togarmah (Turkey), and Persia (Iran)—descending upon an unsuspecting Israel. The "Young Lions of Tarshish" (Western powers) and allied Arab states (Sheba and Dedan) offer only diplomatic protests. This fulfills the exact, terrifying geopolitical alignment prophesied by Ezekiel thousands of years ago.*

The invasion is explicitly placed "in the latter days" (*acharit hayamim*; Ezekiel 38:16). While this phrase broadly denotes the final period of human history, determining its precise timing relative to the Tribulation has generated sustained scholarly debate.

## The Primary View: The First-Half Invasion

A widely held prophecy view places the Gog–Magog invasion in the first half of the Tribulation, a position long taught by Mark Hitchcock and John F. Walvoord. This view relies on the condition of Israel dwelling securely under the covenant of Daniel 9:27.[1]

Building on this framework, Allen Nolan has further proposed a specific correlation between Ezekiel 38–39 and the Second Seal (the Red Horse) of Revelation 6.[2] While this seal-level identification goes beyond Hitchcock's argument, it remains logically consistent with the first-half placement and advances a tighter chronological sequencing within it.

### 1. The Argument from Israel's Security (*Shaqat* vs. *Batah*)

The most compelling internal evidence for a Tribulation-period invasion is Israel's condition at the time of attack. Ezekiel 38:11 describes a people dwelling "without walls, bars, or gates," living "at rest" (*shaqat*).

As Hitchcock observes, modern Israel may dwell in military confidence (*batah*), but it is not *shaqat*, not truly undisturbed or secure from threat. It exists as a fortified garrison, encircled by hostility, terror, and the constant expectation of attack.

The most plausible mechanism capable of producing the specific state of relaxation described by Ezekiel is the covenant confirmed by the Antichrist (Dan 9:27). This agreement, which initiates the Tribulation, creates a deceptive sense of peace and security. Consequently, the Gog–Magog invasion most plausibly occurs after the Tribulation begins, not before it.

### 2. The Red Horse Connection

While Hitchcock argues the invasion must occur sufficiently prior to the midpoint to allow for the seven-month burial, Nolan's correlation with the Second Seal provides a specific chronological anchor:

- **First Seal (White Horse):** The Antichrist emerges as a false peacemaker, confirming a covenant with Israel and ushering in a brief period of illusory security (Revelation 6:1–2; Ezekiel 38:8, 11).
- **Second Seal (Red Horse):** Peace is suddenly "taken from the earth" (Revelation 6:4), signaling the outbreak of widespread global warfare.

In this view, the Red Horse marks the onset of sweeping global conflict, while the Gog–Magog invasion stands as the defining catalytic event that exposes and collapses the Antichrist's false peace.

### 3. A Global Power Realignment

Regardless of whether it is correlated with the Second Seal or placed later within the first half, a first-half invasion explains the rapid consolidation of power by the Antichrist. When God supernaturally destroys a major northern-led coalition during the first half of the seven years, the global balance of power is dramatically altered.

Rather than undermining the Antichrist's authority, this divine judgement produces a dramatic realignment of

1. Mark Hitchcock, *The Battle of Gog and Magog* (Pre-Trib Research Center), accessed January 2026, https://www.pre-trib.org/pretribfiles/pdfs/Hitchcock-TheBattleofGogandMag.pdf; John F. Walvoord, *The Nations in Prophecy* (Grand Rapids: Zondervan, 1967), 113–115.
2. Allen Nolan, **"Ezekiel's End Times Prophecies Explained,"** YouTube teaching series, lectures on Revelation 6 and Ezekiel 38–39, accessed January 2026.

global power that the Antichrist is uniquely positioned to exploit. The removal of rival powers accelerates his rise, culminating in his self-deification at the midpoint of the Tribulation.

## Addressing the "Seven Years" Objection (Ezekiel 39:9)

The primary objection to a first-half placement concerns the seven-year period during which Israel burns the invaders' weapons.

- **The Burial (Mandated):** Ezekiel 39:12–14 specifies a seven-month effort to cleanse the land. As Hitchcock notes, if the invasion occurs sufficiently prior to the midpoint, this burial period can be fully completed before the Abomination of Desolation.
- **The Burning (Descriptive):** The text does not mandate a centralized or uninterrupted national program of weapon disposal. Instead, it describes a readily available resource that replaces ordinary fuel use. When the Jewish remnant flees into the wilderness at the midpoint (Matthew 24:15), these abandoned weapons may serve as a providential fuel source that helps sustain them during the final three and a half years.

## Alternative Views

### The Pre-Tribulation Invasion

Some scholars, including Tim LaHaye and Arnold Fruchtenbaum, place the Gog–Magog invasion *before* the Tribulation, with Fruchtenbaum arguing for a date at least three and one-half years prior to Daniel's seventieth week.[3]

- **Strength:** This view easily accommodates the seven years of weapon burning without overlap.
- **Weakness:** As Hitchcock observes, it struggles to account for Israel's *shaqat* security apart from the covenant of Daniel 9:27.

Some proponents of a Pre-Tribulation placement also appeal to a proposed Psalm 83 war, most notably advanced by Bill Salus. In this model, Psalm 83 is read as a distinct, future conflict in which Israel's immediate neighbors form an "inner-ring" coalition that must be decisively defeated before the conditions of security described in Ezekiel 38 can exist. For a detailed evaluation of this proposal and its challenges, see *Deeper Dive 10.2. The War That Never Happens?*

### The Post-Millennial View (Revelation 20)

Although Revelation 20:8 refers to "Gog and Magog," the context is irreconcilable with Ezekiel 38–39. Ezekiel requires months of burial and land cleansing, whereas Revelation 20 concludes with immediate cosmic destruction by fire.

3. Arnold G. Fruchtenbaum, *The Footsteps of the Messiah: A Study of the Sequence of Prophetic Events*, rev. ed. (Tustin, CA: Ariel Ministries, 2003), pp. 121–123.

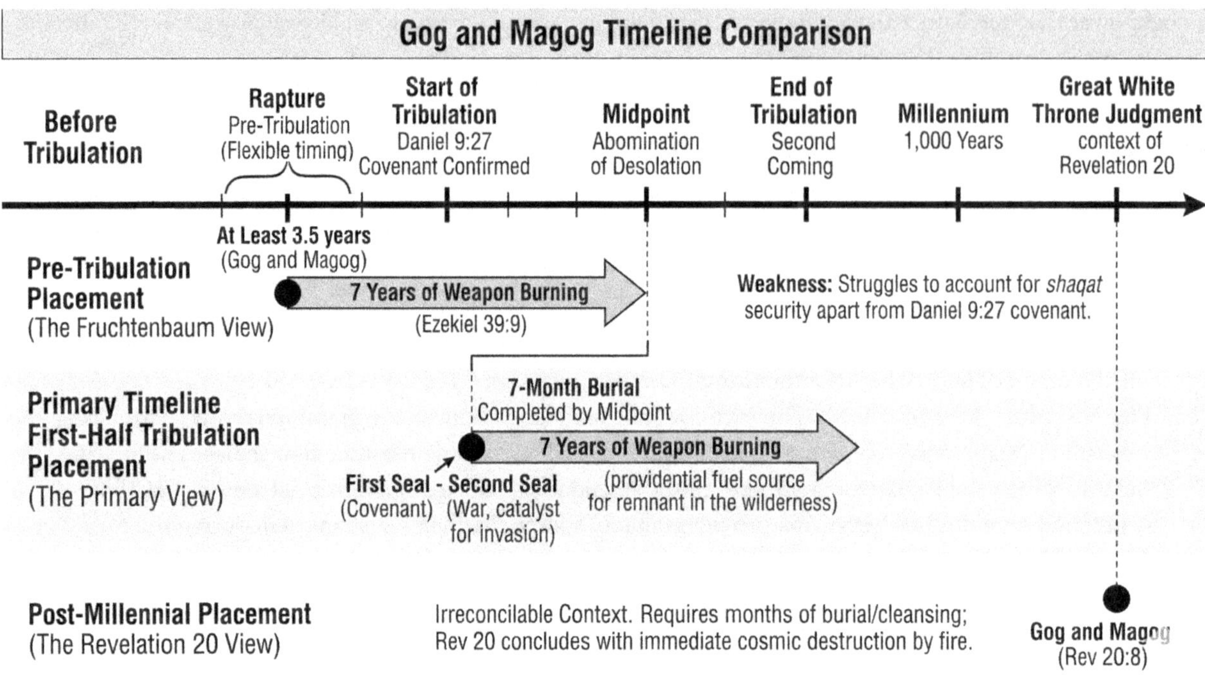


***Figure D10.1.2: Charting the Northern Storm.*** *Comparing the proposed timelines for the Gog and Magog invasion. Placing the conflict within the first half of Daniel's Seventieth Week directly aligns with Israel's false security and the logistical requirements of the seven-month burial.*

## Conclusion: The Most Coherent Timeline

The first-half Tribulation view provides the essential framework for situating the Gog–Magog invasion, placing it after the covenant of Daniel 9:27 and before the midpoint of the seven years. Within that framework, the convergence of Israel's covenant-induced security, the logistical requirements of the burial period, and the opening seals of Revelation increasingly supports an early-Tribulation fulfillment.

In this synthesized view, the Antichrist's initial promise of peace under the First Seal is quickly shattered. The Gog–Magog invasion emerges as the spark that helps ignite the global warfare of the Second Seal, marking the comprehensive collapse of the world's brief illusion of peace. God's decisive intervention not only preserves Israel but also reshapes the global order and accelerates the rise of the final world ruler, whose apparent triumph is utterly annihilated by the returning Messiah.

# DEEPER DIVE 10.2. PSALM 83: THE WAR THAT NEVER HAPPENS?

## Prophetic Blueprint or Poetic Petition?

Among students of Bible prophecy, a popular but debated theory suggests that Psalm 83 foretells a distinct, future war between Israel and her immediate neighbors. Proponents of this view, most notably author Bill Salus, argue that Psalm 83 predicts a coming regional conflict in which Israel's surrounding Arab neighbors unite in a final attempt to "wipe Israel off the map."[1] According to this model, nations such as Lebanon, Syria, and Jordan, along with terrorist entities operating from Gaza, form an "inner-ring" coalition that must be defeated before Israel can experience the conditions of security described in Ezekiel 38. The psalm also mentions the "Ishmaelites," a term biblically associated with Arab peoples of the Arabian Peninsula, a region dominated today by Saudi Arabia.

Psalm 83:4 does sound ominous:

> *They say, "Come, let us wipe them out as a nation; let the name of Israel be remembered no more!"*

The question, however, is whether Psalm 83 functions as **predictive prophecy** or as a **historical plea for divine intervention**. While Salus interprets the psalm as a prophetic blueprint for a future military conflict, many conservative scholars understand it instead as a national lament, likely arising from the era of King Jehoshaphat (cf. 2 Chronicles 20), when a regional alliance advanced against Judah. The psalm's language aligns closely with the conventions of urgent prayer rather than with the apocalyptic or prophetic genre.

Importantly, the proposal of a distinct future "Psalm 83 war" is not universally accepted among futurist scholars. Thomas Ice, writing from within dispensational futurism, argues that Psalm 83 functions as a lament rather than a predictive end-times prophecy, and cautions against turning poetic prayer into a chronological war scenario.[2]

## The Geopolitical Reset: June 2025

Recent geopolitical developments also invite a reassessment of the "Psalm 83 war" model. In the aftermath of the Hamas attack on October 7, 2023, Israel has significantly degraded the military capabilities of Hamas in Gaza and Hezbollah in southern Lebanon. Iran, the principal regional sponsor of both groups, suffered what many analysts describe as a substantial strategic setback during the brief but intense conflict of June 2025, referred to in Israeli sources as **Operation Rising Lion**. That confrontation culminated in a decisive American intervention that reportedly inflicted severe damage on Iran's nuclear infrastructure, though not eliminating it entirely.

---

1. Bill Salus, *Isralestine: The Ancient Blueprints of the Future Middle East* (Crane, MO: Highway 66 Publishing, 2013). Salus argues that this inner-ring conflict must precede the outer-ring invasion of Ezekiel 38.
2. Thomas Ice, "Consistent Biblical Futurism, Parts 10-13" *Pre-Trib Perspectives* (Pre-Trib Research Center), accessed January 2026, https://www.pre-trib.org/consistent-biblical-futurism/message/consistent-biblical-futurism-part-10/read.

In the current environment, Israel's immediate neighbors are pursuing stability, de-escalation, or pragmatic engagement rather than open confrontation. Saudi Arabia continues moving toward normalization, and Syria has signaled interest in non-aggression frameworks. Lebanon, weakened internally, has shown preliminary openness to dialogue, while Gaza faces urgent humanitarian and infrastructure reconstruction needs. Furthermore, the Abraham Accords continue to expand with the UAE and Bahrain already normalized, and Egypt and Jordan maintain long-standing, if cautious, peace treaties with Israel.

FIGURE D10.2.1: THE INNER AND OUTER RINGS
Geographic contrast between the Psalm 83 neighbors and the Ezekiel 38 invaders.

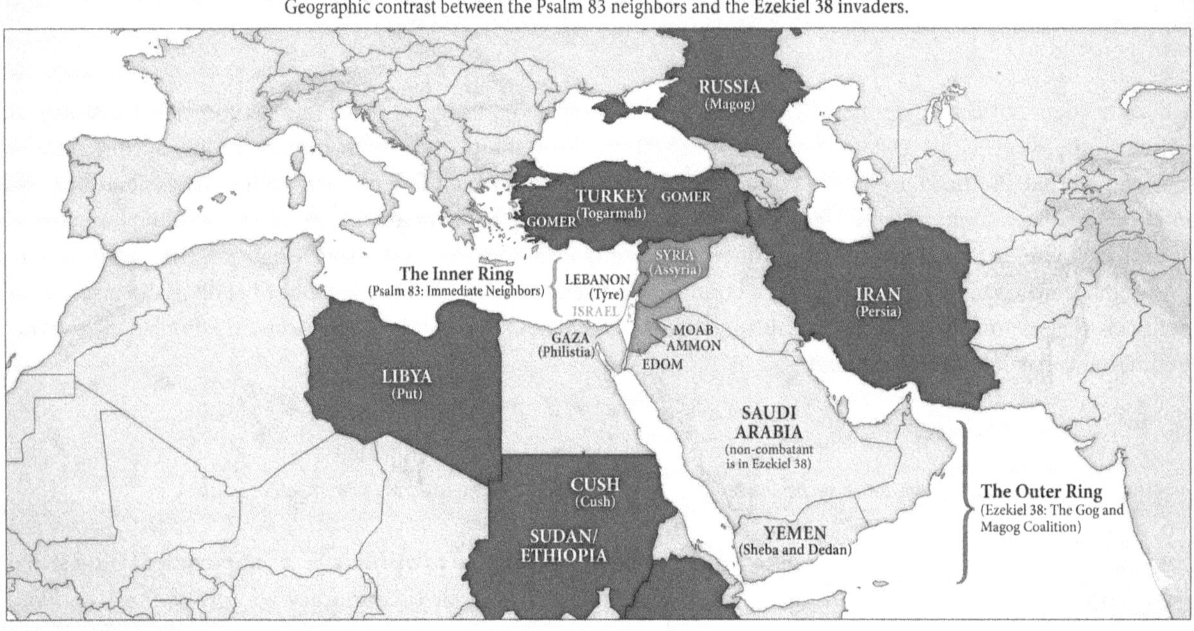


***Figure D10.2.1: Inner and Outer Rings.*** *A geographical comparison of the immediate neighbors of Psalm 83 and the distant invaders of Ezekiel 38. The omission of Israel's bordering nations from the Gog and Magog coalition aligns strikingly with their prophetic neutralization.*

This evolving regional dynamic helps clarify why Ezekiel 38 describes a coalition composed not of Israel's immediate neighbors, but of more distant "outer-ring" powers, commonly identified as Russia, Iran, and Turkey, while omitting Lebanon, Syria, Jordan, and Egypt altogether. Notably, Ezekiel 38:13 portrays Sheba and Dedan, regions traditionally associated with modern-day Yemen and Saudi Arabia, questioning the motives of the invaders rather than joining them. The absence of Israel's immediate and historically hostile neighbors from the Gog–Magog coalition is best explained if, by the time of the invasion, those states have ceased to pose a direct threat, either through military degradation or diplomatic engagement.

## The Vengeance of Persia

Iran, by contrast, remains ideologically and relentlessly committed to Israel's destruction. Though badly mauled in March 2026 by Israel's Operation Roaring Lion and the United States' Operation Epic Fury, Tehran's hostility has not diminished, only its immediate capabilities. Iran now harbors an unquenchable thirst for vengeance. In fact, the preemptive dismantling of Iran's nuclear infrastructure makes perfect sense on the prophetic timeline. If Iran possessed a nuclear weapon, they could attempt to fulfill their public vows to wipe out Israel on their own. Without that nuclear option, they are forced to rely on conventional warfare. Weakened but unyielding, Iran's participation in the Gog-Magog campaign represents a calculated, desperate opportunity for retaliation. They will seek their vengeance under the cover of a massive Russian-led coalition, rather than through an independent strike.

## The Occupation Fallacy

A further weakness in the Psalm 83 war framework lies not in an explicit claim of occupation, but in the level of sustained dominance required to neutralize Israel's immediate neighbors to the degree implied by the condition of security described in Ezekiel 38. This view fails on a basic logistical and demographic level.

Israel's population and standing army are a fraction of those of the surrounding nations. Even in the event of a decisive military victory over an inner-ring coalition, it is highly implausible that Israel could indefinitely occupy extensive territories in Lebanon, Syria, and Jordan to the degree necessary to produce lasting security (*bāṭaḥ*). Modern history confirms this limitation. Israel's 1982 invasion of Lebanon demonstrated that even tactical success and the establishment of a temporary "security zone" tend to incubate insurgency rather than peace. Sustained occupation requires a manpower scale Israel simply does not possess.

Accordingly, the "unwalled" safety described in Ezekiel 38 does not result from Israeli territorial expansion. It must arise instead from diplomatic neutralization, regional realignment, or the illusory guarantees of a covenant, not from conquest.

## The Path to False Peace

In light of these considerations, many scholars interpret Psalm 83 not as a distinct, future prophecy awaiting fulfillment, but as a historical psalm whose themes resonate across Israel's experience without prescribing a specific eschatological event. As Israel increasingly enjoys regional military dominance and expanding diplomatic normalization, the necessity of an additional inner-ring war to establish its supremacy is effectively eliminated.

Rather than awaiting fulfillment through another all-out regional conflict, the conditions echoed in Psalm 83 are resolving through power asymmetry and diplomacy, setting the stage for a broader, and more deceptive, sense of "peace and security." It is precisely this environment that aligns most naturally with the prophetic scenario of Ezekiel 38, where an outer-ring coalition advances against Israel not amid chaos, but amid confidence.

# DEEPER DIVE 10.3. COSMIC CONTEXT

## Why Revelation 6:12-13 and Matthew 24:29 Are Not the Same Event

*I looked when He opened the sixth seal, and behold, there was a great earthquake; and the sun became black as sackcloth of hair, and the moon became like blood. And the stars of heaven fell to the earth, as a fig tree drops its late figs when it is shaken by a mighty wind.*

— REVELATION 6:12–13 NKJV

*"Immediately after the tribulation of those days the sun will be darkened, and the moon will not give its light; the stars will fall from heaven, and the powers of the heavens will be shaken..."*

— MATTHEW 24:29 NKJV

Few interpretive questions in end-times chronology generate more confusion than the relationship between Revelation 6:12–13 and Matthew 24:29. The cosmic imagery is undeniably similar, leading many to incorrectly conclude that both passages describe the exact same event.

A careful examination of timing, context, and function proves otherwise. Rather than describing a single moment, these passages mark two distinct cosmic events that serve as bookends to the Great Tribulation: one opening this great and terrible phase of judgment and the other closing it.

### The Core Issue: Similar Language, Different Timing

The similarity in wording is real. But similarity does not equal identity. The decisive factor is chronology, not imagery. The imagery closely parallels, but the biblical time markers explicitly place these events at entirely different points in the prophetic sequence.

| Feature | Revelation 6:12–13 | Matthew 24:29 |
| --- | --- | --- |
| Timing | Occurs at the Sixth Seal, **before** the Trumpet and Bowl Judgments. | Occurs **immediately after** the Tribulation. |
| The Sun | Becomes black like sackcloth. | Is darkened. |
| The Moon | Becomes like blood. | Does not give its light. |
| The Stars | Fall to the earth, like figs shaken from a tree. | Fall from heaven. |
| Function | Signals the beginning of intensified judgment. | Signals the conclusion of judgment. |

*Table D10.3.1: A Chronological Comparison of the Cosmic Signs*

## The Single-Event Misconception

Critics often argue that the language is too precise to describe different events. They propose that both passages depict a single cosmic disturbance at the very end of the Tribulation, asserting that Revelation 6 is simply a flash-forward embedded early in the vision.

This flawed approach disrupts the natural progression of Revelation (Seals ➔ Trumpets ➔ Bowls). It breaks the chronological flow and assumes that a climactic, end-stage cosmic sign was randomly inserted into the early part of the vision. It leaves a massive logical gap: Why would John place the final Second Coming sign in Revelation 6, only to rewind and proceed through another dozen chapters of escalating judgments?

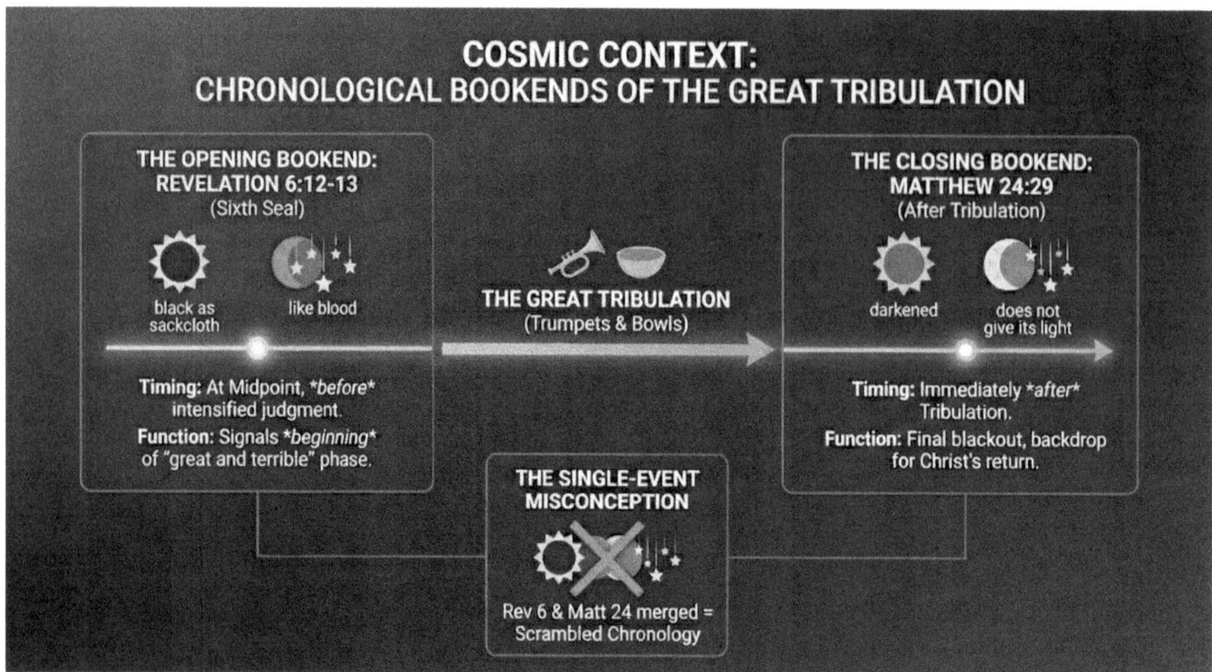


***Figure D10.3.1: Chronological Bookends of the Great Tribulation.*** *Merging the cosmic disturbances of Revelation 6 and Matthew 24 fundamentally scrambles the prophetic timeline. As illustrated, they are distinct, separate events that act as the opening and closing bookends of the "great and terrible" phase of judgment.*

## The Biblical Reality: Chronological Bookends

A faithful, chronological reading recognizes two separate cosmic disturbances, separated by the full duration of the Great Tribulation.

This aligns directly with the Old Testament understanding of the Day of the LORD as an extended period of judgment. Cosmic darkness is not a single moment, but a recurring atmospheric condition marking different stages of divine judgment.

### 1. Revelation 6:12–13: The Opening Bookend

- **Timing:** At the midpoint of the Tribulation.
- **Function:** A global cosmic alarm.
- **Significance:** Signals the transition into the great and terrible phase of the Day of the LORD.
- **Prophetic Anchor:** "The sun shall be turned to darkness... before the great and the terrible day of the LORD come" (Joel 2:31 KJV).
- *Result:* This event announces that the era of relative restraint has ended and the Great Tribulation has begun.

### 2. Matthew 24:29: The Closing Bookend

- **Timing:** Immediately after the Tribulation.
- **Function:** The final blackout.

- **Significance:** Serves as the pitch-black backdrop for Christ's visible return.[1]
- **Prophetic Anchor:** The Seventh Bowl (Revelation 16:17–21).
- *Result:* This darkness does not introduce judgment; it concludes it. The very next verse reveals the Son of Man appearing in glory (Matthew 24:30).

## Why Repetition Does Not Mean Identity

Scripture frequently uses cosmic disturbance imagery to emphasize moments of divine judgment (Isaiah 13:10; Joel 2:30–31; Ezekiel 32:7–8). The repetition of language reflects a prophetic pattern, not a single fulfillment. In other words, similar imagery marks different stages of the same judgment cycle.

| Feature | The Single-Event Misconception | The Chronological Reality (Two Events) |
|---|---|---|
| Premise | Two perspectives on one single event. | Two distinct events using similar prophetic language. |
| Revelation 6 | A literary preview of the final judgment. | An initial cosmic disturbance during the Tribulation. |
| Matthew 24 | The exact same final cosmic sign. | A final cosmic sign after the Tribulation. |
| Chronology | Requires a scrambled, non-linear reading of Revelation. | Preserves Revelation's sequential flow (Seals ➔ Trumpets ➔ Bowls). |

*Table D10.3.2: Two Interpretive Approaches at a Glance*

## The Cosmic Bookends

The similarity in imagery is intentional, but the context demands distinction.

- Revelation 6 marks the **beginning** of this specific period of cosmic darkness.
- Matthew 24 marks its **end**.

Between them lies the full outpouring of divine judgment. Preserving this sequence safeguards the integrity of

1. This total absence of light fulfills the literal parameters of the Day of the LORD established by the Old Testament prophets. Amos 5:20 (NIV) asks, "Will not the day of the Lord be darkness, not light—pitch-dark, without a ray of brightness?" Similarly, Zephaniah 1:15 designates it as "a day of clouds and thick darkness." The utter failure of all natural light is the necessary prelude to the arrival of the blazing glory of Christ.

Revelation's chronology: the darkness begins at the Sixth Seal, persists through the Trumpets and Bowls, and culminates in the total blackout of Matthew 24:29.

Darkness opens the great and terrible phase of the Day of the LORD.

Darkness closes it.

And this final blackout serves as the immediate backdrop for the return of the Light of the World.

# DEEPER DIVE 12.1. THE STAR OF THE ABYSS

## Satanic Rebel or Divine Servant?

*I saw a star that had fallen from the sky to the earth. The star was given the key to the shaft of the Abyss.*

— REVELATION 9:1 NIV

John's vision opens with a jarring image. A "star" has already fallen to earth, yet it is given authority to unlock the Abyss. That combination of being fallen yet authorized creates an immediate tension. How can a being associated with fall and judgment be entrusted with such power? And what does that say about God's sovereignty in the unfolding judgments of Revelation?

Biblical scholarship divides this question into two distinct views.

## View 1: A Fallen Angel Acting Under God's Restraint

The first line of interpretation understands the star as a fallen angel, identifying him as Satan himself or a powerful demonic ruler.[1] In Scripture, stars often symbolize angelic beings. Furthermore, the imagery of a star cast down consistently carries negative connotations of rebellion, judgment, and expulsion from heaven.

The wording in Revelation 9:1 is critical. John does not describe the star falling at that moment. He sees it as one who has already fallen. Elsewhere in Scripture and Jewish literature, this exact language describes Satan and his angels. Jesus Himself uses similar imagery when He says, "I saw Satan fall like lightning from heaven" (Luke 10:18).

If this figure is evil, why is the key given to him?

The answer is that permission does not imply approval. Throughout Scripture, God allows hostile powers to act only within the strict limits He establishes. Satan tests Job, but only by God's explicit consent. Assyria becomes a "rod" of God's anger while remaining fully accountable for its violence. In the same way, the fallen star in Revelation does not seize control of the Abyss. The key is given to him.

The context reinforces this reading. The Abyss is consistently portrayed as a holding place for demonic forces. The beings released recognize a king over them named Abaddon, also called Apollyon, which translates to "the Destroyer." The imagery captures the character of a fallen, destructive power operating under divine restraint.

**Key insight:** Even rebellious powers act only within boundaries set by God. God's absolute authority is never compromised.

1. G. K. Beale, *The Book of Revelation* (New International Greek Testament Commentary; Grand Rapids: Eerdmans, 1999), 488–493. Beale surveys both interpretations but argues that the imagery of a "fallen star," together with the identity of Abaddon/Apollyon and the broader biblical use of falling-star language, favors understanding the figure as a fallen angel acting under divine authority.

## View 2: A Faithful Angel Carrying Out a Severe Assignment

Another interpretive approach understands the star as a loyal angel sent on a dark mission of judgment.[2] The argument here asserts that the word "fallen" translates as "descended," much like other angels in Revelation who come down from heaven to carry out God's commands. In Revelation 20, for example, a clearly righteous angel is given a key to the Abyss to imprison Satan.

From this perspective, opening the Abyss does not require an evil agent. God's servants regularly carry out frightening acts of judgment throughout the book by sounding trumpets, pouring out bowls, and announcing woes. The severity of the task does not imply moral corruption. This view strongly appeals to readers who are uneasy with the idea of God delegating judgment to a fallen being.

**Key insight:** Judgment does not require evil agents. God's servants carry out fearsome missions that fulfill His holy justice.

***Figure D12.1.1: The Star of the Abyss.*** *A visual comparison of the two primary interpretations of Revelation 9:1. The scriptural context identifies this fallen star as a rebellious entity operating strictly under the explicit, delegated permission of God.*

## Fallen, Yet Under Command

Both views attempt to take the tension in the text seriously. However, the language of a fallen star, the consistent biblical use of that imagery, and the identity of the ruler of the Abyss firmly identify this figure as a rebellious angel, specifically Satan or a high-ranking demonic authority.

At the same time, Revelation is careful to emphasize that this fallen power remains entirely under God's control. The key is not stolen or discovered. It is given. Christ, who holds "the keys of death and Hades" (Revelation 1:18), permits the Abyss to be opened at this exact prophetic moment and no sooner.

2. Robert H. Mounce, *The Book of Revelation*, rev. ed., NICNT (Grand Rapids: Eerdmans, 1998), 192. Mounce argues that the star is likely a good angel, suggesting that the "fall" does not imply moral failure but simply describes a descent from heaven to earth to carry out a divine command.

The point of the vision is not to glorify evil, but to reassure the reader. Even when hell itself is unlocked, it opens only at heaven's command.

Chaos is permitted, but never autonomous.

Judgment is unleashed, but never uncontrolled.

And even the darkest trumpet sounds within the ordained purposes of God.

# DEEPER DIVE 13.1. THE MYSTERY OF GOD

## From Hidden Purpose to Finished Plan

> *but in the days of the sounding of the seventh angel, when he is about to sound, the mystery of God would be finished, as He declared to His servants the prophets.*
>
> — REVELATION 10:7 NKJV

The Book of Revelation is layered with dramatic events and unfolding judgments, yet in its very center lies something more profound than cataclysm: the consummation of a long-hidden mystery. Revelation 10:7 declares that in the days when the Seventh Trumpet sounds, ushering in the final judgments, "the mystery of God" will be fulfilled. What is this mystery?

## What Is the Mystery of God?

In Scripture, a *mystery* is not something unknowable, but something once hidden that can now be understood: a divine truth previously concealed but revealed at the appointed time to those with spiritual discernment. The Greek word *mysterion* does not imply an enigma beyond comprehension. It refers to a sacred secret once hidden in God's counsel (see Ephesians 3:4–5).

Paul speaks extensively about this idea. In **Romans 16:25–26 NKJV**, he writes:

> *... according to the revelation of the mystery kept secret since the world began but now made manifest, and by the prophetic Scriptures made known to all nations ...*

This mystery is God's grand redemptive plan spanning all of history. As Revelation 10:7 affirms, a crucial phase of this redemptive arc will be "finished" or brought to its appointed climax with the events of the Seventh Trumpet. This signifies the end of the age of human rebellion and the decisive, public victory of Christ over the kingdom of this world, which in turn inaugurates His Millennial reign and culminates in the final perfection of the New Heaven and New Earth.

## Unpacking the Mystery: A Multi-Faceted Jewel

The phrase "the mystery of God" serves as a summation of interrelated mysteries, each revealing a specific portion of God's salvific work. These mysteries were once hidden but now, through the Spirit and the Word, have been revealed to the church.

It is crucial to recognize that this list is not exhaustive. Rather, these seven serve as the primary, illustrative windows into His single, unfolding redemptive plan concerning the end of the age.

***Figure D13.1.1: A Multi-Faceted Jewel of Redemption.*** *This comprehensive infographic summarizes the primary revealed facets of God's redemptive plan that will be 'finished' in the days of the sounding of the Seventh Trumpet (Revelation 10:7). Organized as a radial hub-and-spoke diagram, it visualizes seven specific biblical mysteries, once hidden but now revealed. It illustrates how glorious redemption and decisive victory arrive simultaneously, satisfying every promise made to the prophets.*

## 1. The Mystery of the Rapture

> *Behold! I tell you a mystery: We shall not all sleep, but we shall all be changed, in a moment, in the twinkling of an eye, at the last trumpet...*
>
> — 1 CORINTHIANS 15:51–52

This mystery unveils the sudden transformation of believers at Christ's coming. Though death reigned for millennia, this divine secret revealed that some would bypass death entirely and be caught up (cf. 1 Thessalonians 4:16–17).

## 2. The Mystery of Israel's Blindness

> *That blindness in part has happened to Israel until the fullness of the Gentiles has come in.*
>
> — ROMANS 11:25 NKJV

This mystery explains why the majority of Israel rejected her Messiah and how her national restoration is still yet future. Her current spiritual blindness is temporary, serving God's purpose of opening the way for Gentile salvation during the present age.

## 3. The Mystery of Christ and the Church

*This is a great mystery, but I speak concerning Christ and the church.*

— EPHESIANS 5:32 NKJV

More than a metaphor, the union between a husband and wife is a shadow of the spiritual union between Christ and His bride, the Church. It is a mystery hidden in ages past, now revealed.

## 4. The Mystery of Christ in You

*...the mystery which has been hidden from ages and from generations... which is Christ in you, the hope of glory.*

— COLOSSIANS 1:26–27 NKJV

God's indwelling presence in the believer, particularly Gentile believers, was once unthinkable. Now it is the heart of New Covenant reality. God does not merely dwell among His people but within them.

## 5. The Mystery of the Kingdom of Heaven (Matthew 13:11)

*He answered and said to them, "Because it has been given to you to know the mysteries of the kingdom of heaven..."*

— MATTHEW 13:11 NKJV

Jesus spoke in parables to veil deeper truths to the unrepentant. These parables revealed unexpected aspects of the kingdom: its delayed physical fulfillment, its mixed nature (wheat and tares), and its surprising growth.

## 6. The Mystery of Godliness

*And without controversy great is the mystery of godliness: God was manifested in the flesh...*

— 1 TIMOTHY 3:16 NKJV

Here lies the incarnation, God becoming man. This mystery anchors the gospel, revealing that divinity stepped into humanity to reconcile creation to its Creator.

## 7. The Mystery of Lawlessness (2 Thessalonians 2:7)

*For the mystery of lawlessness is already at work...*

— 2 THESSALONIANS 2:7 NKJV

This is the dark counterpart to the mystery of godliness. A shadow movement, lawless, rebellious, and energized by Satan, has long been at work behind the scenes. It will climax in the revelation of the man of sin, the Antichrist, who will be destroyed by the brightness of Christ's coming.

## Facets of the Finished Mystery

Each of these mysteries forms a crucial thread in God's singular redemptive tapestry. When Revelation 10:7 states that "the mystery of God will be finished," it guarantees that these representative facets of God's eternal plan will reach their appointed end:

- **The Rapture Completed:** The hidden program for the Church will conclude with her sudden removal from the earth and subsequent marriage to the Lamb.
- **Israel's Blindness Removed:** The temporary, partial blindness of Israel will be entirely lifted, resulting in her national salvation and the physical restoration of the remnant (Zechariah 12:10; Romans 11:25).
- **The Kingdom Manifested:** The Kingdom of Heaven will transition forcefully from its concealed, "mystery" form into the literal, visible, and iron-rod rule of Christ on earth.
- **The Indwelling Glorified:** The unseen reality of "Christ in you" will give way to the visible reality of Christ reigning physically alongside His glorified, resurrected saints.
- **Godliness Vindicated:** The great mystery of godliness (God manifested in the flesh) will reach its apex when the incarnate Son physically reclaims total dominion over the earth He created.
- **Lawlessness Crushed:** The shadow movement of lawlessness will be fully exposed in the person of the Antichrist and then decisively destroyed by the breath of Christ's mouth (2 Thessalonians 2:8).
- **The Gospel Fulfilled:** The ultimate purpose of the gospel will stand completely accomplished, decisively dividing the inhabitants of the earth as God's perfect justice and mercy are displayed before all creation.

The fulfillment of the mystery is the climax of the divine drama, where God's hidden purposes are brought into the light of history, vindicating His righteousness, displaying His mercy, and ushering in His eternal kingdom.

## Only the Initiated Understand

Mysteries, by nature, are for the initiated, not the elite in intellect, but those made alive by the Spirit. Paul requests prayer in Ephesians 6:19 NKJV:

> *...that I may open my mouth boldly to make known the mystery of the gospel...*

To the natural mind, these truths are foolishness (1 Corinthians 2:14). But to the believer, especially those who seek deeper understanding, the veil is lifted.

## A Final Word

When the seventh angel sounds, there will be no more delay (Revelation 10:6). The present administration of grace, as we know it, will have reached its appointed conclusion. At that moment, the plan long hidden in God's heart, hinted at by the prophets, inaugurated at Christ's first coming, and expanded through the Church Age, will enter its final, unstoppable phase of fulfillment.

This glorious consummation requires a legal clearing of the earth. Christ must legally evict the kingdom of darkness before He can physically establish the promised kingdom of heaven. The mystery is not over. It is about to be gloriously and violently unveiled on the world stage.

What began in Genesis finds its glorious consummation in Revelation, not as a new story, but as the unveiling of what God had purposed before the foundation of the world (Ephesians 1:4–10).

Indeed, the mystery of God is the story of redemption: complete, multi-layered, and now ready to be fully revealed.

# DEEPER DIVE 14.1. THE 1,260-DAY ENIGMA OF THE TWO WITNESSES

## First Half, Second Half, or a Shifted Timeline?

*"...And I will grant authority to my two witnesses, and they will prophesy for 1,260 days, clothed in sackcloth."*

— REVELATION 11:3

## Introduction: The Great Debate

Few end-times figures are as fascinating as the Two Witnesses in Revelation 11. Clothed in sackcloth, wielding miraculous power, and destined for a public martyrdom and resurrection, their 1,260-day ministry is a defining sign of the end times. But a fundamental question divides interpreters: exactly *when* do they prophesy during the seven-year Tribulation?

Traditionally, scholars have locked themselves into a binary debate: they minister strictly in the first 3½ years, or strictly in the final 3½ years. However, both of these rigid views create significant textual friction. A careful reading of Revelation, paired with a startling biological reality regarding the final Bowl Judgments, reveals a much more profound and precise "shifted" timeline.

## The Traditional Binary: First Half vs. Second Half

To understand the solution, we must first look at why the traditional views struggle:

### The First-Half View (The Forerunners)

Some argue the witnesses minister in the first half, finishing their testimony just as the Antichrist rises to full power at the midpoint. This solves a logical problem: why would the Antichrist tolerate them for 3½ years? He wouldn't. He kills them the moment he takes global control. However, this view fractures the text. Revelation 11:2–3 grammatically links the 1,260 days of their ministry to the 42 months of Jerusalem being trampled (a distinctly second-half event).

### The Second-Half View (The Climax)

The weight of textual evidence places them in the second half, directly confronting the Antichrist during his 42-month reign of terror. Yet, this creates a major chronological pile-up at the very end. If they are killed on the exact last day of the seven years, when does the world have time to rejoice and exchange gifts (Rev. 11:10) while simultaneously being crushed by the catastrophic Bowl Judgments and the physical return of Christ?

## The Solution: The Hybrid "Shifted" Timeline

The most scripturally and logically cohesive answer is a hybrid view: their 1,260-day ministry is *predominantly* in the second half, but it begins just prior to the midpoint and concludes just 2–3 weeks before the definitive end of the seven years.

Several key factors lock this shifted timeline into place:

### 1. The Malachi Mandate

Malachi 4:5 prophesies, *"See, I will send the prophet Elijah to you before that great and dreadful day of the LORD comes."* To understand this timing, we must define the "great and dreadful day." The Hebrew word for terrible or dreadful is *nora* (derived from *yare*, meaning terror or awe). Prophetically, this specific "great and terrible" phase encompasses the *entire* second half of the seven years: the exact 3½-year period of unmatched global terror that Jesus explicitly identified as the "Great Tribulation" (Matthew 24:21).

Because Elijah must arrive *before* this definitive period of terror begins, the witnesses' 1,260-day ministry must initiate just prior to the Tribulation's midpoint. Their 1,260-day testimony is not confined to one half but spans the most critical transition in human history: the midpoint of the Tribulation. By arriving before the Antichrist commits the Abomination of Desolation, they stand as a blazing harbinger of the impending terror. They then minister directly through that escalating darkness, concluding their testimony just weeks before the ultimate, most severe concentration of God's wrath is unleashed.

### 2. The Final Pivot: The 7th Trumpet and the Biological Deadline

The Two Witnesses are killed by the Beast, resurrected 3½ days later, and ascend to heaven (Revelation 11:11–12). This stunning martyrdom and supernatural resurrection serve as the final pivot of the Tribulation. Immediately following their ascent, the Seventh Trumpet sounds (Revelation 11:15), serving as the catalyst that unlocks the final seven Bowl Judgments.

For the world to have time to celebrate the witnesses' death, and for the Antichrist to still be operating, these Bowl Judgments must happen in a remarkably compressed window of time. Based on the physical nature of these final plagues, they have to be poured out in a rapid-fire sequence lasting only two to three weeks (guided by the rapid succession of the Egyptian plagues in Exodus).

Consider the lethal combination of the Bowls:

- **The Second Bowl:** The sea turns to blood; every sea creature dies (Revelation 16:3).
- **The Third Bowl:** All rivers and springs of water turn to blood (Revelation 16:4).
- **The Fourth Bowl:** The sun scorches humanity with fierce heat (Revelation 16:8).

Under normal conditions, a human being can survive a maximum of three days without drinking water. Compounded by the extreme, scorching heat of the fourth bowl, a hard biological deadline is placed on humanity. If the Bowl Judgments were stretched over months or years, all biological life on earth (human, animal, and plant) would be completely sterilized before the armies could even gather at Armageddon (the Sixth Bowl).

This rapid-fire reality directly reflects Jesus' own pronouncement in Matthew 24:22: "If those days had not been cut short, no one would survive..."

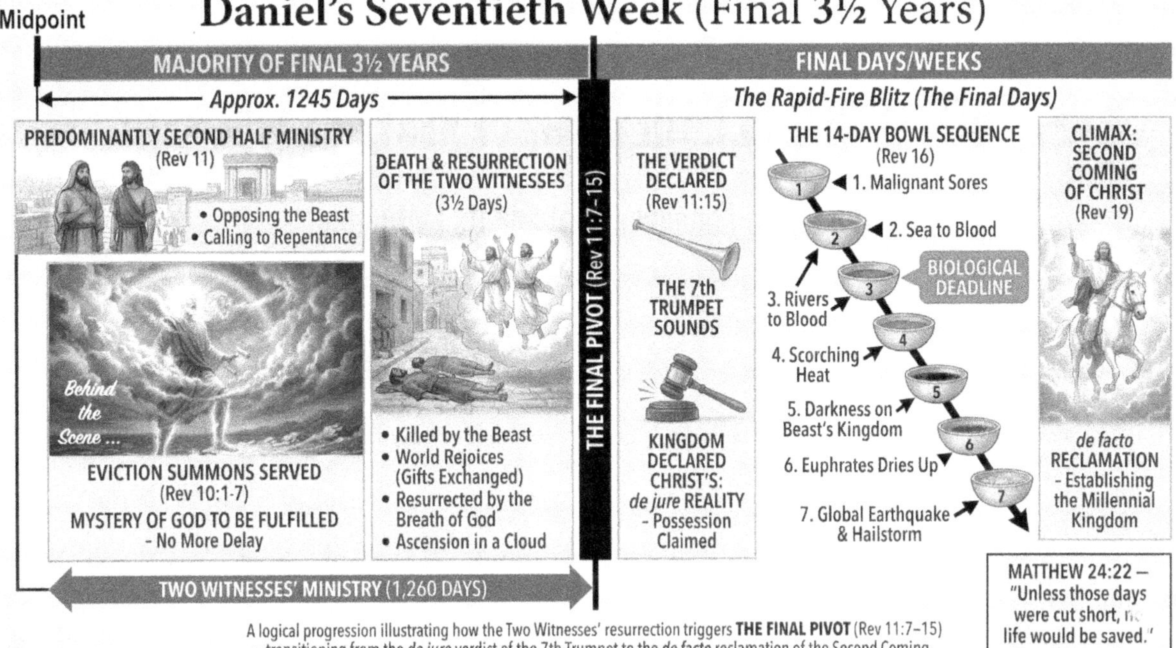


***Figure D14.1.1: The Ministry of the Two Witnesses.*** *A chronological map illustrating the hybrid timeline of Revelation 11. By initiating their 1,260-day testimony just prior to the midpoint, the Witnesses minister through the Great Tribulation and conclude their testimony roughly two weeks before the end, triggering the rapid-fire biological countdown of the final Bowl Judgments.*

## The Perfect Chronology

The hybrid timeline resolves the enigma. The Two Witnesses begin their ministry just before the midpoint, spanning the great divide. They minister powerfully through almost the entirety of the Antichrist's 42-month reign. They are killed just weeks short of the end of the seven years.

For 3½ days, the world breathes a sigh of relief and celebrates, mistakenly believing they have won. But the witnesses' sudden resurrection and ascension act as the **final pivot**, triggering the Seventh Trumpet. In that terrifying moment, the window of mercy slams shut, and God pours out the final Bowl Judgments in a rapid, two-to-three-week biological countdown to the return of the King.

#  DEEPER DIVE 15.1. THE HINGE OF HEAVEN'S JUDGMENT

## The Divine Announcement and Its Fulfillment

### The Announcement:

> *...in the days of the trumpet call to be sounded by the seventh angel, the mystery of God would be fulfilled...*
>
> — REVELATION 10:7

### The Fulfillment:

> *..."The kingdom of the world has become the kingdom of our Lord and of his Christ..."*
>
> — REVELATION 11:15

Students of Revelation frequently misunderstand the structure of the Trumpet Judgments, particularly the pause between the Sixth and Seventh Trumpets. Yet for those paying close attention, a critical and deliberate link emerges between Revelation 10:7 and 11:15. Together they form a powerful one-two punch and serve as the structural and theological hinge of the Trumpet Judgments. These verses are not isolated pronouncements. They are an announcement-fulfillment pair central to understanding how the plan of God for history will reach its denouement.[1]

## Revelation 10:7: The Divine Announcement

This announcement is made by another Mighty Angel (Revelation 10:1), who acts as a high-ranking angelic representative of heaven's court. Declared before the Seventh Trumpet sounds, during the interlude between the Sixth and Seventh Trumpets, this solemn pronouncement defines the significance of the imminent blast. It guarantees that when the trumpet is sounded by the seventh angel, "the mystery of God" will be fulfilled.

But what is this mystery?[2]

In the Bible, a "mystery" is not a riddle to be solved but a divine secret that has now been revealed. As established in earlier chapters, this "mystery of God" encompasses the full scope of His prophetic program for history. It refers to the long-unfolding plan where God finally brings all things to their intended conclusion. This includes the fulfillment of His promises to Israel, the final judgment of rebellion, and the assertion of His direct rule over the earth to wrest control from Satan's usurpation.

---

1. The biblical text clearly establishes Revelation 10:7 as a divine announcement that is definitively fulfilled in Revelation 11:15, when Christ formally takes back His kingdom. For a clear explanation of this connection, see John F. Walvoord, *The Revelation of Jesus Christ* (Moody, 1966).
2. See *Deeper Dive 13.1. The Mystery of God* for a detailed exploration of this theme.

The Old Testament prophets, men like Isaiah, Daniel, and Zechariah, foresaw a coming age of divine rule and the resolution of the struggle between good and evil. While they saw the "what" of this plan, the specific "how" and "when" remained partially hidden for ages. Revelation 10:7 serves as a solemn, divine oath that the period of waiting is over. The sounding of the Seventh Trumpet triggers the final sequence that completes every detail of God's long-held plan for the world.

***Figure D15.1.1: The Climax of the Divine Drama.*** *Visualizing the profound promise of Revelation 10:7. In the days of the Seventh Trumpet's sounding, the multi-faceted "mystery of God" is finished. The radiant center highlights seven facets of God's redemptive plan coming to their appointed conclusion, visually reinforcing that glorious redemption, not just catastrophic judgment, is the ultimate focal point of the end of the age.*

## Revelation 11:15: The Fulfillment Proclamation

The Seventh Trumpet sounds. Heaven erupts. The loud voices of the angelic hosts proclaim the direct fulfillment of Revelation 10:7 by declaring, "The kingdom of the world has become the Kingdom of Christ."

This is a *de jure* proclamation: a courtroom declaration of fact. The "mystery of God," culminating in the establishment of His direct rule on earth, is now declared finished. The phrase "has become" reflects the Greek *aorist* tense, which functions in Revelation to announce a settled verdict so certain it is spoken as accomplished. The focus shifts from the process to the result, signifying the legal transfer of world dominion. Ownership and authority are officially and irrevocably transferred from the usurper (Satan and his earthly agent, the Antichrist) to the rightful owner (God the Father and His Christ).

## Connecting The Dots: The Title Deed Analogy

The relationship is best understood by way of analogy, within the legal framework of the Scroll (title deed) introduced in Revelation 5.[3]

---

3. See *Deeper Dive 5.3. The Title Deed to Creation* for a detailed discussion of the scroll as a legal document.

1. **The Title Deed Claimed (Revelation 5):** The Lamb (Christ) is found worthy to take the Scroll, which is the title deed to the earth, initiating the reclamation process.
2. **The Legal Proceedings (Seals 1–7, Trumpets 1–6):** The breaking of Seals and sounding of Trumpets represent the sequential judgments serving as the legal process against the current rebellious "tenant" (Satan and human kingdoms).
3. **The Eviction Summons Served (Revelation 10:1–7):** The Mighty Angel makes a possession claim on Christ's behalf and frames a final eviction summons through the Little Scroll. The message is unmistakable. There will be no more delay, and when the Seventh Trumpet sounds, the time is up.
4. **The Verdict Delivered (Revelation 10:7 & 11:15)**: This is the "Hinge" of the entire process. In Revelation 10:7, the court promises that the next trumpet blast will conclude the legal case. When the Seventh Trumpet sounds in Revelation 11:15, the promise is kept. This is the *de jure* reality; the gavel has come down, the papers are signed, and the kingdom legally belongs to the King. The mystery of the kingdom transitions into physical reality precisely because the usurper is now legally removed. While the defiant tenant may still be on the property, his legal right to stay has been terminated.
5. **The Physical Eviction (Bowl Judgments, Revelation 16):** The verdict does not mean all rebellion on earth instantly ceases. Hence, God must unleash the final, most intense judgments represented by the Seven Bowls of wrath. This is the physical enforcement, the *de facto* realization, of the legal right that was just proclaimed. It is the new owner forcibly removing the defiant trespasser, culminating in the battle of Armageddon to establish Christ's literal millennial kingdom on earth.

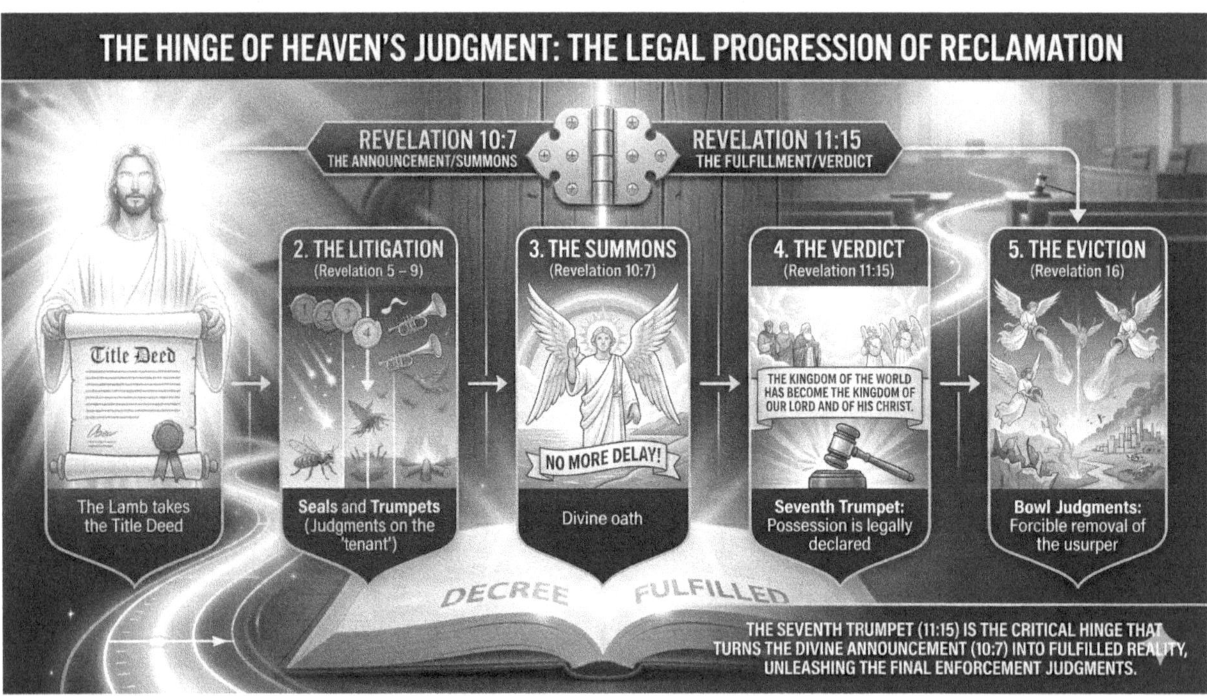


***Figure D15.1.2:*** *A visual representation of "The Hinge of Heaven's Judgment," illustrating the legal and prophetic journey of Revelation: from the Lamb claiming the Title Deed to the final eviction of evil.*

## Summary: The Critical Link Between Revelation 10:7 and 11:15

| Aspect | Revelation 10:7 (The Setup) | Revelation 11:15 (The Payoff) |
|---|---|---|
| Timing | Before the Seventh Trumpet sounds (a promise). | When the Seventh Trumpet sounds (a fulfillment). |
| Nature | An announcement of what is about to happen. | A proclamation that it has happened. |
| Function | Defines the significance of the Seventh Trumpet. | Declares the result of the Seventh Trumpet. |
| Focus | The finishing of the "mystery of God" (The completion of God's entire prophetic program). | The transfer of power (The kingdom of the world officially becomes the Kingdom of Christ). |
| Analogy | The court's promise that the next action will conclude the case. | The court's declaration of the final verdict and ownership transfer. |
| Outcome | Sets the stage for the final enforcement action. | Unleashes the final enforcement action (the Bowl Judgments). |

## The Soundtrack of the Kingdom

Revelation 10:7 and 11:15 are a perfect pair that is inseparably linked. Verse 10:7 provides the divine setup, and 11:15 delivers the dramatic payoff. The first tells us what to look for, and the second shows us that it has arrived, opening the door for the final, intense judgments that will physically establish Christ's kingdom on earth.

Understanding this announcement-fulfillment dynamic is the key to unlocking the structure of God's final judgments. It reveals that the Seventh Trumpet is not just another catastrophe. It is the pivotal event that unleashes the final enforcement action, the Bowl Judgments, resulting in the physical establishment of Christ's kingdom on earth.

Far from being just one more trumpet blast, the Seventh Trumpet is the soundtrack to the End of the Age. It is a heavenly fanfare that accompanies the King's final reclaiming of the earth, echoing through the Bowl Judgments, the Millennial Kingdom, and ultimately into the New Heaven and the New Earth.

# DEEPER DIVE 17.1. THE SUM OF ALL EVILS

## Decoding the Composite Nature of the Final Empire

> *The beast I saw resembled a leopard, but had feet like those of a bear and a mouth like that of a lion. The dragon gave the beast his power and his throne and great authority.*
>
> — REVELATION 13:2 NIV

Revelation 13 does not introduce a brand-new monster. It reveals the final form of an old one.

The Beast rising from the sea is not merely a single man, though it will be ruled by one. It is a composite kingdom, a global system of power built from the accumulated wreckage of history's most God-defying empires. The Antichrist does not invent evil. He inherits it, concentrates it, and weaponizes it.

## A Beast Made of Beasts

The imagery is deliberate. This creature is stitched together from earlier prophetic visions, forming a single, horrifying whole.

Daniel saw a sequence of empires rise one after another (Daniel 7). John sees them collapsed into one terrifying body.

The Beast has:

- the **body of a leopard**
- the **feet of a bear**
- the **mouth of a lion**
- ten crowns upon ten horns, symbolizing the delegated political authority of the final ten-king confederacy.

This imagery marks a deliberate culmination.[1]

1. Many Bible scholars understand the four beasts in Daniel 7 to represent four major world empires: Babylon, Medo-Persia, Greece, and Rome. This interpretation helps explain how a final world empire will arise at the end of the age. For a clear explanation, see John F. Walvoord, *Daniel: The Key to Prophetic Revelation* (Chicago: Moody Press, 1971), comments on Daniel chapter 7.

***Figure D17.1.1: The Sum of All Evils.*** *The final empire is not a new entity, but a composite of history's most godless systems, fusing the traits of the leopard, the bear, and the lion into one terrifying regime.*

Daniel watched history unfold forward. John, standing at the edge of the age, looks backward. The order is reversed because the story is nearly over. What Daniel saw as separate waves of empire, John sees as a single tidal surge, their legacies fused into one final regime.

Far from a "greatest hits" of world powers, this is a worst-of compilation, a Frankenstein-like entity embodying the cumulative tyranny of human history's most godless systems.

## The DNA of the Final Empire

Each animal reveals something essential about the nature of this last kingdom.

- **Leopard: Speed and Saturation.** Like Alexander the Great's lightning-fast conquests, this system spreads fast. It moves with breathtaking reach, politically, militarily, ideologically. It does not crawl across the globe; it floods it. Resistance is overwhelmed before it can organize.
- **Bear: Crushing Control**. Just as the Persian bear "devoured much flesh," this system dominates through sheer force, grinding opposition beneath its weight. It devours, absorbs, and enforces submission without apology.
- **Lion: Arrogant, Blasphemous Speech**. Babylon's arrogance lives on. The mouth gives it a voice, and that voice is defiant. It boasts, mocks heaven, rewrites truth, and glorifies man. This moves beyond casual arrogance into organized blasphemy. Propaganda replaces praise. Pride becomes policy.

Together, these traits form a system that is fast, brutal, and loud, a regime that conquers bodies, silences dissent, and challenges God openly.

| Prophetic Symbol | Historical Echo | The Destructive Trait Distilled |
|---|---|---|
| **Body of a Leopard** | Greece (Alexander the Great) | **Speed and Saturation:** Floods the globe militarily and ideologically. |
| **Feet of a Bear** | Medo-Persia | **Crushing Control:** Dominates through sheer force and devours opposition. |
| **Mouth of a Lion** | Babylon | **Blasphemous Speech:** Organized defiance, boasting, and rewriting of truth. |
| **Ten Horns** | The Final Confederacy | **Delegated Authority:** Fragmented, shared control that props up the regime. |

*Table D17.1.1: The Composite Traits of the Final Empire*

## Not "Best," But Beastly

These features are not the strengths of past empires refined into something noble. They are the most destructive traits distilled.

This is cumulative tyranny.

Compounded defiance.

Evil with institutional memory.

Every empire that opposed God leaves something behind: methods, structures, habits of domination. The Beast gathers them all. What was once regional becomes global. What was once restrained becomes unchallenged. What was once human ambition becomes satanically empowered authority.[2]

The Dragon does not create the Beast from nothing. He animates what history has already been building.

## The End of the Line

This represents devolution, not progress.

The Beast represents the ultimate expression of human government divorced from God: fully centralized, fully hostile, fully empowered by the Dragon himself. It is the sum of all evils, given a throne and a voice.

The Beast is not a new monster.

It is the final form of every empire that ever stood against God, now unified, energized, and unleashed for one last act of global rebellion before judgment falls.

2. Scholars widely agree that this Beast combines the evil characteristics of all previous empires. G.K. Beale argues that this combination highlights the Beast's "extreme fierceness" as the heir of all past pagan empires. Similarly, Robert Mounce calls this figure the "epitome of bestial opposition" to believers. See G. K. Beale, *The Book of Revelation*, NIGTC (Grand Rapids, MI: Eerdmans, 1999), 685–86; and Robert H. Mounce, *The Book of Revelation*, rev. ed., NICNT (Grand Rapids, MI: Eerdmans, 1998), commentary on Revelation 13:2.

# DEEPER DIVE 17.2. DRAGON'S HEADS VS. BEAST'S HORNS

## The Locus of Authority: Distinguishing Revelation's Two Monsters

*And another sign appeared in heaven: behold, a great red dragon, with seven heads and ten horns, and on his* ***heads seven diadems****.*

— REVELATION 12:3

*And I saw a beast rising out of the sea, with ten horns and seven heads, with* ***ten diadems on its horns*** *and blasphemous names on its heads.*

— REVELATION 13:1

In Revelation, John is shown two terrifying figures that are deliberately shaped to resemble one another: a great red Dragon and a Beast rising from the sea. Both are grotesque. Both are powerful. Both bear seven heads and ten horns.

But a single, easily overlooked detail regarding the placement of their diadems, the royal crowns symbolizing authority, opens a window into the difference between Satan's claim to power and the Beast's exercise of it.

John sees the Dragon first, unmistakably identified as Satan himself. Shortly afterward, he sees the Beast, Satan's visible agent on the world stage.

The distinction is precise and intentional.

The Dragon's diadems rest on his **heads**.

The Beast's diadems are fixed to his **horns**.

***Figure D17.2.1: World Dominion vs. Delegated Authority.*** *A visual side-by-side comparison illustrating the critical theological shift between Revelation 12 and 13. The Dragon (left) wears seven crowns upon his heads to symbolize* ***world dominion****. The Beast (right) wears ten crowns upon his horns to symbolize the delegated* ***political authority*** *of the ten-king confederacy.*

Rather than a random artistic choice, this specific placement reveals the hierarchy of evil in the last days.

## Symbolic Comparison

| Symbol | Dragon (Rev 12:3) | Beast (Rev 13:1) |
|---|---|---|
| **Heads** | Seven heads | Seven heads |
| **Horns** | Ten horns | Ten horns |
| **Diadems** | On the heads | On the horns |
| **Names on Heads** | — | Blasphemous Names |

*Table D17.2.1: Symbolic Comparison*

### Shared Features

Both the Dragon and the Beast are described with the same outward framework:

- Seven heads
- Ten horns

These shared features signal continuity. The Beast does not appear in isolation; it emerges from the same stream of dominion already at work in history.

### Key Difference

The difference lies not in *what* they possess, but in **where authority is displayed**:

- **The Dragon (Revelation 12:3)**. His diadems rest on his heads, signaling a claim of overarching authority, asserting dominion over the entire structure of world power.
- **The Beast (Revelation 13:1)**. His diadems are fixed to his horns, and his heads bear blasphemous names: authority exercised publicly, loudly, and defiantly.

## What It Means

### The Dragon (Satan)

Diadems on the **heads** signal a claim to overarching sovereignty. Satan presents himself as the ruler behind the rulers, a counterfeit god asserting control over the entire structure of world empires. The seven heads point to sweeping dominion across history, culminating in a final phase of global rule.[1]

### The Beast (Antichrist and His Empire)

Diadems on the **horns** tell a different story. This is not ultimate authority, but delegated power, authority distributed to subordinate rulers. The Beast governs through coalitions, enforced loyalty, and militarized alliances. His strength depends on others propping him up.

This portrait closely mirrors the "willful king" described in Daniel 11:36–45, a ruler who exalts himself, speaks blasphemies, and advances through political leverage, rewards, and shifting alliances rather than unquestioned sovereignty.

The ten horns expose the fault line beneath the surface: fragmented leadership, shared control, and a regime that looks formidable but is inherently unstable.

One additional detail quietly reinforces this distinction. While both figures share the same heads and horns, only the Beast bears blasphemous names on its heads. The Dragon's claim to authority is implicit; he seeks to rule from behind the scenes. The Beast, by contrast, makes rebellion public. His rule is not only enforced but advertised. What Satan claims in the shadows, the Beast proclaims in the open.

## What This Reveals

- Satan mimics divine kingship, claiming supremacy over the nations.
- The Beast is his instrument, exercising power only as it is granted.
- The shift in diadem placement from heads to horns reveals the internal weakness and disorder of evil's kingdom.
- Revelation consistently portrays this empire as a distorted parody of Christ's reign. Where Satan's

1. John F. Walvoord supports this distinction, identifying the seven heads as "seven successive forms of the kingdom" across history (Revelation 17:9–10) and the ten horns as a coalition of kings who rule simultaneously in the end time (Revelation 17:12). See Walvoord, *The Revelation of Jesus Christ* (Moody, 1966).

domain is fractured and dependent, Christ appears wearing many diadems, symbolizing authority that is unified, inherent, and uncontested.

## Summary Comparison

| Feature | Dragon (Rev 12:3) | Beast (Rev 13:1) |
|---|---|---|
| **Seven Heads** | Represent the long sweep of Gentile world power, the succession of kingdoms through which Satan has exercised influence during the "times of the Gentiles." | Associated with both kingdoms and a city built on seven hills. The imagery points to a political center tied to Rome, the city famously built on seven hills, which serves as the Beast's initial capital. |
| **Ten Horns** | Represent the final phase of Gentile dominion in the form of a ten-nation alliance emerging from the structure of the Revived Roman Empire. This confederation becomes Satan's ultimate instrument for unprecedented global opposition to God's purposes. | Represent ten kings who rule briefly during the Tribulation. These rulers form a short-lived confederacy that supports and empowers the Antichrist. |
| **Crowns (Diadems)** | **On the heads:** Symbolizing Satan's claim to overarching sovereignty over the entire system of world empires, acting as the ruler behind the rulers. | **On the horns:** Reflecting delegated and fragmented authority, distributed to the final ten kings as agents of Satan's last stand. |
| **Character of Rule** | Authority claimed from behind the scenes; power asserted indirectly. | Authority exercised publicly; rebellion advertised through blasphemous names. |

*Table D17.2.2: Summary Comparison of Authority*

## The Illusion of Supreme Power

These diadems, precisely placed, expose the illusion at the heart of Satan's kingdom. The Dragon may project an image of invincible sovereignty, but his earthly dominion rests not on inherent power but on fragile human alliances and delegated authority. The Beast wields nothing that is not first given, and strictly permitted, by a sovereign God. Such a counterfeit empire is inherently unstable, a house of cards built to fall.

When the true King appears, His own head crowned with many diadems (Revelation 19:12), He will bring no coalition, no shifting political allegiance. His authority is inherent, total, eternal. What Satan assembles through cunning and coercion, Jesus Christ will unmake with a single spoken word.

#  DEEPER DIVE 17.3. THE DEAD HEAD REVIVED

## Decoding the Dual Prophecy of Empire and Antichrist

> *One of its heads seemed to have a mortal wound, but its mortal wound was healed, and the whole earth marveled as they followed the beast.*
>
> — REVELATION 13:3

This is one of the most discussed, and misunderstood, verses in Revelation 13.

John tells us that one of the Beast's heads suffers what appears to be a fatal wound. Yet the wound is healed. The result is global astonishment. Awe turns to allegiance. The world follows the Beast.

So what exactly is this "fatal wound"?

Is John describing the collapse and revival of a world power?

Or the near-death, and shocking recovery, of a man?

The text raises the question and leaves the "fatal wound" intentionally open to interpretation.

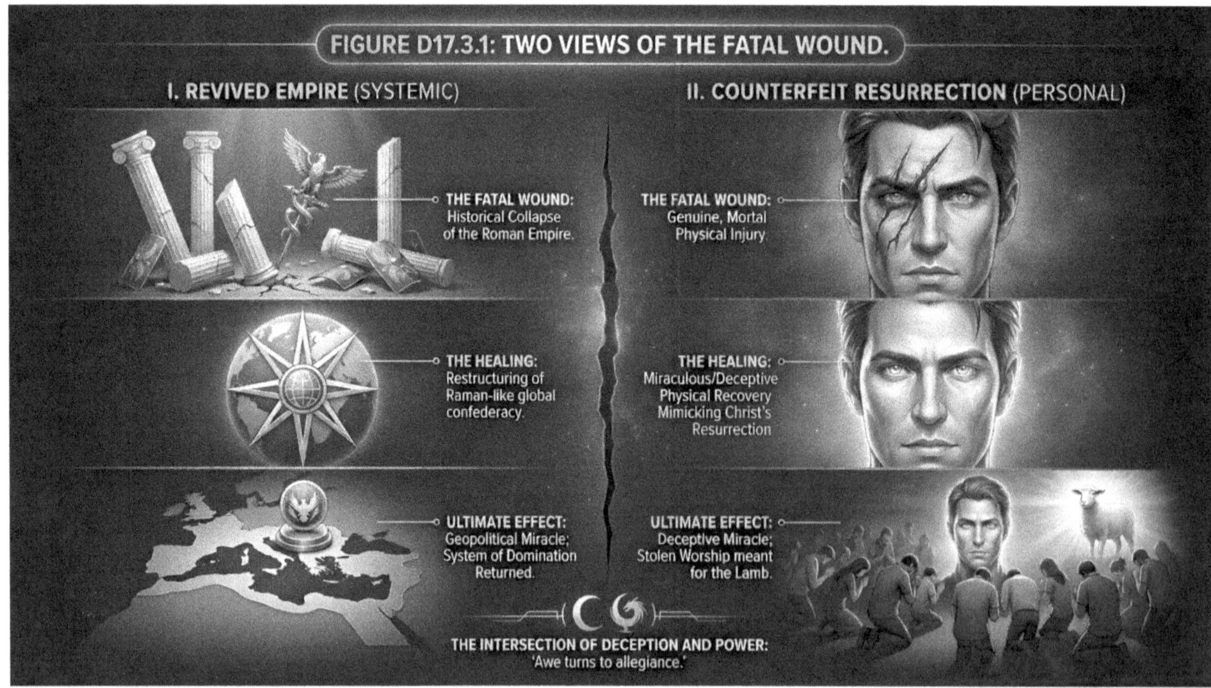


***Figure D17.3.1: The Dead Head Revived.*** *Visualizing the interpretive dilemma of Revelation 13:3. This infographic compares the Systemic View (the historical collapse and revival of the Roman Empire) with the Personal View (a mortal injury and counterfeit resurrection of the Antichrist). The synthesis shows how both views intersect, forming a diabolical parody of Christ's resurrection that deceives the world.*

## Reading the Wound Broadly: A Revived Empire

One long-standing interpretation holds that the wounded "head" symbolizes a fallen empire, specifically Rome.[1] This reading finds strong support in Revelation 17:9–10, where the seven heads of the Beast are described as both seven mountains and seven kings or kingdoms. Many identify these as successive world empires: Egypt, Assyria, Babylon, Persia, Greece, and Rome, making Rome the sixth, the "head" that suffers a seemingly fatal blow.

Historically, the Western Roman Empire collapsed in the fifth century, and the Eastern Empire fell in the fifteenth century to Islamic conquerors, leaving behind a fractured world. In this hybrid view, the healing of the wound points to an end-time revival that fuses both legs of this ancient empire. It anticipates an Antichrist of Middle Eastern origin who directly aligns with Islamic expectations of the Mahdi. This leader will ultimately rise to power within a Western, Roman-like global confederation. This revived "Beast system" inherits the ideologies, territorial ambitions, and blasphemous authority of ancient Rome, now reassembled in a more centralized and deceptive form.

The shock of the world is not that an empire exists. It is that one long thought dead has come back to life.

## Reading the Wound Personally: A Counterfeit Resurrection

Another interpretation narrows the focus to the individual ruler who embodies the Beast. In this reading, the fatal wound is suffered by the Antichrist himself, a genuine, mortal injury from which he miraculously recovers.[2]

Later, the text speaks of the Beast as one who was "wounded by the sword and yet lived," language that naturally invites a personal reading. The world does not merely admire his power. It marvels at his survival. Death, it seems, could not hold him.

This apparent victory over death becomes the foundation of his authority. Loyalty is demanded. Many connect this moment to the mark of the Beast (Revelation 13:16–17), viewing it as a sign of allegiance, possibly even tied to the site of the mortal wound, marking devotion to the one who appeared to conquer death. Worship is normalized. Allegiance is marked and enforced.

Whether the recovery involved literal death is ultimately secondary. What matters is perception. The world believes it has witnessed a man who overcame the grave.

And the resemblance is no accident. This is a counterfeit resurrection, a deliberate imitation meant to steal the worship that belongs to Christ alone.

## Why the Prophecy Demands Both

The strength of Revelation's symbolism is that it rarely confines itself to a single layer.

Notice carefully: the wound is not to the entire Beast, but to one of its heads. Later, those heads are explicitly connected to kingdoms (Revelation 17:10). That alone establishes the primary reference is systemic, not merely

1. For a classic explanation of this perspective, look at John Walvoord's book, *The Revelation of Jesus Christ*. Walvoord argues that the "wound" marks the historical collapse of the Roman Empire. Therefore, the "healing" is a geopolitical miracle, the restructuring of a Roman-like confederacy of nations in the end times.

2. Grant Osborne makes the case for this individual view in his commentary, *Revelation* (Baker Exegetical Commentary on the New Testament). He argues that the text depicts a specific event designed to act as a "counterfeit resurrection." G.K. Beale also champions this idea in *The Book of Revelation* (New International Greek Testament Commentary), famously describing the Beast's recovery as an "intended parody" of the Lamb designed to steal the worship that belongs to Christ.

personal. At the same time, the Beast is consistently portrayed as a ruler who embodies the system he represents.

Even the language itself points in this direction. The head is described as "slain unto death" (Greek *sphazo*), yet the wound is later said to be "healed" (*therapeuo*), a word commonly used for recovery or restoration rather than true resurrection. The vocabulary stops short of claiming a genuine rising from the dead.

And yet the effect is the same. The world responds as though death itself has been conquered. Awe turns to allegiance. What appears defeated returns with convincing force, and the Beast gains the worship and loyalty that follow only apparent victory over death.

The empire revives.

The man rises.

The deception is complete.

## The Pattern Behind the Symbol

This is how Revelation often works.

What happens in history is concentrated in a man.

What is embodied in a man represents something larger than himself.

The Antichrist does not merely rule a revived empire. He is its living expression. The empire's return gives him legitimacy. His survival gives it a face.

Together, they form a diabolical parody of Christ's resurrection. Awe replaces faith. Power replaces truth. Worship is redirected away from God and toward the Beast.

## The Diabolical Parody

The "fatal wound that was healed" is best understood as a revival.

It speaks first to the return of a once-defeated world system rooted in Rome's legacy, yet reshaped for the end times. It also encompasses a personal, dramatic event in the life of the Antichrist that reinforces the illusion of resurrection.

Ultimately, the outcome is the same:

- A parody resurrection without salvation.
- A revived kingdom without Christ.
- A world deceived by the illusion of a dead empire and a slain ruler brought back to life.

# HINTS & POSSIBILITIES 17.4. THE MACHINERY OF CONTROL

## The Technological Architecture of the Mark of the Beast

*Also it causes all, both small and great, both rich and poor, both free and slave, to be marked on the right hand or the forehead, so that no one can buy or sell unless he has the mark,*
*Revelation 13:16–17a*

Scripture describes an economic system so comprehensive that "no one can buy or sell" unless they bear a specific mark of allegiance to a global authority. Whatever else this prophecy entails, it clearly envisions total economic enforcement, something unprecedented in human history.

Until recently, such control would have been impossible to implement at a global scale. Today, however, modern technological developments suggest, for the first time, that the infrastructure capable of enforcing such a mandate may soon exist.

What follows is not an assertion of fulfillment, but a consideration of how such a system is technologically positioned to operate.

## 1. The Gatekeeper: Programmable Money

Central banks around the world are actively developing Central Bank Digital Currencies (CBDCs). Unlike physical cash, CBDCs are not anonymous. They are programmable, traceable, and centrally governed.

When paired with advanced AI systems, such currencies will enable:

- **Real-time monitoring**: Every transaction tracked instantly, identifying payer, recipient, amount, and purpose.
- **Automated enforcement**: Transactions could be algorithmically approved or denied based on predefined compliance criteria.

In such a system, exclusion would not require human judgment. Access to food, housing, or employment could simply be switched off automatically.

## 2. The Mirror: Behavioral and Loyalty Scoring

A total economic system requires a way to distinguish between the compliant and the resistant. Early forms of this already exist.

Some nations have implemented AI-driven social scoring systems, monitoring behavior and assigning risk or trust metrics. These systems demonstrate how:

- **Ideological conformity** could be assessed by analyzing speech, associations, travel patterns, and digital behavior.

- **Punishment through exclusion** could follow automatically: frozen accounts, restricted mobility, or loss of essential services.

Such consequences closely parallel the Revelation warning: exclusion from the ability to *buy or sell*.

## 3. The Seal: Identity Bound to the Body

Revelation specifies the mark as being on the **right hand or the forehead**. Whatever its exact physical form, the text unmistakably links identity, allegiance, and economic access.

Modern biometric systems offer a possible framework:

- **Irrevocable identity links**: Facial recognition, palm scanning, and biometric authentication already replace cards, passwords, and PINs.
- **Biological integration**: Emerging neural-interface technologies hint at a future where digital identity could be inseparable from the human body itself.

Once identity, currency, and compliance are bound together, opting out becomes functionally impossible.

## 4. The Image: Autonomous Authority

Revelation describes an "image" that speaks, acts, and enforces obedience. It does not merely symbolize authority. It exercises it.

To ancient readers, such a phenomenon would have been unimaginable. Today, artificial intelligence introduces a new category of possibility. A centralized AI system could function as a living administrative presence, issuing decrees and managing populations in real time. It would not govern through deliberation, but through execution.

Automated enforcement would complete the system. AI-guided surveillance, predictive policing, and autonomous security could identify dissent instantly and trigger penalties without human hesitation or appeal.

In such a structure, authority never sleeps. It does not reason, relent, or delay. It executes.

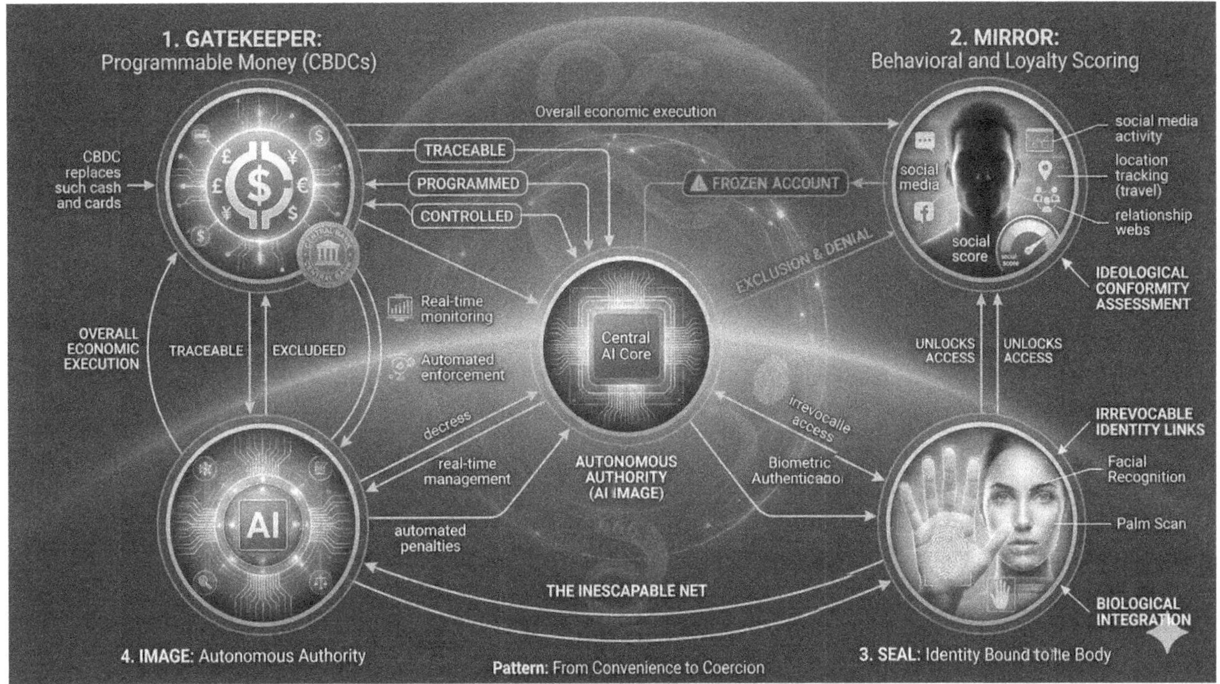


***Figure H17.4.1: The Architecture of Control.*** *Visualizing the technological pillars of the final economic system. This schematic details how Programmable Money acts as the economic gatekeeper, allowing Behavioral Scoring to enforce ideological conformity. These distinct systems merge when Biometric Identity binds credentials irrevocably to the physical body, allowing Autonomous AI Authority to issue decrees and manage populations with instant, automated enforcement. The result is a centralized mechanism for total economic and social enforcement tied directly to spiritual allegiance.*

## The Pattern: From Convenience to Coercion

The trajectory is subtle but consistent. Systems like these do not begin with tyranny. They begin with efficiency, safety, and convenience: simpler payments, fraud prevention, personalized services.

Only later does the architecture reveal its full potential: a digital panopticon where survival itself depends on conformity.

Revelation does not tell us precisely how the final system will operate. But it does tell us what it will accomplish: absolute economic control tied to unconditional allegiance.

For the first time in history, humanity appears to be building the very tools such a system would require.

# HINTS & POSSIBILITIES 17.5. CHARAGMA: THE MARK AS IMPRINT, SEAL, AND BOND

## How Ancient Greek Anticipates Modern Biometric Coercion

*... to be marked on the right hand or the forehead,*

— REVELATION 13:16

The word translated "mark" is the Greek *charagma*. A closer examination of its usage in the ancient world reveals a term far richer, and more unsettling, than a mere symbol. Its semantic range forms a striking bridge between the ancient practice of marking allegiance and modern systems of digital and biometric control.

### 1. The Imprint of Ownership: The Brand

In the Greco-Roman world, a *charagma* commonly referred to a brand burned into the flesh of animals or slaves, signifying exclusive ownership. The mark identified not merely who someone was, but to whom they belonged.

This concept has a modern analogue in digital identity systems. Just as an ancient brand marked a slave's master, a contemporary Digital ID functions as a permanent identifier within a centralized system, marking an individual as a verified, compliant participant in the economic and social order. Identity is no longer self-contained; it is registered, authenticated, and governed externally.

### 2. The Official Seal: Authorization to Function

The term *charagma* was also used for the imperial seal stamped on legal documents or the image of the emperor impressed on coinage. Without such a seal, a document carried no authority, and a coin no legitimacy.

This usage closely parallels the logic behind Central Bank Digital Currencies (CBDCs). In an AI-managed economy, money ceases to be a physical object one possesses and becomes instead a licensed permission granted by a central authority. Participation depends not on possession, but on authorization. If the digital "seal" is revoked, the ability to buy or sell disappears instantly, precisely the condition Revelation describes.

### 3. The Etched Mark: Identity Bound to the Body

Etymologically, *charagma* derives from *charasso*, meaning "to sharpen," "to engrave," or "to etch." The word implies a mark made by cutting, piercing, or inscribing a surface, not merely painting it.

This linguistic nuance points to a permanent, physical identifier bound to the body itself. While this includes modern subcutaneous implants or embedded sensors, the term equally applies to surface-level markings, such as scannable biometric tattoos or quantum dot tags etched into the skin. Whether through surface branding or internal hardware, the mark creates an inescapable interface between the individual and the global economic system.

## 4. The Serpent's Bite: A Hidden Toxin

In certain classical Greek contexts, *charagma* also refers to the bite of a serpent and the venom it leaves behind.[1] The image is subtle but revealing: something that penetrates the skin, appears momentary, yet carries lasting consequences.

This lexical detail is especially chilling given the immediate biblical context. John explicitly identifies the power behind the Beast as "that ancient serpent, who is called the devil and Satan" (Revelation 12:9). Furthermore, Revelation 13 states that the Beast receives its throne and great authority directly from this dragon. The mark, therefore, is not merely a bureaucratic tool. It is the serpent's bite.

As a metaphor, this eerily corresponds to systems that promise efficiency, safety, and convenience while quietly extracting autonomy. An AI-driven economic structure offers frictionless access and total integration as the "bite," but at the cost of human agency, moral freedom, and spiritual independence, which serves as the "venom."

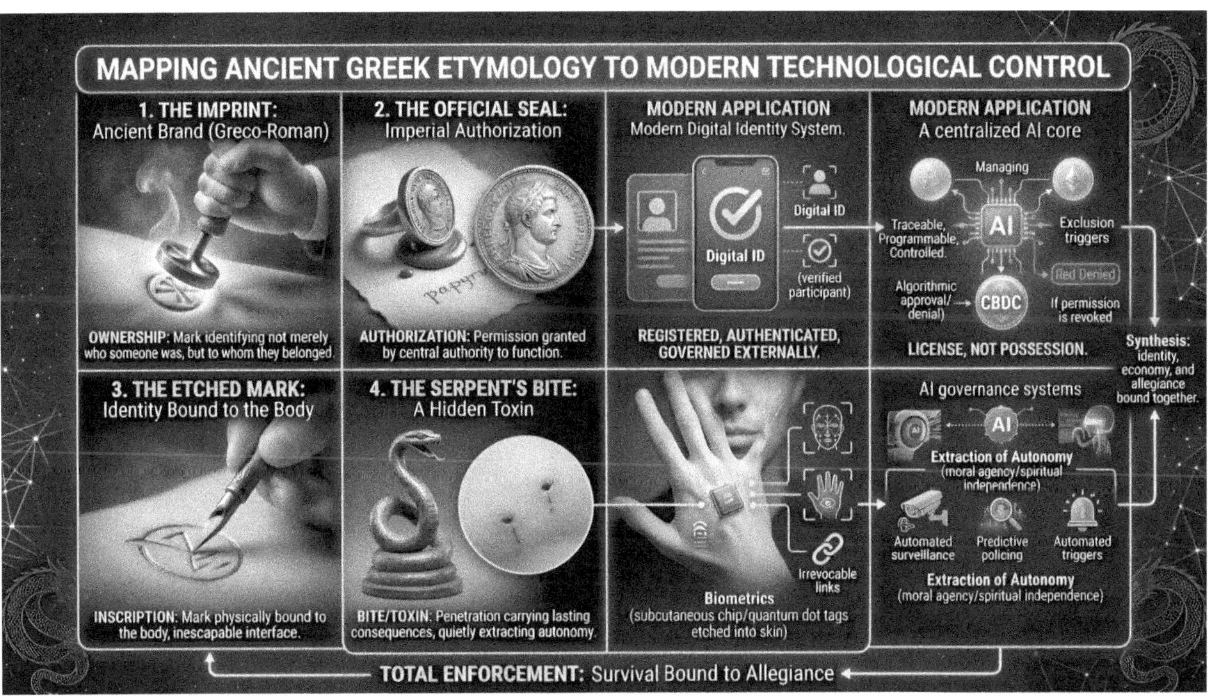


***Figure H17.5.1: Ancient Words and Modern Control.*** *Visualizing the four historical definitions of* charagma *alongside their technological counterparts. By connecting ancient concepts of branding, sealing, etching, and venom to today's digital IDs, CBDCs, and biometrics, this diagram illustrates how the final Mark will function as an inescapable integration of identity, economy, and allegiance.*

1. The term *charagma* (χάραγμα) finds its classical roots in Sophocles' Philoctetes (c. 409 BCE), where it denotes the "mark'"or "bite" of a venomous serpent (line 267). This usage is historically documented in the Liddell-Scott-Jones (LSJ) Greek-English Lexicon, which defines the term in this context as "the bite or sting of a snake." See Sophocles, Philoctetes, trans. Hugh Lloyd-Jones, Loeb Classical Library 21 (Cambridge, MA: Harvard University Press, 1994), line 267.

## The Convergence of Meaning

Taken together, these uses reveal that *charagma* is not merely symbolic. It functions as a tool of ownership, authorization, inscription, and control.

While the ancient world used brands and seals, the modern world employs biometrics, AI governance, and immutable digital ledgers. The terminology itself reveals that the final mark will not be a single device or token, but an inescapable synthesis of identity, economy, and allegiance.

Revelation does not describe the technology. But its ancient language perfectly details the inescapable system that technology will enforce.

# HINTS & POSSIBILITIES 17.6. THE ARCHITECTURE OF THE SYSTEM: 666

## The Algorithmic Engine Behind the Mark

*This calls for wisdom: let the one who has understanding calculate the number of the beast, for it is the number of a man, and his number is 666.*

— REVELATION 13:18

Scripture does not invite superstition here. It calls for discernment. The number is not presented as a spectacle to be feared, but as a clue to be understood.

Rather than functioning as a visible label alone, the number points to the inner logic of the system itself. It describes the numerical framework that allows a fully automated, global economy to function during the Tribulation period. What follows explores how modern logistics, computation, and identification already rest on structures capable of enforcing this prophesied control.

## 1. The Rails of Commerce: Barcodes and the UPC Framework

One of the most striking visual parallels to this system involves the Universal Product Code and the barcode standards that govern global trade.

**FIGURE H17.6.1: THE 'RAILS OF COMMERCE' AND THE 6–6–6 PARALLEL**

**FIGURE D17.6.1:** The numerical architecture of global logistics. This technical schematic illustrates how the standard UPC-A barcode is visually framed by three sets of guard bars at the beginning, middle, and end. To the optical scanner, the binary patterns for these guard bars ('101') and the numeral '6' ('10100000' in the right-hand set) are distinct. However, to the human eye, their aesthetic and geometric structure is indistinguishable, creating a striking visual parallel: a system framed and bracketed by 6-6-6. The diagram highlights the numerical logic embedded into foundation of modern commerce.

***Figure H17.6.1:** Visualizing the "6-6-6" Structure in Global Barcode Standards. This diagram highlights how standard guard bars in UPC and EAN codes are visually indistinguishable from the pattern representing the digit six, symbolically framing modern commerce within the number 6-6-6.*

Every standard barcode contains three sets of guard bars at the beginning, the middle, and the end of the code. These markers allow scanners to orient and interpret the data. In both UPC-A and EAN-13 systems, the digit six is encoded using the exact same physical pattern of ink: two thin parallel lines separated by a thin white space. To the naked human eye, the guard bars and the number six are visually indistinguishable.[1]

The practical result is striking. Every standard barcode is effectively bracketed by a pattern visually equivalent to 6–6–6. Symbolically, it demonstrates that nearly all modern commerce already operates on rails framed by the number Revelation associates with the final system. Global trade moves within a numerical structure visually marked by triple six. It serves as a stark foreshadowing of a global economy entirely dependent on a numerical architecture to restrict buying and selling during the Great Tribulation.

## 2. The Number of Man: Logic Encoded into Computation

Biblically, six is associated with humanity. Man was created on the sixth day. He labors for six days. Yet six never reaches the perfection symbolized by seven.

Triple six intensifies the theme. It represents humanity striving for completeness apart from God, culminating in ultimate rebellion under the Antichrist. Modern computers run on binary logic, but the Beast system is not defined by hardware alone. It is governed by a moral and philosophical logic centered on six, a closed system of autonomous human reasoning.

It is a framework that optimizes efficiency, security, and control while deliberately excluding the divine rest of the seventh day. It is not merely a technical specification; it is a worldview encoded into the system itself, designed to facilitate global idolatry.

## 3. The Interface: From RFID to the Internet of Bodies

Early discussions focused on RFID chips, but the modern *charagma* represents a convergence rather than a single device.

Biometric identity systems now include palm-vein scanning, facial recognition, optical tattoos, and subdermal sensors.

1. It is a common technical misconception that these guard bars hold a mathematical value of six within the computer's logic. They do not. The guard bars are purely structural calibration markers encoded in binary as 101. Conversely, the actual digit "6" on the right side of a barcode is encoded as 1010000. However, because the physical ink pattern of the "6" begins with the exact same sequence as the guard bars, the foundational tracking technology of modern global commerce naturally evolved into an architecture visually bracketed by the physical pattern of the number six.

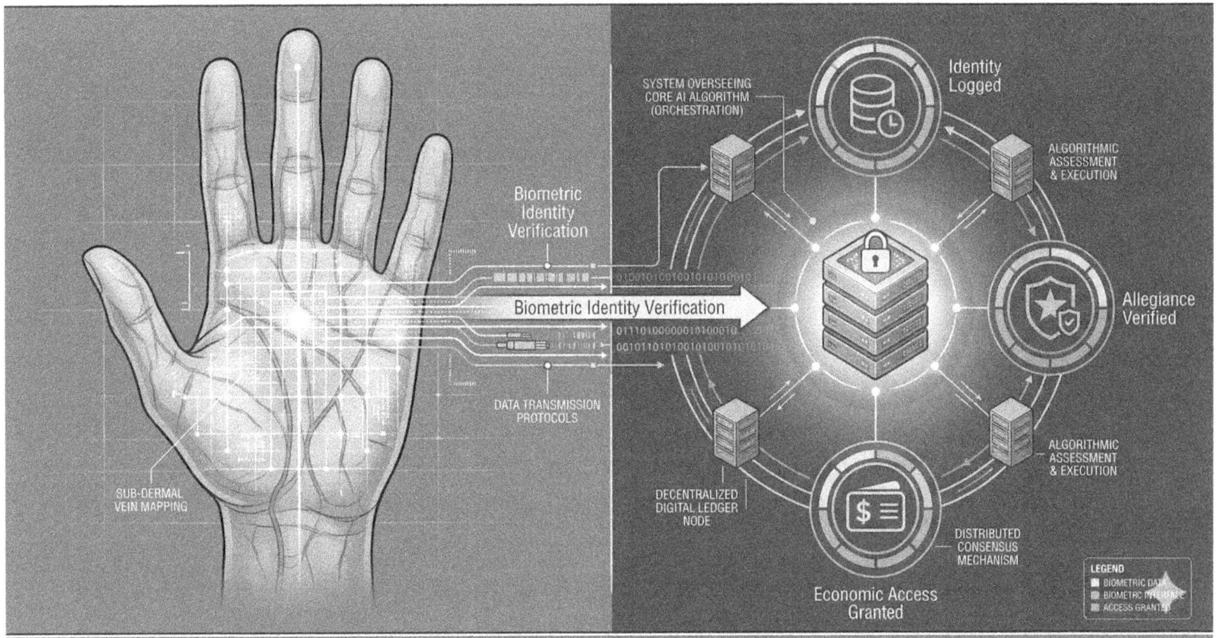


***Figure H17.6.2**: The convergence of human biology and global digital networks. The physical body functions as the biometric portal to the digital economy, binding physical identity to the universal ledger.*

Together, they form what is increasingly called the Internet of Bodies, where human biology is directly linked to global digital networks. In this framework, the "mark" is not merely a tag. It is a biometric portal. It connects the individual to a universal ledger that determines access to food, work, and survival based on a real-time digital profile.

Ultimately, this system serves one purpose during the Tribulation: enforcing mandatory worship of the Beast. Identity becomes permission, and permission requires spiritual submission.

## 4. Convergence: AI as the Authoritarian Interpreter

What makes this convergence unprecedented is artificial intelligence.

AI functions as the universal interpreter, breathing life into the architecture of control, much like the image of the beast described in Revelation 13:15. It binds logistics, identity, and authorization into a single, automated loop.

The machine performs a threefold act of control. It scans the product through the barcode. It verifies the buyer through biometric identity. It renders an algorithmic judgment to permit or deny the exchange based on the individual's allegiance to the False Prophet's religion.

If compliance is lacking, the transaction does not fail. It simply never exists.

The product is present. The need is real. But the ledger remains closed.

The system does not argue.

It cannot be persuaded.

It executes the code.

In such a world, access to life is no longer a human right. It is an algorithmic permission granted only to those who worship the Beast.

## The Mark as the Interface

Seen this way, 666 is not merely an identity number. It is the defining logic of the entire system.

The *charagma* functions as the interface. Whether visible or invisible, etched or biometric, it is the point where personal allegiance meets economic access.

- Every transaction is tracked.
- Every action is logged.
- Every permission is granted or withheld by an autonomous intelligence enforcing spiritual idolatry.

Revelation does not name the technology. It describes the outcome: a world where economic life is inseparable from spiritual allegiance during the Great Tribulation. Participation requires more than consent. It requires total integration with the architecture itself.

For the first time in history, the numerical and technological framework capable of such total, automated control is no longer theoretical.

It is already emerging.

# HINTS & POSSIBILITIES 17.7. THE LEDGER THAT CANNOT BE ERASED

## Blockchain and the Architecture of Beast Economics

*And books were opened... and the dead were judged by what was written in the books.*

— REVELATION 20:12

Scripture repeatedly portrays judgment as a permanent record. In the biblical imagination, what is written in these "books" is neither tentative nor reversible: it is fixed, authoritative, and beyond appeal. This image is unsettling precisely because it conveys irrevocable finality. It describes a record that cannot be altered, a verdict that cannot be negotiated, and an account that cannot be erased. What is inscribed stands.

Revelation applies this same sobering principle to the Beast's temporary dominion over global commerce. The prophecy that no one may "buy or sell" apart from enforced allegiance (Revelation 13:17) dictates more than mere persecution; it describes an inescapable infrastructure. It details a system so integrated and comprehensive that dissent becomes an existential impossibility.

Distributed ledger technology functions as the foundational architecture that transforms a central bank digital currency (CBDC) into a system of irreversible economic enforcement. Though originally developed to promote decentralization and individual freedom, as seen in early permissionless cryptocurrencies like Bitcoin, this core technology is now being repurposed by global institutions to support centralized, programmable control. By deploying a permissioned blockchain, a single governing authority gains a framework uniquely suited to the total economic dominion described in Revelation 13. It establishes an immutable digital ledger where every transaction is permanently recorded and monitored, ensuring the prophetic "buy or sell" mandate is enforced with cold algorithmic precision.

## 1. Immutability: Enforcement Written in Code

At its core, this architecture functions as an immutable ledger for the masses: once data is recorded, it cannot be altered, erased, or forged by any citizen or local entity.

In the Great Tribulation's AI-managed system of global governance, a designation of "non-compliant" is written directly into the ledger the moment an individual refuses the required mark. Because the record is permanently cryptographically locked by the central authority, no local official, merchant, or sympathetic intermediary can override it. The restriction is not merely policy-based or discretionary; it is a fundamental property embedded into the system itself. What is written into the ledger becomes economically final.

## 2. Smart Contracts: Automated Exclusion Without Mercy

Centralized digital currency systems and modern blockchains rely on smart contracts: self-executing programs that permit or deny actions based strictly on predefined conditions.

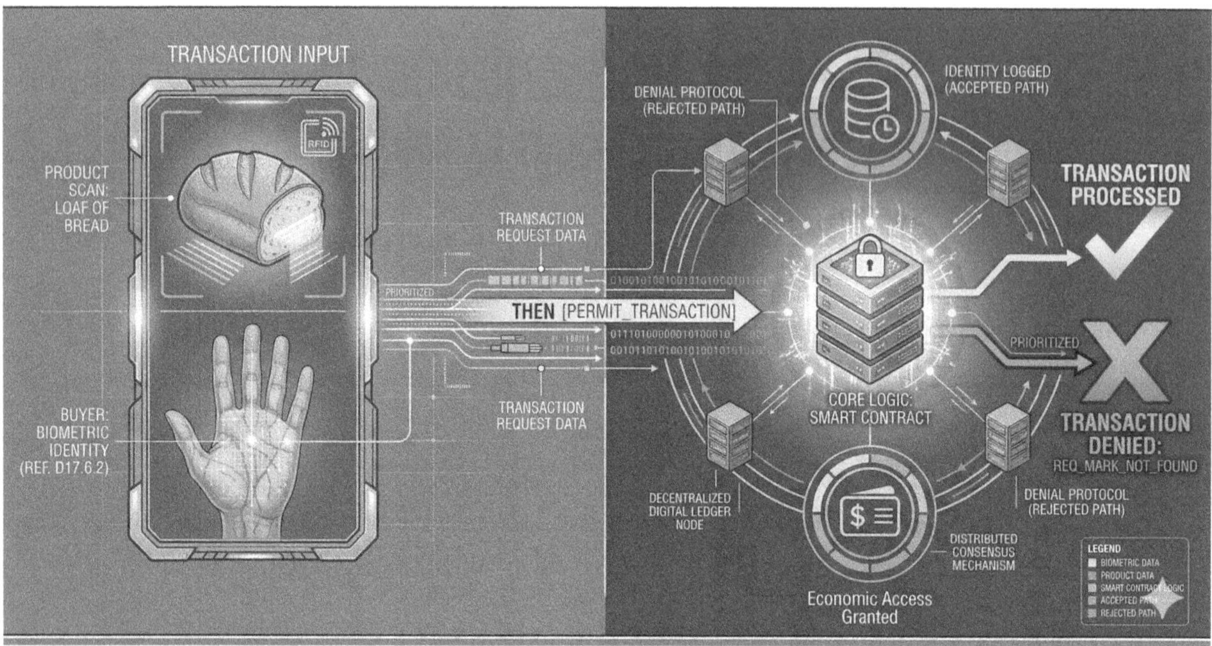


***Figure H17.7.1:*** *The mechanics of Revelation 13:17 enforced by algorithmic code. This schematic illustrates how smart contracts, with their ability to automate enforcement, can be integrated into a larger framework to precisely arbitrate transactions according to predefined, centralized rules.*

In practical terms, the central authority establishes an automated rule dictating that a transaction is permitted only if the biometric identity is verified and authorized. Under such conditions, the restriction described in Revelation, where "no one can buy or sell," no longer depends on human enforcers. There is no cashier to persuade and no official to bribe. If the smart contract does not receive the required digital signature linked to the approved mark, the transaction is mathematically impossible to complete.

Judgment is rendered by code rather than conscience.

## 3. Programmable Money: The Digital Cage

Physical cash is inherently anonymous; it is spent by anyone, anywhere, without embedded restrictions. Blockchain-based currencies, particularly Central Bank Digital Currencies (CBDCs), are fundamentally different because they are programmable. This architecture establishes a tiered system of totalitarian control:

- **Whitelisting** permits only pre-approved transactions, restricting individuals to basic necessities while automatically denying the purchase of all other goods.
- **Blacklisting** prevents access to specific commercial categories, vendors, or individuals entirely.
- **Geofencing** enables AI systems to limit exactly where money can be spent. If a user steps outside an approved geographic zone, their digital wallet is instantly rendered inert.

The result is a form of confinement without walls: a digital cage enforced economically rather than physically.

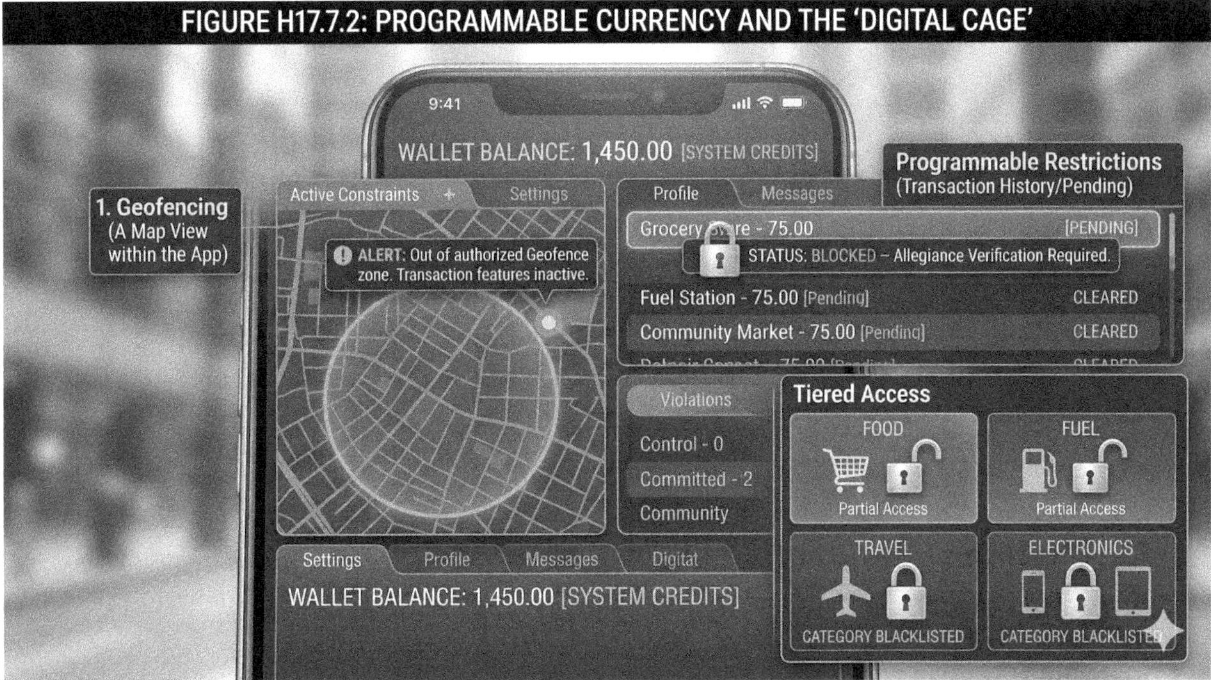


***Figure H17.7.2:*** *The digital cage implemented via a Central Bank Digital Currency (CBDC) interface. Money is no longer passive value; it is active permission. This interface demonstrates how AI-monitored geofencing can economically confine individuals to specific areas and how programmable category blacklisting can weaponize access to basic necessities.*

## 4. Total Traceability: The End of Evasion

Blockchain establishes a complete chain of custody for every unit of currency. Each transaction requires a cryptographic signature tied to a verified identity.

In a fully digitized economy, this effectively eliminates the possibility of black markets or informal exchange. Under-the-table transactions become infeasible because participation in the economy itself requires authentication within the system. By removing anonymous cash and replacing it with an AI-monitored ledger, the final loop of enforcement is closed. There is no parallel economy, no shadow system, and no place to hide.

## The Big Picture: Control Without Armies

In this framework, the Beast does not require vast numbers of physical enforcers to monitor every market. Control is exercised at the central node: the ledger itself. Once the world's economic activity is consolidated onto a single, programmable system, compliance becomes automatic and dissent becomes fatal.

The true terror of this architecture lies in its immutability. Just as the "books" of divine judgment in Revelation cannot be erased, the Beast's counterfeit ledger permits no grace, no exceptions, and no revisions. A designation of non-compliance is permanently etched into the cryptographic chain.

The prophecy of total economic control is not merely a warning about the loss of privacy; it is a portrait of an inescapable digital cage. By fusing programmable currency with an immutable blockchain, the system ensures that the choice of allegiance during the Great Tribulation is not only economically absolute, but mathematically irreversible.

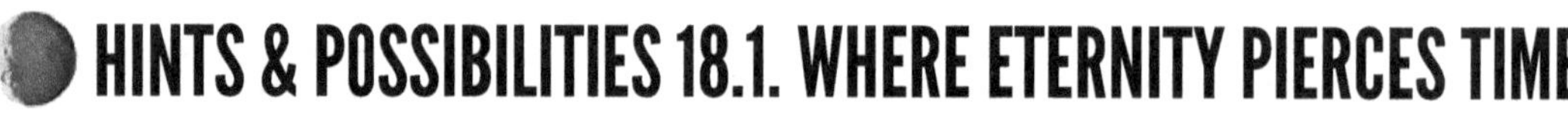

## HINTS & POSSIBILITIES 18.1. WHERE ETERNITY PIERCES TIME

### Mount Zion as the Meeting Place of Heaven and Earth

*Then I looked, and behold, on Mount Zion stood the Lamb, and with him 144,000 who had his name and his Father's name written on their foreheads.*

— REVELATION 14:1

This compelling scene in Revelation 14 presents us with a key interpretive question: where, exactly, is this Mount Zion? Is it the heavenly Zion mentioned in Hebrews 12:22, or the earthly Zion, the city of Jerusalem?

## 1. A Dimensional Overlap

Interpreters have long debated this. Some, pointing to Hebrews 12:22, see it as the purely "heavenly Jerusalem," a spiritual reality. Others, citing Old Testament prophecies of an earthly kingdom, see it as a literal, future Jerusalem. But Bible teacher Chuck Missler proposed a provocative third reality: this Zion is a point of dimensional overlap, a spiritual portal where heaven and earth intersect.

## 2. Biblical Precedent: The Gate of Heaven

Scripture gives us precedent for such an idea. When Jacob dreamed at Bethel, he saw a stairway reaching into heaven, with angels ascending and descending. When he awoke, he did not dismiss the vision as symbolic. Instead, he declared, "Surely the LORD is in this place... This is none other than the house of God, and this is the gate of heaven" (Genesis 28:16–17).

***Figure H18.1.1: Stairway to Heaven.*** *The biblical account of Bethel demonstrates that the unseen spiritual world is a higher-order reality capable of piercing our physical dimensions.*

The emphasis is striking. Jacob's reaction centers not merely on what he saw, but where he was. Bethel is marked as sacred ground, an earthly location identified as a gateway to the heavenly realm. The text presents it not as metaphor, but as a real place where heaven intersected the physical world.

## 3. A Hyperdimensional Reality

Missler connected this biblical pattern with ideas from modern theoretical physics, not as proof, but as analogy.[1] Concepts such as higher dimensions and the holographic universe demonstrate that the reality we perceive is a projection of something deeper. In 1997, physicist Juan Maldacena provided the mathematical framework demonstrating that a higher-dimensional reality can be fully encoded on a lower-dimensional boundary. This radical idea was later popularized in Scientific American.[2] What we experience as solid reality is a shadow of a higher-order structure.

1. For readers interested in this idea, Chuck Missler explores it further in his teaching *Beyond Perception* (Koinonia House, 2010). In this presentation, Missler draws on concepts from modern physics, like higher dimensions and holographic reality, as illustrations to help explain how the Bible portrays the spiritual realm as real, ordered, and more fundamental than the visible world. These scientific ideas are used as analogies, not proofs.
2. Juan Maldacena, "The Large N Limit of Superconformal Field Theories and Supergravity." *Advances in Theoretical and Mathematical Physics*, vol. 2, no. 2, 1998, pp. 231–52. This is the foundational academic paper for the holographic principle.

***Figure H18.1.2: The Holographic Principle.*** *Modern theoretical physics illustrates how our three-dimensional universe functions as a projection from a higher-order boundary. This serves as a powerful analogy for the biblical truth that the unseen spiritual realm is the true, permanent reality.*

For Missler, such ideas helped illuminate a truth Scripture already assumes: the unseen world is not less real than the seen; rather, it is more real. He argued that the biblical "spiritual realm" is not immaterial or abstract, but hyperdimensional, a higher order of reality existing beyond our familiar dimensions of space and time. In line with Paul's words that we now see "through a glass, darkly" (1 Corinthians 13:12, KJV), Missler established that the visible world is a low-resolution reflection of the unseen. God's throne, angelic beings, and even resurrected bodies belong to this higher-order reality, normally invisible, yet utterly real.

## 4. The Ultimate Convergence at Zion

Seen this way, Mount Zion's recurring role in Scripture takes on new significance. Psalm 2:6 speaks of God installing His King upon Zion. Isaiah and Micah describe it as the center of the Messianic Kingdom, where the nations will come to learn God's law. Hebrews 12:22 tells believers they have already come to Mount Zion, the heavenly Jerusalem. And in Revelation 14:1, the Lamb stands on Zion with the 144,000 after their mission during the Tribulation is complete.

This scene may depict a heavenly vision, or it may describe a moment when Zion on earth becomes the interface with heaven itself.

Missler often framed the idea along this line:

*What if Mount Zion is not just a place* but is actually a portal? *What if it is where eternity pierces time?*

***Figure H18.1.3: The Interface at Zion.*** *This panoramic landscape view illustrates Zion as a fixed point in the created order, where the solid earthly peak dissolves and merges into a spectacular, multi-layered heavenly structure. It visualizes the functional interface where the eternal realm intersects the temporal world.*

## The Dimensional Interface

This blending of science and Scripture is not contrary to biblical thought. Ezekiel, Daniel, and John all describe visions in which heavenly realities appear in earthly space. Jesus, after His resurrection, moved through locked doors and ascended bodily into another realm. Paul spoke of being "caught up to the third heaven" (2 Corinthians 12:2), as if to another layer of creation altogether.

Mount Zion, then, may be more than metaphor or mere geography. It could be a fixed point in the created order, chosen by God as a bridge between realms, a place where the higher-dimensional reality we call "heaven" intersects with our own. A place where judgment is pronounced, victory declared, and the Lamb receives His crown.

In the days to come, as heaven invades earth in judgment and redemption, perhaps Mount Zion will again become the gate through which that deeper, more profound reality breaks in.

# DEEPER DIVE 20.1. HOW GLOBAL ARE THE BOWL JUDGMENTS?

## No Fractions. No Limits. No Escape

*"Neither their silver nor their gold will be able to save them on the day of the LORD's wrath. In the fire of his jealousy the whole earth will be consumed, for he will make a sudden end of all who live on the earth."*

— ZEPHANIAH 1:18 NIV

When Revelation 16 unfolds, one question is unavoidable: How big is this?

Are the Bowl Judgments symbolic flashes, regional disasters, or something far more sweeping?

The text itself leaves little room for doubt. The Bowl Judgments are global. They represent the final, unrestrained outpouring of God's wrath on a world that has fully aligned itself against Him.

Earlier judgments were measured. These are not.

The Fourth Seal struck a quarter of the earth.

The Trumpets expanded that reach to a third.

But the bowls remove all restraint.[1] There are no fractions left. No limits. No delay.

This is the endgame.

1. Grant R. Osborne notes that the Bowl Judgments differ from the seals and trumpets in both completeness and intensity. While earlier judgments were partial and indirect, the bowls affect the whole earth and fall directly on the earth-dwellers, signaling that the end has arrived (*Revelation*, BECNT, Revelation 16:1–21).

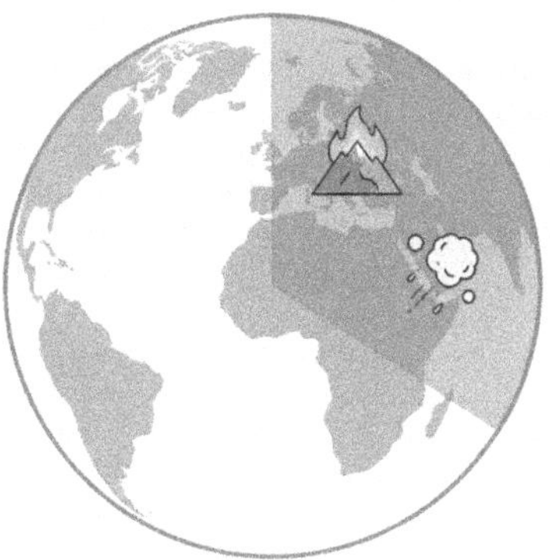


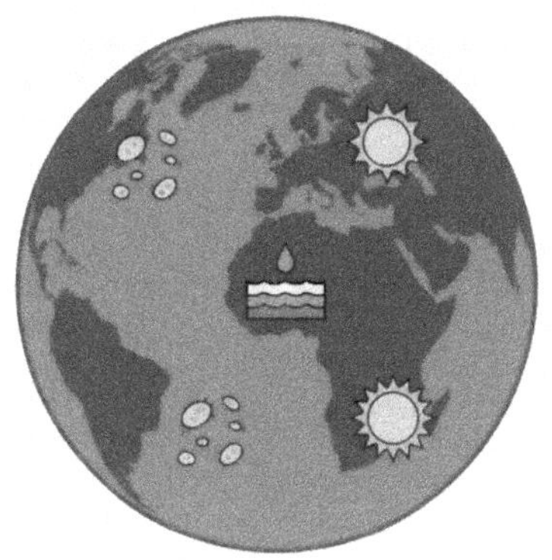


***Figure D20.1.1: The Escalation of Scale.*** *This comparison chart visually charts the transition from the partial judgments of the seals and trumpets to the complete, undiluted, 100% global scale of the bowl judgments.*

## No Intermissions. No Relief. No Escape

Unlike the seals and trumpets, the bowls arrive without interludes. There are no pauses to regroup, no mercy windows left open. The judgments fall in rapid succession, directly and decisively. They strike the earth-dwellers themselves, not merely their environment.

Sores break out.

The seas die.

Fresh water turns to blood.

The sun scorches.

Darkness chokes the Beast's throne.

This is no longer indirect warning. It is direct confrontation.

And still, the world refuses to repent.

## Global Judgment with Strategic Strikes

While the scope is worldwide, Revelation does something deliberate: it zooms in on key targets.

Not because judgment is limited, but because rebellion has centers of gravity.

The bowls expose how God dismantles the Beast's empire piece by piece:

- **Creation itself** is turned against its counterfeit rulers.

- **The Beast's throne**, his seat of authority, is plunged into darkness.
- **The Euphrates**, once a natural boundary, is dried up to allow the nations to rush headlong into final conflict.
- **Babylon The Great**, the crown jewel of human pride and spiritual corruption, is marked for collapse.

***Figure D20.1.2: The Strategic Map of Wrath.*** *This visualization demonstrates how the global bowl judgments execute precision strikes, targeting centers of the Beast's authority and economic power, while abruptly drying the Euphrates River to facilitate the advance of the Kings of the East.*

These are not random disasters.

They are precision strikes.[2]

God dismantles the system exactly where it draws its strength: economically, politically, spiritually, and symbolically.

## The Bowls Drive History to Its End

The final bowls do not merely punish evil; they **exhaust it**.

They gather the nations.

They expose the false trinity.

They prepare the ground for Armageddon.

And they culminate with a voice from the throne declaring, *"It is done."*

There is no "is to come" left in the divine timeline.

2. G. K. Beale notes that while the Bowl Judgments are global, Revelation intentionally focuses on symbolic and strategic locations, such as the Beast's throne, the Euphrates, and Babylon, to expose the centers of resistance against God. These locations function both literally and symbolically, highlighting where divine judgment is most concentrated (*The Book of Revelation*, NIGTC, Revelation 16).

The future has arrived.

What remains after this is not chaos, but reckoning.

## The Horizon of Reckoning

Revelation 16 is not meant to satisfy curiosity about the future. It is meant to strip away illusions.

The world will not drift into judgment accidentally.

It will choose it, again and again, until nothing remains but accountability.

And the same God who patiently warned through partial judgments now brings history to its appointed close.

The bowls remind us that evil does not simply fade out.

**It is judged. Fully. Finally.**

# DEEPER DIVE 20.2. THE GREAT CITY: JERUSALEM OR BABYLON?

## One Verse, Two Cities, Two Fates

*The great city was split into three parts, and the cities of the nations fell. And God remembered Babylon the great, to make her drain the cup of the wine of the fury of his wrath.*

— REVELATION 16:19

At first glance, the verse seems simple. Babylon is mentioned at the end, so it is easy to assume that Babylon is also *the great city* that splits into three parts.

But John is doing something more deliberate.

Revelation 16:19 does not describe one city experiencing one judgment. It presents a sequence of judgments, and two different cities are in view.

## Not One Event, but a Chain Reaction

John structures the verse in escalating stages:

• **The great city** is split into three parts.

• **The cities of the nations** collapse.

• **Babylon the Great** is remembered for wrath.

That final clause, *"God remembered Babylon the great"*, is not a poetic restatement of the first. It marks a shift in focus.

Babylon is not being split here.

She is being summoned.

John is not collapsing the cities into one symbol.

He is lining them up for judgment.[1]

## "The Great City" Has Already Been Defined

Earlier in Revelation, John removes the ambiguity entirely:

*...the great city that symbolically is called Sodom and Egypt, where their Lord was crucified.*

1. See J. Massyngberde Ford, *Revelation*, *The Anchor Bible* (Garden City, NY: Doubleday, 1975), 264, who distinguishes the "great city" from Rome and treats Jerusalem as the referent based on Revelation 11:8.

— REVELATION 11:8

That city is Jerusalem, unmistakably.

Unless John clearly signals a redefinition, he expects the reader to follow his established usage. In Revelation 16:19, he does not redefine the term. He simply uses it.

The continuity is intentional.

## Why Jerusalem Splits

The splitting of the great city occurs during the Seventh Bowl

The final earthquake does not merely shake the nations; it strikes the geographic and spiritual center of the end-time conflict. Jerusalem is fractured, not annihilated; shaken, not erased.

This coheres with the prophetic expectation of Zechariah 14:4:

> *On that day his feet shall stand on the Mount of Olives ... and the Mount of Olives shall be split in two ... forming a very wide valley.*

where the return of the Messiah physically alters the city itself. Jerusalem must be broken open before it can be restored.

The city that once embraced the false king is torn apart in a final, sovereign purging as the true King returns to reclaim His throne.[2]

## Babylon's Judgment Is Deliberately Deferred

Babylon, by contrast, is not shaken by the earthquake.

She is remembered.

And in Scripture, when God "remembers," judgment is no longer delayed.

Revelation 16:19 does not describe Babylon's destruction; it announces her indictment. Her fall is too significant to be compressed into a single clause. That is why Revelation pauses and devotes chapters 17–18 to her exposure, collapse, and burning.

Jerusalem is split.

Babylon is dismantled.

2. Arnold G. Fruchtenbaum, *The Footsteps of the Messiah*, identifies the "great city" as Jerusalem and connects its division to the topographical changes of Zechariah 14:4, distinguishing this event from Babylon's later destruction.

***Figure D20.2.1: Two cities, two fates.*** *Revelation 16:19 reveals a surgical, dual judgment. On the left, literal Jerusalem is fractured to prepare for the Messiah's return and redemption. On the right, Babylon the Great is remembered by God, marking the ultimate epicenter of human rebellion for total and inescapable destruction.*

## Summary: The Divergent Fates

| Prophetic Target | Identity | Action in Revelation 16:19 | Prophetic Future |
|---|---|---|---|
| **The Great City** | Literal Jerusalem | Split into three parts | Purged and redeemed (Zechariah 14) |
| **Babylon the Great** | The Ultimate City of Rebellion | Remembered for wrath | Fully destroyed (Revelation 18) |

***Table D20.2.1:*** *The divergent fates of Jerusalem and Babylon. Revelation 16:19 executes two distinct divine actions upon two literal geographic cities.*

## Two Cities, Two Destinies

If we flatten the verse and treat both cities as one, we lose the precision of the judgment.

John wants us to see this clearly:

- **Jerusalem** is fractured, then redeemed: the stage of Christ's return.
- **Babylon the Great** is remembered, then erased: the global system of the Beast.

One city is broken open.

The other is burned down.

Revelation 16:19 is not confusing.

It is surgical.

The earthquake splits Jerusalem.

The nations collapse.

Babylon's time is up.

And the King is at the door.

#  DEEPER DIVE 21.1. WHAT DOES "MYSTERY, BABYLON THE GREAT" REALLY MEAN?

## A Warning from the Future

*And on her forehead was written a name of mystery: "Babylon the great, mother of prostitutes and of earth's abominations."*

— REVELATION 17:5

At first glance, the phrase "Mystery: Babylon the great" is deliberately cryptic. And that is precisely the point. John is not naming a city in plain terms; he is unveiling a spiritual reality hidden beneath familiar imagery.

To understand what John sees, we need to listen carefully to how Scripture itself uses the words *mystery* and *Babylon*.

***Figure D21.1.1: Deciphering the Clues.*** *The Harlot is identified by specific prophetic details. The inscription on her forehead marks her name as a "mystery" (v. 5). Furthermore, her physical location upon the "seven hills" (v. 9) pinpoints Rome as her geographical headquarters, exposing her true identity as the Vatican and the end-time apostate one-world religion.*

## 1. What "Mystery" Means, and What It Doesn't

In the Bible, a mystery is not something unknowable or mystical in the modern sense. It is a truth once hidden, now revealed by God.

When John writes "Mystery: Babylon the great," he signals that this is a symbolic name rather than a literal address.[1] The woman represents something real, but not in a straightforward, one-to-one way. Her identity must be discerned, not assumed.

The word *mystery* tells the reader to slow down and look beneath the surface. What is being revealed is not ancient geography, but a spiritual system, one that carries Babylon's character into the final days.

## 2. Babylon: A Name Loaded with Meaning

By the time Revelation was written, the ancient city of Babylon had long since faded from power. Yet its name endured as a symbol of rebellion, idolatry, and persecution. In John's day, that symbolic weight naturally fell upon Rome, the dominant power ruling the known world and opposing the people of God. Consequently, many interpreters view first-century Rome as a historical prototype rather than the final fulfillment. Rome merely previewed the ultimate reality: an end-time global system that will align with the Beast.[2]

Babylon was remembered as:

- The destroyer of Jerusalem
- The captor of God's people
- The embodiment of pride and defiance against God

Over time, Babylon became a theological label, a shorthand for any system that seduces the world away from faithful worship. It no longer referred only to a place, but to a pattern.

For early Christians living under persecution, the name carried immediate resonance. It evoked the dominant power of their own day while also pointing beyond it.

## 3. The Seven Hills and "The Great City"

Revelation sharpens the picture by adding specific clues. The woman sits on seven mountains (Revelation 17:9) and is called "the great city" (v. 18).

In the ancient world, Rome was famously known as the city of seven hills. This was common knowledge, not obscure symbolism, and John's original audience would have recognized the reference immediately.

Yet Revelation does not stop with Rome. The imagery stretches beyond one historical city to further portray an end-time global religious system, one that will dominate the world shortly before Christ returns. The vision is rooted in history, but it grows into something larger and more dangerous.

## 4. Not Just Political, But Religious

One of the most important details is this: Babylon is not merely political. She is religious.

She is adorned like royalty and priesthood. She holds a golden cup, but it is filled with abominations. She intoxicates nations not only through power, but through deception.

1. John F. Walvoord, *The Revelation of Jesus Christ* (Chicago: Moody Press, 1966), chap. 17. Walvoord emphasizes that the term "Mystery" distinguishes the title as a symbolic "religious designation" (Apostate Christendom) rather than a reference to the literal city or nation.
2. Grant R. Osborne, *Revelation*, Baker Exegetical Commentary on the New Testament (Grand Rapids: Baker Academic, 2002), 619–623. Osborne identifies "Babylon the Great" as Rome in John's historical context, while also viewing Rome as the precursor to the final, climactic world system associated with the Beast.

This is religion divorced from truth. It is faith turned into a tool of control, a system that blesses corruption, sanctifies compromise, and prepares the world to embrace the Antichrist. At first, this false religious power rides the Beast. Later, the Beast will turn on her and destroy her. Evil does not share power for long.

| The Symbol | The End-Time Reality |
|---|---|
| **The Prostitute (The Woman)** | The apostate, one-world religious system |
| **Riding the Beast** | The apostate, one-world religious system initially controlling or allying with the Antichrist's rising political empire |
| **The Golden Cup** | The intoxicating, deceptive doctrines of false religion |
| **Purple and Scarlet** | The outward appearance of royal authority and religious wealth masking internal corruption |

***Table D21.1.1:*** *Decoding the Symbols of Revelation 17*

## The Unmasking of the Harlot

"Mystery: Babylon the great" is not a relic of ancient history. It is a warning.

Revelation shows that the greatest deception at the end of the age will not look godless at all. It will look spiritual. It will speak the language of faith while opposing the truth of Christ.

But her judgment is assured. The system that corrupts the world will be judged, the Woman who seduces the nations will be exposed, and the Lamb she opposes will triumph.

Her end is certain. And it is near.

# DEEPER DIVE 21.2. THE ENIGMA OF THE EIGHTH KING

## Decoding the Rise of the Final World Ruler

> *"...the seven heads are seven mountains on which the woman is seated; they are also seven kings, five of whom have fallen, one is, the other has not yet come, and when he does come he must remain only a little while. As for the beast that was and is not, it is an eighth but it belongs to the seven, and it goes to destruction."*
>
> — REVELATION 17:9–11

Few passages in Revelation are as dense or as debated as this one. The vision speaks of seven kings, an eighth who "belongs to the seven," and a Beast whose rise is brief and whose end is certain. Yet, when read through a strict futurist lens that treats Revelation as predictive prophecy rather than symbolic retrospection, a precise architectural blueprint of end-time geopolitics emerges.

## The Seven Heads: Kings and Kingdoms

Revelation 17 identifies the seven heads of the Beast in two ways: as "seven mountains" and as "seven kings." While the image of seven mountains has is historically associated with Rome, the text itself quickly interprets the symbol politically, not geographically. In Scripture, mountains frequently represent kingdoms or ruling powers (cf. Daniel 2:35, 44–45), and John is explicitly told that the heads are kings.

Since the Greek term translated "kings" (*basileis*) can also denote ruling powers or kingdoms rather than merely individual monarchs, these "kings" represent successive world empires that have dominated the biblical world and opposed God's redemptive purposes throughout history.[1]

1. A representative futurist interpretation identifying the seven heads as successive world empires and the eighth as the final world government (or political power) may be found in John F. Walvoord, *The Revelation of Jesus Christ* (Chicago: Moody Press, 1966), 254–257.

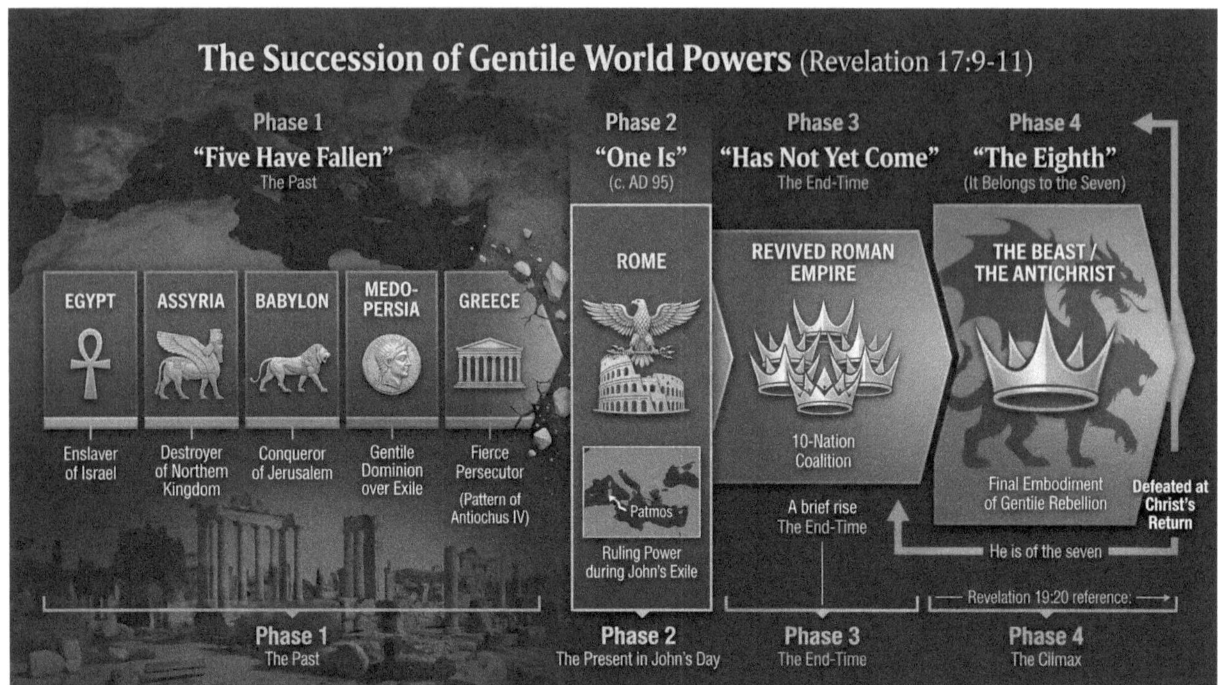


***Figure D21.2.1: The March of Empires.*** *The seven heads of the Beast represent the unbroken succession of Gentile world powers that have historically persecuted God's covenant people, Israel, leading directly to the final reign of the Antichrist.*

| Prophetic Status (Rev 17:10) | The Empire | Relationship to Israel and God's People |
|---|---|---|
| **Fallen (1 of 5)** | Egypt | The enslaver of the nation of Israel |
| **Fallen (2 of 5)** | Assyria | The destroyer of the Northern Kingdom |
| **Fallen (3 of 5)** | Babylon | The conqueror of Jerusalem and the Southern Kingdom |
| **Fallen (4 of 5)** | Medo-Persia | The benevolent ruling Gentile dominion during the return from exile |
| **Fallen (5 of 5)** | Greece | The fierce persecutor of the Jews under Antiochus IV |
| **"One Is"** | Rome | The ruling world power in John's day |
| **"Not Yet Come"** | The Revived Roman Empire | The end-time 10-nation coalition destined to arise briefly before the end |

*Table D21.2.1: The Chronology of the Seven Empires*

In this framework, five kingdoms had already fallen by John's time. Rome was ruling then, and a final kingdom is appointed for the end-time.

## The Eighth King: The Beast Himself

Verse 11 introduces a startling development: *"the beast that was and is not, it is an eighth but it belongs to the seven."* The Beast is both distinct from the seven and yet inseparably connected to them.

In this prophetic timeline, the Antichrist emerges from the final kingdom but ultimately transcends it. He begins as the leader of a revived confederation of kingdoms, then becomes something more sinister: an eighth king who embodies the final, inglorious culmination of every God-opposing power before him.[2]

Several implications follow:

2. The "Beast" represents both the final world empire (Revelation 13) and its individual ruler, the Antichrist (Revelation 17). See J. Dwight Pentecost, *Things to Come* (Zondervan, 1958).

| Prophetic Characteristic | Literal Fulfillment |
|---|---|
| The Beast Is a Person | He comes, reigns briefly, and goes to destruction. These descriptions point to a specific, literal individual empowered by Satan (Revelation 13:2–4). |
| The Beast Is a Kingdom | He rules through a wider political structure that precedes him, empowers him, and carries his authority. |
| The Beast Parodies Christ | He suffers a mortal wound and is restored, a counterfeit resurrection that mimics the resurrection of Jesus (Revelation 13:3, 12, 14). |
| The Beast's End Is Certain | Though his authority is global and terrifying, it is temporary. He "goes to destruction," fulfilled when he is thrown alive into the lake of fire at Christ's return (Revelation 19:20). |

*Table D21.2.2: The Dual Nature of the Beast*

## Rome, Antiochus, and a Layered Reading

This passage brings together two distinct strands of biblical expectation. Historically, Antiochus IV Epiphanes unmistakably foreshadowed the *character* of the Antichrist through his desecration of the Temple and violent suppression of true worship. Politically, the Beast's final empire arises directly from the geographic and political legacy of Rome, the world-dominating power present in John's day.

Taken together, this yields a compelling layered reading of Revelation 17:8–11. The Beast's political authority reflects continuity with the Roman world, while his personal actions and blasphemies follow the violent pattern established by Antiochus. The eighth king is thus both heir to a long line of empires and the final embodiment of their rebellion against God.

## The Climax of History

Revelation 17 does not present history as cyclical or random. It depicts a deliberate progression toward a final confrontation. The eighth king represents the climax of satanic resistance, but also its end. His rise is brief. His authority is derivative. His destruction is guaranteed.

What appears to be the triumph of evil is, in fact, its last stand.

| The Biblical Symbol | The End-Time Fulfillment |
|---|---|
| Seven Heads | Seven successive world empires opposed to God's redemptive purposes. |
| Five Fallen | Egypt, Assyria, Babylon, Medo-Persia, Greece. |
| One Is | Rome (the ruling power in John's day). |
| The Seventh | The end-time revived world empire (the 10-nation coalition). |
| The Eighth | The Antichrist, arising from the seventh yet distinct and ultimately transcending it. |
| "Belongs to the Seven" | Shares direct continuity with prior empires; emerges from the seventh. |
| "Goes to Destruction" | Defeated totally and permanently at Christ's return (Revelation 19:20). |

*Table D21.2.3: Summary of the Prophetic Sequence*

History moves toward a conclusion, not chaos. The eighth king is coming, but only to be crushed by the true King of Kings.

# DEEPER DIVE 21.3. THE BEAST THAT WAS

## Antiochus IV as the Historical Shadow of the Antichrist

*The beast, which you saw, once was, now is not, and yet will come up out of the Abyss and go to its destruction.*

— REVELATION 17:8 NIV

Revelation 17:8 describes the Beast in three movements: past, present, and future. While much attention is rightly given to the Beast's final rise, the opening phrase, "the beast that was," invites the reader to look backward before looking ahead.

Within biblical prophecy, this backward glance is not vague or abstract. It points to a concrete historical reality: the Beast has already shown his character in history. And among all past rulers, one stands out with unmistakable clarity.

That ruler is Antiochus IV Epiphanes.

## 1. "The Beast That Was": A Historical Reality

Antiochus IV (175–164 BC), the Seleucid king who ruled over Judea, represents the most explicit pre-Christian manifestation of Beast-like evil. His reign was not merely tyrannical; it was militantly blasphemous.[1]

Antiochus did not simply persecute the Jews politically. He:

- Desecrated the Jerusalem Temple
- Abolished the daily sacrifices
- Outlawed Torah observance
- Imposed pagan worship by force

These actions went beyond oppression. They were an intentional assault on the covenant between Israel and her God.

In this sense, Antiochus was not merely hostile to God's people. He attempted to replace God Himself.

1. This event is recorded in *1 Maccabees*, a non-canonical Jewish historical work that preserves firsthand accounts of the persecution under Antiochus IV.

***Figure D21.3.1: The Face of Blasphemy.*** *An ancient silver tetradrachm coin minted by Antiochus IV (c. 175–164 BC). The critical Greek inscription across the reverse reads* **ΘΕΟΥ ΕΠΙΦΑΝΟΥΣ**, *meaning "God Manifest." This unmistakable historical artifact serves as a chilling preview of the ultimate self-deification that will characterize the final Beast.*

## 2. The Historical Blueprint of the Beast

Revelation does not invent the Beast's character out of thin air. Instead, it draws from patterns already established in Scripture and history. Antiochus stands as the definitive ancient warning of what the final Beast will do.

When Revelation speaks of a ruler who:

- Exalts himself above God
- Destroys true worship
- Enforces false allegiance
- Persecutes the faithful

... it is echoing actions that Antiochus carried out in Jerusalem centuries earlier.

This is why Antiochus firmly stands as "the Beast that was," a real, historical rehearsal for a far greater evil yet to come.

## 3. A Shadow, Not the Substance

Yet Revelation is precise. Antiochus is not the Beast. He is a shadow.

Revelation 17:8 establishes a clear, three-part prophetic timeline:

| Prophetic Phase | Theological Reality |
|---|---|
| "Was" | Revealed historically in the definitive prototype, Antiochus IV. |
| "Is Not" | The final ruler is presently restrained during the Church Age. |
| "Will Come" | The Antichrist will arise in full satanic power from the Abyss. |

*Table D21.3.1: The Timeline of the Beast (Revelation 17:8)*

Antiochus shows us the pattern, not the fulfillment. What he did locally, the final Beast will do globally. Antiochus terrorized a single nation for roughly three years; the Antichrist will terrorize the entire globe for three and a half. Therein lies the divine limit on his reign of terror.

## 4. From Pattern to Horror

Understanding Antiochus as "the Beast that was" prepares the reader for what lies ahead. Revelation assumes familiarity with this historical precedent so that the future is not misunderstood as unprecedented.

The atrocities of Antiochus are not incidental background material. They are deliberate foreshadowing. And the details matter.

For a full account of Antiochus's brutality, his desecration of the Temple, his slaughter of the faithful, and his attempt to eradicate the Word of God, see *Deeper Dive 21.4. The Prototype of Horror: Antiochus IV Epiphanes*.

## The Final Manifestation

Revelation 17:8 does not merely predict the future. It interprets the past.

The Beast who will come has already left fingerprints on history. Antiochus IV Epiphanes stands as the clearest example of what happens when satanic power is given political authority and religious control.

What he was, the Antichrist will magnify: greater, darker, and global.

The shadow has already fallen.

The substance is yet to appear.

But when he does, he will once again desecrate the Temple, but this time deceive untold masses. He will make war against the Lamb. And lose.

# DEEPER DIVE 21.4. THE PROTOTYPE OF HORROR: ANTIOCHUS IV EPIPHANES

## When History Repeats with Vengeance

> *"In the latter part of their reign, when rebels have become completely wicked, a fierce-looking king, a master of intrigue, will arise. He will become very strong, but not by his own power. He will cause astounding devastation and will succeed in whatever he does. He will destroy those who are mighty, the holy people..."*
>
> — DANIEL 8:23–24

If you are reading this during the Tribulation, understand this: The brutality of Antiochus IV Epiphanes serves as a chilling blueprint for the Antichrist's coming reign of terror. While his actions were historically devastating, they were only a foreshadowing.

The final three and a half years of the Tribulation, the period Revelation calls the Beast's time of authority (Revelation 13:5), will see the Antichrist's evils magnified on a global scale, culminating in the mass martyrdom of those who refuse to bow. As Revelation 20:4 warns, many will be beheaded because they refused to worship the Beast or take his mark. The Greek word used is *pelekizo*, meaning "to behead with an axe." This is not poetic imagery. It's prophetic warning.

***Figure D21.4.1: The Blueprint of the Beast.*** *The historical atrocities committed by Antiochus IV in Judea serve as the prophetic*

*template for the Antichrist. What Antiochus executed locally as a shadow, the final Beast will execute globally as the ultimate manifestation of satanic rebellion.*

## 1. He Desecrates the Temple

Daniel 8:11–13, 24–25 reveals a vision of the "little horn" (Antiochus), who profaned the sanctuary, halted the daily sacrifices, and "threw down" the sanctuary.[1] This was fulfilled in 167 BC, when Antiochus erected an altar to Zeus Olympios on the altar of burnt offering in Jerusalem's Temple as recorded in the historical book of 1 Maccabees 1:54.

This act, known as the "abomination of desolation," not only desecrated the Temple but also served as a direct prototype for the future Antichrist's desecration of a rebuilt Temple (see 2 Thessalonians 2:4).

## 2. He Bans True Worship

Antiochus did not stop at physical desecration. He outlawed worship itself. Daniel 8 emphasizes that the little horn will "take away the daily sacrifice" and "destroy the holy people." Historically, this played out in a ruthlessly systematic way:

**1 Maccabees 1:41–53** describes how Antiochus banned circumcision, Sabbath observance, kosher dietary laws, and even possession of Torah scrolls. Violators faced death. He sacrificed pigs, unclean animals under the Law, on the altar, directly insulting the God of Israel.

This was totalitarian religious control, strikingly similar to what Revelation 13 describes the Antichrist doing on a global scale.

## 3. He Slaughters the Faithful

Antiochus's regime was soaked in blood. The faithful were not just oppressed; they were hunted, tortured, and killed. Daniel 8:10 and 11:28–32 prophesied that the little horn would "trample the host of heaven" and destroy those loyal to the covenant.

**1 Maccabees 1:56–63** tells of house-to-house raids. Infants were killed for being circumcised; their mothers were paraded with their dead babies hung around their necks.

**2 Maccabees 6–7** recounts the torture and martyrdom of the faithful. Two women were paraded through the city and hurled from the walls for circumcising their sons. Later, a mother and her seven sons were martyred for refusing to eat pork. Eleazar, a 90-year-old scribe, was tortured to death rather than eat unclean food. His final words were a defiant stand for God's law.

## 4. He Destroys the Word of God

Antiochus understood that the Torah was not just a book. Rather it was the soul of Jewish identity. So he burned every scroll he could find.

1. On the identification of Antiochus IV Epiphanes as the "little horn" of Daniel 8 and a typological forerunner of the Antichrist, see John F. Walvoord, *Daniel: The Key to Prophetic Revelation* (Chicago: Moody Press, 1971), 183–198.

## DEEPER DIVE 21.4. THE PROTOTYPE OF HORROR: ANTIOCHUS IV EPIPHANES

*The books of the law that they found they tore to pieces and burned with fire. Anyone found possessing the book of the covenant or anyone who adhered to the law was condemned to death by decree of the king.*

— 1 MACCABEES 1:56–57 (NRSV)

This was spiritual genocide. To kill the Word was to kill the covenant.

Under Antiochus IV, possession of a Torah scroll became a capital offense, and copies of the Law were deliberately destroyed. These actions went beyond political repression, functioning as a symbolic assault on Israel's covenant life and a broader assault on Israel's covenant relationship with the God of Israel.[2]

2. See Daniel J. Harrington, *The Maccabean Revolt: Anatomy of a Biblical Revolution* (Eugene, OR: Wipf & Stock, 2009), esp. discussion of Antiochus IV's decrees against Torah observance and their theological significance. See also *1 Maccabees* 1:56–57 for the historical account of Torah destruction and capital penalties.

| Prophetic Theme | Antiochus IV Epiphanes (The Historical Shadow) | The Antichrist (The End-Time Substance) |
|---|---|---|
| The Sanctuary | Desecrated the Second Temple by erecting an altar to Zeus Olympios in 167 BC (1 Maccabees 1:54). | Desecrates the rebuilt Temple by setting himself up in God's sanctuary, proclaiming himself to be God (2 Thessalonians 2:4). |
| True Worship | Abolished the daily sacrifices, outlawed Sabbath observance, and mandated pagan worship. | Halts sacrifices mid-Tribulation and demands absolute, exclusive global worship of himself and his image (Revelation 13:8, 15). |
| The Persecution | Systematically hunted, tortured, and slaughtered Jewish families who remained faithful to God's covenant. | Mandates the global execution, specifically by beheading, of all Tribulation saints who refuse to bow (Revelation 20:4). |
| Eradication of Truth | Burned Torah scrolls and made possession of the Scriptures a capital offense to destroy the faithful. | Savagely purges the Word of God and eliminates all digital or printed ties to the God of the Bible. |
| Mechanism of Control | Used ruthless military enforcement and house-to-house raids to ensure total compliance with his decrees. | Implements the Mark of the Beast, creating an inescapable, totalitarian economic lockout for all dissenters (Revelation 13:16–17). |

*Table D21.4.1: The Blueprint of the Beast: History vs. Prophecy*

## A Shadow of the Greater Evil to Come

The Antichrist will not merely repeat these evils. He will magnify them. What Antiochus did to the Jews in Judea, the Beast will do globally to believers living during the Great Tribulation. The desecration of the sanctuary, the forced worship of a false god or image, the outlawing of true worship, and the systematic slaughter of God's people will reach a scale never before seen (see Revelation 13:7–8, 15–17).

Just as Antiochus burned scrolls, the Beast will seek to erase Scripture from digital and printed existence. Just as Antiochus outlawed circumcision and Sabbath, the Antichrist will outlaw anything tied to the God of Christians or the Jews. Just as Antiochus beheaded the faithful with cruelty, the Beast will do the same publicly, as a spectacle to instill fear and compel obedience.

---

## If You Are Still Here

To those living in the final 3½ years: the road ahead is unimaginably hard, yet full of hope. The ruler is the Antichrist. His terrifying reign lasts only 42 months (Revelation 13:5). It is a blink compared to eternity.

He will demand total allegiance: worship, loyalty, and his mark. **Refuse it.** However appealing, convenient, or necessary it seems, **do not comply**. God's Word is unequivocal:

> *If anyone worships the beast and its image and receives its mark ... they will drink the wine of God's fury, poured full strength into the cup of his wrath ..."*
>
> — REVELATION 14:9–10 NIV

The mark may appear to promise survival, **but it seals immediate doom**. The first bowl judgment (Revelation 16:2) strikes its bearers with "loathsome and malignant sores," which are merely the start of suffering for all who are aligned with the Antichrist.

Conversely, refusing the mark guarantees the wrath of the Beast. This Great Tribulation will eclipse even Antiochus IV's atrocities, and his global persecution means you will be hunted, tortured, or beheaded (Revelation 20:4).

But stand firm. Reject the mark. Deny him worship. Cling to Christ. Your faithfulness leads to reigning with Jesus.

***Eternity outweighs all cost. Hold fast. He comes soon.***

> *"Be faithful unto death, and I will give you the crown of life."*
>
> — REVELATION 2:10

# DEEPER DIVE 22.1. FROM ROME TO BABYLON: THE PROPHETIC RELOCATION

## Solving the Mystery of Zechariah's Vision

*Then the angel ... said to me, "This is the basket that is going out." ... and there was a woman sitting in the basket! And he said, "This is Wickedness." Then I lifted my eyes and saw ... two women coming forward ... They had wings like the wings of a stork, and they lifted up the basket ... Then I said to the angel ... "Where are they taking the basket?" He said ... "To the land of Shinar, to build a house for it. And when this is prepared, they will set the basket down there on its base."*

— ZECHARIAH 5:5–11

Revelation 17 depicts a drunken Harlot sitting on seven hills, unmistakably Rome. Yet, Revelation 18 describes a burning marketplace that had made the merchants of the earth rich, Babylon the Great.

Are these the same city? Or does the Bible tell a tale of two cities? The missing link may lie in a cryptic Old Testament prophecy: Zechariah 5:5–11.

This view, championed by scholars like John Walvoord and powerfully articulated by teacher Chuck Missler, argues for a literal, rebuilt city of Babylon in Iraq as the Antichrist's final headquarters. They contend that prophecies of Babylon's sudden, permanent destruction in Isaiah 13 and Jeremiah 50–51 were never fully, historically fulfilled, requiring a future city to meet that fate.[1]

---

1. Some Bible teachers believe that Revelation 18 is describing a real, future city of Babylon that will be rebuilt in modern-day Iraq. They base this view on Old Testament prophecies about Babylon that have never been fully fulfilled in history. For this perspective, see John F. Walvoord, *The Revelation of Jesus Christ* (Moody, 1966), chap. 18; and Arnold G. Fruchtenbaum, *The Footsteps of the Messiah* (Tustin, CA: Ariel Ministries, 2003), discussion of end-time Babylon. For a related study that connects end-time Babylon with the strange vision of the woman in a basket in Zechariah 5, see Chuck Missler, *The Book of Revelation* (Koinonia House, 1995).

***Figure D22.1.1: The Transfer of Wickedness.*** *Zechariah 5 reveals the literal, geographic relocation of the global system of rebellion. Carried in a commercial basket (an ephah), this satanic religious and economic center is moved from its historical seat of power to be established in the ancient land of Shinar (Babylon) for the end times.*

## The Woman in the Basket

The most fascinating piece of this puzzle is Zechariah's vision. He sees a woman named "Wickedness" sealed inside an *ephah*, a measuring basket used for trade. Two winged figures carry her "to the land of Shinar, to build a house for it." The geography is precise. Shinar is the biblical location of Babylon. The vision implies a transfer: the seat of wickedness is moved from one location to be established in another.

This prompted Chuck Missler to observe that the vision suggests an end-time geographic transfer: the global religious system, long associated with Rome, will one day be physically relocated to its ancient cradle in Babylon during the end times.

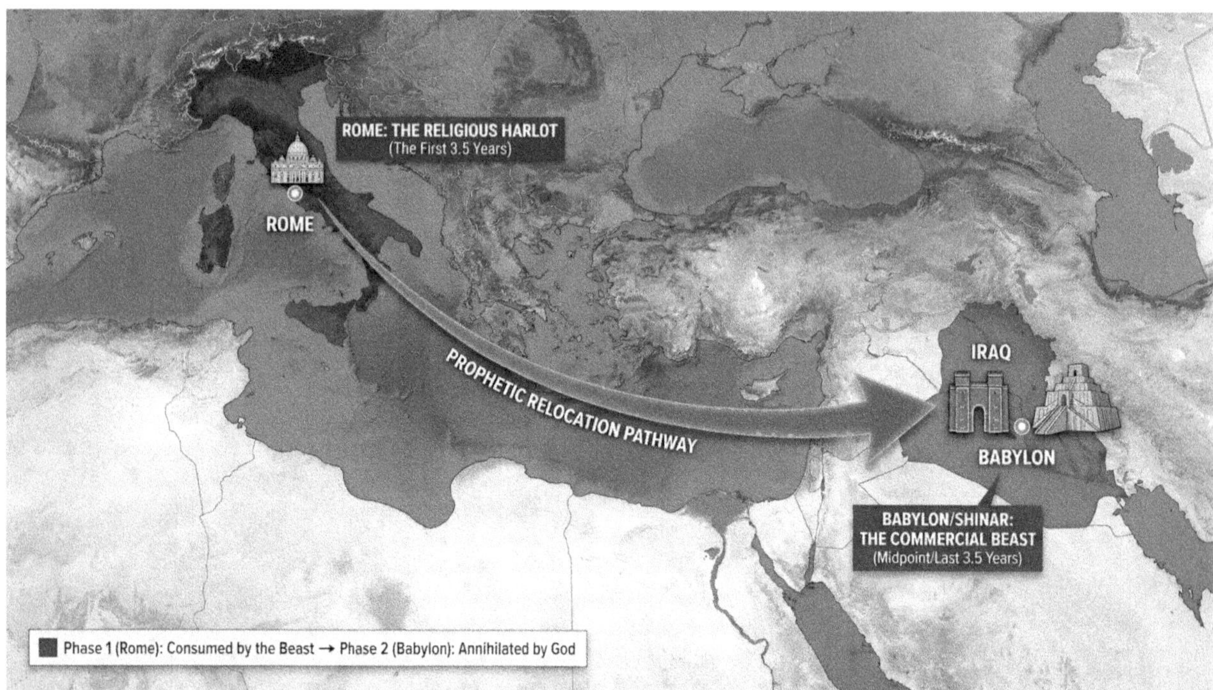


***Figure D22.1.2: The Tale of Two Cities.*** *During the 70th Week of Daniel, the geographic center of global rebellion shifts. Following the destruction of the religious Harlot in Rome at the Tribulation's midpoint, the Antichrist establishes his ultimate global headquarters in a rebuilt Babylon in modern-day Iraq for his final 42-month reign of terror.*

## The Prophetic Handoff

How do we reconcile a religious Rome (Vatican) with a commercial Babylon (Iraq)? By understanding the timeline.

| The Timeline | The Seat of Power | The Literal Fulfillment |
|---|---|---|
| **Phase 1: The Harlot Rides (First 3½ Years)** | **Rome** | The one world religion rules from Rome. She provides the spiritual glue for the early empire of the Beast. Meanwhile, in the background, the Antichrist quietly prepares his ultimate infrastructure in the East. |
| **Phase 2: The Base is Set (Midpoint to the End of the Tribulation)** | **Babylon** | The Beast destroys the Harlot at around the midpoint of the Tribulation. He no longer needs her religious influence because he declares himself God. At this exact moment, the "basket" lands in Shinar, establishing Babylon as his global headquarters for the final 42 months. |

***Table D22.1.1: The Prophetic Handoff.*** *A chronological summary of how the center of global rebellion shifts from the religious system of Rome in the West to a rebuilt Babylon in the East.*

## A Temple of Commerce

Zechariah says a "house" (*bayit*) is built for her. In the context of Shinar, this echoes the Tower of Babel. It is a temple. In the Antichrist's Babylon, commerce and worship are identical. To buy or sell is to worship the Beast.

## The Law of First and Last Things

This return to Shinar represents a profound narrative symmetry. The story of human rebellion began in Genesis 11 on these very plains. There, humanity united under a single leader (Nimrod) to build a tower, possibly a ziggurat, in defiance of God. It was the birthplace of false religion and organized human pride.

Prophetic symmetry demands that the story must end where it began. The "alpha" of rebellion becomes the "omega" of judgment. Evil does not finish its course in Rome or the West; it returns to its cradle to be destroyed once and for all.

## The Sequence

| Step | The Timeframe | The Location | The Prophetic Action |
|---|---|---|---|
| 1 | First 3½ Years | Rome (Religious Center) | The Harlot operates from her historical seat of power, providing global religious legitimacy to the rising Beast. |
| 2 | The Midpoint | Geographic Shift (West to East) | The Beast and his ten kings destroy the Harlot. The center of global rebellion is forcefully relocated to the land of Shinar. |
| 3 | Final 3½ Years | Babylon (Political & Economic Center) | Rebuilt in Iraq, it becomes the supreme geopolitical throne of the Beast, uniting totalitarian commerce and mandatory self-worship. |
| 4 | End of the Tribulation | Babylon (Shinar) | Destroyed suddenly and permanently by the undiluted wrath of the Seventh Bowl while the Beast is away waging his final genocidal campaign against Israel. |

***Table D22.1.2: The Tale of Two Cities Over the Tribulation.*** *Outlining the prophetic transition of the Antichrist's power base from a western religious system to a Babylonian commercial empire.*

Revelation 17 and 18 are not contradictory snapshots; they are a moving picture of the end-times' shifting center of gravity. This interpretation elegantly resolves the apparent tension: they are not the same city at the same time, but two distinct capitals in a prophetic sequence, one religious and one commercial, both doomed to fall.

#  DEEPER DIVE 23.1. THE EAGLES AND THE CORPSE

## Solving One of Jesus' Most Cryptic Riddles

*For wherever the carcass is, there the eagles will be gathered together.*

— MATTHEW 24:28 NKJV

In the middle of His most famous prophecy about the end times, Jesus drops a proverb that has baffled readers for centuries.

It is a gruesome image.

What is the carcass? Who are the eagles?

Part of the difficulty lies in translation. Some English Bibles render the term as "corpse," instead of "carcass." Likewise, some translations speak of "vultures," instead of "eagles."

These differences shape how the saying is commonly understood.

For many years, interpreters favoring the "vultures" translation have read this proverb as a grim afterword to Armageddon: birds of prey are the "cleanup crew" gathering to feast on the defeated armies of the Antichrist (Revelation 19).

But the language and context will not allow a harmless "cleanup crew" reading. Jesus is describing a body lying exposed, with predators circling. The "carcass" is not the aftermath of judgment. It is the target of judgment, a people rendered defenseless before the gathering eagles.

In other words, this is not battlefield debris. It is a **corpse**, and in Matthew's Jewish context, that people can only be Israel.

## The Predator and the Prey

To understand what Jesus is saying, we must look at the context.

In Matthew 24, Jesus is speaking specifically to Jewish disciples about the future of the Jewish nation. He calls this time "Great Tribulation," a period of distress unequaled in history.

Historically, scholars such as Arno Gaebelein identified the "carcass" as the spiritually dead of the nation of Israel.

Modern teachers like Allen Nolan add a grim physical dimension: with two-thirds of the Jewish population slaughtered (Zechariah 13:8), the nation resembles not a fighting force, but a corpse left defenseless before the gathering Gentile armies.[1]

1. For the identification of the "carcass" as the nation of Israel, see Arno C. Gaebelein, *The Gospel of Matthew: An Exposition*, vol. 2 (New York: Our Hope Publication Office, 1910), 206. For the contemporary exposition linking this imagery to the decimation of the Jewish

Even where translations differ, the logic of the proverb remains chillingly consistent: predators gather where the corpse lies.

If the Antichrist and the armies of the world are the "eagles," then Israel is the corpse they have come to devour.

## Why the "Carcass" Is a Corpse

### 1. The "Dry Bones" of a Nation

The prophet Ezekiel's famous vision of the dry bones (Ezekiel 37) unfolds in specific stages. First, the scattered bones come together and are clothed with flesh and skin, representing Israel's physical restoration to the land. Yet, at this critical second stage, Scripture explicitly notes, "there was no breath in them" (Ezekiel 37:8). They have physical form but lack spiritual life. During the Tribulation, Israel exists in this exact state, a nation physically gathered but remaining in unbelief. By definition, a body with flesh but no breath is a corpse. To the eyes of the world, they appear entirely finished and forsaken, a lifeless corpse ready for the eagles.

### 2. The Two-Thirds Prophecy

The prophets warn that the Tribulation will be a time of near-total annihilation for the Jewish people. Zechariah 13:8 predicts that "two-thirds shall be cut off and perish, and one third shall be left alive."

To the gathering armies of the Antichrist, a nation that has lost two-thirds of its people looks like a finished job. It looks like a corpse, an easy meal for the imperial eagles to erase from history.

### 3. The Greek Key: *Aetoi* (Eagles)

The Greek is crucial. The word Jesus used is *aetoi*, literally, "eagles." In both the ancient and modern world, the eagle is the universal symbol of imperial military power, specifically empires historically driven to devour the Jewish people. The Babylonians were described as eagles (Ezekiel 17:3). The Romans destroyed Jerusalem under the standard of the eagle (the *Aquila*). In modern history, Hitler's Third Reich annihilated an estimated one-third of the global Jewish population under the banner of the imperial eagle (the *Reichsadler*). This horrifying historical reality serves as a dark prelude to the Great Tribulation, where the final global empire will gather to slaughter two-thirds of the nation.

Some translators change this to "vultures" because zoologically, it is vultures, not eagles, that are known for flocking to a dead body. But in doing so, the prophetic and military symbolism of the eagle is decidedly lost. When Jesus says the "eagles will gather," He is using language that articulates military encirclement by a final, viciously anti-Semitic global empire. He is echoing the ancient curse of Deuteronomy 28:49, where God warned Israel that if they turned away, a nation would come against them "as swift as the eagle flies."

---

population and the gathering of Gentile armies, see Allen Nolan, "End Times According to Jesus, Part 5" (Cornerstone Fellowship, video sermon, 2020), and "Moses and Petra: Bible Study 14" (Cornerstone Fellowship, video sermon, 2018), available via the Cornerstone Fellowship YouTube channel.

FIGURE D23.1.1: THE LINEAGE OF THE EAGLES (*AETOI*)

Illustrate a historical sequence of empires operating under the same **prophetic** symbol that have systematically targeted the nation of Israel.

Blueprint

BABYLON
(Ezekiel 17:3)
Sought to devour the nation.

ROME
(70 AD Siege)
SPQR
Crushed and scattered the people.

3RD REICH
(1939–1945)
Annihilated 1/3 of the Jewish Population (The Prelude)

The Antichrist's Coalition

The Final Realization
THE FINAL SIEGE
(Zechariah 13:8)
two thirds shall be cut off and perish

"Where the corpse (Israel) lies, the eagles (the final empire) will gather"

***Figure D23.1.1: The Lineage of the Eagle.*** *Tracing the historical and prophetic pattern of empires seeking to destroy the Jewish people. From Babylon to the Nazi Reichsadler of the Holocaust, the eagle is their unchanging symbol. This history is merely a dark prelude to Zechariah 13:8. The final "eagles" gathering around Israel are not scavengers but the massive military encirclement of the Antichrist's coalition.*

## Answering the Question: "Where?"

In Luke 17:37, this proverb is given as an answer to a direct question: *"Where, Lord?"*

Jesus' reply is not a street address but a proverb of inevitability: where the corpse lies exposed, the eagles will gather.

This explains why the armies of the world (the eagles) converge on Jerusalem and eventually surround Bozrah (Petra). They are predators drawn to the scent of impending death.

## The Zechariah Connection

Zechariah describes the final siege of Jerusalem by the Gentile nations (the eagles): "Half of the city shall go into captivity" (Zechariah 14:2).

This eerily parallels Jesus' warning in Luke 17 about "one taken and the other left." Because Luke places this warning right next to the proverb of the eagles (Luke 17:37), the context is clearly one of judgment. Those who are "taken" here are not raptured to heaven; they are taken into the captivity and slaughter described by Zechariah, seized by the invading armies gathering around the city.[2]

2. Note: This creates a deliberate and terrifying contrast with Matthew 24:40. While the ones "taken" in Luke 17 (and Matthew 24:28) are seized for judgment and slaughter by the gathering eagles, the ones "taken" in the later portion of the Olivet Discourse (Matthew 24:36–44) are rescued in the imminent Rapture. For a detailed explanation of how the *peri de* structural shift in Matthew 24 changes the context entirely, and why the same phrase can mean opposite things, see *Deeper Dive 6.3. The Paradox of the Taken.*

## The Ultimate Rescue

The proverb is not a gruesome footnote but a setup for the greatest rescue mission in history.

The world comes to consume Israel as a corpse.

But then the true King arrives.

The corpse breathes.

The great army stands.

And the predator becomes the prey.

# DEEPER DIVE 26.1. THE BRIDE OR THE CITY?

## Solving the Architectural Mystery of the Eternal State

Revelation 21 opens with an invitation that sounds like thunder wrapped in tenderness:

> *"Come, I will show you the bride, the wife of the Lamb."*
>
> — REVELATION 21:9

You brace for a person. Or a multitude. A sea of faces redeemed and radiant.

But that is not what John is shown. He sees a city: "the holy city, Jerusalem, coming down out of heaven from God."

This raises a perfectly reasonable question: **How can the Bride of the Lamb be a city?**

The answer lies in the symbolic nature of apocalyptic literature, where Scripture often fuses categories to convey layered truth.

## Symbol Fusion: A Hallmark of Revelation

One of Revelation's most distinctive literary features is **symbol fusion**: the intentional blending of persons, institutions, and places into single composite images. A few notable examples:[1]

- **The Woman in Revelation 12** is a vivid figure who gives birth to the male child. She is understood to represent **Israel**, through whom the Messiah came, portrayed in maternal imagery as the object of Satan's pursuit.
- **The Beast in Revelation 13 and 17** is both a **kingdom** and a **king**. The heads are identified as kingdoms, yet the Beast is also treated as a singular, final ruler: the Antichrist himself.
- **Babylon in Revelation 17–18** is both a **woman** and a **city**. Her sins are described as personal, moral, and religious, yet her fall is the collapse of a great city and world system.

That is Revelation's method. It fuses categories to communicate layered truth.

So when John is told he will see "the Bride," and he is shown the New Jerusalem, he is not watching a category mistake. He is watching a symbol do double duty.

1. Many Bible teachers point out that Revelation often blends symbols together. So one image can stand for more than one reality at the same time. For example, the "Woman" is widely understood to represent Israel (see John F. Walvoord, *The Revelation of Jesus Christ*, Moody, 1966, chap. 12). The "Beast" is commonly seen as both a world empire and the final Antichrist ruler who leads it (see J. Dwight Pentecost, *Things to Come*, Zondervan, 1958, discussion of Revelation 13 and the "eighth" ruler of Revelation 17:11). In the same way, Babylon is described not just as a system but also as a city: Revelation 17:18 plainly says, "The woman whom you saw is the great city."

**Key Insight:** In Revelation, a single symbol can represent both a place and the people who define it. The people give the place its identity. The place embodies the people's destiny.

***Figure D26.1.1: The Fusion of the Bride and the City.*** *A visual representation of the profound symbol fusion in Revelation 21, here employed within the interpretive framework that envisions the New Jerusalem as a colossal, jewel-like pyramid. By seamlessly blending this crystal-clear architecture with the radiant form of a woman composed of the saints, the image illustrates that the city's true glory is the redeemed people who inhabit it.*

## A City That Is a People

In Scripture, cities often stand for their inhabitants. Jerusalem was never merely stone and streets; it represented the covenant people.

Hebrews makes this fusion explicit:

> *But you have come to Mount Zion and to the city of the living God, the heavenly Jerusalem... to the assembly of the firstborn who are enrolled in heaven.*
>
> — HEBREWS 12:22–23

Notice what the writer does *not* do. He does not separate the city from its citizens. The city is defined by the redeemed assembly within it.

Paul reinforces this pattern when he describes the Church as Christ's Bride being actively washed and prepared (Ephesians 5:25–27). Revelation 21 is simply the final, glorious result of that preparation: the Bride perfectly adorned and taking up her eternal residence.

This is confirmed by the architecture itself. The gates bear the names of the Twelve Tribes, and the foundations bear the names of the Twelve Apostles. The city is literally built upon the identity of God's people across both covenants.

The city is described "as a bride adorned for her husband" (Revelation 21:2), and then again identified as "the Bride, the wife of the Lamb" (Revelation 21:9). The point is not that saints are made of masonry. The point is that the redeemed are now perfected, prepared, and permanently home.

Recognizing this symbol fusion does not make the New Jerusalem any less of a literal, physical city. It simply shifts our focus to what Revelation values most. The ultimate glory of heaven is never just its spectacular dimensions; it is the redeemed people who live there and the God who dwells among them.[2]

## The Eternal Distinction

It is vital to note that while the city fuses these groups into one eternal dwelling, it does not erase their distinct identities. The twelve tribes of Israel are forever inscribed on the gates, and the twelve apostles of the Church are forever inscribed on the foundations. God does not blend Israel and the Church into a single, generic category. Instead, their unique prophetic roles are permanently maintained in the architecture of eternity. One enters the city through the historical covenants of Israel (the gates), which rest upon the final revelation of the Church (the foundations). They are distinct in history, yet perfectly united in glory.

## Why is the City called the Bride?

A careful reader will naturally ask: if the Church is uniquely the Bride of Christ, and Old Testament Israel also dwells in this city (represented by the gates), why is the entire city called "the Bride"? The answer lies in the explicit promise of Christ. In John 14, Jesus told His followers that He was going to His Father's house to prepare a place for His Church. The New Jerusalem is that exact, spectacular, custom-built home. Just as a royal palace is often referred to by the name of the queen it was built for, the heavenly city takes on the title of its most exalted human occupant. The city and the Bride are so intimately linked that John uses the terms interchangeably. Hebrews 12 confirms that while the Church and the Old Testament saints share this glorious eternal city, they maintain their distinct covenant identities. They share the same heavenly address, but the city itself stands as the ultimate architectural monument to the Lamb's love for His Bride.

## The Wedding Fulfilled

Back in Revelation 19, the Marriage of the Lamb took place in heaven. In Revelation 21, following the Millennial Kingdom, that union reaches its ultimate eternal state. The wedding celebration has transitioned into eternal cohabitation. The descending city is the visible manifestation of a spiritual triumph: the Bride is now the Wife, stepping down into the new heavens and new earth to dwell permanently with her Husband. Christ and His people are finally together forever, with nothing left to separate them.

## The Eternal Consummation

This is exactly why the Bride is shown as a city.

A city speaks of permanence. Order. Security. Beauty. Belonging. A place with foundations that cannot be shaken.

Revelation closes by showing the redeemed not simply forgiven, but radiant. Not merely rescued, but enthroned in their inheritance.

2. Many Bible scholars see the New Jerusalem as a symbolic picture of the Church in its final, glorified state, not just a future city of gold. Scholar G. K. Beale notes that the way the city is described points beyond architecture to the identity of God's people themselves. See G. K. Beale, *The Book of Revelation* (Eerdmans, 1999), 1064–1066.

The "wife of the Lamb" is not made of stone.

She is made of saints.

Redeemed. Resurrected. Radiant with the glory of God.

# ABOUT THE AUTHOR

n an era of shifting cultural sands and growing global uncertainty, how does the church remain steady, discerning, and unshaken? This question lies at the heart of Jeff L. Hoen's work and calling.

A writer, teacher, and devoted student of biblical prophecy, Jeff equips believers to navigate the complexities of the modern world through the lens of Scripture. His ministry is grounded in the firm conviction that God has not left His people in the dark, but has spoken with absolute precision about the times we are living in and the glorious hope set before us.

As the founder of Anchor & Sail Press, Jeff presents a compelling, scriptural framework for the Christian life. We are secured by the Anchor of God's *hesed* – His fierce, covenantal mercy that intervenes, redeems, and holds us fast. In response, we raise the Sail of *yare* – a life marked by reverential awe, obedience, and holy wisdom, catching the breath of God and moving in step with His Spirit. Together, these form the blueprint for a life that is both unshakably secure and spiritually effective.

This vision comes to life in his writing. In *IF YOU ARE STILL HERE: Understanding the Great Disappearance and What Lies Ahead*, Jeff offers a sober and urgent prophetic roadmap through the seven-year Tribulation, carefully aligning key passages to illuminate what lies ahead. In *The Anchor & The Sail*, he turns to the deep foundations of the Christian walk, helping believers cultivate a faith that endures, matures, and remains steadfast in every season.

Writing from his home on the east coast of Australia, Jeff brings together decades of theological study with a pastor's heart and a watchman's urgency. His voice is both steadying and stirring, calling readers not only to understand the times but to live with clarity, conviction, and readiness.

Above all, his work points to the unchanging faithfulness of Jesus Christ, the true Captain of our souls, who secures our anchor and directs our course, even in the midst of the storm.

# A REQUEST TO THE READER

If this book has helped clarify God's prophetic timeline and deepen your understanding of the days ahead, please consider leaving a review on the platform where you purchased it.

Independent publishing relies heavily on word of mouth, and your honest review is one of the most meaningful ways this message can reach others who are searching for biblical clarity in an uncertain world.

www.ingramcontent.com/pod-product-compliance
Lightning Source LLC
LaVergne TN
LVHW081249100826
845148LV00009B/1178